The Business of Politics and Ethnicity

A History of the Singapore Chinese Chamber of Commerce and Industry

SIKKO VISSCHER

NUS PRESS
SINGAPORE

© 2007 NUS Press
National University of Singapore
AS3-01-02, 3 Arts Link
Singapore 117569

Fax: (65) 6774-0652
E-mail: nusbooks@nus.edu.sg
Website: http://www.nus.edu.sg/npu

ISBN 13 978-9971-69-365-7

National Library Board Singapore Cataloguing in Publication Data

Visscher, Sikko, 1967–
    The business of politics and ethnicity : a history of the Singapore Chinese Chamber of Commerce and Industry / Sikko Visscher. – Singapore: NUS Press, c2007.
    p. cm.
    Includes bibliographical references and index.
    ISBN-13 : 978-9971-69-365-7 (pbk.)

    1. Singapore Chinese Chamber of Commerce & Industry – History.
    2. Boards of trade – Singapore – History. 3. Chinese – Singapore – History.
    4. Singapore – Commerce – History. I. Title.
HF331
381.0605957 -- dc22   SLS2007005662

Cover image is by Elvin Chng

Typeset by: SC (Sang Choy) International Pte Ltd
Printed by: Mainland Press Pte Ltd

To Tabitha

Contents

List of biographical sketches

Acknowledgements

FIRST AND FOREMOST, WRITING THIS book would have been impossible without the many informants in Singapore who agreed to tell me their story. I spent countless hours listening to them recount their experiences in the Chamber, their businesses, their cultural organizations, their social clubs and their political parties. Many of them preferred to stay anonymous and therefore I cannot list them here. I thank all of them.

I thank Heather Sutherland, my dissertation supervisor, for her unfailing support and her contagious enthusiasm for my project, and Jan Pluvier and Raymond Feddema for introducing me to Modern Asian History. NWO/WOTRO, known in English as the Netherlands Foundation for the Advancement of Tropical Research, employed me and funded my doctoral research awarding a grant under project number W47-198. The Centre for Asian Studies Amsterdam, one of the two constituent chambers of the Amsterdam School for Social Science Research (ASSR), took me on as a candidate. Leo Douw, Peter Post and Mario Rutten sat on my supervisory committee while Leo became co-supervisor during the final stages of writing the dissertation. I am grateful to Dick Kooiman, Henk Schulte Nordholt, Jan Pluvier, Peter Post and Mario Rutten for being on my reading committee.

During fieldwork the Institute of Southeast Asian Studies (ISEAS) granted me visiting associate status, which provided me with a base in Singapore and a place to analyze my findings. The library staff of ISEAS was particularly helpful. Rewriting the dissertation into a book for a larger audience was made possible through a four-month contract as Senior Visiting Fellow at the Asia Research Institute at the National University of Singapore. Additional financial support for rewriting and publishing the book was generously provided through a grant from the International Institute for Asian Studies in Leiden, The Netherlands, and made the inclusion of photographs possible. Paul Kratoska at Singapore University Press liked the manuscript early on and stuck with it. I thank two anonymous reviewers for their comments and constructive criticism.

Many academics gave generously of their time, expertise and network in the course of this project. The list here is surely incomplete and I apologize to all those unwittingly omitted. I thank Tony Saich, Richard Boyd, Ruth McVey, Wang Gungwu, Jamie Mackie, Tony Reid (to whom I am grateful for extending a Cushman Foundation grant enabling me to visit Australian National University, and for offering me the re-writing contract at ARI), Kevin Hewison, David Ip, Loh Wei Leng, Lee Kam Hing, Robert Cribb, Frank Pieke, Tong Chee Kiong, Leo Suryadinata, Cheng Lim Keak, Edgar Wickberg, Chan Kwok Bun, Lynn Pan, Lim Pui Huen, Lim How Seng, Lim Guan Hock, Yao Souchou, Paul Kratoska, Ng Chin Keong, Diana Wong, Chui Kwei-chiang, Huang Jianli, Carl Trocki and Michael Godley.

The staff and leadership of the SCCCI need special mention here. I am very grateful to the presidents Kwek Leng Joo and Tay Beng Chuan for allowing me to use the Chamber library and for granting me access to the Chamber's minutes at the National Archives. Other individuals in Singapore proved to be gatekeepers in different ways: I mention Twang Peck Yang, Sim Gwan Tek (whom I thank for making it possible to interview a retired Chamber leader in Hong Kong), Lee Peng Shu (my first contact in the Chamber) and Kua Soon Khe. Uncle Sia Yong introduced me to numerous friends and connections. I am deeply grateful to him for turning the bar of the Tanglin Club into my personal classroom and research site.

The administrative and executive staff of the ASSR was indispensable in many ways during my years as a doctoral candidate. To be surrounded by colleagues from so many disciplines was a true pleasure and an enriching experience. Discussions on life and work with Wu Xiao'an, Erik Bähre, Alex Claver, Arjan Veering, Pepijn van de Port, Richard Yntema, Oskar Verkaaik and Harald Bekkers proved crucial to my academic and personal well-being. I thank Lion and Ani, Amber and John and Ute for putting me up at various times. Kay and Richard were extremely gracious hosts during later visits to Singapore. The gang at Sunset Bay (the other half of the Petronas Twin Towers), US H4 and H3, Pollenboys, and the friends responsible for the incessant call for Q21 provided social contexts.

My parents instilled in me a love for and appreciation of history. The long road to this book started with the two of them reading to me at bedtime. They never ceased to believe in me and support me, and I am deeply grateful to them both. Over the years, my wife Tabitha has provided overwhelming love and support. She was editor, coach, inspiration and so much more. *Dankjewel lief!* Although this book could not have been written without all the people mentioned above, I am solely responsible for its contents and its shortcomings.

Abbreviations

ACCCM	Associated Chinese Chambers of Commerce of Malaya
AFC	ASEAN Finance Corporation
AMCJA	All Malayan Council of Joint Action
ASEAN	Association of Southeast Asian Nations
BMA	British Military Authority
BOC	Bank of China
CAB	Chinese Advisory Board
CCCs	Citizens' Consultative Committees
CDAC	Chinese Development Assistance Council
CDL	China Democratic League
DP	Democratic Party
DBS	Development Bank of Singapore
EDB	Economic Development Board
EOI	export oriented industrialization
Exco	Executive Council
FDI	foreign direct investment
FEFC	Far Eastern Freight Conference
GSP	Generalized System of Preferences
GLCs	government-linked companies
ISI	import substitution industrialization
KMT	Kuomintang
Legco	Legislative Council
LF	Labour Front
LP	Labour Party
MAS	Monetary Authority of Singapore
MC	Management Committee
MCA	Malayan Chinese Association
MCP	Malayan Communist Party
MNCs	multinational companies
MP	Member of Parliament
NIDL	New International Division of Labour

NOL	Neptune Orient Line
NTUC	National Trade Union Congress
NWC	National Wages Council
OCBC	Overseas Chinese Banking Corporation
OUB	Overseas Union Bank
PAP	People's Action Party
PMCJA	Pan Malayan Council for Joint Action
PP	Progressive Party
PRC	People's Republic of China
RAS	Rubber Association of Singapore
SCBA	Straits Chinese British Association
SCCC	Singapore Chinese Chamber of Commerce
SCCCI	Singapore Chinese Chamber of Commerce and Industry
SCSSCA	Singapore Chinese School Staff Committee Association
SDF	Skills Development Fund
SFCCA	Singapore Federation of Chinese Clan Associations
SFCCI	Singapore Federation of Chambers of Commerce and Industry
SICC	Singapore International Chamber of Commerce
SMA	Singapore Manufacturers' Association
SMEs	small and medium enterprises
SMR	Standard Malaysian Rubber
SNSC	Singapore National Shippers' Council
SSR	Standard Singapore Rubber
TDB	Trade Development Board
UCB	United Chinese Bank
UMNO	United Malays National Organisation
UOB	United Overseas Bank
URA	Urban Redevelopment Authority

Introduction

So a guy like you comes all the way from Europe to study this Singapore Chinese Chamber; why?" (Singaporean taxi driver, January 1998)

DURING THE CHINESE NEW YEAR celebrations at the Chamber, an unforeseen scenario started to play out. Having come in to do academic fieldwork for my dissertation, to listen to the speeches, observe the festivities and perhaps take some pictures of SCCCI celebrities, I found myself receiving unexpected attention. I had hoped to be able to approach some leaders and ask them whether they would agree to be interviewed, but all of a sudden the very individuals I was aiming to approach came up to me to ask me a favour. In the middle of the great hall of the Chamber building at 47 Hill Street stood a large mandarin orange tree, donated by the Bank of China to signify prosperity for the New Year, with the mandarin oranges symbolising lumps of gold. Standing at least two and an half meters tall, the tree provided a magnificent centrepiece. The people coming up to me had their cameras in hand and wanted to pose with me beside the tree. Being just over two meters, I was easily the tallest person in the crowd and this was the reason they wanted me to be in their pictures. "Such a big tree and such a tall man; this way our fortunes will also grow to heaven in the New Year", was what one man said to me.

While I have not received any news that these specific people experienced an exceptional year or struck it rich, this example serves to illustrate how academic work, similar to life in general, will present us with unexpected turns. Likewise, I had expected that the fruits of my scholarly work would have a restricted readership of fellow academics and perhaps a few family members. When the opportunity presented itself to rewrite my dissertation into a book for a wider audience, I jumped at it. Here was a chance to tell the remarkable story of the Singapore Chinese Chamber of Commerce (and Industry) (SCCC(I)),[1] to more people than I ever deemed possible, at a time when the Chamber was gearing up to celebrate its 100th anniversary in style.

First and foremost, this book is a history of the SCCC. Second, it also serves as an alternative reading of the history of Singapore, a history from the perspective of a leading civic institution rather than from the perspective of the state. On a third level, it is a story of how Chinese networks actually work. If the 21st century will be the century of China, an understanding of how the overseas Chinese organize themselves, link together across the globe and connect back to China and its burgeoning economy will be important to us all. But why and how did I end up in Singapore studying the Chamber in the first place? In this introduction, I will answer these questions and will explain why I think a book on the history of this organization is worth reading.

The heady mix of money, power and ethnicity has an irresistible lure to many. From the street cleaner to the marketing manager, from the tabloid journalist to the tall academic, we are all fascinated by the question how people become rich and powerful and whether ethnicity plays a role in the process. When I set out on the intellectual journey to answer these questions in the mid-1990s, my quest was to find an ethnic Chinese organization involved in business, culture and politics, in a country in Southeast Asia that had been at the centre of what was then described as the "Asian Miracle". When using this term, the World Bank meant the remarkable economic growth and social transformation experienced by some societies in Asia after World War II. Because I wanted to look beyond companies and business deals, I searched for an institution that connected the economic, cultural and political arenas.

As the largest Chinese business organization of the region, the SCCC(I) was a logical choice. I was surprised to find that no one had written a substantial academic account on the post-1957 history of this organization despite its age, status, size and importance.[2] Founded in 1906, the Chamber immediately became the leading Chinese organization of Singapore. More than merely a business club, the Chamber was indeed a social, cultural, political as well as an economic organization. By membership size it was the largest Chinese as well as business representative[3] and throughout its history the wealthiest and most influential businessmen of Singapore were its leaders.

This book will take the reader on a journey starting in 1819, first introducing the colonial and immigrant society that was Singapore and the role that Chinese merchants played in it. After recounting the founding of the Chamber and the turbulent decades before the Japanese occupation, the next five chapters will concentrate on developments after World War II. The story's leading role will be played by the Chamber, and its theme will be to detail internal developments of the Chamber as well as the changing fortunes it experienced in its external activities. The state is cast in the role of the main power the Chamber encountered in the outside world. This is an elusive character that takes on different guises: Colonial, Federal Malaysian and Singaporean. In these multiple forms it was the actor the Chamber co-operated with, was sheltered by and also sometimes fought against. I will make clear how the Chamber represented the Chinese community and the Chinese business sector during the journey of decolonization and state formation that Singapore experienced.

Money, power and ethnicity formed the three crucial ingredients of this journey and the Chamber embodied them all. Singapore, as had many young countries after World War II, had a specific and well-defined goal: establishing an independent, sovereign nation-state and a steady progress towards modernity. Generally speaking, modernity, in this context, was understood above all as sharing in the institutions and economic prosperity of the industrialized countries.[4] But there are many ways in which such a history can be told. Some would focus on the market and on economic theories and developments, arguing that ultimately the economy produces society. The assumption, propagated by neo-liberal economics, that rational choices by economic actors are in accordance with economic "laws" and will lead to a coherent and logical economic system dominates this approach. Generally speaking, I do not think human behaviour is that easily explained.

Others would reverse the logic of the neo-liberal approach saying that culture, and the social order it gives life to, will result in an economic system in keeping with moral and cultural tenets. Ethnicity and identity are the central determinants in this system. The danger of this approach is that it could present ethnicity and identity as static and unchanging, creating the illusion of an essential stereotype. In contrast, in this book, I will view ethnicity and identity as strategic and pragmatic: as masks that people can switch between and chose to use in different situations.

A third way to write history would be to focus on the role of the state, which centres on the relationship between state, society and economy. The crucial variables in this approach are power and control in the political game and it emphasizes the central role of the state in initiating, shaping and controlling social and economic processes. The inherent danger of this approach is that it will underestimate or neglect the role of socially based networks and associations that are rooted in civil society. It is the relationship between state and society that should be the focus of attention. This representational relationship can be seen as a two-way street involving three parties. At the top is the state, in the middle the elite and at the bottom the constituency connected to that elite, and information and communication flow back and forth along this street. The elite is the pivotal link in this communication process but the skills and services the former can offer must match the demands and expectations of both the state and the constituency. If these two other parties no longer feel the need for communication, have alternative channels or lose trust in the elite, the latter's middleman role can suddenly disappear.

All three of these approaches have their merits and demerits but a combination of the three will be able to enjoy the strengths of all while correcting their weaknesses. This is why the history of the SCCC(I) makes such a beautiful case, because market, culture and the relationship between state and society come together in one organization. The final ingredient of this enticing cocktail is "time". The Chamber's history of one century, and the fact that it has functioned under very different circumstances and within the context of numerous forms of the state, allow for a comparative perspective. Changes in the market, evolution of culture and shifts in power can all be understood over time and can be seen in comparison with earlier and later events. To understand the main dynamic of Singapore history, let us take a bird's eye view.

Singapore is an island of roughly 600 square kilometres in size, situated just north of the equator at the tip of the Malay Peninsula. Its modern history began in 1819 when the British established a port settlement on the island to exploit both the Straits trade of jungle and agricultural products of the region, and long distance commerce with Europe, India and China. The island was almost entirely populated by a wide variety of migrants, but from soon after its founding the Chinese constituted the majority. Its role was to be a trading entrepot and a centre of commerce and finance for the region, and the colonial *laissez-faire* policy upheld the free market principle for most of the economy.

Singapore has always been a very Chinese city: for most of its modern history 70 per cent of its inhabitants have been Chinese. On the other hand, however, Singapore has been very dependent on the region for its food, water, and, crucially, for its trading products. For an immigrant society and nation, the ambiguities of ethnicity within the regional and global context could be pressing. From the earliest days of the British settlement, ethnicity had been an organizing principle, both geographically (in planning and building the city) and socially, through a system of indirect rule placing communal responsibility on the leaders of an ethnic community. Social order in colonial Singapore was achieved along the lines of ethnicity. Viewing ethnicity as political and strategic is therefore particularly important because individual ethnicity became a key political marker and even a prerequisite for participation in the political process, and a leader's ethnic identity included obligations in the eyes of his community constituency.

Due to the migrant nature of the community and the structural arrangements of colonial Singapore, the Chinese elite of the Chamber performed not one but multiple and mutually reinforcing tasks or roles: social, cultural, religious, political and economic. The leaders of the Chinese community constituted a multi-purpose elite. Attaining and maintaining a position within this elite depended on the magic triangle of power, status and money. The economic logic of Singapore as a trading entrepot, and the multi-purpose role expected from the elite, meant that merchants were the most successful individuals. They had the money to support and take care of a constituency and in return were accorded status and positions of power within the community. This status made them the likely candidates to be appointed by the British to be responsible for their ethnic community.

Ethnicity also played a highly politicized role in the decolonization of Singapore, both on the island itself, in the struggle of connecting ethnicity and political rights, and regionally, as the territory's short-lived independence through merger with Malaysia (1963–1965) encountered strong ethnic opposition both in Malaysia as well as in Indonesia. In the ideologized world of the Cold War, the spectre of ethnic collusion in the extension of the communist ambitions of the People's Republic of China (PRC) in the region loomed large. As a Chinese city in a Malay region, the Chinese ethnic profile of Singapore led it to be seen as a possible communist fifth column in Southeast Asia.

After it became a fully independent nation in 1965, Singapore achieved remarkable economic growth, becoming Asia's second most prosperous nation behind Japan and overtaking its former colonial master Great Britain in per capita income. The stereotypical view of Singapore is that of a free market centre for commerce, finance and manufacturing. As a majority Chinese city and playing a key role in the Chinese diaspora, Singapore is also seen as a successful hub in this so-called "bamboo network". In addition, it has the popular image of a squeaky clean and highly efficient managerial developmental state.

Along this historical path, a number of changes to economy, society and the political arena took place. The market, the trading and entrepot role of Singapore continued unabated after independence in 1965, but the country also managed to establish a role as a production site for multinational and local industrial production within the global economy. Its comparative advantages of geographical position and a relatively cheap labour force meant Singapore could create a niche in the new international division of labour (NIDL) in the global capitalist system of the 1960s and 1970s. From the 1980s, Singapore developed its tertiary sector, and upgraded the educational level of its labour force and its industrial production to higher value-added activities for the information technology sector. Throughout, the state played a crucial role in shaping the market place and in creating and maintaining comparative advantages. The territory drew its life-blood from economic exchange, but was also vulnerable to changes in the regional and world market. In this respect it is interesting to consider that the Chinese in Southeast Asia, and certainly in Singapore, were citizens of the world market before they were citizens of a nation. Singapore has been forced to be sensitive to regional and world market logic, the supply and demand of goods and services, the shifts in trading routes and product flows.

In changes concerning ethnicity, the pattern of indirect rule through the leaders of ethnic communities, which had been the cornerstone of the colonial system, came under pressure in postwar Singapore with the advent of the developmental, interventionist state that redefined and limited the roles it wanted and expected the elite to play. However, the ethnic ordering principle prevailed after independence, as any resident of Singapore must be formally classified as Chinese, Indian, Malay or "Other". Ethnicity was much more than a classificatory aspect of an individual, because it was appropriated by the state as a defining factor of the political and social arena. Political authority was the key characteristic of the strong state, which demanded absolute loyalty to the nation-state, and commitment to the organic national community and the consensual goal of national economic development. The state elite, which in Singapore consisted of the leadership of the People's Action Party (the PAP; the only political party to have ever formed a government after independence), presented itself as the moral "guardian" as well as the expert-manager of society. This left very little room for civil society to continue to play a role, particularly the ethnically-based organization of the colonial era. The Singapore government expanded its power deep into the management of economy, society and ethnicity.

Changes in the political sphere occurred when the process of decolonization and state formation set in motion a process of redistribution of power and influence between state and society in Singapore. It entailed a development from a non-political (in the narrow sense) system of late-colonial petitioning and informal influence, via a highly politicized period of populist politics, to an authoritarian de-politicization by a dominant party-state. From being an elite endeavour of informal co-optation, the basis of mobilization and power became rooted in ideologically informed, class based populist electoral politics, which was later transformed into a strong state authoritarian framework.

Two observations on the representational role of the Chinese elite are important. First, the British colonial system, in which the Chinese elite was anointed as the sole representative of the Chinese community with no alternative representational channels, was replaced by a populist-based political system of elections, which limited the elite roles expected of the Chamber and developed state-controlled representational alternatives. Second, throughout this transformation, constituency needs should be understood as multiple and changing. In the narrowest sense factions within the Chinese elite could represent their own elite interests, or at the broadest end of the spectrum the entire Chinese population could be the Chamber's constituency.

These changes in the characteristics of the state and state power were important because of their implications for the organization and orientation of society. The realities of political power defined the arena of representation, contestation and competition, and set the parameters within which mediating organizations such as the SCCC(I) could operate. Market, culture and state were highly integrated in Singapore. The free market context and the ethnic composition of Singapore had a significant influence on the formation and organization of the state, while the state had, on the other hand, a very visible role in managing aspects of the market environment as well as ethnicity and culture.

Two contrasting images can represent the dynamic change of postwar Singapore. The first is that of colonial, *laissez-faire* Singapore as a highly self-regulating entity, in which ethnic communities were responsible for their internal self-government. This organizational pattern was built on informal sources of power and representational channels, which reflected the limited reach and interest of the colonial state. The Chinese elite and the SCCC had a complementary relationship with the British rulers: politically and culturally because they controlled the Chinese community in lieu of the colonial authorities, economically because they gathered Straits produce through the entrepot, distributed imports over the region, and gave shape to local industrialization. The second image is that of the dominant, ever-present, corporatist PAP state in which the Chinese elite and the Chamber became incorporated and trimmed down. Politically the SCCCI had lost its role of link between people and government, while its cultural and social roles had been shifted to other, state-approved, organizations. Economically it had become a partner serving state interest in the small and medium enterprise sector, trade, and brokering business with China.

The process by which Singapore moved from the first to the second image is the story of decolonization and state formation, entailing a restructuring of market, culture and state. However, large historical processes such as these are seldom simple and never one-dimensional. By taking the history of the SCCC(I) as a focus, we can look at the various aspects of this journey in detail and begin to understand and appreciate the intricate and delicate forces at work.

A note on currencies

Originally the Indian rupee was the currency enforced by the East India Company until 1867. However, the Spanish silver dollar was the local currency of choice for a large part of this period. The Straits dollar was introduced in 1867, which was fixed to the pound sterling from 1903 until 1967. The name of this currency was changed in 1939 to Malayan dollar. In 1967 the first Singapore dollar was released by Singapore although the currency remained interchangeable at par with the Malaysian dollar (Ringgit). In 1973 the two currencies were completely disconnected and no longer interchangeable. Throughout this book, sums of money will be denominated in dollars ($). It is implied that this refers to the currency valid and operational at the point in time described.

CHAPTER ONE

Historical introduction: Singapore, the quintessential trading port

THE FUNDAMENTAL FEATURES IN THE history of Singapore were that it always was a centre for trade and a destination of migrants, especially for the Chinese. Because of this, a local colonial context developed, which will be presented in this chapter. It will introduce the balance of power in the colonial state, commerce and its role in Singapore society, and what it meant to be Chinese. How did the Chinese organize their lives and how did their institutions and needs eventually lead to the establishment of the Singapore Chinese Chamber of Commerce (SCCC) in 1906?

Colonial Singapore developed from a commercial frontier settlement founded in the early 19th century to a full-blown high-colonial society by the first half of the 20th century. From the perspective of the Chinese elite in Singapore, this development can roughly be divided in three periods. The first, from 1819 to 1867, comprised the frontier days of the settlement, when Chinese merchants were drawn to Singapore because of its economically strategic position and free trade policy. Formal political activity and interaction between merchant society and colonial state were kept to a minimum by mutual consent but informal, multi-racial business networks flourished. The second period, from 1867 to 1906, started when formal representation of the Chinese was introduced and saw the development of a more locally grounded Chinese elite within the framework of the Singapore economy and polity. The third period, from 1906 to 1941, started when the Chinese organized their own representation through the Singapore Chinese Chamber of Commerce and was characterized by tempestuous economic development and the advent of ideologically inspired Asian nationalisms. In all three periods, money, status and power were defining factors for outlining and understanding the changes in the nature and composition of the Chinese elite, the economic sectors in which they were active, the structure of the Singapore polity and the position of Chinese society within it. The next section sketches the regional trading port pattern, which Singapore entered upon its establishment, and the colonial system of governing that resulted.

A migrant and merchant worldview characterized Singapore Chinese society and the social and institutional hierarchies the Chinese built reflected these fundamental realities. This was equally true for the founding of the SCCC and its internal organization. While political and military events in Mainland China affected the Chinese of Singapore, they also increasingly developed local ties, activities and strategies. The Japanese occupation of Singapore constituted a turning point for Singapore. Bringing violence and suffering, it also carried the seeds of social, economic and political change.

1. Trading port context

Any study on Singapore needs to be constantly aware of the fact that the essence of the island inhabitants' endeavours lies in economic activity. The very reason for the establishment of modern Singapore in 1819 was to create a British foothold at the tip of the Malayan peninsula to improve the Empire's commercial position vis-à-vis the Dutch over the China trade. The settlement was a construction based on economic logic.

In 1819, when Stamford Raffles, an employee of the British East India Company, moored at the mouth of the Singapore River, the island housed only a small settlement of about 1,000 inhabitants, a large part of whom were sea-faring nomads. For Raffles the attraction of an apparently inhospitable island covered with mangrove forests and salt-water marshes lay not in the people but in its geographical features and location. Singapore is situated at the narrowest point of the Malacca Straits, the body of water between Sumatra and the Malayan Peninsula that connects the Indian Ocean and the South China Sea. Its location there also confers a strategic position on the shipping and trading route between the mainland Southeast

Asian harbours of Burma and Siam in the north and the island Southeast Asian harbours in the Indonesian Archipelago in the south. The island itself also had a few features that made it especially attractive as a location for a trading settlement. A hill provided both dry land close to the river estuary amidst the marshes and also a source of potable water from a spring. Close to the mouth of the river, a natural deep-water harbour allowed moorage of the largest contemporary ships. Natural resources, and a perfect location from both a strategic as well as an economic point of view, were the reasons for Raffles' choice and thereby for the birth of modern Singapore.[1]

Indeed, it is necessary to specify "modern" Singapore here, because settlements had previously existed on the island and for exactly the same reasons of political, strategic and economic logic that had attracted the British. At the end of the 14th century, Temasek, which was situated on present-day Singapore Island, was a dependency of Srivijaya and later of Majapahit.[2] When the settlement became a vassal of the new Malay kingdom of Malacca, the name "Singha Pura" or "Lion City" was first used. Finally, in 1613, the Portuguese destroyed the Malay fort at the mouth of the Singapore River in a bid to eliminate Malay naval and political power. Through the ages, then, Singapore played a role as a strategic outpost and base in regional political development. But political and military aspects of Singapore's development were subordinate to economic advantages offered by its location at the confluence of trade routes, guaranteeing trading opportunities as well as a base for pirate activities.

Regionally speaking, Singapore played a part in larger networks of sea routes connecting various trading cities, which all had their own hinterlands and power bases. This pattern had been established 1,000 years before the first Western traders and conquistadors arrived in the late 15th century and linked the Arabic region, the Indian subcontinent and Imperial China.[3]

After the arrival of Western commercial colonialism, several of these key cities under European control, such as Malacca, Batavia, Macau and Manila, grew more rapidly than non-colonial cities such as Pegu, Ayutthaya and Hoi An. The economic logic and the commercial goals of, especially, the Dutch and British, connected well with the pre-existing pattern and eventually came to dominate a substantial part of the network. In the process, new locations were chosen for developing trading ports to supplement the system. Singapore, accompanied by cities such as Penang and Hong Kong, thus stands in a long line of ports dating from at least the 7th century until the present day.[4] Indeed, colonial drive was but one force influencing change and evolution of the trading system. Regional immigration was another key factor responsible for the implications of the founding of Singapore on the pattern of intra-Asian trade. When Singapore became the focal point of Chinese activity in the region, Southeast Asia emerged as an "articulated trading system".[5]

The Singapore trading network

After its establishment in 1819, Singapore almost immediately became the principal Straits port for Chinese junks to collect Western and Indian goods, and eventually also replaced Bangkok as a Southeast Asian entrepot for trade with China. Bugis traders also sailed their *perahus* to Singapore, which thereby became a nodal point for Western as well as for Asian shipping. Technological progress has been a critical factor affecting networks of transport and communication. And although its first impact, such as the introduction of Western square-rigged vessels in maritime Asia, was dramatic, its full effect took considerable time to become apparent.[6] As late as the 1820s there was still a larger tonnage of Chinese than of European shipping in the South China Sea. Frequently these junks were Southeast Asia-based. *Perahu* shipping remained important, especially for transport from the archipelago to the east and for the Bangkok-Singapore trade. For both Singapore was a natural harbour and entrepot.[7]

The trade of Singapore was almost wholly entrepot, containing very little produce or manufactures of the island itself. European merchants based in Singapore almost exclusively handled the trade with Europe, India and America. Having obtained their goods on consignment, these agents of European houses in Singapore did not dispose of their merchandise directly to regional Asian traders, but sold through Chinese merchants who possessed better knowledge of demand in the various neighbouring markets, and enjoyed special access to them. As the Chinese middlemen seldom had any capital, the European merchants had no alternative but to advance them goods on credit.[8] The merchants of Singapore formed an integrated community within the trading port context and when the Singapore Chamber of Commerce (SCC) was founded in 1837, members of all races were on its first committee.[9]

Trade statistics for the period 1823–1869 confirm that Singapore was a market for the exchange of merchandise and products of Europe, India and China, for the produce of the Malay Archipelago and Peninsula, and the adjacent states of Siam, Cochin China and Cambodia. Straits produce found its way through Singapore to Britain, India and China, while products from those three areas were distributed through Singapore in the region. Furthermore European manufactures and Indian opium made their way to China via Singapore while transhipment of Chinese products for Europe and America took place in Singapore as well.[10]

Significantly, the trade by and through Singapore did not merely constitute a stream of products. The types of goods traded, and the places traded with, reflected social networks as well as economic ones. Next to the British colonial networks, this web of Singapore's trading world had a distinct Chinese flavour. Chinese style foodstuffs moved between producer and consumer, a Chinese labour force was brought from China and dispersed through the region to produce more goods, and hard-earned wages were remitted to families back in China. Merchant communities at both the sending and receiving ends of these flows often housed individuals of the same clan or family.

Singapore's trading network tied the city to the regional and world markets. This merchant outlook on the world, combined with the migrant background of the Chinese linking them to other Chinese settlements in the region and back to their ancestral homes in China, produced a specific worldview. Cultural and social elements were integral to their trading networks. As economic endeavour was the lifeblood of the settlement, the need to consistently uphold and reinforce its free trade status was strong. This necessity led to a colonial governing system based on the logic of free trade economics.

2. The colonial system

The early administrators of Singapore had commercial, military or administrative backgrounds; more often than not they combined these three aspects. However, because the British East India Company (EIC) was their employer, the commercial outlook of local administration was guaranteed. The EIC held a state monopoly on British commerce with Asia and was also entrusted to govern British possessions in the East and make them profitable. Very soon after the British took possession of the island people started flocking to Singapore. The average individual who came to trade or settle in early Singapore was an adult male trader or agricultural entrepreneur.[11] Men of all kinds of ethnic backgrounds arrived but soon the Chinese became the majority ethnic group.[12] For the first 50 years British Singapore was a frontier society of adult male *homo economicus*.

From 1826 to 1867, Singapore was part of the Straits Settlements under British colonial rule from India. Government and administration were proverbially distant and unobtrusive, causing the leading local newspaper to write that: "... there is probably no other government in the world so incapable of addressing the people as that of the Straits".[13] A local state as such did not exist. The administration's goals were clear and undisputed though; to maintain free trade at minimum cost and to limit administrative overheads by a system of indirect rule. Leading individuals of each ethnic group were held responsible for the actions of their part of Singapore society, a colonial practice known throughout Southeast Asia as the headman or *kapitan* system. In Singapore this system was only in operation officially until 1825 but the principle of controlling and ruling ethnic groups by making their community leaders responsible was upheld throughout the colonial period. Although there were no formal representative institutions yet, informal ties between rulers and ruled developed. First and foremost there was commercial interaction. In the chain of produce trading from local fields through Chinese middlemen to the Western trading houses, the gambier and pepper economy held a special significance. From the 1820s to the 1840s, gambier and pepper plantations were set up in Singapore mainly by the Chinese and, by the late 1840s, 6,000 Chinese labourers were employed.[14]

To understand the significance of the link between production and trade, an analysis of the social and financial structures underlying them is necessary. For profitable cultivation of crops, cheap labour was a necessity. With the official suppression of slavery and piracy by the colonial powers in the early 19th century, the coolie trade became the sole legitimate labour supply, and this was protected and monopolized by Singapore.[15] Chinese merchants with the capital to finance the recruitment and shipment of labour from China to Southeast Asia thus controlled the coolie trade. The credit-ticket system, in which the merchant paid for the ticket of the Chinese immigrant in exchange for his labour, indebted the workforce to the financier.

An important element of organization and control was provided by the secret societies or *Tiandihui* (Heaven and Earth Societies), of which the same merchant/financiers were the leaders.[16] They were based on sworn brotherhoods in China with a strong ritualistic character grounded in popular religion. They evolved to include anti-Manchu traits after the 1644 overthrow of the Ming dynasty by the Qing and were outlawed and persecuted in China. In the migrant Chinese world, the secret societies remained a strong organizational force. Throughout the region these organizations provided structure to the Chinese communities as they set up temples and associations. The secret societies were therefore political, ethnic and religious based organizations, and the general view that they were merely criminal entities is limited and misleading.

The martial background of the secret societies was reflected in their ability to mobilize gangs of strongmen, and they thereby provided their merchant leaders with an instrument to control their labour force and defend their investments against rival groups.[17] The importance of the secret society is illustrated by the fact that, after 4,000 members of the Teochew Ngee Heng secret society were expelled from Singapore in 1844, this organization then initiated and controlled much of the planting in neighbouring Johor through the *kangchu* system in which cultivation centred on rivers, often with an administrative settlement (or *kangkar*) at the mouth controlling plantations further upstream. The *kangchu,* or "lord of the river", was the Chinese headman in control of the settlement. The Malay rulers of Johor incorporated this Chinese system in their administrative system through the *surat sungai,* or river document. The document authorized the Chinese *kangchu* to start plantations on a river, and gave him the right to collect taxes in the name of the Malay ruler, exercise the functions of government, and control cultivation within the river valley.[18]

Another important element in the organization of production, the control of labour and the raising of capital was the tax farm. This administrative-financial construction was first introduced in Singapore in the 1820s by Crawfurd, one of the early chief administrators, in order to finance the settlement's expenses while maintaining free trade in the harbour. Under the tax farm system, the government auctioned off the right to collect taxes on a specific product or service, for instance opium, spirits, prostitution or gambling, for a given period of time to the highest bidder. Chinese merchant/financiers were the dominant tax collectors until 1910, when tax farming in Singapore and Malaya was abolished.[19]

The combination of the tax farm, the secret society, coolie labour, and the *kangchu* system united in the hands of the Chinese merchant in Singapore an impressive degree of overlapping financial, entrepreneurial, administrative, "military" and labour control. The overlap of roles in the hands of Chinese leaders also shows that they were a multi-purpose elite. The gambier and pepper economy tied Chinese financiers with frontiersmen and coolies through opium in what was described as "a combination of monopoly and free enterprise in an atmosphere of expansion". The government auctioned off the license to collect taxes on opium that was sold on credit to Chinese coolie labourers by the financiers of the gambier and pepper plantation.

This integrated organization was not only important for the gambier and pepper plantations. Similarly, in the 19th century, Chinese tin mining labour itself could become a source of profit. The "advancer", the same

Singapore or Penang-based merchant, who put up the capital for a mining venture (and in return received tin *at below market price*) provided the necessary labour through the credit-ticket system, and had the sole right to supply loans, provisions and other necessities to the labourers *at above market rates*. The "advancer" was usually a spirits or opium farmer, who used previous farm profits to get the venture going, and could increase his profits by selling alcohol or opium to his captive labour force.[20]

This connection between market and consumer was vital to Singapore. Financially, opium underwrote both the state and the producing economy. Politically, it established a system of social control upon which the British administrative system was based, while financially taxes covered up to 40 to 60 per cent of budgetary expenses. Chinese merchants were crucial to British authority. They gained status by providing the link between ruler and ruled. The working relationship between the British merchant and the Chinese middleman and between the British administrator and the Chinese opium farmer was the foundation of the colonial state.[21] The local Chinese commercial elite in control of the plantations and the opium syndicates, while making a double profit (through sale and taxation) on opium, secured free trade for their other commercial endeavours as well.

Portrait of a Singapore Chinese leader, 1819–1867

A portrait of the typical Chinese leader of the frontier days of Singapore from 1819 to 1867 would be that of a merchant/financier who successfully combined a number of social, political and economic roles. It is in the actions of this typical leader that the connection between money, status and power becomes clearly visible. Wealth, or alternatively the ability to raise capital, was the key variable that sustained the mutually reinforcing relationship between the three elements. The merchant/financier needed money to recruit, ship, and control through indebtedness the labour supply necessary to cultivate crops. He also needed money to successfully bid for the tax farms that helped to make his agricultural and mining endeavours profitable. The practical power he possessed over a large portion of the Chinese community, through his control of labour, credit and provisions, was locked into a system of hierarchical status through the secret societies, temples and the system of Chinese voluntary associations. This power and status enabled him, through the principles of indirect rule, to represent the Chinese community to the British in Singapore and to the Malay rulers on the peninsula. This ability to represent the Chinese community was based on the financial and even physical dependency of his constituency.

The colonial chain of power relations, expressed in indebtedness through opium and the control over the supply of coolie labour, also lay at the root of secret society fights, riots as well as economic and social conflicts, so often attributed to perceived "oriental instability and strife".[22] Essentially, these reflected the efforts of various groups of Chinese entrepreneurs to control the most lucrative economic activities, whether they were tax farms, the rice trade or some other niche.

The resulting violence in the 1850s directly contributed to the British decision to change their style of government, introduce a formal representational structure and thereby create a more involved local polity.[23]

The British intervention in Malaya and changes to the Singapore polity

When London decided to expand its limited commercial focus and, from the 1870s, to impose more political control over the Straits Settlements, it followed what was called a policy of "intervention" in the Malay Peninsula. The British ambition was partly made possible by the significantly shortened lines of communication between Britain and its possessions, resulting from the completion of the Suez Canal in 1869 and the introduction of steam shipping and the telegraph. A first indication of the changes at hand was the conversion of the Straits Settlements of Singapore, Malacca and Penang from a possession governed by the colonial authorities in Calcutta into a Crown Colony administered directly by the Colonial Office in London. A governor was appointed and a consultative system consisting of an Executive Council and a Legislative Council was introduced in 1867.[24] The power of the governor, under supervision of London, remained supreme until 1942 but the system allowed a voice in the councils to a majority of ex-officio members of the administration and also to appointed local residents, Western and Asian.[25] The governor, although instructed to consider the advice of the councils, was in no way obliged to follow it. This system led to a petitionary style of representation of the interests of local residents. A fully-fledged local state did not develop because indirect governing of the ethnic communities was preferred over a deeper penetration of the administration into society. This administrative system enforced the hierarchical structure of the Chinese migrant society because representation was sanctioned as being an elite endeavour. The status and power of Chinese leaders grew because they held a monopoly of access, albeit limited, to the governing system.

The establishment in Singapore of the Chinese Protectorate in 1877 was a further break with the pure *laissez-faire* tradition. The disturbances of the 1850s, the 1867 Penang Riots and more riots in the early 1870s prompted the British to introduce administrative initiatives more directly targeted at, as well as interacting with, the Chinese community and its elite.[26] The new office under William Pickering immediately took initiatives to curb excesses in the coolie trade, prostitution and, most importantly, the secret societies. Governor Cecil Clementi-Smith was especially active with legislation to curb the secret societies. A number of ordinances were passed during the 1870s and 1880s. These culminated in the Societies Ordinance, passed in 1889 and put into effect in 1890, that was aimed at suppressing dangerous societies and registering "benevolent" ones. Although not eliminating the power of the secret societies, the ordinance went some way towards breaking them up into smaller bands and gangs that were easier to police and control.[27]

In 1889 the new power structure was completed with the establishment of the Chinese Advisory Board (CAB) as the official colonial channel of communication with the Chinese community.[28]

The rise of Singapore as a staple port

The opening of the Suez Canal, the steamship revolution and the demand for Straits produce in the world market resulted in a great economic boost for Singapore. The last three decades of the 19th century showed a six-fold increase in trade. This rise in Singapore exports was due to an increase in demand for tin and tropical produce. While Singapore was responsible for neither discovery nor growth in demand of these products, its merchants built on existing knowledge and networks to establish it at the centre of a rapidly emerging pattern of regional economic specialization: Singapore was entering the modern world market fast. The development of Malayan tin and rubber was important because these products did much to foster Singapore's position as a major port in Southeast Asia.

The model Huff provides for the Singapore economy after the 1870s is that of a staple port in which a raw material or resource intensive good is central to the economy. In the case of Singapore tin was its first staple in the 1880s and 1890s while rubber and petroleum provided the second and third from the 1900s until the 1920s. Until about 1850 India and China absorbed most Malayan tin; thereafter it flowed to London. The Chinese dominated and by 1870 controlled most of the tin industry until large Western involvement came after 1912 with the introduction of the bucket dredge.[29]

Rubber took the place of tin as the principal engine of the Singapore economy. Rubber planting in Malaya sprang from a number of experiments in the botanical gardens of Kew, Singapore, and Kuala Kangsar in Perak. In 1897, Henry Ridley, an important pioneer in Singapore, discovered a system of tapping that made estate production a viable economic proposition. One account argues that the first commercial ventures were all European.[30] Another version holds that Ridley convinced a local Chinese, Tan Chay San, to take up planting.[31]

British companies domiciled in the United Kingdom possessed more than half of the rubber estates in Malaya in the 1930s, while the locally registered Western companies owned about a sixth. More than a quarter of the total planted area was owned by Asian capital. The importance of rubber to the Malayan economy becomes clear from the fact that rubber exports as a percentage of total exports rose from only 3.7 per cent in 1906 to 59.5 per cent in 1925.[32]

In conclusion, between 1867 and 1906, Singapore became the centre of British power and administration in Southeast Asia because of its economic success. Intimately connected, through economic and increasingly through colonial administrative ties, to the Malay sultanates known as the Federated Malay States and the Unfederated Malay States, Singapore's other dominant economic relationship was with the Netherlands East Indies.[33] It served as a transhipment point and an entrepot port for regional produce as well as the distribution centre for manufactured products. It was the chief harbour through which cheap labour for mines and plantations entered the region, and a centre for financial services through its colonial and local banks. Commerce was clearly at the centre of the British colonial administration's attention at all times. The colonial state and the representational system that developed enduringly shared an economic logic because both the system of governing and the local immigrant society largely comprised people with commercial interests.

3. Social organization of the Chinese: migrants and merchants

To realize the impact of migration on Singapore, an examination of the statistics on the size of the population and on the number of newly arrived immigrants is revealing. By 1824 the population had reached 10,000 and maintained an annual growth rate of almost 8 per cent. This number was almost entirely due to migration because frontier characteristics and sex ratio prevented growth by natural means. Singapore continued to grow quickly, reaching 100,000 inhabitants in the 1870s, 200,000 in the 1890s and half a million in the 1920s. Since the Chinese comprised the vast majority of new immigrants, their percentage of the total population continued to grow, reaching 70 per cent in the 1890s before stabilizing at just over 75 per cent from the 1920s onwards.[34]

Push and pull factors determined the flow of migrants from China to Southeast Asia.[35] While commercial and economic opportunity attracted many, the deteriorating political and economic circumstances in China, especially since the mid-19th century, contributed greatly to the decision of many to leave their country of birth. Natural disasters such as droughts and floods weakened a faltering agriculture-based imperial system already under great stress from Western powers seeking forceful entrance into China. The Opium Wars waged by Britain in the 1840s and 1850s undermined the Qing state, which also had to contend with internal uprisings such as the Taiping Rebellion (1850–1865). All these factors led many Chinese, especially from the coastal provinces, to seek a better life overseas.[36]

The bang system and Singapore Chinese society

The diversity of geographical origins of the Chinese that came to Singapore, and the enduring identities they derived from it, proved pivotal to the organization of Chinese society in Singapore. The principal dialects historically spoken by Chinese in Singapore are Hokkien, Teochew, Cantonese, Hakka and Hainanese. Statistics for the dialect group breakdown during the first 70 years of colonial Singapore are lacking or at best incomplete. Because Teochew dominated pepper and gambier planting, it could be assumed that they then formed a sizeable group. For the period from 1881 onwards, for which data is available, the numbers present a fairly stable picture. The Hokkien dominated numerically, followed by the Teochew and the Cantonese, which formed sizeable communities. The Hainanese and the Hakka groups, in comparison were much smaller.[37]

The concept of *bang* is central to any understanding of the Chinese social and organizational fabric that developed after 1819. Cheng defines *bang* as "an age-old concept" which in the Singapore context "denotes a Chinese politico-socio-economic grouping based principally on dialect".[38] While *bang* is sometimes used loosely to denote a dialect-based grouping, the term *huiguan*, or voluntary association, always means an actual organization with members, leaders and often a place to gather. In Singapore the hierarchy of the *huiguan* developed to put the *huiguan* of the respective dialect groups at the top of the pyramid. Thus the Hokien Huay Kuan,[39] which all Hokkien speakers could join, became the apex of the Hokkien *bang* at the top of a pyramid of other Hokkien organizations. These were based on more limited organizational principles such as family, clan, village or district. In this way the Hokkien *bang* had a real institution as its seat. However, the *bang* had all Hokkien individuals and organizations in Singapore as its constituents, regardless of whether they were members of the Hokien Huay Kuan.

From the arrival of the first migrants in Singapore in the 1820s, their needs in housing, employment, a support group and a means of defence were met through the *huiguan*. A *huiguan* could be organized on the basis of kinship, geographical origin in China, religious or social organization, economic activity or occupation. The practical purpose of the organizations almost always would overlap with a shared common language of the members.[40] In this the *huiguan* of the Chinese migrants in Southeast Asia echoed the function of the merchant organizations based on shared geographical origin in Imperial China. They took care of fundamental commercial requirements such as standardizing weights and measures and maintaining a stable marketplace.[41]

In Singapore, the *huiguan*, besides assuming a similar role in the economic sector, also organized social, political and cultural affairs. The *huiguan* became the organizational nucleus around which temples, schools, cemeteries, trade associations and many other institutions were established, and the secret societies formed an integral part of this system of organization. Among the *huiguan* in Singapore, a hierarchy developed that was based on size, importance, the width and breadth of inclusion, area of origin in China, and dialect represented. Many categories of the hierarchy are self-explanatory. A village of origin organization would be subordinate to the relevant county or province of origin organization. An organization based on a lineage which originated from a recent common ancestor would be subordinate to one founded on an older common ancestor. The size of the dialect communities in Singapore determined whether a Hakka or Hainanese organization was less influential than a Hokkien one, although the wealth and status of the membership could offset or negate this aspect. For occupational or sectoral organizations, the importance of the activity to the overall economy and the riches attainable within it served as a crude ordering principle that changed as the economy developed. Many of these categories would overlap and reinforce each other. Teochew merchants dominated the rice trade, Hokkien from Anxi virtually monopolized the tea trade and a few Hakka families controlled the pawnshop sector.

In this manner a pyramid of power in the Chinese community was created, which was based on the basis of status, hierarchy and money.

The *huiguan* were self-supporting and depended on the donations of their members to finance their activities. In return for their donations, the rich merchants, who were also the headmen of the secret societies and could afford to bankroll the social system, were rewarded with public leadership positions that provided them with status and invested them with power. The *huiguan* organizations based on common dialect came to constitute the highest level in this *bang*-based system and the richest merchants of the highest status sat on their boards. In this way the *huiguan* were central to the integration of money, status and power through the control of credit, labour, tax farms and the trade, described earlier. The opium economy surrounding the production of gambier, pepper and tin had created a system of dependent representation. Through the *bang* system a wider and more institutionalized connection was forged between Chinese society and its elite in which more categories of Chinese migrants such as shopkeepers, harbour workers, etc. found a place.

Organizational reform of the *bang*-based hierarchical structure did occur. In the 1920s, for instance, a power struggle was played out in the *bang* centres of the Teochew and the Hokkien. In both instances the incumbents were Straits-born Chinese whose leadership was criticized as inattentive to the communities' needs. Public opinion and support was drummed up and sometimes even legal action was taken to dislodge them from power. In the end both organizations were reorganized and fell firmly in the hands of a new elite, who were championing an active identification of the *bang* headquarters with public local interests as well as with native place and Chinese affairs. Chinese *huiguan* thus changed from essentially mutual help establishments into versatile machinery for collective interest articulation and popular mobilization. The reform of the *bang* centres, in particular, enhanced group consciousness and solidarity, and the *huiguan/bang* system became an indispensable operational framework for any large-scale social campaign.[42]

The hierarchical principles of the pyramid laid out above overwhelmingly apply to the first generation immigrant Chinese, called Sinkeh (meaning "new guest") or China-born Chinese. It was this group that set up the earliest *huiguan* because it needed structure and services. It needs to be remembered that sojourning in Southeast Asia was the intention of many Chinese migrants who aimed to return to their hometown in China with enough money to retire. The majority of migrants who became settlers and local residents did not realize this ideal but the dream of returning lingered on well into the 20th century. The *huiguan* were on the one hand strengthened by these feelings, and on the other hand provided the institutional setting and the emotional context to keep them alive. New arrivals fed and expanded this system further, and created loyalties that could endure generations after first immigration.[43] Many residents of 19th century Singapore would have said that these Chinese had an enduring Chinese identity and a greater propensity to return to their home soil.

There was another group, however, largely outside the *huiguan* structure that was made up of Chinese whose families had integrated and partially assimilated into local, Malay society and who had been in the Straits Settlements for generations. These Chinese are commonly referred to as Straits Chinese or Babas. A core group within this category comprised the descendants of Chinese men who had lived and worked in the Malay Peninsula and the region long before colonial Singapore was founded. They had married local Malay wives, learned the languages and evolved hybrid cultural practices. When Singapore was founded, they moved there with all their regional knowledge. These Babas, Straits Chinese, and the local-born Chinese of later date who identified with them, often possessed higher levels of education than the first generation migrants, and included a higher percentage able to speak English and Malay. As a result they were often seen, both by contemporary observers and later scholars, to be more attuned to the colonial government system, and better equipped to enter into business with Western companies and partners as well as with regional traders. Hence they seemed to form a natural elite, able to represent the Chinese community.

While one must be sceptical of the essentialized notions that are often implied in the terms Straits Chinese and China-born Chinese, they are so widely and imprecisely used as to need introduction here. However, definitions of these terms are fraught with great inherent tension precisely because cultural and social behaviour is equated with birthplace and education. However, the definition of Baba or Straits Chinese has changed considerably through time. Jürgen Rudolph has done a magnificent job "reconstructing Baba identities", and his work is by far the best analysis of the complicated patterns of social, cultural, economic and political identities of this special group of Southeast Asian Chinese.[44] The extensive use of the terms local-born/Straits Chinese and China-born/Chinese-speaking Chinese has had a polarizing effect on the interpretation of historical developments in Singapore. Individuals shifted between or combined these identities in their lifetimes, and families did so over generations. This was especially true for the top elite of Singapore Chinese merchants.[45] Still, the colonial government endorsed the term Straits Chinese by making it a statistical category. Even though their definition of the term remains unclear, the percentage classified under this category was around 10 per cent between 1881 and 1901.[46]

Organization and representation

Early Singapore pioneer society had seen much social interaction between Asians and Westerners at the elite level, but distancing later set in for several reasons. First, steamship contact with Britain through the Suez Canal opened in 1869, and the introduction of telegraph service strengthened the social bonds of the colonial authorities and European merchants with the motherland. At the same time the steam revolution allowed Chinese businessmen to bring their families from China. When the British aspired to more direct political control in the Malay states and the Straits Settlements, they introduced the system of the Governor and the colonial councils, as well as a number of organizational initiatives pertaining to the administration of Chinese society. However, organizational forms in the Chinese community itself were also evolving. As the community grew, a greater need for more self-regulation and provision of social services arose, and attempts at pan-Chinese cooperation were made. The founding of the Tong Chai Hospital by leading Chinese merchants in 1885 signified the first institutionalized cross-dialect cooperation. Its board was organized on the principle of proportional representation of the main *bang*, a model that the British followed in the appropriation of seats on the CAB a few years later.

Indeed, when the first CAB was appointed in 1889, the seats were allotted to six Hokkien merchants originating from Fujian Province and six merchants hailing from Guangdong Province. Among the Guangdong group a subdivision was made between the Teochew, the Cantonese and the Hakka. By making the CAB the top representational organization, the British enforced a pyramid of indirect rule, in which the *bang* leaders in the CAB were the middlemen between the Chinese community and the colonial government, and this made the *bang* structure the officially sanctioned channel of the Chinese.[47] The Societies Ordinance of 1889 strengthened this pattern by outlawing the secret societies and registering the *huiguan*, which formed the backbone of the *bang* structure, as benevolent societies.

This meant that this *bang*-based social ladder now also led to positions of formal representation to and brokerage with the British, thus increasing status and possibilities to enhance and expand networks. Importantly, one was not required to be a British subject or be able to speak English to be eligible. English-speaking local-born Chinese did take up a larger than proportional number of seats. Still, the CAB was one more arena in which the elite Chinese merchants of differing dialect and trading backgrounds mingled and interacted. The fact that the elite among the migrants consisted almost exclusively of merchants, or at least individuals with commerce as one of their core activities, united it.

In the socio-economic hierarchy of the Chinese community of colonial Singapore, successful entrepreneurship led to wealth and leadership positions. Control of the leadership of *huiguan* and *bang* organizations in turn supported the ability of these leaders to access and control labour, to pool resources and to petition the government for a favourable policy climate. These circumstances and advantages more often than not led to more wealth, and had worked successfully in the gambier and pepper economy and also during Chinese dominance of the tin sector. New economic opportunities, especially in rubber and banking, reinforced this pattern.

Rubber merchants and bankers

Activity in most products and sectors of the Singapore economy such as in tin, Straits produce and rice, remained stable in volume and price from the 1910s to the late 1930s. Relevant within this context, and indicative of changes to the structure of Chinese business in this period, is the shift in ownership of tin operations in Malaya. Although the Chinese dominated up to 1906, when Western ventures still counted for only 10–15 per cent of production, two decades later the Chinese share had diminished to less than 40 per cent. The takeover was due to technological advances in both mining, with the introduction of the machine-powered bucket dredge, and smelting. Instead of investing heavily in the new mining technology, Chinese capital flowed to rubber, a new sector that presented great opportunities.

World War I and the demand for tires resulting from the advance of the motorcar industry fuelled the rubber boom in the Singapore economy. Malaya's rubber production amounted to half of world net export by 1918. For the Chinese business elite, the rubber sector offered opportunities in estate ownership and trade. The fortunes made in rubber were easily the most conspicuous springboard for industrialization and the growth of local Chinese deposit banking. The establishment of Chinese banks able to finance the rubber industry and pineapple canneries in the early 20th century was indeed a big transition in the formalization of organization and modernization of business institutional arrangements. For the first time, wholly Chinese-owned business ventures were organized as limited liability companies, and Western accounting methods were incorporated. Rubber and commodity production required steadier capital streams, which were perceived as being best provided by banks.

The formalizing and modernizing effect of the Chinese merchants' involvement in banking lay in the fact that in order to do business, they had to conform with modern business standards both in accounting practices and in the employment of a large English-educated group of bank employees. This was not only an institutional evolution; it also encouraged the development of an English-educated Chinese professional and administrative class in Singapore. The link with rubber was obvious; most of the big names in banking had a connection to, a stake in, or a company active in rubber.[48] Rubber also involved the biggest merchants more directly in the world economy. Companies such as Tan Kah Kee Rubber Co., Lee Rubber and Tan Lark Sye's Aik Hoe sold directly to London and New York and thus had extensive contacts with agents and clients in these global nodes.

The biggest Chinese merchants could secure export credit at the European banks, but most others could not and therefore depended on local Chinese banking. The men who ended up establishing and dominating Chinese banking were, not surprisingly, those merchants with access to European banks. There was also a close association between Singapore's industrialization and Chinese rubber entrepreneurs and surprisingly few Westerners were involved in industrial enterprises. The individual businessmen who took part in the new economic developments of industrialization were the rubber barons rather than the pepper and gambier financiers, and they were the prime movers behind institutional initiatives such as the SCCC.[49] Whereas the Teochew merchants had been dominant in gambier and pepper, Straits produce and rice, Hokkien merchants were dominant in rubber and banking. The rubber barons were also closely involved in the establishment of the Chinese deposit banks between 1903 and 1919.[50] From the business backgrounds of the leaders of the Chinese community from 1906 to 1942, it can be concluded that about 60 to 70 per cent of the top leaders were involved in rubber, banking or both.[51]

Singapore and its Chinese elite continued to evolve. Riding the highs of the rubber boom but also feeling the pain of the Great Depression, Chinese entrepreneurs played a major part in Singapore's industrialization. Economically speaking, the attention of the merchants centred more and more on British Malaya, the Straits Settlements and indeed the world market, especially through rubber, banking and transport. The boom years resulted in the expansion of government, increased government spending and therefore more interest in how the latter was spent on the part of the Chinese merchants.[52] In the free trade port and the registration or listing of the biggest Chinese companies in Singapore, the most important party to contend with was the colonial state, leading to a continuously increasing involvement of the Chinese merchants in the society and politics of Singapore.

4. Founding of the Singapore Chinese Chamber of Commerce

The rise of Singapore as a staple port set the stage for changes in organization and representation, not because the British dictated it but because the Chinese needed it. Given their increasing stake in the economic welfare of the colony and the growing welfare needs of its Chinese community, the Chinese business elite needed a supreme organization to crown the *bang* system; an organization that could lead and represent the entire Chinese community politically, socially, culturally and, first and foremost, economically. Through industrialization Chinese merchants had become more intricately tied to Singapore. By the early 20th century, they not only used the island as a base for trade but for production too. Furthermore, their banks and businesses fell under the regulations and policies of the British colonial authorities. As the state became more important to the definition of the market place, the Chinese merchants of Singapore needed a channel to influence and petition that state. This was the main reason behind the establishment of the SCCC. Almost 90 years earlier the first Chinese merchants had come to the island because it was another place to make money. By the early 20th century, however, Singapore had become much more to the Chinese elite than a place to trade. They had sunk roots into the island, the basis of their wealth was there, and so was their constituency – the people they led, who needed them but whom they equally needed, first as labour to produce their wealth, and second for social standing and leadership status.

On April 2, 1906, the *Singapore Free Press* reported:

Chinese Chamber of Commerce for Singapore Inaugural Meeting
A meeting of a large and influential section of the Chinese community of Singapore was held at the Tung Chi I Yuen (Tong Chai Chinese Hospital) Wayang street, on Saturday the 31 ultimo and a resolution was unanimously adopted to form a Chinese Chamber of Commerce in Singapore with the object of affording members the benefits of such an institution. The following gentlemen were then unanimously appointed to form themselves into a temporary committee to lay the matter before the local government

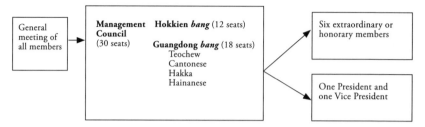

Figure 1: Organizational chart of the SCCC after the 1915 constitution

and to pray for the exemption of the Chamber from the operation of the Societies Ordinance 1889. Goh Siew Ting, Chop[53] An Ho, Fukien Province, Tan Hoon Chui, Chop Joo Hong, Kwangtung Province, Chan Tian Lam and Tan Tek Soon, Secretaries protem.

According to its first statutes, a president, vice president, 10 councillors and 40 committee members managed the organization.[54] The presidency and the vice presidency would both alternate between candidates hailing from Fujian and Guangdong province[55] and were annually elected. In this way the main *bang* would each be assured one of the two top jobs. Of the councillors four had to be from Fujian and six from Guangdong, while of the committee members 16 were from Fujian and 24 from Guangdong.[56]

The committee members embodied the direct link between the organizational pyramid of the *huiguan/bang* system and the Chamber. They were the benefactors and leaders of their family, clan and district *huiguan* and held the top positions in the *bang* organizations of their dialect group. It was precisely because they held those positions that they were thrust forward and elected by their fellow *bang* members to represent their dialect group in the Chamber.

A secretary was elected from among the members of the committee. Goh Siew Tin, a Hokkien ship and sawmill owner, was the first president in 1906. Chua Chu Yong, a Teochew rice and sugar merchant, succeeded him in 1907.[57] The organization grew quickly, and from around 500 founders in 1906 the membership rose to 2,000 by 1909.[58]

The formation of the Chamber did not go without challenge. In 1912 an alternative organization, the Chinese Merchants General Chamber of Commerce (CMGCC), was formed but it was only active for a year or so. Its members were not nearly as wealthy or successful as those of the SCCC, and their driving force was political motives connected to Nationalist China. By 1914 it had completely fizzled out.[59] In 1915 the SCCC constitution was amended and elections were made biannual. The councillors were abolished

The first SCCC building at 47 Hill Street, which was formerly the mansion of Wee Ah Hood.

Courtesy of National Museum of Singapore, National Heritage Board

The Chamber rented, and later bought, the old Chinese mansion of Wee Ah Hood in Hill Street to function as its home. In many ways the Wee Ah Hood mansion was a fitting home for the SCCC. Its location signified one of the organization's main functions: lobbying the British colonial authorities. The Chamber building was situated right on the axis between Fort Canning Hill, the place where Raffles resided and built the fort that embodied British sovereignty, and the Colonial Administration buildings beside the mouth of the Singapore River. Built in 1878, the mansion was one of four in Singapore constructed in the Chinese style. Its architectural features made abundantly clear that it was the home of a Chinese organization. Another mansion, that of Tan Poh Seng which was built in 1869, was also in Hill Street and functioned as the Chinese Consulate. Together they formed a mini enclave of Chinese institutional buildings in the colonial precinct of town.

and in their place six extraordinary or honorary members were appointed. The number of committee members was reduced to 30 (Figure 1).[60]

In the opinion of Song Ong Siang, one of the founder members, the view of certain Europeans that the SCCC was a Chinese government bureau was wrong. He said that although it was indeed registered with the appropriate ministry in Beijing, the Chamber was purely a local, commercial body. Recognition of the Chinese authorities was sought only to afford the members maximum safety when in China. After one decade of the Chamber's existence Song wrote that it had been a successful arbitrator in trade disputes, had mediated between Chinese and non-Chinese merchants and had been the means of bringing the views and wishes of the Chinese to the colonial government. It had assisted the authorities in times of emergency to make the Chinese public acquainted with the intentions of the government, and in every charitable endeavour it had taken a very prominent role. Rice riots, anti-Japanese unrest and plague prevention were among the developments that the Chamber had played a responsible role.[61]

Interpretations of the founding of the Chamber

The establishment of an organization of Chinese merchants in Singapore did not stand on its own. It was part of a larger development in China and Southeast Asia, which saw the chamber of commerce as an organizational form among the Chinese spring up in many cities. Because this process took shape at the initiative of the Imperial court in China and was followed by the overseas Chinese, it is often interpreted as proof that the overseas Chinese in Southeast Asia were still predominantly oriented to China.[62] While this seems a logical assumption, I will show that there were strong local factors at work as well.

Why did the Chinese court want to organize the overseas Chinese, a group that had been outlawed as illegal emigrants up till the 1860s? The answer is to be found in the political situation in China itself. Western forays into China, domestic uprisings and general administrative decay at the imperial court had brought the ruling Qing dynasty to the brink of collapse. Under great pressure from a royalist reform movement, the court decided upon measures to develop the Chinese economy in a belated attempt to save their power position and elevate China's stature in the world. The rich ethnic Chinese emigrants to Southeast Asia were sought out to help finance technical modernization and infrastructure projects. In their quest to improve relations quickly, the Chinese government thought that the Chinese chamber of commerce was most suitable to formalize links with the merchants of Chinese descent abroad.

The Qing court selected Chang Pi-shih, a prominent regional Chinese with business interests in Palembang and Penang, to spearhead the operation in Southeast Asia. He understood the local merchants and commanded their respect and trust.[63] Chang, a Hakka who had gone to Nanyang at 17, had established a vast tax farming and commercial network in Southeast Asia. He was persuaded to become vice-consul for the imperial court in Penang in 1893 and was to be influential in setting up enterprises and organizations both in China and Southeast Asia.[64] Yong Ching-fatt, outspoken advocate of a China-oriented explanation of the phenomenon of the Chinese chambers of commerce, writes that "between 1896 and 1905, there were few pressing social, political and economic pressures within the Chinese community in Singapore for the establishment of a Chinese Chamber of Commerce".[65]

That such an organizations was formed in 1906 after all, was due mainly to the Qing initiative and the active propagation of the scheme by Chang Pi-shih.[66]

However, these China-centred interpretations fail to address the economic, social and political changes among the Chinese in Singapore in the late 19th and early 20th centuries. From the economic perspective, the period 1867–1906 showed unprecedented growth and resulted in great development for the Chinese entrepreneurial elite of Singapore. In addition to the tin and rubber sectors, the regional trade in foodstuffs, focused primarily on the rice trade, was another rapidly expanding sector of the economy. Before World War I, the rice traders, the likes of whom included Chua Chu Yong and Tan Jiak Ngoh, were among the wealthiest and most influential leaders. It was no surprise then that these Teochew rice traders featured prominently among the founders of the SCCC.[67] Huff clearly makes the link between the long-term economic growth, the development of the staple port, which connected the Singapore economy more closely with the world economy, and the founding of institutions such as banks and associations. He observes, "In 1906 the Singapore Chinese Chamber of Commerce was established and soon afterwards, the Chinese Produce Exchange;[68] Singapore's earlier export-led growth no doubt encouraged the formation of both. This was certainly true of the contemporaneous development of the first local Chinese deposit banks."[69]

With new products and sectors, Chinese capital started to flow into banking, rubber, industrial activities and western corporations. As the economic elite of the Chinese were more and more tied into, and were indeed themselves forming, a modern economy, social control within a much more stabilized Chinese community was now possible through institutions such as the Chinese Chamber of Commerce.[70] The economic logic of the elite strategies and identities had a clear influence on the organizational structures they chose to represent their interests.

Therefore, apart from the China-centred explanations, other additional factors should be analysed. The social and political changes in Singapore provided opportunities for political brokers among the Chinese elite to gain wealth and power by fulfilling the role of informal and formal representative. The founding of the SCCC fits into this picture as a local response to the colonial implementation of representational channels. As Singapore evolved from a *laissez-faire* frontier society into a colonial city, the British, from 1867, had increased their level of political and social penetration. At the same time, Chinese society had become more locally grounded and had institutionalized a hierarchical system of power and representation through the *bang* system. The Chamber was more influential than the Chinese Advisory Board precisely because it was more representative of *bang* groups. The leaders of the former were elected by the elite of the Chinese *huiguan* and *bang* structure, while the members of the latter were appointed by the British. Also, the Chamber could impose decisions on members much more readily than the CAB could on the society at large. In principle, both had the sanction of the *bang* system but in the case of the Chamber it was a natural evolution of power bases that led to the choice of dialect group representation. The agency for action came from within the community itself.

The CAB, with its government-appointed members, was seen as a disciplining organization, put in place by the British with the aim of a divide and rule policy. In short, the Chamber was not constrained in a wide array of issues by being a semi-governmental body like the CAB.[71] Most importantly, the CAB had no commercial rationale to it. It mainly addressed social and cultural issues, and was never intended by the British to be the channel of communication for the Chinese business sector. The Chinese merchants of Singapore, as society leaders, needed a body with its own power base in order to command respect from the Chinese community they wanted to represent, and to be able to raise a wide range of issues with the government without being constrained by colonial institutional structures. The SCCC provided them with a united body that was independent of the British, both formally and practically.

5. Nationalism and China politics: migrants and primordial sentiments

Developments in China had their influence on Singapore. With the revolution in China in full swing in the early 20th century, the interest of the Singaporean Chinese merchants in their motherland increased. Different parties and factions in China were vying for the financial and political favour of the overseas Chinese. Organizational activity of the Singapore Chinese concerning China was significant, but it would be one-sided to endorse the suggestion that the dominant characteristic of the Chinese community in this period was a bitter split over events in China. Many developments actually united the Chinese elite, economically, socially and politically. What was significant for the development of the Chinese community was the sense of Chinese identity evoked by the events in China, and more importantly their effects in Singapore.

In his classification of the political behaviour of Chinese migrants in Southeast Asia, Wang Gungwu identifies three types. The A-type was concerned with national politics in China, the B-type was concerned with migrant community politics at whichever location they resided, the C-type was drawn into non-Chinese, hierarchical politics, whether indigenous, colonial or national.[72]

For most of Singapore's colonial history, the B-type was dominant, especially among the community at large. The elite leaders of the community, the merchant socio-political brokers, were inclined to keep abreast of all three types of political behaviour. At the elite level it is possible to combine the types of Wang's classification and indicate their historical dynamics. From 1819 to 1867–1877 the *laissez-faire* frontier type society was not formally politicized and the Chinese elite can be typified as "aBc". With the introduction of formal colonial politics and formal representation of the Chinese through the Chinese Advisory Board, the elite Chinese classification evolved to "aBC". From the late 19th century the elite classification evolved to the "ABC" pattern that would remain dominant until 1945. China politics in the first half of the 20th century, doubtless an important factor in, and a significant influence on, the Chinese community of Singapore, was part of a larger context. Developments in Chinese politics were translated and digested in local context and the worldview of the Chinese leaders was based on Singapore, through local community and formal colonial politics as well as through their business interests.

Some of the salient features of this local context were changing dramatically in the first half of the 20th century. Due to the worldwide economic depression, which hit Singapore hard, immigration restrictions for adult males from China were imposed in 1930. The restrictions had the effect of greatly increasing the percentage of locally born Chinese, from 35 per cent in 1931 to 58 per cent in 1947. It also meant that the sex ratio improved from 166 to 113 to 100 females in 1931 and 1947 respectively.[73] From 1923 onwards, crude birth rates exceeded crude death rates for the first time in Singapore history. Therefore, during a time when a focus on China was important, population characteristics show that grounding in an increasingly settled, local social context was taking place simultaneously.

Three types of China politics in Singapore

The history of China in the first half of the 20th century was tempestuous. Two revolutions, disintegration into warlordism, foreign invasion and an ideologically-based civil war shook the country. It is not surprising that these events had an effect on the Chinese communities overseas. Three different categories of these developments can be discerned: ideological conflict and civil war, natural disaster, and Japanese military invasion.

In the first decade of the century, royalists and nationalists vied for moral and financial support among the overseas Chinese. Later supporters of the nationalist Kuomintang (KMT) were opposed to those favouring the communists and, after 1940, the pro-communist Chinese Democratic League (CDL). All these mainland Chinese parties and movements sent agents and officials to set up Singapore branches and spread propaganda. But what was the effect of all these Chinese political movements at the elite level in Singapore? First they heightened awareness of Chinese identity on the personal level. The second effect was a local introduction of Chinese nationalism as a political-cultural identity. Being focused on China and following organizational initiatives of political organizations there, the resultant Singaporean organizational structures provided opportunities for reinforcing or challenging existing Chinese elite patterns.

Cultural nationalism: royalists and reformers

Changes in China lay at the base of this opposition. Defeat in the Opium War with Great Britain between 1839 and 1842 resulted in the Nanjing Treaty and the establishment of treaty ports on the Chinese coast where British, and soon all other foreign merchants, could trade freely.[74] The Qing concern meant a renewed interest by the court in the Nanyang Chinese. The immigration edict, which had made the act of leaving the country a crime, was relaxed in 1859 and formally revoked in 1893. This enabled much freer travel, trade and communication between the migrant communities and China. Qing officials started frequenting Southeast Asian cities and formal representation was established when consuls were appointed in the 1870s. In Singapore the Chinese consulate was established in 1877 with the familiar figure of Whampoa as Consul.[75]

Increased contact with China was certainly a factor in the rise of cultural nationalism among the Chinese elite in Singapore. A first exponent of this was the Lo Shan She or lecture movement, started in 1881. It aimed to counter Westernization and Babaization by reintroducing and explaining the socio-political doctrines formulated by the Qing emperor Kangxi in the 18th century on the basis of state Confucianism. Many of the merchant patrons such as Goh Siew Tin, the later first Chamber president, were Qing titleholders. The Qing consul, by this time a Chinese diplomat rather than an appointed local, strongly endorsed the movement and regularly opened meetings. A cross-*bang* unifying effect did not come about because the Lo Shan She was a Hokkien-dominated movement and Cantonese and Teochew were overall not willing to attend lectures sponsored by the Hokkien community. Instead they set up their own groups.[76]

The Confucian revival movement was another form of cultural nationalism and had a broader cross-*bang* base. It emerged in 1889 and wanted to revive Confucian values in the overseas Chinese community through religious rather than intellectual means.[77] Lim Boon Keng, the most prominent Straits Chinese around the turn of the century, was actively involved, showing that a focus on, or interest in, Chinese culture and politics was not an activity in which the China-born immigrants were exclusively involved.[78] The Reformists in Singapore were inspired and influenced by a reform movement of young officials in China. The scholar-administrator Kang You-wei propagated the idea that Chinese learning should remain the essence in the Chinese political and social system but that Western learning should be used for practical development. Under the influence of Kang, the Guangxu Emperor staged a far-reaching but short-lived reform attempt in 1898.[79]

When the SCCC was established, it counted mainly Qing loyalists, both royalists and reformers, among its leaders and members. This loyalty expressed itself in celebrations organized on the birthdays of the Empress Dowager and the Guangxu Emperor. Concern over loyalty to the dynasty and over Confucian values and practices are evident in the early Chamber discussions on which flag to fly and on which calendar to use: the Imperial/Confucian or the Western.[80]

Nationalist revolutionaries

After having been disappointed as a royalist reformer, Sun Yat-sen became the founder of the Kuomintang (KMT), China's nationalist revolutionary party. As the Imperial Qing dynasty was replaced by civilian rule in China through the 1911 revolution, the KMT became a major actor in national politics. Very soon, however, the country descended into a period when significant parts of China fell under regional rule by so-called warlords. Backed by armies loyal to them personally, these warlords fought against each other to increase their territory or to ultimately re-unite the country.

A KMT government with Nanjing as its capital remained in control of a large part of China. The Singapore branch of the KMT was set up in Beijing in 1912 as the Singapore Communications Lodge. From 1914–1919 the

KMT operated in Singapore clandestinely under the name of Chinese Revolutionary Party. After 1919 it was known as the KMT of China and operated openly.[81]

By the early 1930s, a sizeable number of the Chinese merchant elite supported or had become involved in the local KMT. The increasing role of KMT supporters in the Chamber is apparent from an incident in the early 1930s. The new office bearers for the period 1931–1932 refused to take office under the traditional oath and ceremony of the Chamber, which was still set in Imperial phraseology because it dated from before the 1911 Chinese revolution. Supporting President-elect Lee Choon Seng, the new committee demanded that a new ceremony, in line with the Chamber of Commerce Ordinance of the KMT government, should be introduced. In the end the outgoing committee stuck with the old and the incoming president introduced the new. Two years later, changes to the Chamber's constitution, which brought it in line with the National Government Chamber of Commerce Ordinance of 1929, were reported.[82]

Leftist revolutionaries

Rooted in the May Fourth 1919 movement, which was essentially anti-Japanese and anti-imperialist, and heavily influenced by the communist revolution in Russia, the Chinese Communist Party (CCP) was founded in 1921 in Shanghai. Initial cooperation with Sun Yat-sen's KMT existed between 1924 and 1927 but after Sun's death in 1925, due to developments in China and the Soviet Union, the KMT and the CCP slowly but surely became adversaries. Sun's successor as the leader of the KMT, Chiang Kai-shek, went on an extensive drive to unify the country and make an end to the period of the warlords through what is known as the Northern Expedition lasting from 1926 to 1928, which also brought KMT and CCP forces into combat against each other.[83]

The earliest leftist revolutionaries in Singapore had their basis in the Tongmenghui, a China-based organization, which had established a local branch in 1906. When the Singapore KMT evolved out of the Tongmenghui in 1912 some left-wing elements stayed out of the new organization. Latent working class feelings were fanned by sporadic anarchist and communist activity in Singapore and Malaya from 1919 onwards. The breakdown of the united front of the KMT and the CCP in China meant that radical politics in British Malaya sought a more defined organizational form. Under strong influence of the Communist International, the Nanyang Communist Party was established in 1928, and the more geographically specific Malayan Communist Party was founded in 1930.[84]

The early radical leftist movements in Singapore and Malaya received very little elite support. Ideological opposition deriving from class roles and backgrounds was the most obvious reason; one of the first leftist activities was an attempt at rallying labour behind its cause. From 1937 onwards some contacts between the left and the merchant elite developed when some elite leaders became more influenced by, and attracted to, the communist side in the Chinese political arena. This was more due to concerns over the stability, unity and welfare of China rather than to deep revolutionary ideological convictions. When a group of Singaporean Chinese leaders around Tan Kah Kee became convinced that the KMT of Chiang Kai-shek was devastating China with its policies, an elite-backed pro-communist organization in Singapore started to take shape.

New ideologically based political organizations in Singapore created additional power structures and hierarchies in which the local merchant elite could participate and compete. The local, Singaporean part of this political dynamic was an important result of an ideological conflict taking place in China. It aroused feelings of nationalism focused on China, but also of individual Chineseness grounded in Singapore, their place of residence. Men like Tan Kah Kee connected these feelings to relief for victims of natural and man-made disasters that befell the motherland. When floods and droughts compounded governmental and administrative disintegration, community leaders in Singapore set up fundraising efforts. The Chamber's records show a long list of relief efforts and discussions on aid, helping victims of floods, droughts, famines and the dreaded overflowing of the Yellow River.[85]

An important feature of these relief efforts was that they were either organized through the Chamber itself or initiated by one of the *bang* organizations and then supported and coordinated by the Chamber. In this manner, the relief activities reinforced both the *bang*-based organizational features of the Chinese merchant elite, and the dominant position of the Chamber therein. This strengthened elite integration across *bang* lines and across political and ideological lines.

The anti-Japanese movement

Even more than these aid efforts, the Chinese community united when the territorial integrity of China was at stake. In 1919, Japanese demands at the end of World War I outraged and united overseas Chinese of all political persuasions, the local-born as well as China-born. Having supported the allied side, Japan laid claim to some of the German possessions in China. The rage of the overseas Chinese were expressed in a number of anti-

Tan Kah Kee: Rubber tycoon, industrialist,
philanthropist and then bankrupt.

*Collection of Tan Kok Kheng. Courtesy of the
National Archives of Singapore*

Tan Kah Kee was born in 1874 in Tongan
County in Fujian Province. As a seventeen
year old he came to Singapore for the
first time to work in his father's local rice
business and would spend most of his life
there until he returned to China for good
in 1950. In 1903 he was forced to fold
the family businesses in Singapore due to
debts, but soon after he ventured on his
own into the pineapple canning business.
In 1906, he was one of the early entrants

in the rubber sector, planting 180,000
seeds amidst the pineapple plants at his
Hock San plantation. Tan developed
into the "Henry Ford of Malaya" when,
in the 1920s, he started the processing
of latex and the manufacturing of
rubber products such as boots, tennis
shoes and tyres. In 1925, at the peak
of his business fortunes, his ventures
made a net profit of almost $8 million.
Eight years later in 1933 his business
interests, principally organized in Tan
Kah Kee and Company Ltd., went
bankrupt. By this time, however, he had
already built up an extensive network
of businessmen who were tied to him
by family bonds or to whom he had
given a first independent business
opportunity after they had worked
in one of his companies. These men
included Lee Kong Chian, his son-in-
law who would become the world's
largest rubber producer and dealer,
and who was pivotal in the merger of
the three Hokkien banks that formed
Overseas Chinese Banking Corporation
in 1932. Another Tan protégé was Tan
Lark Sye who had worked in his rubber
factory and later started up the Aik Hoe

Japanese boycott actions and later, when Japan actually encroached upon
Chinese territory, in war relief efforts.[86]

As Japanese military aggression in China escalated, the level of
organization in Singapore of resistance and support for China and Chinese
victims increased. After the 1928 Jinan incident in which Chiang's KMT
troops were blocked on their Northern Expedition by Japanese forces
intervening on Chinese soil, anti-Japanese feelings were fanned higher.
In Singapore, Tan Kah Kee took the initiative through the Ee Hoe Hean

Rubber Company. These and other men supported Tan Kah Kee's social and political endeavours and donated large sums to keep all of Tan's educational projects afloat. Education was Tan's central philanthropic interest, and he was instrumental in the setting up of primary and secondary schools, and teacher training colleges in Singapore and China. The crowning glory of these activities, and a major drain on his wealth, was Xiamen University in the city of Amoy, close to his native village of Jimei. Tan was one of the founding members of the SCCC and an active member of the Hokien Huay Kuan, which under his leadership was reformed and reorganized between 1927 and 1929. In the latter year he became president of the Hokien Huay Kuan and would hold on to that position until 1950. In 1929 he launched an unsuccessful attempt to reform the SCCC as well. He wanted to get rid of the *bang*-based election system and put the organization on a more professional and administratively efficient footing. His efforts were blocked by the combined efforts of a group of KMT

supporters and non-Hokkien *bang* interests. Tan supporters remained a very active constituency in the Chamber arena, but Tan himself withdrew from this platform. Apart from a very strong *bang* base in the Hokien Huay Kuan, Tan cultivated a network of millionaires in the Ee Hoe Hean Club. After becoming president in 1923, he made strong efforts to attract top leaders from dialect groups other than the Hokkien who had been dominant among the founders. It would remain Tan's principal base of power from 1923 to 1947, and during that period, the club took on an increasingly political nature and became more involved in China-related political activities. Tan had been a member of the Tongmenghui from 1910 but never joined the Singapore KMT, its successor. He was an active supporter of the KMT's unifying efforts in China though, and was involved in a number of specific fundraising initiatives towards those aims. By the late 1930s he opposed Chiang Kai-shek and supported the efforts of the communists in China as well as organizations sympathizing with them in Singapore.[87]

Club to set up the Shandong Relief Fund Committee. Unsurprisingly the Committee was also set up along *bang* lines. The election of its 32 executives, who would aid Chairman Tan Kah Kee, guaranteed solidarity among the dialect groups and a broad base for the Fund. The Committee was very successful and collected $1.3 million within a year.[88]

The Mukden Incident of 1931, by which the Japanese forcefully gained control over all of the northeast provinces that made up Manchuria, infuriated the Chinese community in Singapore and led to more boycott actions and relief efforts.[89] The Marco Polo Bridge incident in 1937, which signalled the Japanese invasion of China proper, led to the establishment of a Chinese community-wide relief association in Singapore headed again by Tan Kah Kee. The Singapore China Relief Fund, in existence from 1937 to 1946, was again set up along *bang* lines. The organization spread its wings to envelop the whole of Southeast Asia in October 1938, when the South Seas China Relief Fund Union, which existed until 1949, was formed. The organization decided to send a Comfort Mission to China in early 1940. After this trip, which included a visit to the communist controlled areas, Tan Kah Kee turned decidedly anti-KMT and this brought him into a direct clash with KMT supporters and with the pro-KMT press.[90]

The effects of China politics on Chinese identity in Singapore

It might appear that much of the socio-political development in the Chinese community of Singapore in the first four decades of the 20th century was dominated by concerns over the situation in China. This trend seems to pertain to cultural movements, ideological viewpoints, natural disaster relief organizations, and to the anti-Japanese and war relief initiatives. The first conclusion often drawn from this picture is that China politics was indeed the dominant factor to explain the historical development of the Chinese community in this period, and that Chinese nationalism and Chineseness were its salient features. The second conclusion often reached is that this China focus divided Singapore Chinese society and its leadership. Yong holds that the Chinese community was "structurally divided along the lines of language and education, contending political ideologies and orientations, divisive institutions and professions".[91]

However, there was more to the picture than China politics. Politically, as a migrant community in Singapore, the Chinese were concerned with their internal community politics, and had to contend on a day-to-day basis with the influence, control and impact of the British colonial state. Recalling Wang Gungwu's model of A-, B-, and C-type Chinese political activity, it is clear that China politics was, in fact, the late-comer of the three. Also, economically, the attention of the average Singaporean Chinese, and certainly of its merchant elite, was focused more on the regional and world economy than on China. Singapore's main export markets were Europe and the United States, while its regional trade and sourcing of goods focused on Southeast Asia. Furthermore, China politics in Singapore did not mean a simple transposition of Chinese cultural and political movements, ideologies or struggles. All these activities were translated and had a distinct and important local component to them. Chinese culture, Chinese politics and Chinese nationalism were integrated and embedded in pre-existing, or newly created, organizational structures and hierarchies that were specific to Singapore and its Chinese community.

Throughout the developments in China it is noteworthy that the majority of the Singapore Chinese elite were not at the forefront when it came to change. At every major junction in China, Singapore Chinese leaders ensured that the resulting power balance was clear after a confrontation before switching allegiance to the new powers-that-be. The elite were cautious and conservative in shifting allegiance and loyalty, but they did shift, which indicates that for the majority ideological conviction was not strong. The SCCC had held on to its royalist based constitution and oath for almost twenty years after the fall of the dynasty. In those two decades, however, warlords had divided China and made it very unclear what the eventual power balance would look like. Only when the KMT under Chiang Kai-shek had united the country and was firmly in control did the Chamber formally change its allegiance. In the meantime, the logic of free market economics had ensured that political identifications in Singapore did not, in most cases, constrain business dealings or cooperation in social initiatives with individuals of different political persuasions.

While developments in China, and the extension of cultural and political structures to the Nanyang, are important to any understanding of Nanyang Chinese political motives and orientation, forces and conditions in Singapore played a decisive part in shaping the stand and modus operandi adopted by Singapore Chinese. Rather than signifying an exclusive China orientation, China politics reinforced local structures and presented new positions of status, networks and business opportunities. The relief organizations, especially the bigger ones, were set up as a big elite umbrella over the dialect group structure, while the practical work was done along *bang* lines, rallying support and gathering donations through the voluntary associations. Therefore, although these efforts were focused on China, organizationally they were very much grounded in local networks and structures.[92]

In this way the large relief efforts also had an integrative rather than a divisive effect at the elite level. A number of prominent Straits Chinese participated in the cultural movements and the natural disaster and war relief efforts. Especially in the Confucian Revival Movement and the introduction of local Mandarin Chinese (as opposed to dialect) education, the figure of Straits Chinese leader Lim Boon Keng loomed large. He later became the Vice-chancellor of Tan Kah Kee's Xiamen University. In the opposite direction many China-born supported English-language education in Singapore. Tan Kah Kee, for example, donated to the Anglo-Chinese School and Raffles College. Just as for war relief for China, fundraising efforts to aid Britain in World War I and early World War II saw support from all types of Chinese.

At the elite level, true to the dominant trading port characteristic of Singapore, business remained the prime common ground on which everybody dealt with everybody as long as there was a profit to be made. In the Chinese Commercial Bank, China-born and early royalist Lim Peng Siang (also in Overseas Chinese Bank, and Ho Hong Bank), cooperated with Straits Chinese Lee Choon Guan and Straits Chinese and early KMT supporter Lim Boon Keng (also in Ho Hong Bank). A number of SCCC leaders were on the board of directors of the English-language *Malaya Tribune*. Straits Chinese S.Q. Wong sat on the board of OCBC, which was dominated by Tan Kah Kee's son-in-law and supporter Lee Kong Chian and other China-born.

At the elite level, shared business interests as well as a shared sense of responsibility in social and cultural affairs drew the Chinese leaders of Singapore deeper into the local arena in which they cooperated and competed. China politics was a part of this dynamic and did not necessarily weaken the connections of the Chinese elite with Singapore. Rather, it contributed indirectly to a strengthening of organizational structures and an early sense of civil society. When war in Southeast Asia broke out in December 1941, the Chinese, China- as well as Straits-born, and pro-KMT as well as pro-communist, joined the Anti-Japanese Defence Council under the British approved leadership of Tan Kah Kee. When the Japanese successfully invaded Singapore, the Chinese paid dearly for this loyalty, which was a loyalty to Singapore rather than a loyalty to China or to Britain.

6. Impact of World War II

Defence activities

A form of local military organization had been in place since 1901, when the Chinese Volunteers of the Straits Settlements Volunteer Force, mainly consisting of Straits Chinese, had been established.[93] In December 1941 they numbered about 2,000. Earlier in May that year, preparations had begun for the eventuality of a Japanese attack. A branch of what would later become the Special Operations Executive was established as a training school for subversion and sabotage behind an advancing enemy. After war with Japan broke out on 7 December 1941 (on 8 December for Asia), the training of "stay behind" groups was stepped up.

On 26 December 1941, Tan Kah Kee was asked to lead a Singapore Chinese general mobilization council. The Mobilization Council was set up on a *bang* representation basis and consisted of a Protection, Labour Service, Propaganda, General Affairs, and Arms department, and a Singapore Chinese Anti-Japanese Volunteer Battalion of about 5,000 was created to aid in the defence of Singapore. The force was ill-equipped, but fought valiantly in January and February 1942 and sustained heavy casualties during the battle of Singapore.[94]

Singapore became Syonan (meaning "Light of the South") on 15 February 1942 when British Lieutenant-General A.E. Percival surrendered unconditionally to Lieutenant-General Yamashita Tomoyuki. The Japanese saw Syonan as the centre of the Southern Region of their Greater East Asia Co-Prosperity Sphere. After the successful invasion, the 25th Army was left in charge of Singapore, Peninsular Malaya and Sumatra with Syonan as its base. In theory the Japanese came to liberate their fellow Asians from the yoke of colonial rule, but in practice imperial needs were put far above local interests.

Sook Ching

It was apparently the policy of the leaders in Tokyo to take a conciliatory approach in the relations of the new regime with the local ethnic communities, as well as the Chinese. The 25th Army took a different view. Many of the soldiers had fought in the Sino-Japanese War, and had met mainly Chinese resistance when they fought their way down the Malay Peninsula and on Singapore. The intimate involvement of Singapore Chinese in anti-Japanese activities dating back to 1908, but especially in the National Salvation Movement from 1937 to 1941, as well as their role in the civil defence, guerrilla warfare and intelligence work in the last-ditch battle of Singapore, made the local Chinese a target.

Three days after surrender, all Chinese men between the ages of 18 and 50 were ordered to report to registration camps for screening. What followed was the *Sook Ching* or "purification through purge" in which thousands of Chinese were killed for allegedly being anti-Japanese. Officially, the search targeted Singapore Volunteer Army members, civil servants, members of the KMT and the MCP, leaders of the anti-Japanese boycotts and the civil defence movements. The Kempeitai, the Japanese Military Police, and its

members, however, condemned and killed at will. It is impossible to state
with certainty how many became victims of the *Sook Ching*. The Japanese
later admitted to killing 5,000 Chinese, but local Chinese sources put the
number at 25,000 for Singapore.[95]

The *Sook Ching* was an extremely traumatic experience for the Chinese
community of Singapore; the fear and bloodletting are etched on the collective
memory.[96] Terror continued with the arrest, imprisonment and torture of
many Singaporeans.[97] In early 1942, a few hundred local women, most of
them Chinese, were rounded up and forced to work in "comfort stations",
which were brothels for the Japanese soldiers.[98] The *Sook Ching* inevitably
alienated most of the Chinese population from the Japanese administration
and drove many young Chinese into the jungle to join the Malayan People's
Anti-Japanese Army, the communist-led resistance movement.

The Chinese elite and the Overseas Chinese Association

Some of the top leaders of the Chinese community had managed to escape
Singapore. Chamber president Lien spent the war in the Chinese capital of
Chungking, Tan Kah Kee went into hiding on Java, and Lee Kong Chian
was in America and later India, where a little community of Malayan elite
members congregated. Those Chinese community leaders who stayed behind
tried to go underground but almost all were caught during the screening
period in 1942. They escaped summary execution during the *Sook Ching*
because Tokyo expected local Japanese authorities to raise their own
revenue, and therefore the richest Chinese were now held at ransom.

In March 1942, the Chinese of Singapore and Malaya were ordered to
collect a $50 million gift to atone for their resistance against the Japanese
in the previous decades. The amount was so high as to make collection
impossible; this was equivalent to a quarter of all the currency officially in
circulation. Tortured and under threat of death, Malayan Chinese leaders
formed the Overseas Chinese Association (OCA). Its Singapore branch
was expected to raise Singapore's $10 million share.[99] Characteristically,
the Singapore OCA was subdivided into seven *bang*-based categories,
which were made responsible for raising money within their dialect group.
Eventually, after a few extensions of the deadline, the OCA took out a
loan with the Yokohama Specie Bank for $22 million in order to reach
the required amount. Presentation of the "gift" to Yamashita took place
on 25 June 1941 at the Singapore Chamber of Commerce premises in the
Fullerton building.[100]

The wartime economy of Singapore

The Japanese occupation was a great social and economic disruption to the preceding twelve decades of peace during which the island had flourished. Extensive Japanese bombing and the Battle of Singapore had severely scarred its infrastructure, but, more importantly, free trade ended. Large Japanese companies such as Mitsui and Mitsubishi enjoyed virtual monopolies in domestic and foreign trade, and strategic raw materials for Japan's war effort were seized and shipped off. Japan had made plans well before the invasion of Malaya for the organization of the region's finances.

On 27 April 1942 all the Singapore banks were closed except for five Chinese banks, which were allowed to reopen two days later.[101] The Japanese military currency, dubbed "banana money",[102] was now the only legal tender. Continuous printing of more and larger denominated notes, but most of all great problems in supplying Singapore with sufficient food, resulted in extensive hardship and mounting inflation. An extensive black market system developed and the wholesale price index rose from 100 in December 1941 to 185,648 in August 1945.[103]

The essence of the Singapore economy, its trading port status, was severely affected during the war. Normal business came to a standstill. Many individual businesses were either wrecked or suffered substantial damage, especially those in possession of factories and industrial structures. However, more than 100 new firms were established in Karimun during the war years, mostly import-export businesses, and the island became the free trade hub of smuggling and black marketeering for the region.[104] Also, as the Singapore economy was based more on the software of trading goods rather than on the hardware of producing them, a fundamental devastation of the Singapore economy did not occur.[105]

Concluding remarks

Having skimmed through roughly 125 years of Singapore history (1819–1945), it is possible to formulate some characteristic features of economic activity, the state, and the Chinese community. Singapore was conceived and built for making money, and therefore, save for the Japanese occupation, that aim was exactly what government sought to serve and the Chinese strove to achieve. The trading port context and economic logic led the colonial state to uphold free trade, keep administrative overheads low, and to leave the population to do its business. This *laissez-faire* approach prevailed up until the Pacific War, although its purest form ended when, by 1867, frontier Singapore started to give way to a more formal colonial society.

Singapore and its Chinese formed a migrant community and the organizational patterns that took shape in Chinese society reflected this. A web of kinship, regional, and occupational *huiguan* crystallized around dialect, making the *bang* organizations the most important, prestigious and influential entities in the Chinese representational pyramid. The colonial state governed this migrant community in an indirect fashion by making use of this pyramid. The Chinese headmen were appointed because they were the *huiguan* and secret society leaders who commanded power and influence over their respective dialect group constituencies. In 1889, the colonial authorities capped the system with the CAB. Again the appointees were the leaders of the *huiguan* organizations that governed and structured Chinese society. Thus, the British sanctioned and strengthened the *bang* principle, a system that would prevail for a century until the Chamber formally abandoned its dialect group election system in 1993. The Chinese man in the street had little contact with the colonial authorities because of the representational system. First the *kapitan* system, later the CAB, from the early 20th century the Straits Chinese British Association (SCBA), and most of all through the SCCC, the Chinese elite functioned as his spokesman and representative, just as they organized his work, and his social and religious life.

A portrait of a Singapore Chinese leader, 1906–1941

If we attempt to paint a portrait of a typical Chinese elite leader and his dominant outlook before the Pacific War, we come to the following description. The Chinese leader was without fail a businessman first and foremost. Most often he would be involved in the agro-industrial production of rice, pepper, tropical produce, pineapple or rubber, and/or the trading of these products. In the first half of the 20th century he could also be engaged in shipping, insurance and banking. With business prowess and wealth as status providers, the Chinese leader was typically active at the top of the pyramid of Chinese organizations, either, as was the case for most, in the *huiguan* and *bang* organizations if they were China-born and Chinese-speaking, or, for a minority, in the Straits Chinese British Association if they were Straits-born. The SCCC was the pinnacle of this system and the most influential Chinese, whether China-born or Straits-born, had a seat on its Management Committee (MC). The top merchants would be appointed to the CAB (1889) by the colonial authorities. If the hypothetical elite leader of this portrait possessed the right language skills and had strong network connections to the colonial state, he would also be appointed to the Municipal, Legislative or Executive Council.

Apart from being a businessman and political actor in both the Chinese community and colonial society, the Chinese leader was ideally also exemplary in the socio-cultural sphere, emphasizing the multi-purpose nature of his elite status. He could be a Maecenas to learning. Indeed, with the responsibility for education left to the community itself, the Chinese leader should donate large amounts of money towards the establishment and running of schools, and would sit on the boards of these institutions. Such donations would be public and actively publicized. In a society where money was a key to status, the Chinese leader led by example. Newspapers would list his donations to charitable causes and to a host of funds aiming to relieve natural and man-made disasters in Singapore, Britain and China. Publicly pledging and donating funds served to prove his moral rectitude as a magnanimous leader who gave back to society and thereby enhanced his status. In his more private public life, he would be a member of several elite clubs where he would cement his informal social and business network while eating, and often gambling. He could also be a member of a political organization outside the *huiguan* structure or join social or cultural clubs in the wider society.

During the first half of the 20th century, the outlook of the Chinese elite leader, although including Malaya, the Netherlands East Indies, China and other countries through business and personal ties, came to be anchored in Singapore. Local Chinese politics and the colonial representational system tied him to the city. His clansmen in his *huiguan* and the local Chinese who spoke his dialect in his *bang* organization, usually small shopkeepers, artisans and petty traders, were his first constituency. They needed him as their banker and supplier of credit, their arbiter for internal affairs and as their representative to other *bang*. In return they voted for him in *huiguan* or Chamber elections, they provided their labour to him, and bestowed upon him the status he needed to rise to higher levels. At the supra-*bang* level, as a leader of the Chamber, he became a representative first for its members but he also assumed responsibilities for the Chinese community of Singapore. As a member of one of the Colonial Councils this responsibility was formalized by the Governor's appointment. Most of his business, which often had a wider Southeast Asian flavour, was conducted in or through Singapore. If he was a pineapple and rubber man, he would source regionally, process there or in Singapore and sell on the world market. As a banker he would provide local and regional financial services to the Chinese business community. The links and dependencies between credit, labour, production, supply and markets were inextricably interwoven through the triangle of money, status and power.

This portrait attests to the fact that he was Chinese. He was born in China or was aware that his ancestors hailed from there, was defined as belonging to the local Chinese community, derived his status from his leadership of, and over, other Chinese, and represented local Chinese interests to the colonial government. He was active in the dissemination of Chinese culture in Singapore through schooling and public campaigns. He was aware of, and involved in, the local translation of China politics but seldom to the point that this would jeopardize or harm either his local and regional business interests or his local socio-political status and network. Furious about Japan's incursion into China, he would be a staunch supporter, contributor and organizer of the war relief efforts. Equally outraged about the Japanese threat to Singapore – his residence, place of business and source of his wealth and status – he would lead the civil defence movement. During the war, spent in hiding or under close scrutiny of the Japanese, his business would suffer a major setback and probably would be affected more fundamentally through the destruction of ships, plantations and factories. His faith in the ability of the British colonial system to protect and serve the local community would be severely damaged, and in his eyes postwar reconstruction would have to include changes to Singapore's system of governing and balance of power.

Members of SCCC presented to the Prince of Wales in 1941.

Collection of Peng Song Toh. Courtesy of the National Archives of Singapore

Tong Chai Medical Hall, birthplace of the SCCC.

Copyright Sikko Visscher

Chamber seal.

*Courtesy of the National
Archives of Singapore*

Thian Hock Kheng Temple on Telok Ayer Street.

Copyright Sikko Visscher

Tan Chin Tuan with Governor Franklin Gimson, c.1950s.

Collection of David Ng. Courtesy of the National Archives of Singapore

CHAPTER TWO

1945–1950
Localization

At one stage [the Chamber's] regular monthly meetings could be likened to a forum for public issues. Although we in the Chamber's Committee were not appointed as leaders by the public, it was perhaps inevitable that the Chamber should have taken on this unaccustomed role because of the increasing political consciousness among the Chinese ... after the war.[1]

IN THE YEARS IMMEDIATELY AFTER the war, Singapore proved to be a city of reconstruction and change, but also of division and political awakening. The damage to the city, its people and its harbour had been extensive and took years to mend. Roads and houses were damaged, the harbour and the waters around Singapore were riddled with shipwrecks, and mines proved a further threat to shipping. Water and electricity systems had to be repaired but would show the beating they had taken by malfunctions and outages.[2] As immigration had slowed to a mere trickle due to colonial policy, the war and the civil war in Mainland China, the Singapore Chinese were slowly making the transition from a migrant society with highly transitory characteristics to a stable, locally-based community. Although by now a sizeable city with about 900,000 inhabitants, public housing of a significant scale was unknown and the people lived in stone shophouses or in townships of wooden houses. There were still plenty of rural areas on the island and driving across to the Causeway to Johor or going to Changi village would take the traveller through rainforest and plantations, and along beachfronts and *kampong-style* fishing villages.

"Singapore is British again! Our day of liberation" headlined *the Straits Times* the day British troops took control of Singapore.[3] But the colonial overlords returned with dented pride and with the myth of white superiority blown to pieces by their inability either to defend the "impenetrable fortress Singapore", or to safeguard its inhabitants from the Japanese occupation. When the British came back, they were supposed to have ridden in on a carefully laid out tactic of winning back the hearts and minds as liberators, which was precluded by the abrupt end of the war. Instead, the communist guerrillas, the only credible counter-force against the Japanese during the war, came out of the jungle talking about "liberation" and "the end of colonialism".[4]

They struck a chord with a working class that was increasingly aware that they lived in a distinctly divided city.[5] In their eyes, the colonial elite enjoyed a privileged position, dressing up in their finery for high tea at the Raffles, cocktails at the Tanglin Club or a ball in one of the posh hotels, while the working man was suffering from a stagnant economy, layoffs and a huge rise in his cost of living due to all sorts of shortages. They would be tempted to look upon the Asian business elite with the same disgust but would partly be held back by the fact that these men, their employers and therefore "class oppressors", had been, and continued to be, their community leaders and their only representation to the colonial government. So while they would perhaps balk at the ostentatious behaviour of some tycoons, like Tiger Balm King Aw Boon Haw driving around in a Rolls Royce with a tiger image mounted on the grill, they would also respect their status and feel that they needed their influence in higher places.

Still, social and economic tensions along class lines were truly awakened and the returned communists and others on the left-wing of the political spectrum used the momentum to organize labour unions and start a class action movement. Strikes were the order of the day and, while fighting an important battle of consciousness and collective strife, also put further pressure on the feeble economy. The list of strikes in February 1947, as reported to the Governor's Advisory Council by Colonial Secretary McKerron, indicated the persistence and breadth of the labour movement. Fifteen strikes were occurring at that time, involving harbour workers, rubber factory and oil mill labourers, bus drivers, fire fighters, builders and municipal labourers.[6]

Singapore still had strong ties with the Malayan peninsula and the British proposals for the transfer of power to local institutions had sparked unrest on both sides of the Causeway. Political action and work stoppages called *hartals*, based on the example of Mahatma Gandhi in India, were aimed against the separation of Singapore and Malaya and against various aspects of the British plans, further fanning the flames of the early instances of anti-colonial action. Communist guerrilla attacks against colonial officials and Western planters became common in the peninsula and soon spread to Singapore with bomb attacks on busses and public places. The colonial authorities answered by declaring the situation an Emergency and tried to combat the guerrilla forces by military means and through relocation of some of the rural Chinese population of Malaya. The rather grim scenario was exacerbated by widespread black marketeering, while robbery and banditry were reported almost daily.

1. The case for localization: income tax and political participation

Amidst this atmosphere of reconstruction, political awakening and early anti-colonial sentiments, the leadership of the SCCC had to formulate its position and devise a strategy to safeguard the interests of the Chinese business elite as well as of the Chinese community at large. The Chamber remained the primary representative of the Chinese community, capping the pyramid of Chinese organizations and including all the leaders of the *bang* in its Management Council.[7] The Chamber leaders went through a process of localization that concentrated around one question. Who would be allowed to participate in politics as voters and as candidates for the elected positions that would be introduced into the local political scene as a first step towards self-government? Two related political discussions in 1947 and early 1948, the introduction of income tax and that of the eligibility to vote and to stand as candidate in the elections of the Municipal and Legislative Councils, will provide insights into how the process of localization took shape and who among Chamber members played crucial roles in these issues.

Income tax

A proposal to introduce income tax in Singapore was first discussed in the Governor's Advisory Council in December 1946. When the Advisory Council, meant to temporarily replace the Legislative and Executive Councils until they could be reintroduced by means of elections, and the Municipal Council were installed after civil rule returned in 1946, these bodies had appointed members only of two categories: the "Official", ex-officio members (top colonial administrators) and "Unofficial" members (representatives of the local elites) appointed by the Governor. The British blueprint was to slowly increase the number of Unofficials on the various councils and subsequently select them through elections. Opposition to the income tax proposal from the Unofficial members was unanimous. The minutes of the meeting show that Lee Kong Chian, an Unofficial member of the Council and the SCCC president at the time, respectfully rose and asked the Honourable the Governor of Singapore Franklin Gimson if he would be allowed to make some comments on the issue. While Lee Kong Chian agreed that income tax was in principle an equitable means to raise revenue for a government, the timing for introduction in Singapore was, in his view, ill conceived. He argued that the economy had not returned to a normal state by far and that it would be hard for residents to meet the tax burden and therefore equally difficult for the government to collect from them. Instead of income tax he suggested that luxury goods could be taxed. Central to his argument was that the issue of income tax should be left until a semblance of local representation in the decision was restored when the new Legislative Council was installed. His speech was greeted by a round of applause from the other members.[8] It seems that the government heeded Lee's call, at least for the time being, because the revised budget did not propose implementing income tax in 1947.[9]

While Lee Kong Chian was probably the most influential Chinese individual in Singapore at the time, neither his opposition to income tax nor the opinions of his Unofficial colleagues on the Advisory Council could prevent the issue from remaining high on the agenda of the colonial government. When the territory's budget for 1948 was prepared and discussed, the issue resurfaced in the political arena.

In anticipation of the government's proposals on the issue, the newspapers were full of articles and opinions on the matter. Arguments for and against the tax centred on issues of budgetary necessity and class. Mr. R. Jumabhoy, an Unofficial member of the Advisory Council and a leading Indian businessman, in his role as community leader had ventured to declare that the "masses would object to income tax". In a letter to the editor an author identified only as "An Economist" wrote that this claim was patently false. He argued that the working classes simply made too little money to have to pay tax and would therefore not object to a tax that would only affect the rich. However, in his view "the trouble is that they are still too disorganised and inarticulate to denounce their self-appointed spokesmen".[10] This exchange of opinions was symptomatic of the arguments exchanged between the leftist and the elite positions in the discussion.

When the report of the Special Income Tax Advisor, Mr. R.B. Heasman was issued, the range of prospective tax payers and of the rates became clear. As an indication, incomes over $500 per month for a married couple without children would be taxed at progressive rates; an annual income of $6,000 would be taxed at $60 while an annual income of $300,000 would be taxed at $57,730. In his report Heasman called the need for revenue "urgent, imperative and vital" for Malaya and Singapore.[11]

Lee Kong Chian: The sage of compromise.
Collection of David Eng. Courtesy of the National Archives of Singapore

Born in Nan'an County in Fujian Province in 1893, Lee Kong Chian at 53 was at the apex of an impressive career as a businessman and a civic leader. He was involved as shareholder, manager, member or chairman of the board of directors of household names such as Great Eastern Life Insurance, Sime Darby, Singapore Cold Storage and the Straits Trading Company. With his hair starting to grey and dressed in impeccable suits, he looked every inch the successful businessman that he was. The combination of vast personal wealth and the image of moral rectitude ensured him the admiration and respect of the Chinese as well as the colonial establishment. He was considered an intellectual and was known as a warm-hearted and kind man with a strongly developed philanthropic disposition. Notwithstanding the fact that he could call almost the entire Upper Ten Thousand, including a number of

governors, personal friends, his start in life was much more humble.

After attending a Chinese school he joined his father, who had set up a small trading firm, in Singapore in 1903. He was taught English and mathematics at Anglo Indian School and studied Chinese at a Confucian school during weekends. In 1908, he was chosen by the Chinese Imperial government to study at Jinan High School in Nanjing, which had been specially established for Nanyang Chinese. Graduating top of his class, he continued his studies in engineering at Qinghua College in Peking and at the Railway and Mining College at Tangshan. Back in Singapore he taught at Daonan and Chung Cheng School while holding other jobs and continuing his studies through a correspondence course in civil engineering at an American college.

Soon, however, his talents were spotted in the Chinese commercial world, where Tan Kah Kee was primarily credited with introducing him to, and preparing him for, his future career. For the rest of his life Lee would remain a businessman first and foremost. When Tan, in 1916, wanted to expand his rubber business directly to the European and American markets he promoted Lee to manage his trading business. Four years later Lee married Tan's daughter. Notwithstanding family ties, Lee ventured out on his own in 1927 when he set up a rubber smoking business in Muar in Malaya, although he continued to assist Tan in his public and private affairs. Lee Rubber, the company he founded, survived the Depression by staying away from speculation, a judicious business style, and because of its small size at the time. He turned it into a private limited company in 1931 and, at the depth of the crisis, bought large tracts of rubber land and a number of companies at rock-bottom prices.[12]

Lee quickly extended his company's activities to include the whole rubber product chain from the plantation to smoking, milling, packing and shipping as well as selling rubber latex and sheets to Europe, America, China and Japan. He was active and prominent in the Rubber Trade Association of Singapore, of which he was chairman for many years before the war. As another pillar of his business empire, he expanded the well-known rubber sideline activity of pineapple planting through Lee Pineapple, canning and exporting the fruit on a huge scale. He employed Yap Pheng Geck as manager of his pineapple business shortly after the war and made a fortune by responding quickly and flexibly to market opportunities in rubber and pineapple. To the general public he was affectionately known as the "Rubber and Pineapple King of Singapore".

Another sector Lee put his stamp on was banking. He was the main architect behind the merger of the three Hokkien banks that amalgamated to form the Overseas Chinese Banking Corporation (OCBC) in 1932. He served the bank as deputy chairman from 1932 and as chairman from 1938 until 1965, by which time the Lee family held a controlling share. British business circles as well as the colonial authorities had great respect for Lee. His broker role between Western and Chinese business enabled Lee Kong Chian to obtain credit from both Western and Chinese banks, and OCBC was reportedly the only Chinese bank that could deal directly with the great colonial financial institutions before the war. It was rumoured that because of the bank's good connections with the British it had managed to secure the exchange of its deposits in wartime Japanese currency before it was declared worthless by the British Military Authority (BMA). In any case, OCBC survived the war well. In its first shareholder meeting after the war, OCBC declared a $3 million profit over the past two years but posted a loss of $2.5 million during the occupation.[13]

In Chinese society Lee held the SCCC Presidency from 1939–1941 and again from 1946–1947, and was very active in the realm of education, serving as Nanyang Chinese High School chairman from 1934 until 1956 and donating to all large educational initiatives. His children received their education in Chinese first but eventually all attended English language colleges. In 1952 he established the Lee Foundation with $3.5 million to promote education and social welfare projects.[14]

Yap Pheng Geck: Trusted associate.

Courtesy of SCCCI

Yap Pheng Geck was a Straits Chinese whose ancestral home was in the Teochew county of Puning in Guangdong province. He was born in 1901 or 1899 in Heping, Johor, where his father was a pepper and gambier planter and the harbour master or *kangchu* of Heping harbour. Educated in Malay and English, Yap obtained a degree in pedagogy at Hong Kong University. Upon his return to Singapore he became a teacher at the Anglo-Chinese School, a job he held until 1932. In that year he joined the Overseas Chinese Bank (soon incorporated in OCBC) as its Secretary, and started working for Lee Kong Chian, a man he would cooperate with in many business and political affairs and who would become a personal friend. While he was not an independent businessman with his own companies but worked as a professional manager, Yap became the embodiment of modern business practice for the leading Chinese-owned companies of his time.

There were those who accepted this need and agreed to income tax as a method that could be accepted under certain conditions. The newly established Singapore Progressive Party (SPP), led by local lawyer C.C. Tan,[15] echoed the earlier Advisory Council Unofficials' opinion of late 1946 that the financial need would have to be made clear and that implementation should take place only with the consent of the elected representatives of the people in the Legislative Council, which was to be elected in 1948.[16]

The Chamber made its position clear early on, when Yap Pheng Geck, a Municipal Councillor and SCCC Vice President, opined that if income tax was to be introduced, there could be no sincerity in the British offer of self-government. The proposal would have to be put before the new legislative council.[17]

The Chamber continued to organize opposition by establishing a subcommittee to study the tax proposal of the government Finance and Revenue Committee.[18] The real decision on the issue was going to be made in the Advisory Council, which met with all members in attendance on 27 November 1947. During the first reading of the income tax proposal, the Financial Secretary, Mr D. Smith, stated that without it Singapore would run a $34 million deficit in 1948. Tan Chin Tuan, a senior SCCC

Socially he was involved in the Straits Chinese British Association (SCBA) and in time would hold the highest leadership positions in this organization. He had joined the Singapore Volunteer Force in 1925 and Yap was in command of a Chinese company during the Japanese invasion of Singapore. An active member of the Rotary club, he was elected as one of its office bearers in 1947. Yap was a typical example of the English speaking Straits Chinese who provided a liaison function between the British colonizers and the Chinese population. He was involved in the Chamber early on, and claimed he was able to do so because he had worked for OCBC before the war and therefore had contact with the Chinese-speaking business elite. "As a member of the SCCC committee, I saw in that role an opportunity to bring about closer relationship between the English-speaking and the Chinese-speaking. I encountered no difficulty at all in my attempt. Some other English speaking members: Tay Lian Teck, S.B. Tan and S.Q. Wong were all given leadership positions."[19] For the Chamber he took the role of interpreter and spokesman and was sent on international missions. In 1949, for instance, he was the representative of the SCCC and the Singapore Indian Chamber of Commerce in the meetings with the Colonial Office in London on the entrepot trade of the colony. In 1950 he would represent the Singapore employers at the Asia regional conference of the ILO. Yap would be awarded an MBE by the British crown in 1952 for his services to the community.[20]

Management Council member and the only Chamber representative on the Advisory Council since Lee Kong Chian had stepped down a few months earlier, spoke out vehemently against the bill. He argued that the budgetary need was not proven, as a number of large expenses on the budget were not of a recurring nature and that, similar to public finance in Europe, short-term borrowing by the government could easily be used. He also stressed that the Singapore Chinese Chamber of Commerce as well as the Singapore Ratepayers' Association, of which he was president, were opposed to income tax at this time. The Unofficials reiterated that a decision on income tax should not be made until an elected local political voice would be included in the process. With unanimous Unofficial opposition to the bill, the income tax ordinance proposal was defeated by ten votes to seven.[21]

Introduction of the tax therefore seemed to be blocked, and Governor Gimson was forced to seek the advice of Governor-General MacDonald in Kuala Lumpur. In a colonial show of force, Gimson and the Governor of the Malayan Union, Sir Edward Gent, decided to override the councillors' vote and to proceed with implementation. Tan Chin Tuan and C.C. Tan resigned in reaction to this flagrant disregard of the Advisory Council.[22]

Tan Chin Tuan: The gritty politician.

Collection of Loke Wan Tho. Courtesy of the Cathay Organisation

Tan was the second close friend and business partner of Lee Kong Chian who performed representational tasks for the SCCC after the war. By the late 1940s he was, with Lee, the central man in OCBC and in many of the companies OCBC acquired. He had the reputation of being a very shrewd businessman who favoured a conservative financial approach to entrepreneurial decisions. A sense of control was important to him, for he would emphasize that full insight in a financial and political situation was

needed to make informed decisions. Strong-willed and sure of his opinions, he was known as a sharp mind and a fierce debater.

Tan did not have a first generation immigrant background because he was born in Singapore in 1908. He was the son of Tan Cheng Siong, a banker and local Hokkien community leader. Educated in English, he finished his Senior Cambridge and a Senior Commercial Class at Anglo-Chinese School. He started working for the Chinese Commercial Bank in 1925 and in 1926 married the daughter of its general manager. When OCBC was formed his star continued to rise.

His first public position in the colonial system came when he was appointed Municipal Councillor from 1939 to 1941, after being elected to the committee of the SCBA. He was co-opted into the Straits Chinese China Relief fund committee but did not take official positions, though he donated handsomely. Further activities included his involvement in the Straits Chinese Fund Raising Committee to support the British war effort in 1939 and in the Malayan Patriotic Fund led by Lee Kong Chian. He took an active part in the civil

Tan Chin Tuan's indignation at the high-handed manner in which the colonial overlord had implemented an unpopular measure against the will of the appointed representatives of the people of Singapore was far from the only bitter reaction to the introduction of income tax. Reactions were furious and fuelled the process of localization because, as Yap Pheng Geck emphasized in his acceptance speech as president of the SCBA, it was now "up to ourselves to take stock".[25] The Chamber organized a meeting of all defence movement when the Japanese advanced on Singapore, but eventually left Singapore because he had been selected to be joint managing director of OCBC with power of attorney to take charge of its overseas operations. He made his way to Bombay where he re-registered OCBC, an action necessary to keep its international business activities going. After the war, upon his return to Singapore he became the sole Managing Director for OCBC and was appointed by the BMA to the Advisory Council. His rise to the top of OCBC was a sensitive issue because some had expected that he would return the special privileges bestowed on him to the pre-war leaders of the bank.

Some of his business tactics are noteworthy. After the war, Tan decreed that any former internee of the Japanese camps could come to OCBC for a $500 or $1,000 loan without collateral, a generous policy that created enormous goodwill. His good connections with the British also stood him in good stead when it came to the circulation of British and Malayan currency. OCBC was the first institution to be issued currency. OCBC again benefited from British colonial decisions when

the Debtor/Creditor Bill of 1947, implemented to demonetize all Japanese bank notes, stipulated that banks were not liable to repay deposits made during the war. One source argues that OCBC benefited to the tune of $20 million.[23]

As one of the bridging personalities between the Chamber and the colonial government, he became Vice President of the SCCC between 1948 and 1950. He was also active in the SCBA, the Progressive Party, the Ee Ho Hean Club, the Garden Club and the Straits Settlements (Singapore) Association. His social and business networks were extensive and ranged from Hokkien speaking rubber magnates such as Tan Kah Kee (a good friend of his father) to English-educated Straits Chinese such as Lim Boon Keng and Song Ong Siang, and to British colonial officials and leaders of other immigrant communities. In the mid 1950s he left active politics, concentrated on business and replaced Lee Kong Chian as Chairman of the Board of OCBC. Throughout his career he was an astute, conservative businessman and he continued to be a dominant force in Singapore business.[24]

trade associations to oppose the principle of income tax and protest the arrogant manner in which the British implemented it without considering local views.[26]

Still, the decision stood and in a special supplement to the Government Gazette, the introduction of income tax on 1 January 1948 was announced and Mr. Heasman was appointed Comptroller of Income Tax for Singapore and Malaya.[27]

Eligibility for political participation

If the income tax issue made clear that the colonial government could decide as it pleased on important policies for the territory, it also reinforced the sense of importance and urgency among the local elite concerning the eligibility for political participation in the near future. At the heart of the second serious collision between the SCCC and colonial policy were the assumptions and expectations of the Chinese business leaders concerning citizenship and the right to vote. If Singapore was slowly moving towards a system of self-government and eventually of independence, these questions of citizenship and enfranchisement were central to that process.

When the first plans for a Legislative Council, which proposed an equal number of official and unofficial members, were presented in 1946 both Lee Kong Chian and Lien Ying Chow publicly reacted. Lee said, "The Chinese should be well represented", and Lien contended that Unofficials should have the majority. Both favoured women members on the council and Lien said that it would be desirable for the council to be open to all nationalities residing in Singapore and that other languages than English should be permitted during its deliberations.[28] Lien's two cornerstones signify that a number of individuals in the elite were already sensitized to these important political matters early on. Singaporeans, regardless of formal nationality, should be given the opportunity to participate in governing the territory in which they lived.

The position of the colonial government was heavily influenced by politics in Westminster, where a new citizenship law for Britain and the colonies was being drafted. Under the new legislation, all those who were British subjects already or born in Singapore after 1945 automatically qualified for naturalization. All others had to fulfil five conditions before 1952 in order to be considered for naturalization: (1) residence in Singapore for five out of the last eight years, (2) being of good character and sound mind, (3) having an adequate knowledge of English, (4) showing intent to reside in Singapore permanently, and (5) declaring exclusive allegiance to the British crown.[29] According to the 1947 census, out of a total population of 450,000 adults, 220,000 Chinese who were China-born would meet these requirements except for the language barrier and the need to take up British nationality exclusively. Issues of dual citizenship lay at the root of this legislation.

The central principles of law underlying the British approach were *Ius Soli*, citizenship based on the soil one was born on, and the singularity of citizenship. The position of the Chinese, and of both the Chinese Imperial state in the past and the Nationalist and Communist state thereafter, was that citizenship was based on *Ius Sanguinis*. This boiled down to the principle that if the father was Chinese the child was Chinese, regardless of where it was born. If local authorities granted local citizenship on other grounds this was accepted as a complementary, and possibly flexible, political identity, whereas Chineseness was seen as a lasting ethnic identity.

In an era of great political and ideological turmoil in China, the British colonial government wanted to exclude dual citizenship because it feared that otherwise Mainland Chinese politics might dangerously influence the Singapore political arena. Therefore, government's point of view on who would be allowed to vote in Singapore was never in doubt. British subjects were to be the only ones so enfranchised.[30]

The Governor's Advisory Council was the forum in which the proposed legislation was discussed, and the main objection of the Unofficial members was that many long-term residents who had made Singapore their home would not be allowed to vote while British subjects from other colonies would be. As Unofficial council member Thio Chan Bee put it, "a man from Madras will have the right to vote after one year's of residence, but a man from, say, Manila or Bangkok or Canton cannot vote even though he has been here 20 or 30 years continuously". Despite this opposition, most Unofficials thought the Bill a step in the right direction and it was passed.[31]

In response to this development, the Chamber started to send memoranda to the colonial government. In its first letter, the SCCC argued that the language restriction should be dropped and claimed that it did not exist before 1920. In a reply Acting Colonial Secretary Brysor stated that he would consider the question of naturalization of non-English speaking Chinese.[32] Within a few months the issue would indeed become pressing.

At the end of 1947, the term of Municipal Councillor Lien Ying Chow, a very prominent Chamber leader and its past president between 1941 and 1946, would come to an end. The governor had appointed Lien to this position, without nomination by the Chamber, when civilian rule had returned in 1946, because of his efforts for Singapore's economic and social reconstruction.

Despite the respect Lien was accorded by the colonial government due to his track record in community leadership and service to the public causes of the territory, the authorities let the new draft law prevail when it came to political appointments. When Lien's term was almost up the colonial government insisted that the Chamber representative in the Municipal Council had to be a British subject, a status Lien did not possess. In an act of defiance, and in conjunction with Malayan-wide actions by all Chinese

Lien Ying Chow: Gregarious networker.
Courtesy of the National Archives of Singapore

Singapore in 1920. There he worked for a chandler business, learned English and made professional contact with the sundry departments of well-known British firms Boustead, Guthrie, Robinson and John Little. In 1929, he founded Wah Hin Company, his own chandler and supplies business, which flourished during the depression because Lien landed contracts to provide food and beverages to the British military in Singapore and Malaya from his good contacts with the procurement officers. Lien was ahead of his time as a young, Chinese-born man who understood the value of a Western-style business model. He wanted to be seen as sophisticated, intelligent and, most of all, modern. With an early flair for public relations, Wah Hin remodelled the top floor of its Robinson Road shop for entertaining clients and was one of the first Chinese companies to hold a cocktail party for its clientele on the occasion of Wah Hin's tenth anniversary.

In the late 1930s, Lien's success and status brought him to the top of the Chinese pyramid of organizations. First, he became chairman of the Teo Yeoh Huay Kuan (the leading Chaoyang organization) and also president of the Provision and Sundries, as well as, the Wine and Spirit Merchants' Association of Singapore. Then, in 1941, he became the youngest President of the SCCCI

Lien was a social animal and a prolific networker. His language skills and natural flair enabled him to move with ease in all kinds of circles at home and abroad. He built his business empire around banking and the hotel industry with Overseas Union Bank and the Mandarin Hotel chain as his flagship companies. He loved hosting and attending parties and knew the importance of putting in an appearance at official occasions with his signature glass of lukewarm XO cognac in hand.

He was born a Teochew in the Chaoyang district of Guangdong province in 1904 in a small village where his grandfather was the village head. His parents died young. After working in Hong Kong, where Lien learned Cantonese, he went to ever. While the position "… involved considerable personal expense. Plainly, the prestige and power were worth the cost for Lien".[33] Active participation in the organization of civil defence against the advancing Japanese and his close connection to the British military forced Lien to flee Singapore shortly before the Japanese invasion. Via Australia and India he arrived in Chongqing, where Generalissimo Chiang Kai-shek appointed him to his Political Council as a representative of the Overseas Chinese. Ever the businessman, he noticed that many bankers had flocked to Chongqing and he coordinated setting up the Overseas Chinese Union Bank with colleagues from all over Southeast Asia. In the aftermath of the war, Lien was based at the Savoy Hotel in London as a special envoy of Nationalist China. While in London, Lord Inverforth of the Ben Line and Lord Tivy, head of the Labour Party, were his colleagues on the Imperial Rehabilitation and Reconstruction Committee.

Back in Singapore he was appointed to various advisory positions, looking into matters concerning economy, commerce and relief work for the whole of Singapore and Malaya. Not surprisingly, from 1946 to 1949, he was involved in various discussions with local leaders about gaining independence for Malaya and Singapore.[34] In 1947, he founded the $10 million endowed

Overseas Union Bank (OUB) with financial backing of prominent figures from various regional cities.[35] In the spirit of the era and in keeping with his modern business approach, OUB taught the local Chinese importers of rice and other commodities how to establish a letter of credit, and how to finance imports themselves without going through the big colonial business houses. Lien was set on running his business as a local from the heart of the colonial economic centre. He had visited the American company Irving Trust, located at 1 Wall Street in New York, and with a keen sense of image and prestige decided he wanted 1 Raffles Place as the place of business for his bank.

After the war, he was elected president of Ngee Ann Kongsi, and in time tapped its most valuable asset, a plot of land on Orchard Street. He donated time and money to educational institutions such as Tuan Mong School, Ngee Ann School and Ngee Ann Girls' School, Nanyang High School, Chinese High School, Nanyang University and Ngee Ann College. Despite his numerous activities in the social, cultural and political arenas, Lien was always clear about how he saw his primary identity. He said, "I myself wanted to be a businessman …".[36]

Chambers of Commerce opposing the British constitutional plans for Malaya and Singapore, Lien was re-nominated. The Chamber urged the local colonial government to be far-sighted by continuing to give civic opportunities to all sections of the people of Singapore.

When the list of appointments was published shortly after in the Government Gazette, it became clear that Lien's nomination had been rejected. The Chamber had argued in vain that non-British subjects had served in the past and that in 1947, the Municipal Commissioners themselves had advised that only the directly elected Commissioners should be British subjects or British protected subjects, but that the nominated members could also fall outside of that requirement.[37]

Soon after, a 10-man delegation of the SCCC led by Lee Kong Chian achieved a "good understanding" with Governor Gimson. Reportedly, the Chamber had asked if non-British subjects among its members would at least be allowed to vote for the Chamber representative and in that manner have Lien Ying Chow's place filled.[38] The Municipal Council proceedings do not name a specific SCCC representative in the following months, but Yap Pheng Geck did have a seat and undoubtedly looked after the Chamber's interests.

Of course the issue of political participation was most pressingly important in the Legislative Council (Legco) election of 1948, the first election in which the eligible voting populace would elect a number of candidates. In what one scholar calls "a feeble attempt to political reform",[39] the Legco was revamped to include six popularly elected members and three appointed representatives of the respective chambers of commerce (the SCCC, the Singapore Chamber of Commerce and the Singapore Indian Chamber of Commerce). Voters had to register in person in order to be included on the ballot roll and vote. After the registration period was over, only slightly more than 22,000 voters out of a total population of 940,756 had put their names on the ballot roll.[40] With the potential electorate at 200,000, only just over 10 per cent of eligible voters participated in the election.[41]

On the apathy of the Singapore electorate over registration for the Legco election, John Eber, co-founder of the Malayan Democratic Union (MDU), an anti-colonial and pro-independence leftist party of English-educated radicals, wrote an extensive article to the *Straits Times*. He argued that with only six of 23 seats being directly elected, the apathy was very understandable. Furthermore, of the 17 other members, three would be appointed by the Governor after nominations by the three largest Chambers of Commerce. Thereby, he argued, "A handful of businessmen will elect half as many members to the council as half the entire electorate of Singapore *(sic)*". With a further four nominated Unofficials, the directly elected Unofficials would be a minority even within their own camp. Therefore, Eber argued, it was not surprising that the electorate was not jumping at the chance to register.[42]

Although political parties had formed in Singapore, only one, the SPP, actually participated in the election. The Malayan-based Pan Malaya Council for Joint Action (PMCJA), led by Malaccan Chinese Tan Cheng Lock, which could have had a shot at a fair share of the seats, put itself on the sidelines in Singapore because of its Malaya-wide boycott of all elections. The MDU had come under communist influence and also decided to boycott the election. After a period of great activity the Malayan Communist Party (MCP) had given up the urban revolution in Singapore. Most communist leaders retreated to peninsular Malaya where the guerrilla actions of the MCP led to the period of Emergency. In the meantime, however, the communists would not play an open role in Singapore party politics.[43]

The great winner of this election was the SPP, which had been set up barely seven months before in August 1947. The Progressives were fully willing to cooperate with the British to promote steady constitutional reform by gradually extending the numbers of elected councillors and eventually creating a cabinet of ministers responsible to a legislative assembly. Importantly, they set no definite target dates for this process. With this limited political platform, and aided by the absence of other parties, the SPP scooped up three of the six available seats. The party attracted English-educated professional men, typically members of the Singapore Association or the Singapore Chinese British Association (SCBA). The Straits Chinese community especially, did not want to see their privileged position towards the British jeopardized. As a result contemporary observers regarded the SPP as quite conservative.[44] The three remaining seats went to independent candidates, a category that included all the other candidates in the election and was dominated by professionals. Because the left-wing parties had taken themselves out of the equation and because the successful candidates represented very small segments of the population, the SCCC continued to be one of the most important representational channels in Singapore society. Tan Chin Tuan was appointed as the Chamber representative in the Legco, a seat he would continue to occupy until 1955.

It is interesting to note that eight months before he was appointed as the SCCC Legco representative, Tan had called the reservation of three seats for the chambers of commerce "repugnant to all ideas of a democracy".[45]

The fact that he still accepted the nomination of the Chamber, of which he had just become the Vice President, indicates that he was either pragmatic enough to put his democratic principles on the back burner, or that he might have been diplomatically pressured by Lee Kong Chian to swallow his pride. He was undoubtedly a very good candidate if the Chamber's ambition was to change the late-colonial system from within. However, as the most forward representative in the colonial political arena, Tan had a degree of independence in his political manoeuvring. In future years he would not always toe the SCCC line but sometimes followed his own principles and agenda.

2. Analysis of localization

The central theme of this chapter is the process of localization, defined in this context as the increasingly active involvement of the Chinese of Singapore not only in the economic, but also in the social and political affairs of the territory. The two issues presented above show that the Chamber put socio-economic and political issues of the immediate postwar years, such as the opposition against the introduction of income tax and the question of eligibility for political participation, high on its agenda. Realizing the political reality of British colonial rule, it decided that implementing a strategy of lobbying the late-colonial system from within was the most prudent way to safeguard the SCCC's goals. To succeed in this "working-with-the-British" strategy, the Chamber utilized members of its leadership that were well-connected and respected in government circles. The process of localization signified a move by the Chinese business elite towards the local political arena when they realized that safeguarding their interests during decolonization would necessitate an active representational stance. Realizing that their future lay in Singapore and that they wanted to be Singaporean, the SCCC leadership took up the challenge of developing its local political profile.

The situation had been quite different not too long before. During the National Salvation movement from 1937–1941 and the war of resistance in China, Chamber leaders such as Lee Kong Chian and Tan Lark Sye had declared China "my country" and Japan "our enemy" and had urged the local Chinese to unite under the leadership of Chiang Kai-shek to "repulse our enemy".[46] When the Chamber council was sworn in on March 1941, the new president Lien Ying Chow had pledged that "We are all citizens of the Chinese Republic". Despite long-standing local roots, many *huaqiao*, or overseas Chinese of the pre-war years still regarded Singapore as their *di'er guxiang* (second homeland). This was so because British paternalistic rule before the war offered little opportunity for the creation and emergence of a Singapore nationalism with a Singapore loyalty as its objective.[47] The war, however, had changed this picture completely. The Atlantic Charter, authored by the USA and the United Kingdom, with its promise of self-determination for colonized peoples meant that the land one lived in could be one's own to rule.

As a gradual transfer of power to the local population became apparent, both the local political arena and the rules it lived by started to change. Initially, the institutional forms were not those of the pre-war era. The period of British Military Administration (BMA), under Lord Louis Mountbatten, from September 1945 until April 1946, was significant in its failure to regain legitimacy for colonial rule and in its incorporation of local advisers. During August and September 1945, Chinese leaders emerged from hiding or returned from abroad and Chinese organizations were revived again. In the case of the Chamber, Vice President Tan Lark Sye announced on 1 September 1945 that the Chamber was back in business.[48]

While the BMA struggled to reconstruct some measure of organization and structure to the former civil service, the focus of the businessmen in the Chamber was on matters economic. The main concerns of the Chinese traders were rationing, supplies of goods, especially foodstuffs, and the availability of legal currency. With the cancellation of the Japanese "Banana" currency, Chinese traders were helpless without British currency. Lee Choon Seng, a Chamber leader who was also the top man of OCBC, was already busy negotiating with the BMA on the status of the Japanese wartime currency.[49] The Chamber's primary interest was the return of the free market in Singapore and it advocated the competitive selling of all commodities except for land. It pledged full support to the BMA and staged a reception for representatives of the Allied Forces present at the surrender ceremony.[50]

In a newspaper interview after his return to Singapore on 8 October 1945, Lien Ying Chow, the Chamber President, explained his plans to increase trade. He revealed that, at the request of the authorities, the Chamber would aid in easing trade bottlenecks, and had set up an organization to act as liaison between owners of Chinese junks and traders.[51] His contacts with the Teochew rice millers in Thailand helped to relieve the rice shortage, while a trip to Hong Kong aided coordination of increased trade between the two territories. He also ironed out transportation problems using his *guanxi* with the shipping line owners. The involvement of Lien and a number of others in the Chinese business elite in reconstruction efforts was an important first sign of localization.

The Chamber was faced with the question of how it would secure a position of political influence in order to safeguard the economic concerns of its membership as well as the wider social and political needs of the Chinese community. The period of military rule ended on 2 April 1946 when Sir Franklin Gimson, the new Governor of Singapore, arrived. At the same time, civilian rule was restored in the whole of British Malaya with Sir Malcolm MacDonald as the new Governor-General of Malaya. The reality for the Singapore Chinese merchant elite was that the British were in command, and therefore, working with the British within the colonial framework seemed to be a political necessity. As a result, the SCCC adopted the work-with-the-British strategy to fill the representational void.

The characteristics of the process that the British envisioned greatly influenced which Chinese leaders could execute the Chamber strategy. The central principle of the British was a gradual transition to increased local participation in politics and government with Singapore as a separate entity from Malaya. The transition was to take place through a step-by-step increase in the number of local representatives on the various colonial councils and in the tasks and responsibilities these bodies were to be given. In early 1946 the informal system of a temporary advisory council was resumed with significant continuity in personnel from the BMA Advisory Council. Lien Ying Chow, Lee Kong Chian and Tan Chin Tuan all remained members. Lien Ying Chow's status and influence were reflected by the fact that he was appointed to committees including the Municipal Council.[52]

Political participation of the Chinese business leaders was now more direct and also more concerned with wider political issues, rather than with community developments in Chinese society. A further indication of the changes in the political arena was the fact that the CAB, the highest formal channel of communication in pre-war Singapore, did not reconvene until 1949. The Chamber was still very well represented on the CAB with 13 of its 26 members being top SCCC people. The responsibilities and issues that remained in the portfolio of the CAB were of much less importance to political developments than what was already happening in the Municipal and Legislative Council at that time.[53]

If working with the British was the prerequisite, it was perhaps to be expected that Babas or Straits Chinese would be prominent among the postwar elite. This was not exclusively the case. Perhaps one explanation lies in the fact that the Babas suffered disproportionately during the Japanese occupation and therefore were preoccupied more with getting their lives and businesses back on track than with politics.[54] There was an additional problem though. While they had easy access to British colonial power, as a group they lacked the connections with the broad base of Chinese society necessary to be its viable representatives. If the Straits Chinese were politically well plugged in but lacked a large enough representational base, the Chinese-speaking elite suffered from the opposite. While they constituted the traditional apex of the Chinese community, they did not possess the political access or the necessary communication tools. Both the Straits Chinese and the Chinese-speaking elite suffered from this mismatch in the supply and demand of politics. Only individuals that could take the better of the two types and combine effective communication with the authorities with broad support from, and appeal to, the various constituencies would fit the bill.

Who then, were the dominant members of the Chinese elite immediately after World War II? Did all pre-war leaders return? Since no new entrants became active in the elite, the answer is yes. However, the power balance had changed. Of the pre-war elite some individuals stepped back, mostly because their businesses and finances were either completely gone or in great disarray. The individuals who did emerge as leaders after the war, Lien Ying Chow, Lee Kong Chian, Yap Pheng Geck and Tan Chin Tuan, shared three characteristics. First, their businesses had been relatively unscathed, or their positioning in their respective markets or sectors had even improved. Second, they felt they had a stake in Singapore's future and were therefore willing, and sometimes eager, to enter Singapore politics. Third, because of their pre-war and wartime activities they had access to, and were respected by, the colonial government. The quartet also possessed both the political tools as well as the constituency support and the necessary appeal. All four bridged the Chinese and the colonial sphere, and also connected the Chinese-speaking and the English-speaking Chinese. Between the four, strong personal connections existed as well. The professional bond between Lee, Yap and Tan – witness their positions in OCBC and other companies in Lee's business empire – was strengthened by close friendship. Lien was also part of the same networks and would regularly meet with the others to discuss the matters of the day. Possessing the means and the networks to execute the work-with-the-British strategy, the four of them dominated the Chamber and represented it in the colonial councils.

While the leadership of the Chamber went through the process of localization in its political agenda, its strategy and its choice of representatives, the Chinese community at large was also waking up to the stakes of the local political game. Feelings about Chinese identity and what it meant to be committed to living in Singapore were central considerations in how local Chinese perceived themselves as political actors. Education policy became an important marker in these identity issues and would remain so throughout the decolonization process.[55] The British devised a *Ten-Year Education Programme*, passed in 1947, which effectively made English the language around which the schooling system would be built. Selected vernacular schools, historically based in and financed by the ethnic communities, would be included in the colonial financial budget on certain terms. These included English language training, approval of teaching material, and the exclusion of ideological issues based on China politics.[56] The express aim of the policy was to educate Malayans and to prepare them for self-government. Chinese schools, however, wanted to retain their independence and many of them turned down the subsidies. When it became apparent that subsidies to Chinese language schools would cease when capacity in English-language schools became sufficient, resistance to the scheme became more outspoken.[57]

For some Chinese the ethnic identity of the Chinese of Singapore had been partly defined through an ideological commitment based on divisions in China politics, and the Japanese invasion of China and the subsequent years of the occupation of Singapore had added an important anti-Japanese aspect to this. After surviving the Japanese efforts to force a language and ideology upon them, the Chinese now felt that the British educational policy aimed to do the same. If they were to change the way in which they shaped their Chineseness, it would not be by taking on English as a unifying element. With the China-based identity waning, the localization process retained a central emphasis on a cultural Chineseness based on education. By starting to disengage loyalty to China from what it meant to be Chinese in Singapore, localization took on an anti-colonial Asian agency. The Chinese of Singapore asked themselves: if we are to be or become Malayans, why would we have to be educated in English?

The feelings of unease among the Chinese caused by developments in educational policy were exacerbated by the fact that the British wanted to make local political participation contingent upon an exclusive British citizenship. This policy automatically deprived many of political rights because of the language clause and forced the others to choose between political allegiance to the UK, a country they had never lived in and had no connection to, and allegiance to China, the country of their birth and the basis of their ethnic identity. The Chinese in Singapore did not want to make this choice. The elite of the Chinese Chamber, as the traditional leaders of the Chinese community, were keenly aware of these feelings among their constituency and a number of them, just like Lien Ying Chow, were in danger of being deprived of a political say themselves.

This explains the focus and determination with which the Chinese elite approached the issues of income tax and political participation. The underlying logic of the Chamber's actions concerning these issues were based on its argument that colonial rule, which had stated the goal of transferring responsibilities to local actors in the near future, could not claim the authority to decide upon the structure of that future while disregarding the views of almost 80 per cent of the local population. This principle provided the fuel for the localization process.

The preceding analysis shows that the political activities of the Chamber and its representatives were crucial to the localization process of the local elite that would ultimately result in a more aggressive anti-colonial strategy. For the time being, the political and constitutional changes in the 1940s heightened the political consciousness of the Chinese elite and enforced the process of localization that was taking place among them. The prominent leadership role played by the SCCC in the 1940s in local politics enhanced the prestige of the Chamber and allowed it to vastly expand its role.

3. China and Malaya: no alternatives to Singapore localization

The question addressed in this section is whether preoccupations among the Chinese in Singapore with politics in China, or with a Malayan perspective of decolonization, could be considered a real counter-current to the process of localization centring on Singapore.

In these postwar years the Chinese in all of Malaya also, for a short period, organized their protest in tandem. Led by Tan Cheng Lock of the PMCJA, the Chinese in several areas boycotted the local councils, the Federal Legislative Council and the various state councils. The citizenship qualifications pertaining to the Chinese were the main bone of contention.[58] In the course of 1948, however, the SCCC opted out of the cooperation and decided to put its money on the work-with-the-British strategy in Singapore.

The next three sections will look first at the demise of China-related politics in Singapore before turning to the Malaya-based developments. Finally, business concerns and matters economic will be shown to have continuously formed a dominant part of the Singapore Chinese business elite identity.

China politics

The first extraterritorial political interest to the Chinese businessmen of Singapore was the ideological tussle in China. It is not difficult to present data that supports the image that the Chamber continued to have strong interest in, and strong ties with, China and especially with the Chinese KMT government. The Chamber's president, Lien Ying Chow, had been a special member of the Overseas-Chinese Affairs Committee, had sat on Chiang Kai-shek's wartime advisory council, and had served as a special envoy to London for the Chinese.[59] Just days after Lien's return to Singapore the most important day on the Chinese Nationalists' calendar, 10 October, prompted the Chamber to organize a big Double Ten celebration, to which Allied commanders and BMA officials were invited. The next day, 100,000 Chinese held the biggest mass rally in Singapore history on the Padang to celebrate the same occasion.[60] In subsequent years the Double Ten festivities were occasions for the Chamber and the Chinese Consul General Wu Paak-shing to co-host receptions or cocktail parties, and the latter was guest of honour at the installation ceremonies of the Chamber's office bearers in both 1946 and 1948.[61] This continuous identification of the Chamber with the Nationalist government in China indicates that the SCCC was pragmatic in its power politics and inclined to maintain its allegiance to the powers-that-be. The work-with-the-British strategy in Singapore should be seen as part of the same pattern of political behaviour.

Since the Chamber as an institution showed no inclination to rashly change allegiance in the conflict that was brewing between those who favoured a CCP government in China and those who would rather see the KMT stay in power, it is no surprise that the most vigorous competition between the two sides was played out outside the SCCC. The principal actors were the local branches of the China Democratic League (CDL) on the leftist side and the KMT[62] on the rightist side. Both organizations tried to penetrate the existing Chinese organizational landscape in Singapore and attempted to gain control of the SCCC. In the case of the CDL this was done through Tan Kah Kee, whose personal secretary, Li Tieh-min, was a prominent leader of the local CDL. Through Hokkien leaders such as Tan Lark Sye, Lee Kong Chian and Li Tieh-min, Tan had significant influence on the Hokien Huay Kuan.[63] On a number of occasions when the Chinese organizations were split, the Hokkien Huay Kuan led the camp that followed Tan and the CDL point of view. The Hokkien support also gave Tan and his CDL views an indirect voice in the Chamber.

The KMT also tried desperately to bring the SCCC under its control through the faction it already constituted in the Management Council.[64] An analysis of the leadership of the Singapore branch of the KMT reveals a significant overlap between prominent Nationalist leaders and a faction of the Chamber elite. It is noteworthy that five individuals of the local KMT top were among the directors of the SCCC.[65]

Despite these attempts, the Chamber elections in the post-war years show that neither side gained any significant control. Rather, while many members were involved in China politics, the realization that another strategy was necessary locally won out. When the Chamber elected its leaders in 1946, Lee Kong Chian became president, while Yong Yit-lin filled the vice presidential position. Chui labels Yong as a neutral, pro-status quo representative, who was also close to the British.[66] Yong, a Hakka, was involved in building and contracting and his connections with the colonial authorities had resulted in many lucrative contracts for, among others, Clifford Pier and a number of other colonial buildings.[67] Both left and right wing again tried to take over the Chamber during its 1948 election; the KMT lobbied hard to get their members into positions of control and the Tan camp did the same. In the end both sides were still minorities in the 32-member board. Confirming the commitment to the work-with-the-British approach, Yong Yit-lin and Tan Chin Tuan were elected president and vice president respectively.[68]

Still, between 1946 and 1949, a number of conflicts in the Chinese community centred on the issue of who would be the legitimate representative for the overseas Chinese to the Chinese government and which government that would be. Tan Kah Kee claimed the chief representative's role and supported the CCP, sending telegrams to US President Harry S. Truman, the Speakers of both US Houses and General George Marshall, asking the recipients to stop military aid to the KMT in what became known as the "Cable Incident" of 1946.[69] Of course the Singapore KMT strongly opposed this action and sent telegrams arguing the contrary.[70] Tempers within the Chamber flared numerous times in the next few years as the CCP and the KMT continued their civil war in China.

When the communist victory was finalized on 1 October 1949 with the declaration of the People's Republic of China (PRC), overseas Chinese were confronted with the question of which China, Mainland or Taiwan, to pledge their allegiance to. On the eve of that year's Double Tenth, it was announced by the colonial government that it would be allowed to fly either the Nationalist or the PRC flag, but on that day few people flew any flag at all.[71] The SCCC, true to character, was more hesitant and its president announced that the Chamber would still hoist the Nationalist flag on 10 October. However, the Chamber soon faced the new political reality: when England recognized the PRC and the Nationalist Consul General Wu Paak-shing was forced to leave, he asked the Chamber to take care of the consular properties and archives, but the Chamber declined. This signifies the switch in the allegiance of the Chamber. On 9 May 1949, the KMT in Singapore and Malaya was proscribed by the British because its activities ran counter to the British attempts to create a Malayan citizenship and national consciousness. Similarly pro PRC voices were also seen by the Singapore authorities as a threat to their attempts to build up a sense of civic loyalty to Singapore and they clamped down on communication and contacts with Peking. When Tan Kah Kee visited China in 1950, the British refused to let him re-enter Singapore, and he never returned.[72]

Malaya-based coordinated Chinese political action

To understand the development of decolonization on a Malayan scale, it is necessary to look further back and consider the British ideas that germinated during the war. In those years a planning unit of the colonial office in London, headed by Edward Gent, prepared blueprints for a British Malaya centred on Singapore, which would eventually include British Borneo as well. Not having any contact with Malaya or its representatives, the planning unit depended heavily on the input of some Malayan Civil Service members in London. They alerted Gent to the fact that his plan would likely cause ethno-political tensions because of changes in the ethnic composition that would arise from the plan. Some slightly differing numbers are available, but all point in the same general direction: Cheah, for instance, puts the percentage of Chinese in British Malaya (all the Malay states, Malacca, Penang and Singapore) just after the war at 44.7 per cent, the total percentage of Malay (including indigenous peoples and Indonesian Malays) at 43.5 per cent, and for the Indians at 10.25 per cent. Of the immigrant communities 62.5 per cent of the Chinese and 49.8 per cent of the Indians had been born in Malaya.[73]

The salient point contained in these numbers is that, if considered as a singular entity, the combination of the Straits Settlements, the Federated and the Unfederated Malay States would result in a state in which the Malays did not form the majority and were not even the largest ethnic group. The Malay rulers and the Malay nationalist political organizations were, therefore, opposed strongly to any self-government scheme along these lines. As early as March 1943, fearing that the Malay Sultans would not sign over their power to the British Crown under these circumstances, Gent turned 180 degrees to a plan for a Malayan Union excluding Singapore altogether. While still recognizing the desirability of including Singapore, the British opted out of any further responsibility for pushing this idea.[74] The issue of which form and institutional structure postwar, and later post-colonial, Malaya should get, would prove to be divisive. Different ethnic groups, with different political and economic goals in different parts of the areas under British rule had different wishes and expectations. This set the stage for an ethnically and economically charged period of political competition in which, for a while, the SCCC played its role.

When Franklin Charles Gimson arrived on 2 April 1946 to take up his position as Governor of Singapore, and Malcolm MacDonald was inaugurated as Governor-General of Malaya, Britain's postwar constitutional proposals took Malaya by surprise.[75] Not much of the Malayan Union plan was known among the general population of Malaya until 22 January 1946 when the British issued a White Paper. The Malay outcry was instantaneous. The emphasis on a Malayan rather than a Malay outlook and the diminished status of the Sultans were the main concerns, while in Singapore, severance from the entrepot hinterland was lamented. As an immediate result, the Malay political organization United Malays National Organisation (UMNO) was set up, and its first president, Dato Onn bin Ja'afar, convinced the Sultans at the last moment not to welcome the new governor with ceremonial pomp. Arrangements for an All Malay-British Constitutional Committee were hastily put in place by the colonial authorities.[76]

Non-Malay support on the peninsula for the British proposal was lukewarm even though the scheme basically presented them with equal political rights and citizenship was available for most. In a change of form rather than substance, Malay-British negotiations led to proposals for a Federation instead of a Union.[77] This idea succeeded during the 25 July 1946 constitutional conference of the British with the Malay rulers and UMNO, which came to a solution based on treaties signed with the individual Sultans.[78] Although the whole Malayan Union scheme went off the table, one crucial aspect remained: the separation of Singapore from Malaya.

In December 1946, provisional approval came from London for the new constitution and a consultative committee was set up to gather the non-Malay views on it. In response, the SCCC submitted a memorandum to the Constitutional Consultative Conference, in which it opposed the separation of Singapore from Malaya as well as the stringent regulations on citizenship contained in the draft constitution. In an attempt to take the case of the Chinese of Malaya to a higher organizational level, the SCCC argued that economic and geographical links should be more important than politics, and proposed an All-Malayan Chinese Chamber of Commerce as a vehicle to express Chinese concerns. Lee Kong Chian and Lien Ying Chow were reported to be among the initiators of this plan.[79] A few months later, Lee Kong Chian vacated his seat as an Unofficial on the Singapore Advisory Committee and the Associated Chinese Chambers of Commerce of Malaya (ACCCM) was established with him as founding member and first chairman.[80]

While this development seems to indicate that there was both intention and opportunity for socio-political representational organizations to be formed by the Chinese of Singapore and Malaya, the new association of Chinese chambers never became the dominant spokesman for the non-Malay. In December 1946, the PMCJA had been set up, and in August 1947 it was renamed the All-Malaya Council of Joint Action (AMCJA) with Tan Cheng Lock as its chairman. It comprised the MDU, the Pan-Malayan Federation of Trade Unions and various communal, commercial, women's and youth organizations. Tan Cheng Lock was outspoken from the start in his criticism of the Federation proposal that stipulated a 15-year residency to attain citizenship.[81] Importantly, although the SCCC through a statement of its president, Lee Kong Chian, agreed with the Council of Joint Action that Singapore should be included in the Federation and that 15 years was too long a period for the residency clause, it did not join the newly formed organization.[82] The Malayan Communist Party (MCP) through its front organizations was an important force in this amalgam, thereby contributing to the British refusal to acknowledge the AMCJA (allied with PUTERA, the left-wing Malay nationalist party) as the representative of non-Malay opinion. MCP involvement seemed to have played a role in the SCCC refusal to join.[83]

This did not mean that the SCCC was not concerned. It sent a memorandum to the government in February 1947, the main points of which are also found in the recommendations sent by the ACCCM to the governor-general on 25 March. This latter document advised: (1) Construction of a Federation of Malaya plan by a Royal Commission, (2) Inclusion of Singapore and equal citizenship rights for all, (3) Acknowledgement for the special position of the Malays but caution on the issue of pro-Malay policy, (4) Redressing the under representation of Chinese in the current proposal, (5) Election of the Unofficial members for the Federation councils rather than direct appointment by the government, (6) Lowering the requirement of 10 years of residency out of the preceding 15 years in the current proposal to five years of residency, in line with the Ceylon situation, and dropping the Malay and English language test altogether, (7) Lifting the colour bar in the Malayan civil service.[84]

The ACCCM proposals indicated willingness for serious dialogue with the British on these issues. Their commercial interests in Singapore and Malaya influenced the ACCCM to cooperate and two leading members were sent as representatives to the Consultative Commission. The AMCJA, however, demanded the outright resignation of the Consultative Commission and boycotted both that forum and the discussion.[85] In May 1947, the colonial authorities published a federation draft agreement, which had been approved by UMNO and the sultans. Now, the AMCJA-PUTERA drew up a counter-scheme called the People's Constitutional Proposals for Malaya, demanding inclusion of Singapore and an executive council responsible to a legislative assembly elected by all adults domiciled in Malaya.[86] Because the Chinese commercial elite of Singapore and Malaya felt bitter over British disregard for their opinion and interests, they now decided that it was time to cooperate with the AMCJA-PUTERA. In September 1947, Tan Cheng Lock persuaded the Malacca Chinese Chamber of Commerce to stage a *hartal* and another followed soon after in Ipoh. Then the ACCCM decided to stage a countrywide *hartal* and invited the AMCJA-PUTERA to participate.[87]

The Malaya-wide *hartal* was held on 20 October 1947, coinciding with the re-opening of British Parliament. It brought commercial and social life in Singapore and Malaya to a standstill. As a result of the strike and the alliance with the AMCJA-PUTERA, the Singapore Chinese elite hardened their standpoint towards the British, temporarily stopping the work-with-the-British strategy in its tracks. On the eve of the signing of the Federation agreements with the Malay rulers, the ACCCM decided to boycott the Federal Legislative Council and the various state councils, which occurred just when the SCCC was embroiled in a conflict with the Singapore colonial authorities over the appointment of Lien Ying Chow to the Municipal Council and over the eligibility of non-British subjects to be appointed as Chamber representative on the Singapore Legislative Council. The SCCC supported the ACCCM boycott.

Since the first *hartal* had been unsuccessful in gaining results, ACCCM leaders were divided on whether to adopt constitutional or extra-constitutional methods of agitation against the Federation of Malaya inauguration on 1 February 1948.[88] The Chinese Chambers refused to respond to Tan Cheng Lock's call for a second *hartal* in January 1948. The pact of the Chinese chambers with the AMCJA-PUTERA had been a cooperation of convenience throughout with the only strong point of agreement being immediate unification of Singapore with the Federation. Neither the ACCCM, nor the SCCC, ever supported the other AMCJA-PUTERA demands for Malay self-government or immediate elections.[89]

While the *hartal* was the high mark of united action among the Chinese business community of Singapore and Malaya, it aroused Malay hostility and kindled little response among the English-educated Malayan Chinese.[90] A desirable solution for the Chinese of Singapore and Malaya on the issue of Malayan citizenship would mean the automatic inception of a Chinese popular majority, which would lead to irreconcilable opposition from the Malay. Considerations by the SCCC leadership on the importance of remaining a partner of the British in Singapore further alienated them from a Malayan solution. In late January 1948, the SCCC defected from coordinated Malayan politics by agreeing to nominate its representatives to the Singapore Municipal and Legislative Councils according to the British rules, ending its temporary coalition with the Malayan counterparts.[91]

When Edward Gent was inaugurated as first High Commissioner for the Federation of Malaya on 1 February 1948, the separation of Singapore from Malaya became a *fait accompli*. As a result, the Chinese business elite shifted their political attention to Singapore almost exclusively.[92] However, true to their traders' pragmatism and Singapore's port history, Malaya, and Indonesia for that matter, remained very important in their economic orientation. They continued to own and operate plantations and processing plants in these two countries and traded extensively with these two territories. However, lobby activities concerning obstacles to trade with Indonesia and Malaya would be organized within the Singapore arena.

Business elite identity and economic concerns

While it appears that China and Malaya politics played a major role in Singapore Chinese elite activities and organizations, we need to ask whether these were the main developments on the minds of the Chinese commercial elite in this period. The cases on localization show clearly that socio-political issues focused their individual attention and their organizational efforts on matters pertaining to Singapore. Their primary identity as businessmen ensured that economic affairs further strengthened this process.

For Chinese businessmen, World War II was a major disruption. Many of their businesses suffered badly or were wiped out. Worst of all, the free market of the trading port context, the environment in which they thrived, came to a standstill. When the war was over, rebuilding their companies and regaining their market access and share was paramount in their minds. The general economic situation was not good; inflation and shortages of critical goods and foodstuffs continued, thus undermining the confidence of the population. The poor showing of the BMA did not help matters. In general, both at the time, as well as in the historical analyses of the period, the BMA was seen as inadequate. It was dubbed the "Black Market Administration" and was said to have destroyed in seven months the goodwill that existed at the time of liberation and to have brought British prestige in Singapore to a lower point even than in February 1942.[93] The Chinese business elite felt hampered by London's concerns about the UK economy, which put the colonies at a distinct disadvantage.

The Chinese merchants would benefit greatly from the competitive selling of commodities, and in its very first statement to the temporary government this was exactly what the SCCC advocated that the BMA should implement.[94] The reality was that the British shielded their home market and decided against free trade with the colonies. To aid reconstruction efforts in the UK, its inhabitants were supposed to "buy British" not imperial. In 1946, Lien Ying Chow revealed that the Malayan market was flooded with cheap British piece goods.[95] The UK was using the colonial market to generate revenue for its postwar manufacturing sector, and local business circles levelled allegations of subsidies and unfair competition against it.

The rubber sector offers a strong case. Rubber was in great demand right after the war and it was a major foreign currency earner for Singapore and Malaya. The first export shipment took place on 26 September, just 19 days after the British returned. By June 1946, the commodity made up half of Malaya's export trade. However, by September there was a glut in the rubber market resulting from overproduction.[96] In addition, the British government included rubber on the list of commodities under price restrictions because of the strategic nature of the product and the immediate postwar problems in creating an efficient system of financing, transportation and marketing. The Singapore rubber sector was greatly concerned about this development.

Other occasions, Chinese traders felt equally ill-treated. In a dispute between Singapore Chinese shippers and the Dutch colonial authorities the British forced the issue and warned Chinese shippers in a strongly worded message not to pursue their claims as they jeopardized relations with the Netherlands East Indies.[97] In a bid to revive trade with other traditional trading partners despite the foreign exchange restrictions, the Chamber lobbied for a barter agreement between China and Singapore.[98] The authorities did not support the proposal and the plan never took off.

In the following years issues other than the civil war in China or the situation in Malaya continued to capture the larger part of the attention of the Chinese commercial elite. The first issue was the new visa regulation in Hong Kong, which was implemented in November 1949. This policy further obstructed the sending of remittances to China already hampered by foreign currency regulations in Singapore. The SCCC objected to these policies, but the British authorities in Singapore passed the buck and blamed the Hong Kong administration. The issue of foreign exchange restrictions in general became increasingly heated when the British clamped down on many businesses and remittance houses for infringements. This development reinforced the opinion among Chinese merchants that Singapore was bearing the brunt of the Empire-wide monetary policies of the British.[99]

Trade with Indonesia was an even more important matter on the minds of the Chinese businessmen. During the war and immediately thereafter, great profits had been made in barter trade and in supplying the Indonesian independence movement.[100] The year 1948 had been a spectacular trading year with total transactions amounting to $467 million, while 1949 proved to be a bad year because, in February, an Anglo-Dutch direct trade pact was signed restricting and formalizing trade. All the chambers of commerce of Singapore, uncharacteristically, united in opposition. They feared that they would be cut out of the market expansion and sent a delegation to London.[101] Trade with Indonesia, especially the big portion with Sumatra, was conducted mostly as barter. In 1949, under the new regulations the Dutch ordered the liquidation of these "barter accounts" by 15 April. They did so with the tacit approval of the British who wanted this trade incorporated in their formal banking system. This new regulation resulted in $1.9 million in unsettled debt for Singapore's traders, mainly due to the illicit nature of the exchanges. Led by the Chamber they protested and in November 1949, the UN commissioner for Indonesia announced a new trade agreement between the British and the Dutch.[102]

The third issue pertained to the new Sterling trade pact between the British Empire and Japan, which would allow Britain and its dominions to export £55 million to, and import £45 million from, that country. In principle this development meant an exciting opportunity for Singapore's traders. Interest focused almost exclusively on the import quota of £5 million or $42 million granted to Singapore and Malaya. The sub-division of this share resulted in a big pulling match in which Singapore's chambers of commerce claimed two-thirds of the share as opposed to parties from peninsular Malaya who wanted a 50–50 split. It took half a year to settle the matter in Singapore's favour and the allocation finally went into effect on 1 July 1950.[103]

Despite the upheaval about the civil war in China and the temporary collective action in Malaya, economic considerations were a very important factor in the process of localization and continued to turn the attention of the local Chinese elite to Singapore. To the SCCC leaders and the Chamber members, the world was first and foremost a place to trade. Chinese migrants had flocked to Singapore for a century and an half because of its trading port characteristics and much of the migrant myths were stories of rags to riches and becoming a towkay. Having fulfilled this dream, the Chamber leaders were very aware that their continued wealth as well as social and political status depended on the success of their business empires. The need to safeguard these economic, social and political interests ensured that the localization of the Singapore Chinese business elite was a logical process. If decolonization and democratization was the road Singapore would travel, they wanted to be at the forefront of the process of defining the rules of the political game.

Concluding remarks

For the period 1945–1950, the dominant development of the Chinese business elite of Singapore was a process of localization. This localization should be understood within the framework of the decolonization of the territory. Chinese businessmen were keen to rebuild their companies after the war and therefore lobbied for the full reinstatement of the free market. They realized quickly, however, that in order to safeguard their economic interests, they needed to involve themselves increasingly in the social and political affairs of the territory. Despite the dented legitimacy of the colonial system, British views on the slow evolution towards increased local political participation were dominant, and the parameters London put in place for this process were the political reality for Singapore. The fact that the British decided early on to separate Singapore from Malaya on the road to independence implied that "local" in this process, would be "Singapore".

China politics was not a viable alternative focus for the Chinese commercial elite. While the rift between supporters of the two ideological sides in the Chinese civil war was large, and certainly gave rise to a spirited fight for influence over the institutions of the organizational pyramid of Chinese society, the Chamber was never dominated by either side and remained focused on local, Singaporean issues. Resolution of the Chinese civil war in 1949 further took the sting out of this conflict. After years of anticipating which side would end up on top, it was now clear which was the dominant power constellation. Ideological fervour on both the winning and the losing side subsided and everybody turned their attention fully to business matters and local politics. The Chinese of Singapore wanted to incorporate Chineseness as a local identity. Now that the chips were down and decisions about Chineseness and localness needed to be made, the identity strands based on ideological China politics were discarded. The outcome of this process was the birth of the Chinese as Singapore citizens.

Malaya-based collective political action also was not an alternative orientation for the SCCC either. The only period of significant Chamber cooperation with parties and organizations on the Malayan peninsula to counter the Federation proposals was in 1947. The *hartal*, unsuccessful in its goal to influence either the British or the Malays, remained the only instance when cross-causeway cooperation found a tangible political form for the Chamber. Matters concerning political strategy and ethnic balance posed significant obstacles to a joint approach. While the multiple identities of the Singapore Chinese business elite most definitely included Malayan and Mainland Chinese faces, the necessity to claim a political foothold in their place of residence and business meant that their efforts would be focused predominantly on Singapore. Economically, socially and politically, the Chamber's activities and strategies were relevant to the local context.

Within this Singapore context, changes in the social and political landscape were taking place. Decolonization, the advent of elections and the formalization of the representation of local residents prompted reactions in local society. New institutional forms, such as political parties and trade unions, were still in their infancy though and the Chamber was therefore well placed to make full use of the opportunities. Issues deemed to be of great importance to the SCCC and its Chinese community constituency, such as the opposition against income tax and the right to political participation, were taken up with great energy. A certain segment of the Chamber leadership was selected to fill powerful positions in both the Chamber hierarchy and the colonial representational system. The four men introduced in this chapter exemplify this group: Lien Ying Chow, Lee Kong Chian, Yap Pheng Geck and Tan Chin Tuan. Their business interests had survived the war relatively well, giving them financial and commercial security. They also had excellent pre-existing connections with the British authorities on which they could build, and they were willing and motivated to lead the Chamber in its work-with-the-British strategy. This strategy was based on the assumption that in order to obtain a voice for Chinese business and for the wider Singapore Chinese society, the Chamber needed to participate in the arenas implemented and endorsed by the colonial authorities.

As the balance between colonizer and colonized shifted, it became necessary for the Chinese business elite to adapt in order to ensure a say in the course of change. If the formalization and expansion of local participation in politics signified the first phase of this power shift, localization was required of the SCCC leadership to participate in the journey to modernization. Logically, the Chamber strategy focused on cooperation with the colonial authorities. In the next phase in 1951, as we will see, the SCCC realized it held a position of strength vis-à-vis the British and became more assertive in its demands.

CHAPTER THREE

1951–1959
The Chamber in politics: Ambiguity and ambition

The chamber of commerce is important as the major organisation in the Chinese community; it is a charitable, cultural and political body as well as a commercial one, and chamber of commerce is really a misnomer.[1]

ON 16 MAY 1949, NG AIK HUAN, a well-respected Hokkien leader and close friend of Tan Kah Kee, spoke prophetic words at an SCCC meeting, "... Singapore has embarked upon the road of democratic self-government and the Chinese community cannot afford to ignore future election campaigns".[2] Apparently, the British did not expect the Chinese-speaking majority, of which Ng was a leader, to understand and take an active part in the politics of decolonization. On 15 July 1949, Governor Franklin Gimson presided over the first postwar meeting of the Chinese Advisory Board (CAB). In a statement replete of the "white man's burden", he said that the Chinese had only recently adopted democracy and continued "it would be the height of folly for the West to attempt to impose on the East a form of Government which took no account of the characteristics for which this ancient civilisation is responsible ... The object of this board is, as I have said, to develop principles of democracy in a form which will make them readily acceptable to the Chinese people and thereby gain for them, if I may say so, the logical outcome of their long civilisation."[3]

Decolonization was a dominant feature of the 1950s in Asia. The process of the transfer of power from the colonizer to the colonized was the central question, which meant that established elites of the colonial system tried to consolidate their power base around access and status, while new elites attempted to construct alternative power bases around concepts of self-determination, nationalism or ethnic identity. Electoral politics would be the guiding principle by which Singapore would become an independent nation. For the SCCC, therefore, if continued power and status was the ultimate reward, the right to vote had to be the goal, and citizenship the key. Citizenship had meant becoming a British subject but increasingly shifted toward a local, Singaporean citizenship. The Chamber was a major force behind this change through its appeals to the colonial government. The British were not so sure about the democratic pedigree of the Chamber, suspecting a rather more elitist and pragmatic rationale. A report on a Chamber delegation to the Governor reads: "The Chinese press supports the Chamber, but many people suspect that the object of these representations is simply to confer on a few alien Chinese leaders the right to be elected to membership of the councils".[4] At first the British did not want to enfranchise non-British citizens, but the inherent logic of decolonization would prove stronger than these British sentiments.

Singapore's economy was still suffering from its postwar predicaments. Dependent as it was on trade, the city-state suffered from the economic disruptions caused by various anti-colonial struggles, the formation of newly independent states in the region, and from Britain's policy of imperial preferences, which disfavoured the colonies. Low trade volume and a struggling economy resulted in high unemployment, which was the ideal seedbed for a strong labour movement, that put great pressure on established and new political elites. Ethnic and ideological violence shook Singapore at times. Ethnic tension in Singapore found an unfortunate release during the Maria Hertogh riots in 1950 in which Malays, angered about a court ruling in a case involving a Dutch girl that had been brought up in a Malay family, took to the streets and a curfew was ordered after 18 people were killed. The bomb attack on the White House Hotel in 1952, and reports of burned buses and arson of factories further attest to the charged ideological and social atmosphere.

The nature of politics and leadership in Singapore changed as the electorate increased and more residents became involved in the political process. Political power became ideologically charged and mass based. In this changing political landscape the SCCC, still by far the largest business representative with 5,000 members, was contemplating the question of consolidating its leading position in business and society. Two groups of Chamber leaders, which I call the Ambiguous and the Ambitious, proposed two distinct sets of answers and strategies to this question. The Ambiguous derived their power basis from their positions in the colonial system and were key actors in the Chamber's work-with-the-British strategy after World War II. The Ambitious, who were dominated by men who had recently acquired great wealth during the rubber boom of 1950–1951 caused by the Korean War, did not want to wait for the British to decide to which local elite they would transfer power but wanted to force a dominant position for the SCCC through an active role in politics.

The Ambiguous and the Ambitious held each other in a delicate balance by alternating the presidency between them and clashed on the goals and strategies the Chamber should pursue. In the Chamber election of 1958 a fierce struggle evolved in which the elite politics strategy was pitted against the popular politics approach. Dominant issues of the time, such as ideology, political power, the changing nature of leadership, and questions of identity and culture were poignantly put in perspective.

1. Political participation: the citizenship issue

The citizenship issue was ignited by a threat to the position of China-born Chinese in Singapore. After the proclamation of the People's Republic of China on 1 October 1949, the British reacted with the Emergency Travel Restriction Regulations followed by the Immigration/Passport Bill in 1950. Both tried to drastically limit the flow of Chinese to and from China. Certificates of Residence for China-born living in Singapore were abolished and aliens had to obtain re-entry permits for overseas travel.[5] Both regulations, because they made a clear distinction between British subjects and non-British subjects, also touched upon the crux of the matter of citizenship: which residents of Singapore would be protected by and could reap the benefits of its laws, and who would be awarded political rights.

In late November 1950, the Chamber MC met to discuss the strategy the SCCC should follow and a clear linkage was made between the issues of travel restrictions and citizenship.[6] On 12 December 1950, the Chamber sent a strongly worded petition to Governor Gimson concerning the passport regulation and the terms of re-entry for resident aliens, requesting that Chinese with Certificates of Admission be allowed to return to Singapore.[7] The November MC meeting also established a special committee to prepare a recommendation to the government on voting privileges for long-term resident China-born Chinese. The argument was that they contributed to the colony and paid taxes and should therefore be allowed to vote. The bias of the Chamber as an economic elite is clear in this reasoning because the great majority of the China-born Chinese did not earn enough to have to pay taxes. Lee Kong Chian, Tan Chin Tuan and Lien Ying Chow led the top brass of the Chamber who were appointed to this committee. The choice of personnel reflects a continuation of the work-with-the-British strategy of petitioning the colonial government through the services of bi-lingual leaders well-connected to government circles.[8]

In early January 1951, the SCCC proposed a new entry pass system treating British subjects and resident aliens alike. It envisioned an immigration council, comprising the Governor, three government officials, three Unofficial Legco members and three Unofficial Singapore residents, to control and supervise the system.[9] The next month, a petition, this time co-signed by 279 Chinese organizations, was sent to Secretary of State for the Colonies Griffiths. "The Singapore Chinese have hitherto always had implicit faith in the promises and assurances of Government. These events have seriously shaken that belief." The petition asked that amendments to the Passport Regulation 1950 be set aside in order to allow the Chinese who had left the colony to return, "before great and possibly irreparable damage is caused between the government and the Chinese community".[10]

On 5 January 1951, the Chamber MC gathered again at the main hall of its premises on Hill Street to discuss the recommendations of the special committee. The members had flocked to the old Chinese mansion purchased from Wee Ah Hood almost 50 years earlier. On this day, though, the Chamber leaders were not dwelling as much on the past as on the future. They were eager to take a step towards their emancipation and empowerment by finalizing the memorandum to urge for franchise and citizenship rights for the China-born Chinese in the colony. Vice President Tan Siak Kew, a Teochew rice trader in his mid-40s, delivered a key speech:

> Times have changed and our hearts are no longer with a China dominated by Chinese Communists. Large sums are invested in Singapore by many Chinese who, because they were born in China, are now regarded as aliens, with no voting privileges and cannot get naturalization papers. We have made our homes here, our children were born here, and our life's interests are in this colony. We feel that the time is ripe now to urge the government to consider allowing us the privileges now only enjoyed by local-born Chinese. Over the decades, domiciled Chinese have proved by their industry and sincerity that the development and progress of Singapore do not depend alone on the efforts of a favoured few but on the majority. Naturalisation requirements are still too restrictive for those who do not speak or write English.[11]

Tan Siak Kew: Cautious conservative.
Courtesy of the National Archives of Singapore

Tan Siak Kew was a Teochew born in the Chao'an district of Guangdong province in 1903. After receiving some primary level education in Chinese, the remainder of his formal education was in English after immigrating to Singapore with his father and older brother in 1910. He attended St. Anthony's Primary School and Raffles Institution but did not finish his education after his father died and he started his own business. His first trading company, Buan Lee Seng, focused on pepper, copra and coffee.[12] Tan's first wife was the daughter of Liau Chia Heng, an influential Teochew and three-term president of the SCCC in the 1910s. Because he was bilingual, Tan was already included in the representational elite of the

Tan Siak Kew met the defining characteristics of the work-with-the-British strategy by asking the government for leniency in applying existing rules. Playing by the existing rules and avoiding risks while maximizing the profitable position of bridging the colonial government and the Chinese community, he was as conservative a force within the process of defining the political strategy of the Chamber as he was in his business dealings.

Some of his Chamber colleagues, led by the Hokkien President Tan Lark Sye, were indeed willing to take more risks and took a clear stand when the MC meeting of February 1951 adopted the draft petition on voting privileges. The proposal went beyond enfranchising the China-born Chinese through British naturalization by advising the government to introduce a local citizenship. The requirements for this new status would be fivefold: (1) Eight years of residency in the previous 10 years, (2) Declaration of no intention of leaving for at least five years except for business or vacation, (3) Declaration of loyalty to the colony, (4) Undertaking not to join any foreign political party, hold any appointment under a foreign government or owe allegiance to another state during the period of residence in the colony, and (5) Ability to read and write either Chinese or English. Local

Chinese and was a municipal councillor in pre-war years. During the war, he was a member of the Overseas Chinese Association, forced into existence by the Japanese to extort $50 million out of the Chinese community.[13] After the war, his star quickly rose as a very successful produce trader. The shortage of staple goods in the years immediately after the war provided great opportunities for this fast-acting merchant whose networks included access to producers of scarce goods as well as to capital to finance trade deals. Tan's connections to the Teochew rice millers in Thailand stood him in good stead. He used his new wealth to buy a controlling stake in the Sze Hai Tong Bank. His activities in the colonial government and his involvement in many statutory boards attracted a lot of business for the bank from official institutions and government boards.[14] In an interview his son described Tan Siak Kew's style of business: "He was very conservative. Extremely cautious. That was his philosophy. He had gone through two economic depressions and survived them. And like Tan Chin Tuan he became somewhat circumspect." The son contrasts the father with some of his contemporaries, saying they "were bolder", "did much better financially" and "thrived on risk".[15] Tan Siak Kew had his feet firmly planted in both the colonial and the Chinese sphere, and was involved in the major Teochew schools and *huiguan* as well as in the Ngee Ann Kongsi.

citizenship would also entitle standing for election and holding office, thereby automatically implying that the representative councils of the colony would operate on a multi-lingual basis.[16]

While Tan Lark Sye managed to add more bite to the Chamber's political style, he could not change its opponent. The British still firmly controlled the political playing field and called the shots. Political enfranchisement through naturalization was the preferred colonial track. The British were only willing to soften the requirements for naturalization, as they did on 11 December 1951, by removing the language clause for the acquisition of British citizenship.

The Chamber reacted quickly and in its MC meeting of 14 December decided to pressure the Colonial Secretary once again.[17] In direct opposition to the newly established rules, the SCCC asked to change the oath of allegiance to the British crown to a declaration of loyalty to the colony. Colonial Secretary Blythe answered the Chamber, rather tersely, that the government firmly dismissed what it regarded as a proposal to grant "full citizenship rights for the China-born in return for a declaration of temporary allegiance".[18] The context of political development in Malaya

Tan Lark Sye: Ambitious gambler.

Collection of Loke Wan Tho. Courtesy of the Cathay Organisation

Tan Lark Sye, who had been elected President in March 1950 after rebuilding his business, was the main force behind this more assertive line of political pressuring. He was born in Tong An county in Fujian province in 1897 and, like Tan Kah Kee, hailed from Jimei. Life there was tough and Tan lost his parents to disease at a young age.

Having received only three years of primary education at the Jimei School that Tan Kah Kee had founded, he came to Singapore at 18 to work in one of Tan's rubber businesses. In 1925 he had learned enough about the business to try setting up a rubber trading company, Lianhe, with his brother. The financier behind this venture was See

Teong Wah, former president of the SCCC and comprador of the Hong Kong and Shanghai Bank. After a slow start the business took off and by 1928 they had started a rubber processing business, Aik Hoe.

In 1933 when the depression was causing many casualties in the rubber sector, Aik Hoe rented a complete factory from Tan Kah Kee. By 1938, Aik Hoe had become the largest rubber company in Singapore and Malaya, owning plants and plantations in Indonesia, Malaya, Thailand and Vietnam, and doing business in New York and London. In October 1938, Aik Hoe was reorganized into a private limited company with a registered capital of $1 million.[19]

His business success gave him the status to assume a leadership position in the Chamber and in 1941 he was chosen as vice president under Lien Ying Chow. During the Japanese occupation of Singapore, having been active in the China Relief Funds, Tan was thrown in prison. After the war, he lost no time working from a half caved-in building on Circular Road, and with the help of his nephew Tan Eng Joo, to rebuild Aik Hoe. Very much the immigrant rags to riches role model, Tan possessed an impressive work ethic but also enjoyed risk-taking in business and in pleasure. He was an avid gambler and was a regular in the Ee Hoe Hean Club of Tan Kah Kee, from whom he took over as president from 1948–1963, and the Goh Loo Club before he set up his own Tanjong Rhu Club where the stakes were famously high.[20] Where possible he would hedge his bets and, despite his credentials fighting for a Singaporean citizenship, he took the opportunity to get some insurance when it came. In 1954, a small front-page article in *The Straits Times* announced that Tan had received his naturalization and was henceforth a British subject.[21]

Family was an important factor in all of Tan Lark Sye's business ventures. Many members of the extended family worked in one of the companies the family owned, controlled or had a stake in. Members of the family held directorates in Chinese businesses such as OCBC, OUB, UOB, Chung Khiaw Bank and Asia Insurance.[22]

Tan Lark Sye was the undisputed leader of the family and ran the businesses with a high level of personal control. One of his contemporaries remembers that Tan actually handled all incoming calls at Aik Hoe, functioning as the telephone switchboard operator. The difference in management style and business vision between Tan and Lee Kong Chian, the other great rubber baron, could hardly be more marked. Whereas Lee was on top of the demands of modern management, the latest commercial and industrial

developments and continuously reorganized his companies into a professionally run conglomerate that could survive very well when he retired, Tan with his personal style and traditional family business ways made it hard for his successors to keep the family business going.[23]

In many ways Tan Lark Sye succeeded Tan Kah Kee, taking over his leadership positions at the top of the Hokien Huay Kuan in 1950 and the Ee Hoe Hean Club. He also shared similar educationalist aspirations and had financially supported Kah Kee's many projects, including Xiamen University. Tan Lark Sye shared with Tan Kah Kee a stubborn conviction that the Chinese, while standing united, could form a strong platform to fight issues important to their community.

Tan was famously described by Professor Lin Yu Tang, the man Tan picked to be the first Vice-Chancellor of his pet educational project, Nanyang University, as a "charming, intelligent, ruthless and cynical businessman".[24]

was important to the British decision. In the early 1950s the possibility was being discussed of independence for Singapore and British Malaya in partnership. The British favoured this approach but left it to the local parties to find a solution to the ethnic and political implications. This idea of partnership was referred to as "merger". At this point in time, however, the British rejected the Chamber proposal, partly because they were under pressure from the Malayan side not to give franchise rights to people who were not naturalized British subjects. They did not want to harden the Malay stand and jeopardize the possibility of merger.[25]

The Chamber tried to prove that it was loyal to Singapore and willing to contribute to its safety and development. During the installation ceremony on 15 March 1952, outgoing president Tan Lark Sye called on the Chinese public to support the national service bill, under which an estimated 80,000 Singaporeans would have to serve for up to two years.[26] A British intelligence report recorded the general approval of the SCCC for the principle of national service. However, it also noted that some Chinese saw support for the national service bill as a good trade off for greater civic rights.[27] This was indeed true; the MC meeting of March supported the call-up for national service and Yap Pheng Geck said: "Chinese are 80 per cent of the population. We want protection and we can get it if we support this bill".[28]

Tan Siak Kew, the incoming president of 1952, continued the direction set by Tan Lark Sye but brought his more conservative style and his sensitivity to the British side of the power equation. Under his leadership, the Chamber supported the government when it tried to get eligible persons to register on the electoral role. The Chamber offered to assist in giving broadcast talks on registration in the different Chinese languages.[29] Due to the citizenship issue, two distinct visions on politics formed within the Chamber and the two groups that advocated them increasingly disagreed about the goals and strategies of the SCCC.

2. Competing leadership groups: the Ambiguous and the Ambitious

In the process of decolonization the Chamber and its leaders actively brokered between the receding colonial administration and the residents of Singapore. It spoke for all Chinese of Singapore in demanding political rights in the late-colonial and post-colonial period and was acknowledged by the British as one of the paramount local organizations. The leaders of the SCCC were faced with the question how best to secure these safeguards and continued Chamber status and dominance. In response, two groups, defined as "the Ambiguous" and "the Ambitious", formed. The British-oriented Ambiguous were of the opinion that continuing to work-with-the-British in a framework of politics as an elite endeavour would be best. As the moderating bilingual liaison between the Chinese business world and the withdrawing colonizer, their answer to the decolonization question was to transform their colonial elite status to a post-colonial power base by means of a British blessing. Therefore, although they saw the need for political action, they were ambiguous about populist politics and an active role of the Chamber therein. The anti-colonial Ambitious viewed politics as a local affair to be decided by locals, not by the colonial overlord. As a result they wanted to popularize political issues in a wider societal context and saw an active, leading role for the Chamber. The two sides clashed because of their differing views on the politics of decolonization, which were based on different social backgrounds, education and different understanding of the nature of leadership and power.

The Ambiguous

The individuals constituting the Ambiguous leadership in the early 1950s were familiar faces: Yap Pheng Geck, Tan Chin Tuan and Tan Siak Kew. The first two were key agents in the Chamber's work-with-the-British strategy, Tan Chin Tuan as appointed Legco member and Deputy Speaker and Yap as Municipal Councillor. Because the Chamber still had appointed positions on these councils and because command of the English language and naturalized British citizenship were prerequisites to occupy them, their skills and status were still needed. In these capacities they continued the work-with-the-British approach and provided the Chamber's connection with colonial elite politics. Tan Siak Kew shared their pedigree of political, social and commercial contact with the British. These men were part of the colonial elite and strove to retain the elite character of politics in Singapore. Their elite status depended greatly upon the utility of their political status, while popularization of politics through a wider electoral system would erode their position immediately. The core of the Ambiguous was part of the bilingual elite of the Chamber and was close to the Straits Chinese elite but generally did not have strong connections with the Chinese-speaking community or its *bang/huiguan* structure. The constituency of the Ambiguous varied in the following years as temporary alignments on specific issues or shared enemies brought KMT supporters and Hokkien reformists into its camp. The Ambiguous, generally, constituted a conservative,

Ko Teck Kin: Savvy operator.

Courtesy of the SCCCI

Ko, a Hokkien born in 1906 in Longxi district of Fujian province, was Vice President during 1952–1954. He had made a meteoric rise through the ranks, considering he only arrived in Singapore from Palembang shortly after World War II.

When his family fled from Palembang to escape an anti-Chinese mob after the Japanese surrender, he used a ship to bring contraband rubber to Singapore. Profits from the sale of the rubber provided his start-up capital. He made his big move when Japanese rubber estates in Johor seized as enemy property were auctioned. He secured some prime estates and made a fortune during the rubber boom of 1950.[30] The way in which he acquired one of these properties shows the savvy with which Ko operated, in economic as well as

moderating force. What the Ambiguous lacked was a broad base in the Chinese population, or a forward-looking vision of Singapore that included the entire Chinese community.

The Ambitious

The Ambitious had a more radical vision of politics. Predominantly Chinese-educated, they believed that they could use their control over the power structure of Chinese society as a basis for dominance in electoral politics. They advocated mass political participation – if under their elite guidance – through enfranchisement of immigrant residents, as well as popular policy concerns such as Chinese education. It was hard, if not impossible to be an influential leader in the Chamber without being successful in business. Not only did it take a lot of private money to finance the projects and causes of the Chamber, wealth was also necessary for the status and connections needed to play the game at the highest level.

in political affairs. Before an auction, Ko struck a deal with Lee Kong Chian, his brother George Lee and Tan Lark Sye. At that time these three Hokkien leaders were among the richest and most influential Chinese in Singapore. Ko, being the junior partner and the least conspicuous, was to bid for all of them to not drive up the price. At the last moment, though, he informed his partners that he would go it alone. In this way he made sure that his strongest competitors would not be able to bid against him, and secured the best estate at a low price. It is interesting to note that neither Lee Kong Chian nor Tan Lark Sye wanted to quarrel about the issue.[31]

In the social arena, Ko also used the channels open to a wealthy businessman. Together with Kheng Chin Hock, a fellow Longxi man who had also come from Palembang after World War II, he used the Longxi Huiguan as a springboard to Hokkien and Chamber prominence. Just after the war, the Longxi Huiguan was not a large or influential organization among the Hokkien for lack of strong and wealthy leaders. Ko and Kheng went on a membership campaign to round up support and became the leaders of the Longxi Huiguan. This entitled them to a voice in the larger Hokien Huay Kuan and put them on the map as players in the Hokkien power game. Leverage within the Hokien Huay Kuan provided opportunities and a power base to join the competition in the Chamber.[32]

In the postwar years and the early 1950s, individuals in a number of sectors took advantage of the opportunities to amass great wealth in a short period of time, putting themselves on the business map as well as lifting themselves to the status of societal leaders. A great opportunity presented itself in the rubber sector at the start of the Cold War in Asia with the outbreak of the Korean War. The great increase in demand for natural rubber for tyres drove world market prices up. At the beginning of 1950, Singapore rubber sold for around 55 cents per pound while at the end of the year prices peaked at 236 cents per pound, a fourfold increase.[33] Singapore was an important centre for the rubber trade as it lay between the major rubber producing areas. Those entrepreneurs who had stakes in, and control of, the entire production process from plantation to export shipping were the ones who made the largest profits. Two characteristic representatives of this group were Tan Lark Sye and Ko Teck Kin. Tan Lark Sye was already an established businessman while Ko was an example of a group of new faces making a fortune.

Ng Aik Huan: Hokkien orator.

Collection of Tan Kok Kheng. Courtesy of the National Archives of Singapore

Ng Aik Huan was a Hokkien who hailed from Nan'an in Fujian Province. He was born in 1906 or 1908 in China, although his father was a merchant based in Singapore. Having attended Chinese private school in China, Ng came to Singapore in 1923 but soon left for Johor where he established a groceries and Straits-produce trading company. He returned to Singapore in 1929 and set up a Chinese wine trading shop with his brother. In 1934, Ng joined Asia Insurance as an assistant manager.

He was involved in the big relief campaigns organized because of the civil war and Japanese aggression in China, and worked together closely with Tan Kah Kee. He spoke no English but his oratory skills in Hokkien were important in both fundraising efforts and for informing and arousing the people to anti-Japanese boycotts and the civil defence of Singapore.

After the war, in 1948 Ng became manager of Asia Life Insurance. Throughout his life, he was active in clan and educational organizations from the Nan'an and Hokien Huay Kuan to primary and secondary schools and Nanyang University.[34]

The newfound wealth of men like Tan Lark Sye and Ko Teck Kin provided them with a source of private capital that was especially important for the funding of communal, public causes such as political organizations and educational institutions. In these ambitions they gained considerable support from established businessmen. The gregarious networker Lien Ying Chow provided the Ambitious with access to London political circles. Having been a key actor in the work-with-the-British strategy before, Lien was the only of the four exponents of that strategy to fundamentally revise his ambitions and goals. On the other side of the spectrum, the Ambitious gained strong support from the older generation that had been close to Tan Kah Kee. Ng Aik Huan was the most active and outspoken.

Lee Kong Chian seemed to be a candidate to support the Ambitious camp, but unlike Lien Ying Chow, he did not openly align with them. At times, Lee would show that he favoured the Ambitious approach to political activity through a statement or by way of one of his associates. Lee remained a man of negotiation and compromise. He was, in that way, a believer in the traditional ways for making such decisions. He liked to create a full majority rather than using his considerable clout to push his opinion through. Therefore, he abhorred open conflict in the Chamber and cautioned against rash action. However, because of his closeness to Tan Kah Kee, his track record on political action, and his zealous work for Chinese education, he quietly supported the Ambitious in some of their projects.

While Lien and Ko were bilingual and could boast social and political connections with the colonial system, Tan and Ng Aik Huan did not speak English. The constituency of Tan and Ko, as well as of Ng, was primarily the Chinese-speaking community, and from them they derived their community leader status through the pyramid of Chinese *huiguan*. Chineseness was an important factor in the tie between leaders and constituency, and it was politicized through the localization of identity and focused on what it took for the Chinese to be involved in their own political future. These characteristics enforced the conviction of the Ambitious that the issue of political rights for the local Chinese-born immigrant community was the key to their own and the SCCC's continued success.

Internal disputes on politics, 1952–1955

Citizenship and decolonization politics were not the only flashpoint of disputes. In a clear indication that a power struggle was brewing in the Chamber, its internal election system came under attack. Throughout the Chamber's history attempts to get rid of the *bang* structure of representation of dialect groups coincided with power shifts or power struggles on other issues. In early 1952, 15 Hokkien wrote a letter to the Chamber arguing that the *bang* system should be abolished. The driving force behind the letter was MC member Colonel Chuang Hui Tsuan.

The 1952 letter requesting the abolition of the *bang* structure serves as an example of Colonel Chuang's latter stand. In it, he argued that the dialect group principle was ill-defined in the constitution, which had led to illogical assignment of seats. He also contended that the *bang* structure weakened the

Chuang Hui Tsuan: Combative colonel.

Collection of Tan Kok Kheng. Courtesy of the National Archives of Singapore

Chuang Hui Tsuan was born in Anxi County in Fujian province. He was educated in Chinese in Xiamen and came to Singapore in 1915 to work for his brother's Chinese produce company. He assisted his sister-in-law in setting up Nanyang Girls' School. Before the Japanese invasion, Chuang was Vice Director of the labour group of the Nanyang Overseas Chinese Relief Fund, which was the reason he left Singapore with Lim Bo Seng and a number of other KMT members two days before the Japanese arrived. They ended up in India where plans were made together with the British to organize a covert resistance scheme for Malaya. Chuang flew to Chungking, the wartime capital of China and received a brief to participate in the British plans and was made a Colonel in the Nationalist army. Back in India he cooperated with Lim Bo Seng and the British to set up the Malayan anti-Japanese guerrilla group Force 136. From 1943 to 1945 he was responsible for the dispatch of Chinese liaison officers, from Chiang Kai-shek's Nationalist Army, to Malaya to undertake anti-Japanese work.

Chamber because it led to competition among the *bang*. Furthermore, he saw the co-optation methods of leadership selection used within the *bang* to appoint MC members as a large obstacle to change and as a hindrance to younger people who wanted to serve the Chinese community.[35] That the letter writers were Hokkien and leaned to the KMT in the political spectrum showed that those supporting non-dominant political groups had a hard time getting into the MC. The KMT group was losing influence fast particularly in the Hokien Huay Kuan, which was dominated by the British-oriented pragmatists and the more PRC inclined anti-colonialists. In the end the MC decided that the constitution would not be changed and the *bang* system would remain in place because too many groups were uncertain whether a change would be beneficial to them.[36]

During the same period, a British report on the Chamber citizenship petition of 1951 shows that Colonel Chuang was also actively working

The British and Force 136 cooperated with communist guerrilla fighters and eventually this led to the betrayal of Major General Lim Bo Seng and many of the KMT agents to the Japanese. The experience made Colonel Chuang even more staunchly anti-communist.

After the war, he returned to Singapore and set up Ma Hua printing house and became a British subject by naturalization. Both before and after the war, he was a supporter of the KMT in the Chinese civil war and was a member of its Singapore branch. He was very active in the early postwar movement that sought Japanese apologies and compensation, and was involved in the Anxi and Hokien Huay Kuan as well as in the Zhuang Clan Association. Colonel Chuang was a fiery and sometimes maverick character. Never skirting from a strongly-worded statement, a cynical turn of phrase or

an emotional personal attack, he was nicknamed "Big Gun Chuang". In the spectrum of Ambiguous versus Ambitious, he embodied the temporary and topical alliances that were struck. His work with Tan Kah Kee and his anti-colonial view of politics put him very close to the Ambitious camp, which he aligned with on several occasions. On the other hand, his democratic feelings, as well as the shrewd pragmatism of a member of the weakening minority KMT group within the Chinese power structure, pitted him against the leading, and predominantly Ambitious, Hokkien and eventually into an alliance with the Ambiguous.[37]

for the Ambitious cause. The British were aware of the two schools of thought within the Chamber and the report describes one group led by Tan Chin Tuan and Yap Pheng Geck that was happy with the Colonial Secretary abolishing the language requirement for naturalization to British citizenship. The other group, led by Colonel Chuang, was described as arguing that British citizenship had disadvantages in the region. It foresaw that Britain would have to abandon the region at some point, leaving these British "locals" with a string attached, preferring a form of local citizenship tied to Singapore, not to Britain.[38]

Citizenship would continue to split the Chamber leadership. In the fall of 1952, the Ambitious' campaign for a Singaporean citizenship received a boost from an unlikely corner. While in London for business, Lien Ying Chow brought up the citizenship issue with Lord Inverforth of the Ben Line and Lord Tivy, head of the Labour Party, who had been his colleagues on the British rehabilitation and reconstruction committee after the war. They both supported his ideas of a Singaporean citizenship for the Chinese immigrants in Singapore. When Lien returned to Singapore, he initiated a discussion in the MC on a new call on the government.[39]

The *Sin Chew Jit Poh* strongly endorsed SCCC leadership in representing the Chinese community at this vital junction. "The Chinese Chamber of Commerce is supported by 80 per cent of the Singapore population who look to it as their leader. It should be able to exert its power as such. We need the leadership of the CCC in many matters. The CCC should play its part with its full strength and the public support of all bodies".[40]

The Ambiguous–Ambitious split became clear in the MC meeting of 29 September, when Lien Ying Chow made a long speech on the need for the Chamber to renew its claims for citizenship rights and Yap Pheng Geck opposed and observed in reference to British naturalization that "the door that was closed is now open, so what is there to claim … By all means claim, but also use the opportunities given". The most vocal support for Lien's proposal came from Colonel Chuang and Tan Lark Sye. Tan complained that the government had not "given the Chamber any face" in this issue, even though it represented 80 per cent of the population of the island.[41]

During the October MC meeting a new memorandum proposing a Singapore citizenship, championed by the Ambitious, was discussed. Tan Chin Tuan presented the Ambiguous case and argued that the government would probably not accept anything short of naturalization to British citizenship. He reminded the meeting that non-English speakers could now naturalize as well and that 52 individuals were granted this status during the previous Legco meeting over which he had presided.[42]

Despite opposition of the Ambiguous, the Ambitious prevailed and the MC endorsed a new memorandum to the Governor. It entailed franchise rights only to vote and stand for election but not to enter the civil service, and an oath of absolute allegiance to the colony as well as a renunciation of all foreign ties. A delegation visited the governor on 20 November to present the memorandum but failed to convince him. The British rejected the proposal on the same grounds as before. The main difference of opinion was that the SCCC saw British naturalization as an effective renunciation of Chinese nationality but regarded local citizenship of a non-independent territory as a totally different issue. They asked themselves why, with decolonization imminent, local Chinese should take on a non-Malayan nationality. The British pointed at the Chinese principle of *Ius Sanguinis*, to prove that dual nationality would remain anyway. They saw a local citizenship as giving in to a de facto dual citizenship.

In the conflict between the Ambiguous and the Ambitious personal attacks were used. Those with the closest ties to the British were increasingly confronted with the disapproval of their peers. Tan Chin Tuan was singled out, because the Ambitious questioned his loyalty to what they saw as the Chinese cause. An analysis of two incidents will illustrate this development. In December 1952, the Legco discussed the gift of £1 million by the colony to Britain. Tan Chin Tuan, in his capacity of Deputy Speaker, moved the proposal and presided over the meeting in which the Legco approved it. There were some in the Chamber who thought that such a substantial gift to the colonial overlord was outrageous and counter to the trend towards decolonization, and that it was Tan's duty to consult with the MC on matters of this magnitude.[43]

Tan Chin Tuan reacted in a very agitated manner, saying that he would resign his Legco seat if the SCCC wanted him to consult on every matter. The next day the president of the Chamber, Tan Siak Kew, had to intervene to prevent such a public embarrassment. Siak Kew defended Chin Tuan saying that the latter was not bound by any rigid rules concerning consultation but that he considered it etiquette that the Chamber's representative in the Legco would stay informed of the views of the MC. He also affirmed that Tan was right in this particular instance to use his discretion, and added that Tan had been an able representative of the Chamber.[44]

Two years later, Tan Chin Tuan was attacked again, this time by Colonel Chuang and others who charged that he had ignored the MC's decision to ask questions on the issue of the use of multiple languages in the Legco. Before the debate in the Legco the MC had written to Governor John Nicoll to petition him on the issue of the use of multiple languages in the Legislative Assembly that would come into operation after the election planned for early 1955, and on the eligibility of non-English speakers to be elected. The petition suggested that if the governor's goal was to have the widest possible participation in the elections, lifting the language requirement would be a "big step".[45]

Despite this petition and despite opposition in the Legco to the Legislative Council Elections Ordinance, the bill was passed as Colonial Secretary William Goode took it through all the stages in one sitting. Thio Chan Bee of the Progressive Party raised objections against the language requirement and said he did so on behalf of Tan Chin Tuan who, as Deputy Speaker, felt he could not speak despite his instructions by the SCCC.[46] At the next MC meeting, Colonel Chuang wanted to move a vote of censure against Tan and by doing so force the issue whether MC members still had confidence in Tan. The MC decided not to take any action in the matter but Tan Chin Tuan surely made few friends when he said he would not do anything in the Legco that he personally deemed foolish and that multi-lingualism was impractical.[47] A week later, during a Chamber meeting discussing a petition to the Queen to ask for a multi-lingual Assembly, Colonel Chuang somewhat cynically stated that he was happy that another Legco member, Mr. Raj, would table a motion to this effect. Then the gloves came off when he said of Tan that "he should give full support when the matter is brought up. Failing this he should resign."[48]

Shortly before the Legco debate, the Chamber discussed the issue again, because Tan Chin Tuan had apparently stated that he opposed a multi-lingual Legislative Assembly. Ko Teck Kin diplomatically stated he expected a full discussion in the Legco.[49] As Vice President, Ko perhaps had to be diplomatic but other Ambitious increased the pressure on Tan through the media. The Chamber had sent Tan the petition to the Queen in order for it to be read during the debate. Lam Thian, a young Ambitious, and Colonel Chuang made clear that they would be attending as observers, and Chuang, in a thinly veiled threat, said to *The Straits Times* that he would take notice of councillors voting for or against the motion for a multi-lingual Assembly.[50]

The next day the motion was defeated after 2½ hours of heated debate by a 13 to 5 vote. During the discussions, the conflict between the Ambitious and the Ambiguous entered directly into the heart of the Singapore political arena. Nominated member De Souza lashed out saying that multi-lingualism "would bring not self-government but government by a foreign power" and that "a few adventurers in the Chinese Chamber of Commerce" inspired the demand. Referring to the remarks by Colonel Chuang the day before, De Souza turned to the public gallery and asked, "Are members of this House going to allow themselves to be intimidated by this type of adventurer who has been described by responsible Chinese as nothing more than a society worm?" Tan said during the debate that he was instructed by the Chamber to emphasize that it had the interest of all races at heart in appealing for multi-lingualism, and also read extracts from the Chamber petition to the Queen. Tan said that he "associated himself with the contention that, as far as practicable, other languages, especially the majority language should be permitted." But he also said: "as the motion seeks to discredit the recommendations of the Rendell Commission of which I was a member, I shall, in view of the rather special circumstances, simply abstain from voting".[51]

A few days later during a meeting at the Chamber, Colonel Chuang moved again for the resignation of Tan from his Legco position because of the abstention. Considering that the Legco had already held its last meeting and perhaps as a way of saving Tan Chin Tuan's "face", the MC decided not to pursue the matter.[52] After this episode Tan Chin Tuan left politics signifying that the arena and the rules of political action had changed; the work-with-the-British approach was no longer a viable strategy. Tan would not figure in the SCCC leadership after 1955.

At this crucial junction in the decolonization process, the Ambitious were ready to play the political game. To better understand why those with more anti-colonial views, whether inspired by political ideology or by the reality of a Chinese-speaking majority and its political and cultural needs, were claiming an independent place on the Chamber stage and in Singapore politics, the political development of the territory over the preceding years will be reviewed.

3. Chinese education and the politicization of Singapore society

Chinese education proved to be the spark for the politicization of Singapore society. To the China-born immigrants of Singapore, Chinese education tied together culture, identity and politics in a manner that Singapore had not witnessed before. A number of incidents concerning this issue were to become defining events in the political development of the territory. Aspects of class and social developments became intertwined with feelings of ethnicity and identity because the majority of the Chinese were Chinese-speaking and working class. The continued economic difficulties weighed heavily on them and resulted in a vigorous labour union scene.[53] As their class consciousness awakened, the issue of Chinese education became a symbol for the struggle of the Chinese-speaking working class against the English-speaking colonial and local elites. Since anti-colonial feelings were linked to issues of Chinese culture and identity, left-wing unions and parties, as well as the Chinese elite, were obliged to engage in the matter of Chinese education.

The Chamber's involvement in the attempts to secure a more prominent position for Chinese education proved to be a dangerous activity for two reasons. First, unlike citizenship and the use of local languages, which were issues of Singapore-wide importance and relevance, Chinese education was ethnically based. As a result, the Chamber was not a societal leader on this point but an ethnic representative. Second, and most important, the issue meant a real or perceived alliance with left-wing organizations. These organizations staged examination strikes, school boycotts and other campaigns fuelled by the alleged inequality of Chinese education vis-à-vis English education.

With the Cold War looming large in Asia, left-wing views, especially when they found expression in public action and agitation, were easily equated with, and connected to, a perceived communist threat. Historian Timothy Harper has lucidly described how the colonial authorities and the conservative local political forces emphasized this threat allegedly posed by the left-wing based on very scant empirical proof. In the later canonization of Singapore history, the left-wing of the 1950s and 1960s is persistently portrayed as "Communist controlled", but this picture is in need of a thorough academic reconsideration.[54] As in other decolonizing societies, a leftist oriented labour movement was an important and legitimate ingredient in the politicization of society and the creation of a popular-based political arena necessary for the introduction of a democratic system. Still, in the political mood of the day, conservative forces could, and did connect the Chamber support for Chinese education with left-wing agitation on this issue and thereby with a perceived communist threat to Singapore society.

The Chamber dilemma

The Chamber dilemma lay in the British intention to shape the education system firmly based on the English language before independence. The colonial government had implemented a 10-year plan in 1947, which was aimed at integrating the separate language streams with English as the common and dominant language. Through a 1951 subsidization plan, Chinese schools were to receive funding, though less per student than English schools, only until enough places were available in the English schools to admit all students.[55]

Widespread opposition arose from schools, teachers' organizations and left-wing groups and this, combined with higher than expected population growth and building material shortages, frustrated the government's English school building programme. In 1953, the British considered a more balanced policy that would entail a bilingual curriculum and an increase in financial assistance to Chinese schools. Nevertheless, in the light of the ongoing Emergency, they still saw the Chinese schools as potential problem spots of both Chinese nationalist and communist activities. To counter this danger, Colonial Secretary Blythe installed a committee, in which the Chinese themselves would advise on improvement of Chinese schools, composed of "qualified individuals of the highest integrity from among the Chinese community".[56]

Lee Kong Chian was intended to be the chairman of the committee, but in a conversation with Blythe he indicated the precarious position of the English-speaking, work-with-the-British, Chamber leaders in this discussion, saying that "... this committee will not be productive of any significant results. Either the committee must strongly support the claims of Chinese schools, in which case the government would regard it as intransigent and would not be disposed to grant their requests, or alternatively the committee's approach to government must be so diluted that the Chinese schools would regard the committee as being merely government stooges".[57] Lee instead proposed a larger framework within which Chinese representatives, government officials and English educators could try to create a practical bilingual system. While such a wide framework did not materialize, discussions on a bilingual system continued between the British and British-oriented Chamber leaders. In July 1953, this produced an agreement on increased grants to Chinese schools, although Lee Kong Chian did say that this would not be satisfactory as a permanent solution. Tan Siak Kew, then Chamber president, was the other senior SCCC representative. Lee and Tan agreed on the utility and desirability of a bilingual system. Young, in his report to the Colonial Secretary, emphasized the importance of this gesture and added that it would be imperative that the government welcomed it and pursued it to the limit.[58]

In the meantime, Ambitious leaders took the matter of Chinese education into their own hands. On 16 January 1953, Tan Lark Sye proposed a Chinese language university.[59] Nanyang University, or Nanda in short, was to be financed through private funding and to that end an island-wide fundraising campaign was started. Tan himself pledged the first donation of $5 million of his newfound rubber wealth, and financial security among the Ambitious Chinese business elite allowed many to donate generously.[60] The idea of a Chinese-language university paid for by the people proved to be very popular with Chinese. The Chinese in the street was proud to donate his or her few dollars to this Chinese project. The British were rather taken aback by the initiative, and were not inclined to give their stamp of approval. However, the leading backers of the plan let the British know that fundraising and planning would continue with or without colonial approval. For the time being, Governor Nicoll was prepared to take a tolerant stand. He thought the scheme was of political origin but expressed that it probably had to do with "face". Nicoll expected the whole enterprise might fail and that the government could then use the Nanda buildings for the realization of a polytechnic plan.[61]

The feeling of empowerment that swept through the Chinese community, when it realized it could shape its own destiny, cannot be underestimated. Establishing its own Chinese language university, while the colonial government acknowledged the equal status of Chinese as a language in the educational curriculum of Singapore, meant that more and more Chinese started to connect their language and cultural identity to their identity as Singaporeans, not just for the present under colonialism but even more so for the future in an independent state of Singapore.[62]

For education policy in general, the principle of bilingualism was approved by the Exco on 15 October 1953. However, a number of provisos were put in place stipulating the hours for teaching English and other subjects using English.[63] Chinese educational bodies pressured the Chamber to lead the protests against these new terms, and in January 1954 a joint meeting of schools and SCCC representatives unanimously resolved to oppose the bilingual education policy in its current form. Lee Kong Chian discussed the matter with the Director of Education and in the following months the British compromised.[64]

The main motivation of the colonial government for this change of heart was the fear that antagonism over Chinese education would jeopardize wider security and state formation issues. There was a growing perception of increased communist activity in education since late 1953. To counter this trend the British now wanted to win the cooperation of the local Chinese in general and the Chinese school authorities in particular for their anti-communist plan. By no longer forcing Chinese schools to change their medium of teaching, the British hoped to gain the support of the Chamber and the more pragmatic educational organizations. The change of tack paid off quickly. Within a few weeks after the endorsement of the new grant-in-aid system by the SCCC and the Chinese School Management/Staff Association, a majority of schools was applying for government aid before the deadline of 31 March 1954.[65]

Merchants and students: the 1954 riots

Soon, the apparent concurrence of opinions was under severe pressure and the Chinese leaders in the Chamber found themselves in an awkward position between student activists and the colonial government. The expressly left-wing leanings of the students only complicated the middleman dilemma that Lee Kong Chian had described to the Colonial Secretary. Now, however, the Chinese leaders were not just representing a politically rather passive Chinese community but had to deal with a very active and ideologically motivated group of students who tried to manipulate them.

In the flowery prose of journalist Dennis Bloodworth the dilemma for the tycoons was that:

> ... since their [the students'] popular rallying cry was no seditious Maoist slogan, but an appeal to all patriotic Chinese to resist the 'barbarous destruction' of Chinese education by the brick-faced British, the tycoons of the Chinese Chamber could not gainsay them without appearing traitors to their own culture. The millionaires were thus shamed into playing into the hands of the communists, having been adroitly 'hooked on culture'.[66]

Things came to a head on 13 May 1954, when a demonstration of Chinese students from Chinese High School and Chung Cheng High School against the National Service Registration led to bloody riots and the arrest of 48 students.[67] The argument of the students was that if Singapore still did not allow their fathers and mothers to become local citizens and if the government turned those with a Chinese education into "second-class citizens", why should they be expected to pledge their lives to its defence. The national service issue was a godsend to the Malayan Communist Party, which had for a considerable time infiltrated the Chinese schools and student groups. The party had operated underground ever since most of its leadership had moved to the Malayan peninsula, but in early 1954 decided to use the call-up for military service to show it was returning to struggle against the British. The students were the ideal vehicle for this cause. In the national service issue, the goal of the communists was to undermine the pro-KMT and SCCC authority in the Chinese schools. The governing boards of these private schools were predominantly from those two groups and presented an obstacle to the MCP in radicalizing the Chinese students.[68] Fresh scholarship will have to determine to what degree the MCP was successful in its attempts.

On 13 May, 900 students gathered close to the governor's residence to support an eight-man delegation that was supposed to discuss their grievances concerning national service with Governor William Goode. Before this could happen, riots broke out. Clashes came to an end when the well-organized students asked the police if they would be allowed to return to Chung Cheng High School. Two thousand students then locked themselves in the school in protest against the arrest of their classmates. They broke up the next day only after Ng Aik Huan had bailed out seven of the arrested students and the Chamber had promised to take up their case for exemption from national service.[69]

Student representatives held a meeting at the Chamber soon after and an "Exemption Delegation" was set up from among them. It drafted a memorandum for the unconditional release of the 48 arrested, which was forwarded to the government by the Chamber. The Chamber initially seemed to support the students in their efforts, even though this would be a reversal of their earlier position on this issue.[70] Remembering the dilemma of Chinese education expressed by Lee Kong Chian, Chamber support for the students can be explained as an attempt to maintain the status of the Chamber in educational and social matters. This proved not to be a viable strategy and when the students occupied Chinese High School on 18 May, it was time for the Chamber to fall back on its original position and to take the sting out of the students' actions. As the governors and board members of the schools, prominent Chamber leaders decided to close them early for the summer holiday.

Nevertheless on 1 June a group of students locked themselves into the Chinese High School. Financial support from sympathizers and strict organization made it an efficient and smooth-running endeavour, and they maintained their stronghold for 23 days. This of course put great pressure on the Chamber leaders closest to the government. In an interview that was conducted years after the events, Governor Nicoll said of Lee Kong Chian that "he was in tears in my office" after a failed attempt to persuade the students to back down.[71] The students were willing to settle for postponement of national service rather than complete exemption but they did not really attract a government reaction initially. When they started a hunger strike, which was to last three days, the government finally agreed to postponement, but accompanied their offer with the stern warning that they would close down Chinese High if the students did not behave themselves. Lee Kong Chian was the one to bring the students this news and persuaded them to end the sit-in. *The Freedom News*, the activist student paper, called him "three-faced", although ironically it had been Lee who had given the Exemption Delegation leader Robert Soon Loh Boon a place at Chinese High School and had paid his fees.[72]

The students' troubled relationship with the Chamber and their claims on its leadership were not over. Later in the year, the students through their legal advisor hired Queens' Counsel Pritt from London for the defence of the students arrested on 13 May at a staggering $30,000, having conned Lee Kong Chian into a promise for financial coverage of legal cost. Lee Kong Chian protested at first but later an internal arrangement was made whereby the Chamber would raise money and Lee would pay the difference.[73]

Student involvement in the anti-colonial struggle and their subsequent need for legal counsel resulted in some other interesting effects on the political scene. Lee Kuan Yew, a young local lawyer active in a group of

Malayan students returned from studies in England, realized that the popular appeal of the causes of the Chinese students would be an excellent way to tie the Chinese-speaking majority to his own political ideas of pan-Malayan independence. Furthermore, Pritt had been one of Lee Kuan Yew's sponsors for his admission to the Middle Temple in London, so he became Pritt's assistant in the case. Goh Keng Swee, who was in Lee's circle, called it "a major breakthrough" saying that "if we formed a new political party and could get the Chinese-educated on our side, we would have a winning combination".[74]

This proved to be true, and because of the heightened profile of anti-colonialism, which was now connected to Chinese education and language, its influence on Singapore politics and on the Chinese business elite was by no means over. The Chinese-speaking population, which was awakening to the importance of political struggle for a greater say in its own future, came to see the issue of Chinese-language education as a key point in its thinking about what Singapore should look like in the future.

4. Elite politics to popular politics: the Chamber in the 1955 election

The Legislative Assembly election of 1955 signified an important transformation in Singapore political development. For the first time a significant part of the executive branch of government was elected at the ballot box. This fundamental change from elite politics to popular electoral politics drastically reshaped the political landscape of Singapore. The incumbent elites had to decide upon their strategy within this development. Conservative as well as progressive groups formed political parties and the Ambitious leaders of the Chamber decided to enter the fray.

The political landscape

British postwar strategy aimed to nurture an English speaking and English-educated elite and prepare them to take over under a limited self-rule arrangement and, in the long run, for leadership during independence. The group the British singled out in the late 1940s and early 1950s to provide this leadership was the Progressive Party, led by local lawyer C.C. Tan. A significant step on this road to independence was to confer executive power on locally elected individuals. In order to guide this transformation, a new constitution that would set out the parameters for such a transfer of power had to be prepared for the colony of Singapore.

The Rendel Commission was created in 1953 to draft this constitution and elections were scheduled to take place in April 1955. The colonial Legislative Council with its ex-officio and appointed Unofficial members were replaced by a Legislative Assembly with members elected from 25 electoral constituencies, three ex-officio ministers and four nominated Unofficials. The party gaining the majority in the elections would assemble a government consisting of a cabinet of nine ministers led by a Chief Minister. Three ex-officio ministers, the colonial Financial Secretary, the Attorney General and the Chief Secretary (the former Colonial Secretary) controlled the crucial ministries of Finance, Justice and Foreign Affairs/Defence. The remaining six ministers were in charge of commerce, industry, labour, immigration, social welfare, education, housing, communication, public works and health. By including in the new constitution the automatic registration of eligible voters, the Rendel Commission made electoral participation easier and generally added to the heightened awareness of political opportunities among the population.[75]

With so much at stake, a major regrouping of political forces started to occur from 1954. There was no shortage of parties with alternative power bases and policy platforms. First of all, there was the Progressive Party, which was expected to dominate the election. It ran on a conservative platform that did not include a definite date for independence. Three parties, the Singapore branch of the UMNO, the Singapore Malay Union and the Singapore branch of the Malayan Chinese Association, prepared an alliance. This initiative originated from the headquarters of these parties in peninsular Malaya whose "Alliance", led by Tunku Abdul Rahman, was the dominant political force. Since the eventual independence of Singapore was viewed by many within the framework of a merger between Singapore and the Federation of Malaya, the political strategies and positions of parties in peninsular Malaya were of influence on Singapore.

While the Chamber, in the period 1951–1953, was unsuccessful in forcing the British to directly give in to their appeals for enfranchisement of local China-born Chinese, it did manage to make the general public aware of the importance of this issue. Partly because of these efforts, other actors in the political arena, such as David Marshall's Singapore Labour Front (LF) and Lee Kuan Yew's People's Action Party (PAP), included demands for increased political rights for local residents in their party platforms. The Singapore Labour Front had developed from the Singapore Labour Party of Francis Thomas and Lim Yew Hock after it had attracted local lawyer David Marshall as its leader. The LF wanted immediate independence within a merged

Singapore/Malaya, aimed to localize public administration within four years and promised to extend Singapore citizenship to include the 220,000 China-born inhabitants.[76] Through Thomas and Lim, the party had extensive union support but primarily of the non-communist influenced kind.

The People's Action Party (PAP)[77] had been established in November 1954 and consisted of two camps in an uneasy alliance. On the one hand a group of students recently returned from the UK championed independence through merger with Malaya on the ideological basis of democratic socialism. Leading individuals in this group were Lee Kuan Yew, Goh Keng Swee and Toh Chin Chye. On the other hand, union leaders led by Lim Chin Siong occupied the left-wing of the party. This group advocated anti-colonial action, an end to detention and banishment without trial under the Internal Security Ordinance, and improvements in the living standard of the common man. For the time being, however, the left-wing needed the conservative wing to participate in electoral politics, while the conservative wing needed the left-wing for its influence over the votes of the working class. It was a matter of access to the power arena and the constituency in order to claim a place in Singapore politics.[78]

The high point of ambition: the Chamber enters popular politics

The Ambitious leaders in the Chamber were not satisfied with merely influencing the policy platforms of political parties. They believed that the Chamber could be active in politics and thereby could assure itself of a leading role in the new political system. The fact that the appointed seats for the business sector representatives in the legislature were to be discontinued only strengthened their resolve. The Chamber protested this development and objected that "a situation might well arise in which trade would be seriously affected by uninformed legislation".[79] What the Chamber feared was that the trading port heritage of Singapore would be squandered away to popular politics. As a result of the new political constellation, the Ambitious undertook several political initiatives.

The voter registration campaign

The Chamber entered the fray in 1954. In March of that year, the Chamber organized its bi-annual election. After the presidency of the cautious conservative Teochew, Tan Siak Kew, it was now the turn of the Hokkien to put forward a candidate for the presidency. At this important political junction the Ambiguous Tan was replaced by the Ambitious Ko Teck Kin who received widespread support in the Hokien Huay Kuan. In the light of the Singapore elections the following year, Ko presented a six-point plan at the installation ceremony. Two strategies were laid out: first, to ensure a high Chinese participation rate in the elections by making the voters aware of their rights and the main issues; and second, to continue lobbying for the retention of the appointed Chamber of Commerce seats in the Legislative Assembly.[80] This second strategy witnesses the fact that the Chamber was still hedging its bets.

As awareness of the upcoming election rose, no doubt aided by all the political attention to the Chinese education issue, the Chamber stepped up a gear. In November 1954, an election and electoral registration committee was formed, and it staged a voter information campaign to explain the issues in mass rallies across the island. A speech-cum-variety show toured the island from 15 January until 1 March. Representatives of different ethnic groups took the floor, and the Chinese population was addressed in several Chinese dialects, while dance and music groups provided entertainment. The first rally was held on 15 January in the Tanjong Pagar district with all the Ambitious Chamber leaders, Tan Lark Sye, Ko Teck Kin, Ng Aik Huan, Lam Thian and Colonel Chuang lined up as speakers, while a lion dance troupe intermittently entertained the crowd.[81]

Extensive newspaper coverage remains of a rally on 6 February in Changi, then a rural and remote district. By this time, the Chinese press had hopped on the bandwagon and strongly endorsed the goals of the campaign declaring that "the Chamber was trying to make the Chinese voice heard".[82] At the rally, 10,000 heard speeches by Tan Lark Sye, Ko Teck Kin, Lim Cher Keng, the Chamber MC member in charge of Changi district, and the Malay chairman of a local electoral committee. Their speeches emphasized the need for Singaporeans from all ethnic groups to vote, but almost all speakers also touched on the issue of safeguarding vernacular education in Chinese, Malay and Tamil.[83] The English language press reported on the rally with a large picture of the lion dance gracing the front page of *The Straits Times*. It quoted Tan Lark Sye instructing the crowd "not to vote blindly if they wanted a truly democratic government". He emphasized that it was well-known that the Chamber had been a "bridge of understanding" between the government and the people.[84]

The pitch was clear. By picturing the Chamber as the traditional connection between the government and the common people, Tan emphasized the need for continuity into the next phase of decolonization. Furthermore, by creating a multi-ethnic platform and by raising issues that considered all Singaporeans, he avoided being labelled as a force for the advancement of Chinese issues alone. The governor expressed appreciation for the voting drive in informal talks with Ko Teck Kin, Tan Lark Sye and Lee Kong Chian.[85] In total, seven "use your vote" rallies were held at a cost of only $858 to the Chamber coffers. Undoubtedly, individual Chamber leaders had picked up the bill rather than let it deplete the Chamber budget.[86]

The Democratic Party and its Chamber links

After a few weeks of persistent rumours, *The Straits Times* reported on 8 February that a new body, the Democratic Party (DP), had entered the fray on the very day that the Rendel constitution came into force. The paper said that the SCCC would finance the party to carry on its battle for multi-lingualism within the Legislative Assembly, and noted that until recently the Chamber Executive Secretary Dr. S.Y. Wang had denied the SCCC would launch into politics and that Vice President Yap Pheng Geck had said that if candidates claimed they were Chamber nominees, they certainly did not have Chamber approval.[87] Three days later the paper reported on the identity of the sponsors of the party and declared they were all millionaires or near-millionaires. DP Secretary Tan Ek Khoo, a Teochew MC member, was the party spokesman and said that nine sponsors made the party financially stable. Of the nine, three were Chamber MC members and the other six ordinary members and the party had its headquarters at the Ee Hoe Hean Club. Still, Dr. Wang reiterated that the party had no official connection to the Chamber, a statement confirmed by her husband, DP president Tan Eng Joo.[88]

The next day the "biggest ever" voter registration event to be held by the Chamber was announced for 13 February at Geylang Serai. Modern Malay dancing and lion dance performances would be staged and Tan Lark Sye, Chuang Hui Tsuan, Ko Teck Kin, and two Malay leaders would deliver speeches.[89] Despite the repeated statements by the SCCC that the DP was not a Chamber party, evidence of the connections with the SCCC, and especially its Ambitious leaders, were overwhelming. Newspapers made the connection that during the following weeks would be made even more clearly.

Indicating that the Ambitious did not have the support of all in the Chamber leadership, the Chamber stood divided on whether to openly fight the polls. During a MC meeting on 28 February, which was the deadline for all parties to nominate their candidates, Tan Lark Sye openly proposed fielding Chamber candidates directly through the DP. He justified this idea by pointing out that the appointed chamber of commerce seats had been scrapped under the Rendel constitution. It would only be fair for the

Chamber to try and hold on to its seat through candidates in the election. Ng Aik Huan supported him but Yap Pheng Geck opposed, asserting that members with the necessary knowledge and qualifications should join a political party and not involve the Chamber directly in politics. Ko Teck Kin, as president and chairman of the meeting, took the middle ground, perhaps giving in to Ambiguous pressure not to link the Chamber directly with the DP.[90]

Yet, according to one of the DP candidates in the election, Ko had been directly involved in the idea of setting up the DP together with Tan Lark Sye and Lee Kong Chian, and Governor Nicoll had actively pushed and supported the idea.[91] One academic observer argued that Tan Lark Sye and Lee Kong Chian "did not commit their persons to the various parties but sought to exercise their control indirectly through the medium of patronage whilst they themselves remained in the shadows. It was the substance, not the appearance of power that they wanted".[92] Governor Nicoll divulged later that Tan Lark Sye blamed the Progressive Party for the dropping of the nominated chambers of commerce seats in the Legislative Assembly and for blocking multi-lingualism, and he therefore "cordially hated the Progressives".[93] Mr. Rajah of the PP even said that Tan set up the DP with the deliberate intention of "ditching" the PP, which Tan thought otherwise would win.[94]

The linkage of the Ambitious in the Chamber and the DP became even clearer when the DP's constituency organizations were revealed. Many of the Chamber voter registration committee members in charge of electoral districts now stepped forward as DP candidates for the election and the party fielded candidates in 20 districts. In reality the DP was entirely made up of, and funded by, Chinese merchants from within the Chamber leadership, with the lone exception of the intriguing figure of Murray Brash, a Scottish lawyer and Singapore resident of 20 years who stood for the DP in Queenstown.[95] Popularly, therefore, the party was known as the "Chamber Party" or the "Millionaire's Party".[96] Other parties deliberately attacked the DP on its pedigree. The Progressives objected to the DP's use of the lion as its party symbol, saying it was too much related to Singapore (Singha Pura) in general and was not specific for the party. They wanted to break the link forged in the electorate's mind between the voter registration campaign and its lion dances and the DP, but their objection was turned down.

David Marshall of the LF jibed in an interview that the DP were "potbellied millionaires" and Brash rejoined that "while a number may answer to the adjective, I know of very few that answer to the noun." Labour candidate Lee Yong Min said that DP had introduced a new kind of democracy: "the millionaire democracy and now they want the power to go with it." The Independent candidate Mr. Raj said that if the DP would come to power Singapore would be turned into a "slave camp as their aim was not to better the peoples' lives but that of free trade".[97]

Devoid of any regular members, the DP was composed only of its governing committee and the candidates it had nominated and, according to one source, its manifesto was "composed in three hours over a convivial dinner".[98] It contained these points: (1) Free trade, (2) Local and foreign investment in secondary industries, (3) Housing development schemes and hospitals, (4) Multi-lingual legislature, Singapore citizenship for all who lived in Singapore for more than 10 years and swore allegiance, and the right to vote and be elected, (5) Equal grants-in-aid to schools of all races.[99]

Trusting their traditional position on top of the Chinese pyramid of organizations, the DP leadership leaned heavily on these social power structures and networks to secure votes. This was achieved through the clan, district and *bang* organizations of which these chamber leaders were the presidents and financiers. Tan Eng Joo explained later that by "leashing" the liberal Progressives and checking the potentially "dangerous" Labour Front, they could win communal votes without becoming involved in ideological disputes.[100]

Proof that the demands of Singapore citizenship and multi-lingualism, championed by the Ambitious leaders of the SCCC, had made a great impact on the political arena, the profile of candidates in the 1955 election were considerably different compared with the 1951 Legco election. In 1951 there were only four Chinese candidates compared to 56 out of 79 in 1955.[101] The DP fielded 20 candidates who were all described as businessmen or merchants in the constituency-by-constituency discussion of candidates provided by the *Singapore Free Press* in the run up to the elections. With one exception they were in their 30s and 40s and many had graduated from Chinese High School. The exception to the younger men was Ng Sen Choy, a 69 year old who exemplified the party's connection to the pyramid of Chinese organizations. He was one of the leaders of the Cantonese *bang* and a former member of the CAB.[102]

Campaigning was lively and sometimes fierce. On 24 March, Radio Malaya held an Election Forum live on the air with Lee Kuan Yew of the PAP, David Marshall of the LF and Murray Brash for the DP. During the debate, Brash tried desperately to ward off the equation of the DP as a party of the rich but he failed miserably. The transcript of the discussion shows that Lee Kuan Yew made his customary reference to the millionaires of the DP who stayed at the Ee Hoe Hean club in Bukit Pasoh.

Brash: "Where is this club? I have never seen it."

Lee Kuan Yew: "But the address is on your own manifesto."

Brash: "I said, I hadn't seen it."

Lee Kuan Yew: "Good Lord, that's terrible. How will we know where to find the man?"

Marshall: "Perhaps they have shifted to the Chinese Chamber of Commerce."[103]

Despite the likelihood that these allegations would stick in the voters' minds, but perhaps because of the enthusiasm at the voter registration meetings and the popular support for multi-lingualism, the DP had high expectations of the election. In *The Straits Times* of the morning of polling day, Tan Eng Joo crowed: "I have every confidence that the Democratic Party will win an overwhelming majority".[104]

The outcome of the 1955 elections was a surprise in a number of ways. The comfortable victory for the Progressive Party, for which the Rendel constitution seemed to have been tailored by the British, did not materialize. The PP only managed to win four seats due to the change in political atmosphere over 1954–1955. It was now seen as a pro-British party in an increasingly anti-colonial Singapore. To the great disappointment of its leadership, the DP did even worse by securing only two seats. To their frustration, the DP came in second in eight constituencies. Both the PP and the DP were simply seen as right-wing and elite parties and therefore could not do well in an electorate awakened to social issues.[105] The DP with its championing of Chinese culture, language, education and citizenship had pulled off two feats. First, it had weakened the PP by attracting 20 per cent of the total votes.[106] Second, it heightened awareness of the citizenship and education issues in the elections. Partly due to these pressures, the Labour Front had given these issues a prominent place in their policy platform.[107] David Marshall's party was the great victor of the elections, securing 10 seats. With the support of the ex-officio ministers, the three Singapore Alliance members and two of the nominated unofficials, the LF formed a left-wing minority government.

After all the effort and the apparent success of the voter registration campaign, the initiators of the DP must have been surprised at their poor showing. Although they won two seats in the Legislative Assembly, they learned that popular electoral politics was a different arena from the pyramid of clan and dialect organizations. The political aspirations and strategies of the Ambitious in the Chamber had patently failed. As a result, the Chamber's activities in politics remained a point of heated internal discussion.

Singapore politics after the election: riots and education

With the establishment of a local, largely elected, government, a new phase in the SCCC's political action started. Next to the continuing appeals and demands presented to the British, David Marshall, the newly elected Chief Minister, became the target of the Chamber's political agenda. Since his Labour Front had won the election on a platform promising local citizenship, the Chamber was determined to pressure his government.

Apart from reminding the LF of its election promises on local citizenship and a multi-lingual Legislative Assembly, the Chamber pushed the issue of vernacular education. In reply to a Chamber memorandum of 25 April, Chief Minister Marshall said that Chinese and other vernacular schools should get equal treatment. He reiterated that the Chamber's work for a multi-lingual assembly was not in vain, and that further representations could be made to a special committee of the Legislative Assembly.[108] Before the new government could start implementing its policies, the unions and the students once more took centre stage.

A strike over the dismissal of 200 members of the communist-controlled Singapore Bus Workers' Union at Hock Lee Bus Company led to a full scale riot involving both students and union members on 12 May 1955, the eve of the first anniversary of the riots of 13 May the previous year. The grim tally of the riots came to four killed and 19 injured.[109] The next day 20,000 workers went on strike as well. Chief Minister Marshall answered by closing Chinese High School and Chung Cheng High School but 2,000 students barricaded themselves in Chung Cheng High as the strikes spread to five more schools. The unions fully supported the students and pledged to keep the workers' strikes on until student demands were met. In the newspaper reports on the school strikes, no mention is made of Chamber involvement or of attempts by the students to gain support from the Chamber leaders at this time.[110] The events of the year before had left even the Ambitious leaders in the Chamber hesitant to get involved with the students. Soon though, the students and the unions on their part would seek to use the Chamber for their political purposes in the discussion on Chinese education.

In the midst of the post-riot mayhem, on 16 May the LF government was severely attacked in the Legislative Assembly on its education plans. Two days later, the LF proposed an All-Party Committee (APC) on the issue of Chinese education.[111] For the DP, and for the Ambitious forces in the Chamber, Lim Cher Kheng, one of the two successful DP candidates, sat on the committee.[112]

Arguing that forces favouring Chinese education should combine to send a strong message to the APC, unions and student organizations pressured the Chamber. Lim Chin Siong, leader of the left-wing of the PAP, as chairman of 16 unions publicly stated that the Chamber should convene a mass meeting on Chinese education. Five hundred organizations, comprising clan associations and educational bodies as well as student organizations and unions, sent representatives. Representatives of the student organizations and unions quickly took control and strong-armed the meeting into a vote for overturning the rules agreed upon to exclude the floor from the discussion.[113] It appeared that the leftists were going to be successful once again in highjacking the Chamber's name to further their views. This time the Chamber leaders were unwilling to succumb to the mounting pressure. A definite break between Ambiguous Chamber leaders and the students occurred at that 6 June meeting. Yap Pheng Geck tabled a motion calling to stop all student involvement in political and industrial disputes, but the students and the unions made sure it was defeated in a noisy show of hands.

Although left-wing forces had great influence on the meeting, unrealistic demands concerning Chinese education were formulated. In the end five points were adopted: (1) Government should uphold equality for schools of all races, (2) Government should retain the excellent tradition of Chinese education and emphasize education in the mother tongue, (3) Government should grant equal assistance both in the construction and the administration of all schools, (4) Teachers in Chinese schools should receive equal benefits compared to teachers in English schools, (5) Students in Chinese schools should enjoy six years of free education. Newspapers reported that these points were included in the Chamber's written presentation to the APC prepared by Ko Teck Kin and Yap Pheng Geck.[114] This time, the Chamber distanced itself decisively from the student organizations and the unions compared to the student strikes of 1954.

As the APC reacted to the public representations and started to air some of its own views, it became clear that it agreed, in principle, with the five points in the Chamber's written presentation.[115] When the APC published its report in February 1956, it stressed the need for bilingual education.[116] Its recommendations were taken over by the government in its April 1956 White Paper on Education. It was another year before the government presented its new education act, in which multi-lingual principles were incorporated. It brought a degree of closure to the Chamber's struggle for Chinese education.

Resolving the citizenship issue during 1955–1957

After the 1955 election, the Chamber still pursued a dual track approach to the citizenship issue. On the one hand, it continued to appeal to the British authorities, both locally and in London, to expedite change, while on the other hand, it increasingly directed its efforts towards coaxing the local government into action. Of these two approaches, the former seemed to lose importance as the British tried to distance themselves. After the appeals made by the Chamber in the early 1950s and after its lobbying of officials and a number of lords in London, the British seem to have decided by 1954 to leave the problem to "local political forces". In the opinion of the British, the Indonesian-PRC dual citizenship agreement provided a blueprint for solving the problems. Under this agreement the PRC government would drop claims of *Ius Sanguinis* on Chinese who obtained Indonesian citizenship.[117]

The Chamber received confirmation of this British stand when it sent a citizenship proposal to the Secretary of State for the Colonies together with a memorandum restating the plea it had made for a multi-lingual Legislative Assembly.[118] In a reaction to the proposal, the Colonial Secretary said that it was reasonable and that matters should be resolved by the Singapore government.[119] This did not mean that the British did not have a role to play in the end game of this issue. After all, they were still an active and controlling part of those "local political forces" through their control over defence, foreign relations and internal security.

In July 1955, as a result of promises in the LF election platform and perhaps also due to continuing pressure from the Chamber, Chief Minister Marshall presented a proposal for a scheme of local citizenship next to British naturalization. The SCCC liked the proposal, but for the first time serious Malayan opposition against a solution to this Singapore issue presented additional complications. Marshall's plan increased mainland fear of being swamped by politically-enfranchised Chinese, thereby complicating the question of independence through merger of Singapore and Malaya. The Tunku even told Marshall that the UMNO would refuse a merger outright if Singapore were to proceed with the plan.[120] Under this kind of pressure it was hard for Marshall to provide a solution. The Chamber reacted with a vicious letter accusing him and his government of tardiness and lack of commitment, contending that "the public cannot help but doubt the sincerity of the government" concerning the language issue and "the public cannot help but have misgivings about the government's real motives" regarding local citizenship.[121]

Marshall reacted as if stung by a bee. He released a public rebuttal through the Chinese language press. He pointed out that it would take a constitutional change to introduce more languages in the Legislative Assembly, something it could not do itself. Changes therefore had to wait until the constitutional discussion with the British. Not without venom he added "the SCCC has not, under any circumstances, made any practical suggestions on these matters". Regarding the Chamber's reading of the developments on local citizenship, he said it was untruthful and that the Chamber should know better as they had participated in meetings with societal and government representatives. He reminded the Chamber that Tan Lark Sye, Ko Teck Kin and Yap Pheng Geck had been present when it was decided to hand the drafting of a new citizenship bill over to an international lawyer. Marshall warned the Chamber not to bring racial and political issues into this constitutional discussion.[122] The reality was that race, ethnicity and politics were at the heart of the citizenship issue, especially within the framework of merger with the Federation of Malaysia.

Given the nature of the development of the political process in Singapore, denial of political rights to the largest segment of the local population had become unthinkable. Local democratic socialist parties could ill-afford to exclude a majority of the working class electorate, and the British had agreed that local political forces would decide the matter. After discussions between a delegation of Singapore politicians and Secretary of State for Colonies Lennox-Boyd in London in April 1956, the British agreed with a proposal for Singaporean citizenship. This agreement was the basis for the Singapore Citizenship Ordinance, passed on 24 April 1957 by the Legislative Assembly, which made virtually all 220,000 China-born residents Singapore citizens.[123]

The passing of the Ordinance meant that the dominant political issue for which the Chamber had fought since the late 1940s had been solved in its favour. With the principle of bilingual education also enshrined in law in 1957, and with the use of local languages in the Legislative Assembly imminent, the three political campaigns of the SCCC had been brought to a successful conclusion. The Chamber leaders took great pride in these achievements. The Chinese, localized in the 1940s and 1950s, had been led by the 1950s Ambitious rubber tycoons who had managed to make an ethnic-political connection. However, when left-wing political forces appropriated education and Chinese identity the Chamber started to lose out. This appropriation had an incendiary effect on the representation of Chineseness, because it connected ideology with ethnicity once again. As the rules of the Singapore political arena changed, the leaders of the SCCC continued to disagree among themselves over the role of the Chamber in politics. This disagreement culminated in the SCCC election of 1958.

5. The 1958 SCCC election

The political role and direction of the Chamber in the Singapore political arena was the most important issue underlying the 1958 Chamber election. With the elections for limited self-rule scheduled for May 1959, the SCCC had to decide whether to remain active in politics, representing not only the commercial interests of the rich but also the views of Chinese society at large, or to fall back on its official core purpose as a commercial organization. The negative experience of the 1955 election had resulted in a return to the Ambiguous point of view, and in 1956 the Chamber elected the conservative Tan Siak Kew as president. He selected a Hokkien vice president, Ng Quee Lam, who was opposed to the Ambitious playing an active role in politics through the Chamber.[124] In 1958, the battle between the Ambiguous and the Ambitious would be rejoined when it was the turn of the Hokkien to supply the president.

The election system

Jockeying for position by manipulating votes at the Chamber level was a prominent feature of the campaign for the election. It is therefore necessary to look at the election process. Elections for the council were held biannually and an election committee took inventory of the membership roll and allocated seats to each *bang* accordingly. At election time each individual or firm member could cast one vote for only one of the candidates of his *bang*. The Hokkien, for instance, would only vote for Hokkien candidates to fill the number of seats allocated to the Hokkien. After the council was formed, the new council members elected a president and vice president, as well as sub-committee chairmen. Only the council members themselves were eligible for these positions. In addition, the presidency had to alternate between a Hokkien and a non-Hokkien, and the president and vice president had to belong to different dialect groups. The Hokkien, by far the largest group both in Chinese society in Singapore and in the Chamber, always had a dominant voice if not a majority in the council.

By the 1950s, the election process within the *bang*, and especially within the Hokkien *bang*, had become more elaborate. According to a long-time Hokkien leader, the incumbent Hokkien council members in the Chamber would nominate suitable candidates. Then, by secret ballot only these incumbents would determine the Hokkien nominees for the Chamber council election. This seems to have been a closed, elite-dominated political system. There was, however, another option open to aspiring Hokkien leaders who were not selected. After the various *bang* had nominated their candidates for the Chamber election, the Chamber would publish the nominees for each *bang*. There was then a period in which each regular Chamber member was allowed to nominate another candidate from his *bang* to stand as well. If no additional candidates were nominated, the original *bang* nominees would occupy the allocated seats unchallenged. If new candidates were nominated, however, an election round would be forced. All members of that particular *bang* in the Chamber then had the right to cast one vote for any of these candidates.[125] For anyone wanting to challenge the incumbent elite in their respective *bang*, manipulating and controlling votes among Chamber members from his own *bang* was, therefore, the first step in securing a position through the general election round.[126]

The contenders and the issues

The main contenders for the presidency were two Hokkien rubber tycoons, Ko Teck Kin and Ng Quee Lam.

The Ambitious Ko Teck Kin

Ko was proud that the major political figures of the day such as Lee Kuan Yew, Lim Chin Siong and Lim Yew Hock, the Labour Front leader who had taken over the position of Chief Minister, sought his opinion and support. He had a wide variety of contacts among the China-oriented Chinese as well as the Straits-born and also with the British. Ko saw an active political role of the Chamber as a crucial strategy for continued prominence of the SCCC. In the past he had shown this Ambitious conviction through his activity in the Chamber campaigns for citizenship and Chinese education and his involvement in the Democratic Party. In Ko's view of the future of Singapore, a successful local businessman could be, and had to be, an active politician.

When he was rounding up support for his candidacy, Ko needed to secure the backing of the senior Hokkien leaders. Among these leaders there were two groups, those who had rallied around Tan Kah Kee during the civil war in China and had been very outspoken on Chinese education, and those who had taken a more moderate stance. The former were more likely to be Chinese-educated, while the latter included those with a higher level of education and knowledge of English who were more attuned to working within the colonial system. The crucial person linking these two groups was Lee Kong Chian. Ko approached one of Lee's lieutenants to find out if he could count on the support of Lee Kong Chian. When the lieutenant relayed the question, Lee said that he favoured Ko because of his past record in social and public affairs.[127] Although this was a rather vague statement Ko understood the message. Lee was on record as a strong advocate of increased Chinese involvement in the politics of Malaya and Singapore. His political views were definitely more in synch with Ko than with Ng.

Ng Quee Lam: Ambiguous or ideological

Ng Quee Lam's allegiance to the KMT viewpoint re-introduced the old rivalry between the Tan Kah Kee supporters of the PRC and the KMT supporters into Chamber politics. Ng tried to win support from the Ambiguous, and believed in and used some of their arguments to try to defeat his Ambitious opponents. He did so by stating publicly that he did not favour an active political role for the Chamber. From the available sources, it does seem that Ng was not active in the three main political issues the Chamber promoted in the 1950s: citizenship, a multi-lingual legislature and Chinese education. During the election campaign he was quoted as saying: "Trade is the main concern. This is the business of our Chamber. We will not meddle in politics".[128]

It is no surprise that Ng's main backing came from other die-hard KMT followers such as Colonel Chuang. A number of others such as S.Y. Wong, Lim Keng Lian and Ong Kiat-soo were also either MCA and former KMT leaders, or had been connected to the anti-Japanese guerrilla group Force 136 during World War II. The Chungking headquarters of the KMT, the ruling party of one of the Allied Forces, had been involved in the Force 136 plans from 1943 and Colonel Chuang had liaised to provide KMT agents. The British were the executing power behind Force 136 and they insisted on involving communist guerrillas. The betrayal to the Japanese by MCP leaders of the ranking KMT officer in Force 136, Major General Lim Bo Seng, and numerous other KMT agents resulted in the strong anti-communist stand of these Ng supporters.[129] The fact that their Ambitious opponents were championing Chinese education and political action was an indication that the former were bringing the Chamber perilously close to the unions and student organizations, whom they regarded as communist-controlled. With such a strong ideologically inspired platform, Ng can hardly be described as apolitical. He was not averse to politics at all, but favoured the elite lobbying variety.

Ng Quee Lam: The KMT contender.

Courtesy of the National Archives of Singapore

Ng Quee Lam, younger than Ko Teck Kin at a mere 38 years old at the time of the election, hailed from Hui'an district in Fujian.

Admirers of his rubber empire, second only to Lee Kong Chian's

Lee Rubber, nicknamed him the "rubber wizard". The rubber boom made him a multi-millionaire in his early 30s.[130]

Ng did not have nearly as broad a social base as Ko, within or outside Chinese society. He took an active part in leading business organizations such as the Singapore Rubber Packers' Association and the Malayan Rubber Export Registration Board. He also held some social leadership positions, especially on the board of Tong Chai Medical Hall, the Nanyang Girls' High School and in the fundraising committee of Nanyang University.

Ng's general political leanings were quite clear: he was a staunch supporter of the KMT and a member of its Singapore branch until its deregistration by the British in May 1949.

Ng had shown a definite opinion on another ideologically charged issue in the recent past: trade with the People's Republic of China. On this political issue he and his KMT supporters had also suffered defeat, strengthening his conviction that his opponents would lead the Chamber astray to the communist camp. Throughout the Korean War the British had enforced a ban on trading with New China, and this embargo was enforced even when hostilities ended because a formal peace accord was not reached. Under pressure from the rubber merchants and those involved in the trade of Chinese products, the authorities were willing to follow the policy of other countries in the region and allow barter trade. Under these conditions, Britain lifted its trade embargo against the PRC in 1956, causing many of the less staunch Nationalists in Singapore to drop their ideological objections and adapt to the new situation. The Chamber and other commercial organizations sent a number of official trade delegations to China; Ko led the first one in 1956.

Support for the Nationalists, who were now occupying Taiwan, did not vanish overnight. After deregistration of the Singapore KMT, many of its leaders became involved in the Singapore branch of the Malayan Chinese Association (MCA), through which they advocated pro-Taiwan policies.[131] Many of them were also still on the MC. As a counterbalance to the trade missions to the PRC, they tried, in 1957, to organize a Chamber mission to Taiwan. It was a thinly disguised attempt by Ng, who was the Vice President at the time, to have the Chamber make a political gesture of recognition towards the Nationalist regime. At first Ng had the tacit approval of President Tan Siak Kew. But when Ko and his following applied pressure, accusing the president of breaking Chamber rules by involving the organization in open international politics, Tan Siak Kew backed down.[132]

The core of Ng's support, therefore, rested primarily on ideological grounds but other issues rallied support to his camp as well. Colonel Chuang would seem a very likely supporter because of his KMT and Force 136 connection but had also played an active role in the citizenship campaign and the Democratic Party, openly supporting the Ambitious, as indeed had S.Y. Wong. The reason why they decided to team up with Ng now was connected to their conviction that some of the Hokien Huay Kuan leaders, who happened to be the Ambitious that Ng was facing, were using the *bang* election mechanism to monopolize power. Colonel Chuang had attacked Ko and Tan Lark Sye on this issue before, in 1952, and now backed Ng in an attempt to bring KMT leaders back to the top of the Chinese pyramid. Ng felt confident that his challenge for power had enough support.

The positions of the two camps were clear: Ko advocating a pro-active political stance for the Chamber and Ng emphasizing that politics should be left to the politicians because he did not like the ideological flavour of the Ambitious political agenda.

When elections are near, the membership grows

The first signs of election campaign activity were reported in late November 1957, and by the beginning of 1958, the race was on. Both sides were trying to increase their electoral base, and hundreds of new members were accepted. Newspapers reported that the Hokkien membership had mushroomed to 2,009, which constituted an increase of around 50 per cent over January 1957. Gradually, the Hokkien were divided into two camps gathering around their respective candidates. The two were identified in the papers as the "Progressives" of Ko, favouring effective measures to "encourage Chinese to be loyal to Malaya", including Lee Kong Chian and Tan Lark Sye. In their eyes, this loyalty would be best expressed by active Chinese involvement in the politics of Singapore and Malaya. The list of Ng's "Conservatives", who stood for a politically low profile and more focus on trade, consisted of the core KMT group.[133]

The large increase in Hokkien membership had great destabilizing effects. Since the Hokkien grew proportionally within the Chamber and thus secured a larger share of the fixed number of seats on the council, smaller *bang* suffered losses.[134] The Sanjiang or Northern Chinese ended up with only two seats instead of the three they had held previously. Already very unhappy with the situation, the Sanjiang were incensed when reports surfaced of 13 Hokkien businessmen who were surprised to see their names published as Chamber members since they had never joined. The Sanjiang suspected foul play and threatened collective resignation of all of its 226 Chamber members if the election committee did not act. However, Tan Siak Kew, outgoing Teochew president and chairman of the election committee, explained, "the election committee for the election of the new board of directors has already been established. All matters related to the election are currently under preparation. To convene a general meeting now and to adjust the directorial numbers of each clan is difficult and, I am afraid, inappropriate".[135]

Three days later, the stakes were raised when Colonel Chuang also insisted that a thorough investigation be held. By this time 11 of the 13 businessmen in question had stated that they had simply forgotten that they had become members and nothing was wrong. The fact that the Ng camp still insisted vehemently on an investigation suggests that they thought they could damage Ko. There had been rumours that many new members were registered at Ko's brother's business address. The situation was grave enough for Tan Siak Kew to call a secret meeting with the two Chamber elders, Tan Lark Sye for the Hokkien and Yeo Chan Boon, one of the only remaining founding members of the Chamber, for the Teochew, in an attempt to smooth things over.[136]

Attempts by neutral Hokkien to persuade the two sides to be content to split the 16 available Hokkien seats failed. Instead, more than 100 Hokkien members signed a letter demanding that ballot counting be postponed until the matter of the false membership applications was resolved.[137]

Election day

On election day, however, counting did proceed, but not until after two hours of heated debate during an emergency Election Committee meeting. Ng Quee Lam, in his capacity of incumbent vice president, chaired the meeting because Tan Siak Kew was away. Chuang led the attack for the Ng camp from the floor, providing information on just six addresses where more than 200 new members were registered. He claimed that under these circumstances, a new board could never be credible, and therefore the votes should not be counted. Lim Cher Kheng, the Teochew council member, DP Legislative Assembly member, and strongly anti-KMT, rejoined that the 400 members for whom Chuang deposited membership fees on 31 December 1957, a grand sum of $20,000, were equally suspect. It is interesting that the practice of introducing new members to secure votes was not seen as morally wrong among the leadership of the Chamber. Yet this type of behaviour was not in keeping with the idealized picture of leaders of high moral stature, and publicizing this information was a tactic designed to harm the opponents' respectability, and sway undecided voters.

The main argument of the Ko camp, as well as of the neutral council members, was that procedure should be followed and that the rules of the Chamber prescribed that the members, once approved, had the right to vote. The 100 protesters only constituted a small minority; thus, the election should proceed. More mudslinging followed, with the Sanjiang and Hokkien members combining their arguments, saying that these were legitimate concerns that could have an important influence on the outcome of the election. The strategic co-operation between the Ng group and the Sanjiang is noteworthy. A minority group such as the Sanjiang normally would not make waves lightly for fear of alienating the Hokkien leaders. The struggle for power gave the Sanjiang the opportunity to ride on the coat-tails of the Ng group. Co-operation was smooth because a number of Sanjiang were KMT supporters.

As caretaker Chairman of the Election Committee, Ng made a feeble attempt to gain time. He argued that the letters from the Sanjiang and Hokkien members were addressed to both the president and the vice president, so he could not be held responsible; Tan Siak Kew should be consulted upon his return to Singapore. Although there is no conclusive evidence why Tan Siak Kew was absent, it seems significant that he was not present. He had endorsed Ng's position earlier, but must have realized that Ng was going to lose the election. Tan's concern for his "face" meant that he did not want to be associated with Ng's defeat. Not being part of Ng's moral team of ideologically like-minded KMT supporters, Tan conveniently switched sides for pragmatic reasons. He apparently did not want to denounce Ng in public, but also did not want to miss the opportunity to jump ship. It seems likely that Tan Siak Kew was intentionally absent.

Ng's argument for postponement was easily brushed aside, and those in favour of proceeding clearly had the upper hand. Realizing this, the principal players in the Ng camp, including Chuang and Ng himself, walked out of the meeting in protest. Minutes later, the three attending Sanjiang members did the same. With only Ko Teck Kin supporters left, the votes were then counted and the elections resulted in a resounding victory for Ko. Ng managed only enough votes to become third alternate member for the Hokkien, effectively sidelining him, while none of his supporters fared any better.[138]

Continuing opposition: a legal battle in the making

In the last meeting of the outgoing council on 28 February, the Ng camp made an attempt to improve its position. A lawyer had sent an official letter, on behalf of Colonel Chuang, demanding that the application forms and the voting slips of the 13 suspect Hokkien members be sent to the government chemist for official investigation. The lawyer stated that if the signatures were forged he was instructed by his clients to ask the High Court to declare the elections null and void. Lim Cher Kheng tabled a proposal to disregard the letter altogether and after much discussion, won just enough support to have his proposal passed by 12 votes to 10.[139] That the Ng group would resort to such a frontal attack shows that they had either run out of internal networking options, or that they thought that this public and legalistic approach would do maximum damage to the credibility and face of their opponents. In a further attempt to block the installation of the new MC, Ng tried to prevent approval of the annual and financial report over 1957 by the Annual General Meeting on 1 March. Questions were raised why the MC had not responded to written enquiries about the elections. The response argued that because the election was the responsibility of the outgoing council, the issue had to be discussed before the council could finalize its official duties. In the end, a vote on the 1957 report was held and, although a fight almost started when two members disagreed on the counting of hands, a large majority passed the report.[140]

The losing side did not give up, and filed the request to the High Court to declare the election results null and void. A summons was served to Ko, Vice President Yap Pheng Geck and the 15 Hokkien council members. It seems that the court case was initiated as a matter of pride rather than with any expectation that the elections could be reversed. By early 1959 the case still had not started, and later that year the case was dropped.[141] Colonel Chuang, Ng's staunchest supporter, was to be active in the Chamber as a dissenting voice for another decade, but Ng Quee Lam had nothing more to do with the Chamber.

This detailed look at the 1958 election skirmishes serves to show how important considerations of political strategy in the Singapore-wide arena were to the Chamber. As the old PRC versus KMT rivalry again entered the Chamber and the KMT supporters used the arguments of the Ambiguous to try to beat their opponents, proponents and opponents of an active SCCC political role clashed. The victory of the Ambitious over the Ambiguous bears testimony to the larger changes taking place in Singapore politics. With the transition from elite politics to popular electoral politics, the Ambitious argued successfully that it was of paramount importance for the Chamber to be at the forefront of decision making. They saw this as a prerequisite for effective representation of the interests of their own businesses as well as for the wants and needs of the Chinese community.

Concluding remarks

The politics of decolonization and the race for political, social and economic dominance in post-colonial Singapore were central to the Chamber's activities in this period. As politics in Singapore was modernized and formalized, the rules of politics and the characteristics of the political arena changed. From being an elitist endeavour, the basis of mobilization and power quickly became rooted in left-wing, non-communal populist politics. The split between the Ambiguous and the Ambitious in the Chamber in the period 1951–1959 was essentially a clash of alternative views on the position of immigrant Chinese businessmen in a decolonizing world. The Ambiguous were thoroughly inculcated by 150 years of British colonialism and believed that a continuation of the work-with-the-British strategy would best safeguard Chinese business interests. The advent of popular, left-wing politics was anathema to their elite view of politics, and they felt strongly that the Chamber should not aspire to an active role in that dangerous game.

The Ambitious were inspired by the liberating idea of self-determination that swept through the colonized world after World War II and believed that their traditional status in the pyramid of Chinese organizations would automatically qualify them as leaders on the road to Singapore's independence. Aided by the great wealth they acquired during the rubber boom of 1950–1951 they unfolded ambitious initiatives in politics and education such as the Democratic Party and Nanyang University. Although the presidency alternated between the two groups, the Ambitious dominated the Chamber's political initiatives and were aware of the change in social and political capital necessary to prevail in politics. They managed to popularize the central political issues of the day through the Chamber's campaigns concerning citizenship and language. But in this success also lay the defeat of the political dreams of the Ambitious. There existed an inherent contradiction in their political position. On the one hand they wanted to be modern, populist, democratic and enlightened. On the other hand, they still depended for their elite status and power in a paternal, hierarchically-based communal structure in which ethnicity and tradition were key elements.

In their concern for Chinese ethnic identity, culture and education, they felt compelled to defend Chinese education and to involve themselves with the Chinese student organizations. However, this attempt to link up with the new left-wing populist base in politics backfired when they were strong-armed by left-wing forces, and consequently backed away from supporting the students. The self-image of being modern popular leaders inspired the Ambitious to campaign vigorously for political rights for the Chinese community. The success of this ambition meant that the electorate was greatly enlarged and that the nature of politics changed. However, the Chamber could not play a central role in the populist electoral political game controlled by democratic socialist parties because, contrary to the self-image of the Ambitious leaders, the voting public considered it an elite organization with an elite agenda. The electoral failure of their Democratic Party in the national election of 1955 and the constitutional and legislative solution to the citizenship and language issue emasculated their political ambitions as other actors and forces started to dominate the political arena. Eventually, the Ambitious determined the struggle of the two alternative political views in their favour during the Chamber election of 1958. In many ways this proved to be a Pyrrhic victory. Their platform of an active political stance won but the rules of the political game had already changed.

One scholar observed,

> … the campaign for a Singapore citizenship and a policy of cultural pluralism was a major development in the island. The offer of political rights to the China-born through a local citizenship completed the transformation of Singapore's migrant Chinese from a transient to a domiciled community. … the citizenship-language campaign, being a key factor behind the rise

of a politically-conscious Chinese community, contributed significantly to the emergence of an anti-colonial movement in the island.[142]

Ironically the Ambitious leaders of the Chamber were instrumental in changing the political landscape but at the same time failed to adjust to the consequences of these very changes. In the period that followed, they themselves, and the Chamber as an institution, would pay the price for their ambition.

Police in action at the Hock Lee Bus riots, 1955.

Ministry of Information, Communications and the Arts. Courtesy of the National Archives of Singapore

Cartoon reproduced from *The Straits Times*, 12 February 1955 on the DP "millionaire's party" campaign.

Photograph by courtesy of SPH – The Straits Times

Hokien Huay Kuan building, opened in1955.

Courtesy of the National Archives of Singapore

Registering for citizenship at the old SCCC, 1957.

Courtesy of the National Archives of Singapore

Opening of Nanyang University, 1958.

Courtesy of the National Archives of Singapore

CHAPTER FOUR

1959–1966
Paradox of the PAP state: Disciplining and courting the Chamber

I would like to hear the end of all this. Language, culture, religion: They are not political issues. ... I was deeply grieved when I saw that it was the intellectuals of the Chinese Chamber of Commerce – men responsible for the commerce and industry of our country, our nation – who have said these very unwise things.[1]

THE STRUGGLE EETWEEN LEADERSHIP STYLES, embodied in the encounters between the Ambiguous and the Ambitious, was won by the latter. Still, new challenges arose for these leaders after the 1959 election. The early 1960s were a period of unrest in Southeast Asia, as the last, sometimes violent stages of decolonization, combined with the growing pains of nation-building, resulted in a tense arena of regional politics and business.

The relationship between the Chamber and state greatly changed in the period 1959–1966 as colonial rule made way for independence. Three elites with distinct styles, backgrounds and constituencies competed in a power struggle: the modern technocratic elite of the PAP, based on knowledge, the traditional multi-purpose elite of the SCCC, based on wealth and status, and an oppositional, ideological elite of the PAP left-wing and later the Barisan Sosialis, based on class. The dynamics of the relations and competition between these three constituted much of the political developments in this period.

The Chamber-government relationship was influenced by two sets of developments: the political struggle between radical and conservative forces within Singapore, and the rocky trajectory of Singapore's merger into and expulsion from Malaysia. As the technocrats took firm control of the PAP, its left-wing established the Barisan Sosialis party. The Barisan constituted an ideological elite, which used culture, ethnicity and identity as tools for their class struggle goals, and competed with the merchant leaders for the Chinese-speaking constituency. The ideological elite both challenged and appealed to the Ambitious, who in their role of traditional leaders of the Chinese community supported non-government views on education and culture. In doing so, they made the Chamber a competitor of the PAP. Since the PAP aimed for its policy apparatus to have the greatest possible autonomy from society through the exclusion of alternative power bases, it effectively exterminated the ideological elite and severely disciplined the multi-purpose elite of the Chamber. Cultural issues such as education, ethnicity and language were declared out of bounds.

The shift towards modern politics dominated by the technocratic elite was not absolute, as traditional leadership and status still had strength and utility. The SCCC successfully put the issue of Japanese payment of reparation for the atrocities committed during World War II on the political agenda. It could do so partly because the PAP government courted the Chamber for its influence on the Chinese population to win its political battles. The SCCC publicly supported the government proposal for merger, but once within Malaysia, the Chamber found itself at times fighting joint battles with the PAP against the government in Kuala Lumpur. Politics of ethnicity eventually led to the expulsion of Singapore from the Federation of Malaysia. Thus, the PAP became the government of the independent nation-state of Singapore, and further enhanced its modern, technocratic and paternalistic resolve. In the seven years from 1959 to 1966, the PAP marginalized the Chamber and its leaders politically, socially, culturally and economically.

1. New power constellations

The year 1959 exemplifies the arrival of the local state as the strongest force in the political arena of Singapore. The new power constellation that started to evolve centred on this modernizing state, which embodied the formalization of politics taking place in Singapore since the early 1950s. The introduction of the technocratic, dominant style of governing meant a change in the nature of leadership in the city-state. The Chamber was aware of these changes and tried to maintain its elite status through leadership initiatives and internal reform.

Self-government celebrations

The implementation of the Rendel constitution called for general elections in order to form a government. In the light of the anti-colonial action, political activity and social upheaval described in the previous chapter, this was a significant step and Singaporeans took pride in taking it. The Chamber realized a big event was called for and on 1 August 1958 the idea of a large trade fair, the Exposition, was officially announced on the day that Royal Assent was given to the State of Singapore Bill. The purpose of the exposition, as defined by Ko Teck Kin, was:

> ... to commemorate Singapore's emergence from the colonial status to self-government. We, the Chinese of the Chinese Chamber of Commerce, feel that this historical change is an important event for the 1½ million people of Singapore. We will not be satisfied with self-government in name only but we are determined to show the world that we, the people of Singapore, are capable of determining our own destiny and will continue to strive in the cause of freedom until we gain complete independence. ... We, on behalf of the people of Singapore, need to make a significant gesture at this historic occasion and resolve that we shall prove ourselves capable of fulfilling the responsibilities of self-government. ... Another purpose is to emphasise the fact that Singapore is one of the key stations in international trade – an important international market and a thriving free port.[2]

There could hardly have been a more clear statement by the Ambitious Chamber leaders, who were prepared to put their money where their mouths were. The Exposition was a big undertaking but the pockets of the Chinese business elite were deep. The total cost was estimated at $10 million with $5 million spent on construction alone. The site chosen for the occasion was the old Kallang airport, of which half was occupied by an ambitious government building project while the other half, on the sea-side, was planned as a public park. It was envisioned as the new Padang and together with the housing estate would be a symbol of the proud new Singapore. Two large fountains, illuminated by coloured lights at night, were constructed; a Bailey bridge jetty was built so visitors could come by *sampan* from Clifford Pier, and both the Government and the City Council had large pavilions showing the blessings of modern life.[3]

After much preparation, Chief Minister Lim Yew Hock opened the fair on 31 January 1959. He said that the site was aptly chosen because it was from the same spot that the Malays saw the East India Company ships sail in. "What was founded as a trading settlement for men of all nations has now become the homeland of her citizens".[4] According to the Chamber's own figures, as many as 30,000 patrons flocked to the

Exposition grounds every night, among them, on 22 February, the Duke of Edinburgh, Prince Phillip.[5] The Chamber was proud of the role it had played in decolonization and had every intention of retaining its position of economic, social and political leadership.

The nascent state

The Chinese merchants of the SCCC did, of course, have their preferences and expectations, and as well as their apprehensions and fears regarding the 30 May 1959 election. The PAP clearly appealed most to the Chinese-educated voter because of its position on education and on merger with Malaysia. As businessmen and employers, however, the Chamber leaders were wary of the party's close connection with the unions. Few observers in Singapore had expected the PAP to win, let alone attain an absolute majority. On the day, though, the PAP swept the polls, as it won 43 of the 51 seats. The opposition failed to unite or, as in the case of the Labour Front (LF) and its leader Lim Yew Hock who had taken part under the new name of the Singapore People's Alliance, was presented the bill for having been a local government under British control. The most important reason for the PAP's success was the introduction of automatic registration of voters and compulsory voting under the Rendel constitution. In combination with the 1957 Citizenship Ordinance, these measures meant that the electorate was vastly enlarged and included a large proportion of Chinese-educated and lower-income voters. The PAP, with its union-based character, anti-colonial pedigree, and mass-based organization, was best equipped to appeal to them.

A contemporary Chamber leader said that many Chinese merchants feared the impact of a class struggle by the unions and the left-wing of the PAP.[6] Still, continuing its role of community leader, the SCCC took the initiative to organize an official celebration of self-government. Seven hundred organizations took part in the meeting held at Victoria Hall on 8 August.[7]

The new government had its work cut out, for Singapore was not in a good position to generate the rapid economic growth it so desperately needed. The International Bank for Reconstruction and Development thought Singapore would need to curb population growth, discipline its labour force and achieve an expanded domestic market with the Federation if it wanted to attain significant economic development.[8] Austerity and the need for all Singaporeans to contribute their bit for the common good were the early buzzwords of the government.[9]

Lee Kuan Yew: Omnipotent progressivist.

Ministry of Information, Communications and the Arts. Courtesy of the National Archives of Singapore

Lee Kuan Yew was born in Singapore in 1923 and attended English-language primary and secondary school before entering Raffles College on scholarship. With an anglophile grandfather and with the experience during the Depression of seeing people in commerce, like his father, suffer while professionals fared well, he decided to study law in England. He attended Fitzwilliam College at Cambridge University after the unsettling period of the Japanese occupation, which taught him that the British did not have a God-given right to rule.

While in England, he was involved in the Malayan Forum, a group of students from British Malaya and Singapore. Some of his later collaborators in the PAP were members too and together they discussed independence and the future of their homeland. Lee obtained a double First and was called to the bar at Middle Temple.

Back in Singapore, he worked for a local lawyer, John Laycock, who was active in the Progressive Party (PP)

The PAP government that went to work in June 1959 was dominated by the Western-educated technocratic wing of the party and was led by Prime Minister Lee Kuan Yew.

Lee's closest collaborators were Finance Minister Dr. Goh Keng Swee who held a doctorate from the London School of Economics, and party chairman Dr. Toh Chin Chye, a physiologist trained at the University of London. Many of these men were fiercely proud of their intellectual and academic achievements. Lee Kuan Yew often referred to his double First at Cambridge in speeches and interviews. Goh Keng Swee's pride was demonstrated to me when I reported at the desk of his secretary saying that I had come to interview *Mister* Goh. She quickly corrected me saying that I must have come for *Doctor* Goh and added that he was very particular about being called by his title.

Additional modern-minded progressivists were enlisted to provide efficient leadership. From its inception, the PAP was fiercely anti-colonial and was elected to the Legco in 1951. Lee became legal advisor to a number of unions and eventually involved his Middle Temple sponsor QC D.N. Pritt in the defence of the students arrested during the riots on 13 May 1954. Although the case was lost, Lee had made a lasting connection with the left-wing unions and student organizations. When he and a number of his colleagues from the Malayan Forum started the People's Action Party in November 1954, these left-wing organizations provided some of the founding members an important link to mass-based politics.

According to one of the most recent and well-researched books on "the beliefs behind the man", Michael Barr asserted that progressivism and elitism are the two most important building blocks of Lee's character. The former is a thoroughly Western culture of continual achievement, whereby both Lee and his society had to "advance". According to this analysis, Lee also believes deeply in the superior quality, also genetically, of the elite and sees elite rule as the only reasonable and efficient way to govern. This is the source of his conviction that democracy and notions of egalitarianism should not be allowed to constrain the power or privileges of a ruling elite.[10]

In keeping with his progressivist outlook, Lee valued achievement and intelligence but loathed stupidity and weakness. To some extent, he always retained the style of a courtroom lawyer: flexible and thinking on his feet, eloquent and efficient with words, goal-oriented towards convincing his judges, and cornering opposing council or witness to leave them powerless.

but led by Western-educated men with a strong appreciation for knowledge. Traditional bases of power, whether in the colonial or in the communal hierarchies, were an anachronism to them. The PAP advocated that entrance into positions of power and leadership should be based on knowledge and merit, thus coining the phrase that PAP-led Singapore was a "meritocracy". Collectively these PAP government leaders formed a technocratic elite, which saw that its task was to lead the territory to a future of development, modernity and independence.[11]

It is perhaps indicative of the outlook of the PAP elite that I found a stack of copies of Plato's *The Republic* in the bookstore of the National University of Singapore in 1996 or 1997. Curious to know why the book was sold, or at least stocked, in such great number, I bought a copy. In the introduction by the translator, Desmond Lee, I found two passages that seem highly applicable to Singapore. First of all, commenting on Plato's vision for "philosopher rulers", Lee wrote, "they represent the highest talent,

Kheng Chin Hock: Organizer and agitator.

Courtesy of SCCCI

A Hokkien originally from Longxi, Kheng had come to Singapore from Palembang shortly after the war. Kheng was a produce trader also involved in shipping.

Kheng belonged to the Ambitious camp during the 1950s and was a close ally of Ko Teck Kin with whom he used the Singapore Longxi Huiguan as a power base. This entitled them to a voice in the larger Hokien Huay Kuan and put them on the map as players in the Hokkien power game.[12] Kheng's cooperation with Ko Teck Kin was instrumental in gaining the latter the Chamber presidency in 1954 and again

are given the highest training and are put at the disposal of the state: … they have a duty to their fellow-men, and that they discharge by doing the work of government for which their training has fitted them; they are a dedicated minority ruling in the interest of all".[14] And commenting on Plato's ideal society he writes, "… what Plato wanted was an aristocracy of talent, and we must see the principles behind his detail. And if we want a modern brief description of his kind of society, '*Managerial Meritocracy*', is perhaps the nearest we can get: it emphasizes the need for qualifications and competence in government …".[15]

This view on leadership was markedly different from the traditional ideas underpinning the Chinese community. The *huiguan* were still the bedrock of Chinese society and the Chamber stood at the apex of their hierarchical pyramid. Power in these organizations was based on wealth, status and seniority. The Ambitious leaders of the Chamber had a firm footing in this system and some, such as Ko Teck Kin, skilfully used it to attain their top positions. For men like Ko, it was a logical conclusion that they would lead the Chinese community on all fronts – socially, culturally, politically as well as economically: a true multi-purpose elite. They were convinced that their wealth and status entitled them to substantial influence in the political arena.

The news that the PAP wanted all clan groups to be abolished must, therefore, have been disturbing and threatening to the Chamber leaders. A in 1958. His strong organizational skills were an important asset in strengthening power bases and bringing to fruition various social projects in the Chamber and the Hokien Huay Kuan. He never gained a large fortune like Ko but he did command respect and, more importantly, controlled a large block of votes within the Hokkien clan. Ironically, while Kheng used the opportunities of the power structure, he was vehemently opposed to the dialect group election system of the Chamber. This reiterates the dilemma of the Ambitious leaders simultaneously aspiring to be modern while basing their power on traditional structures.

Kheng was an outspoken man and was seen by some as creating too many problems for the Chamber with his combative style and confrontational approach, both in internal discussions and in dealing with parties outside the Chamber. One contemporary, who knew Kheng well, observed that Kheng had a bit of an inferiority complex. He was short in stature, short-tempered, a little vindictive in nature, and because his business had failed, he felt he had lost face.[13]

PAP party publication declared that *huiguan* were supposed to go now that Singapore had become self-governing. In the authors' view the associations only catered to a limited group of clansmen or families and belonged to the past. On the way to independence, there was no room for these old ideas.[16]

Modernization in the Chamber: the 1959 constitutional change

The SCCC leaders, keenly aware of the tide of modernization sweeping the island, understood that the images of modernity and progress were becoming an important aspect of leadership in Singapore society. They were closely linked to the issues of self-determination and independence for which the Ambitious had fought so hard during the 1950s. Now there were some among the leadership who thought that the time was right to modernize the internal workings of the SCCC. Driven by the mood of the changing times, the Chamber Management Committee (MC) decided to call a special general meeting on 26 April 1959 to discuss two points: a new building and the constitution of the Chamber. Kheng Chin Hock, who was one of the initiators of the meeting, held a press conference the following day and announced his points for change: (1) Increase MC membership, (2) Two vice presidents, (3) A professional administration/ secretariat, (4) A property trust committee, (5) Abolish the clan election system, and (6) Multiple consecutive terms for presidents.[17] The fact that these proposals came from Kheng indicated that they emanated from the Ko Teck Kin camp.

Kheng and Ko, although working as a strategic partnership, had specific personal interests contained within the proposals. Point five, on abolishing the clan based election system, was clearly Kheng's input whereas point six, allowing more consecutive presidential terms, would be of great benefit to Ko Teck Kin in achieving his ambition to make his mark in Chamber history by initiating and overseeing the building of a new headquarters.

Initially, point five received the immediate attention of members and of the media. Significantly, Yeo Chan Boon, *éminence grise* of the Teochew and the last surviving founder member of the Chamber, together with Teo Han Sam, another senior Teochew, raised doubts about abolishing the *bang* system as soon as the plan was announced.[18] The Teochew opposition was not surprising, considering the Hokkien formed the numerical majority in the Chamber. Any form of free election system would, in Teochew eyes, only serve to concentrate more power in Hokkien hands. In contrast, the press coverage was favourable and in the week before a Special Annual General Meeting, *Nanyang Siangpau*, controlled by the family of Lee Kong Chian, a known champion of constitutional change, dedicated two editorials to it, supporting gradual change away from the *bang* system.[19] The *Sin Chew Jit Poh* also applauded a move away from the old *bang* system. It expressed the hope that the Chamber would "take on a new look" and said that the Chamber could not "evade a heavy task in politics".[20]

A constitutional change committee worked on the theme of modernization. In line with Kheng's proposals, three issues were singled out for amendment. First, the size of the Management Council would be increased from 32 to 51 members (Figure 2). Second, the existing six "special directors" would become six Trade Association directors, to be elected by the member associations. The president (maximum three terms) and vice presidents could be re-elected, and two vice presidents would be elected per term but not from the same *bang*. In addition, the new position of honorary president would honour past leaders, and permanent sub-committees on several specialist issues were introduced.[21] The issue of abolishing the *bang*-based election system received no more mention. Only after the proposals had been approved by the MC was a statement released saying the *bang* system would remain.[22]

The new constitution was drawn up and, in December, a celebration was held to commemorate its implementation.[23] Significantly, this celebration coincided with the government-declared national loyalty week, which was

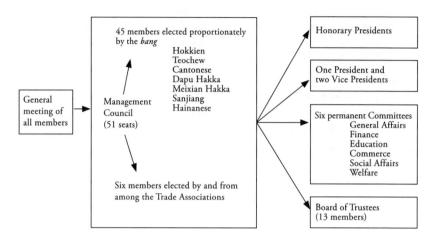

Figure 2: Organizational diagram of the SCCC after the 1959
constitutional amendment

the week following the installation, on 3 December, of the country's first
Malayan-born head of state, Yang di-Pertuan Negara, Yusof bin Ishak. With
this new constitution, the Chamber leadership indicated its continuing
ambitions regarding its elite status in Singapore while making clear that
it was sensitive to the changing times and would be a constituent part of
modern Singapore.

With the new constitution in place, the road was clear for re-election,
in 1960, with Ko Teck Kin as president. Since the new constitution called
for the election of 51 council members, little competition was necessary
because the extra 19 new seats could be used to satisfy different *bangs*
and factions. Six permanent committees were established: general affairs,
finance, education, commerce, social affairs and welfare. The chairmen
for these committees were appointed from among the senior leaders of
the various dialect groups. Ko's closest Hokkien allies, Ng Aik Huan and
Kheng Chin Hock, held the most important posts of general affairs and
finance respectively.[24]

Ko's ambitions concerning the realization of a new headquarters for the
SCCC had not come to fruition yet. The need for a new building for the
Chamber had been pressing for many years. It still held its meetings in the
same old building on Hill Street. The issue that had prevented any council
or sitting president from initiating the planning and construction of a
new headquarters was that the task was simply too big to be accomplished
in one term. If a president was to put in all the time and effort, not to

mention the largest personal donation, he definitely wanted to take all the credit and still be in charge when the new building was opened. After the election, with Ko's power reaffirmed, the MC appointed a building sub-committee. Kheng was in charge of the building fund; it was no small task as an estimated $2 million would be required.[25] Although considerably wealthy by this time, Ko did not make the largest contribution to the building fund. Lee Kong Chian, who had given his support, if hesitantly, to Ko in the heated election of 1958, took that honour. Possessing the highest status and a dominant business empire, Lee commanded respect and great moral authority. Although he did not attend Chamber meetings anymore, his opinion and support were sought on all major issues. In this case, Lee pledged to raise all actual donations by 10 per cent, the largest single contribution by far. The project would not be finished until late 1964. In the meantime, Singapore went through some significant changes.

2. Politics of economic growth

The PAP's policy of economic development was the practical issue dominating the Chamber's external commercial concerns. In the arena of economic policy, the SCCC encountered the government, which made clear that macro-economic state intervention would be used to deal with Singapore's economic and social woes. Job creation and economic growth were central to the government's approach and industrialization would be the spearhead rather than trade and commerce. This new approach, as one economic historian observed, "successfully combined authoritarian interventionism at home and international free trade".[26]

Some aspects of the government's early interventions to achieve a sounder basis for economic growth were welcomed by the SCCC and by employers in general. Creative labour regulations, modelled on the Australian example, suppressed and prevented strikes through compulsory procedures before an arbitration court. This initiative instilled some confidence in the government's intentions towards sound, growth-oriented socio-economic policies among entrepreneurs, but there were also fundamental points of contention.

The Chamber's trade perspective

The difference between the economic plans of the government and the commercial logic of the Chinese business elite was indeed fundamental. While the government stood for intervention and industrialization, the

Chinese merchants wanted free trade, *laissez-faire* and a continued dominance of commerce. The SCCC, with roughly 75 per cent of its membership involved in trade, transportation and services, remained the main voice of the Chinese merchants because the alternative business organizations had different aims or membership structures.[27] Western business dominated the two largest among the alternatives, the Singapore Chamber of Commerce (SCC) and the Singapore Manufacturers' Association (SMA). The SMA, in particular, had an industrial orientation. Trade promotion and the removal of obstacles left over from colonial days were first on the SCCC agenda. Within a month of the PAP coming to power, Ko Teck Kin had a discussion with Lee Kuan Yew on a new trade policy for Singapore. Lobbying for the interests of the Chamber members, he tried to impress upon the new Prime Minister the importance of entrepot trade to Singapore. Ko claimed that the entrepot trade constituted 80 per cent of Singapore income[28] and, therefore, barriers to trade should be lifted.[29] The Chamber's position and desires were clear but the government had different plans.

Shotgun wedding

The government did not conceal its resolve to set up an economic policy with speed and determination. Its first goal was job creation and economic growth. Whether this was achieved in or through Singaporean companies was not a priority. Goh Keng Swee, the minister for finance, gave a clear warning at the Chamber's installation ceremony in 1960. He called on local entrepreneurs to expand Singapore industry. "If you do not avail yourself of this opportunity, then you cannot blame the government if we ask people from abroad to start on these ventures and receive the reward from them. But we wish, as far as possible, to give preference to local businessmen, whenever they are willing to move into these new ventures".[30] The government did recognize the need to communicate and in July 1960, Ko Teck Kin was elected the first chairman of the Consultative Committee on Commerce and Industry, which comprised the three local chambers of commerce, the SMA and the Exchange Banks Association.[31]

Over the next year, as tensions between the left-wing and the conservative technocrats in the PAP, that is, in the government, started to rise, economic policies still had a limited effect. The political struggle translated into labour unrest, which in turn led to low investor confidence, whether local or foreign. The government invited a United Nations Technical Assistance Board team for guidance. Its brief was to survey the proposed Jurong Industrial Estate and advise on suitable types of industries.[32] The team, which arrived in October 1961, was headed by Dr. Albert Winsemius, a Dutchman with experience in public administration and industrialization policy who also was an accomplished businessman and consultant.[33]

While entrepot trade and port activities were highly developed in Singapore, the UN mission observed that unions had pushed up wages, causing manufacturing industry employment to drop by 20 per cent. The number one prerequisite was that "everybody puts his shoulders to his task, that he sees further than his own direct interests, further than today, and over Singapore's frontiers where the customers are. ... only an expansion of manufacturing industry can keep stride with the growing population". The report emphasized that the international customer would not be interested in a sheltered position for Singapore entrepreneurs, and that only price and quality would determine the viability of the export sector. The key to reaching that would depend not only on the intensive involvement of the government in the economy but especially on the cooperation between employers and employees.[34]

Winsemius hit home a stronger message behind closed doors. During one of his earliest conversations with Lee Kuan Yew, he said that two elements would be essential,

> Get rid of the communists; how you get rid of them does not interest me as an economist, but get them out of the government, get them out of the unions, get them off the streets. Number two is: Let Raffles stand where he stands today; say publicly that you accept the heavy ties with the West because you will very much need them in your economic programme ... If you want to be a socialist, you have to be a businessman first. You have to plan the income before being a socialist.[35]

On the question of who would be the entrepreneurs to create the jobs, the report was vague. The UN mission understood that it would be hard for the Singapore government to sell the idea that foreign investment was to be the cornerstone of the economic plan. Both Winsemius and Goh Keng Swee, however, attest to the fact that in top government circles, a clear awareness of the need to turn to foreign investment was present. Winsemius said later: "There was no local industrial sector to speak of, and we did not advise to build such a sector up either. It simply would take too much time."[36]

Based on the UN mission report, a four-year economic plan was launched, which stressed economic development and industrial growth, with the government participating directly and providing infrastructural services. Both foreign and local investors were wooed with incentives in the form of tax holidays for pioneering industries and low rates of taxation for export-oriented manufactures, together with temporary protective tariffs against imports. In practice, the plan was dependent on and geared towards foreign investment, a fact confirmed by Goh Keng Swee.[37]

This did not mean the government ceased to engage local business and the Chamber. From an electoral point of view, it would have to be seen as presenting the local entrepreneurs with at least equal opportunities. It called on Singapore businessmen to take part in industrialization, as Goh Keng Swee did again at the 1962 Chamber installation ceremony: "We must not be too dependent on overseas manufacturers to establish industries here. Our own capitalists should make a contribution and the government will give them every assistance to embark on new industries."[38] However, if these entrepreneurs decided not to do so, it would be their loss; the development plan would continue, financed as it was through foreign capital.

This long-term planning decision distanced the government from the local business elite and, therefore, diminished the influence of the SCCC and increased the importance of the SMA. In time, the government's choice of economic development strategy greatly influenced the balance of power between itself and civil society. The government became the planner as well as the executor of economic growth while it was not primarily dependent on local entrepreneurs. This development also signified a change in the nature of leadership and power. The traditional elite of the Chinese business community, which was based on the wealth and status created in trade and commerce, was overshadowed by a modern technocratic elite based on knowledge and expertise. The transformation of economy and politics went hand in hand.

3. Redefining power relations: the Chamber chastised and courted

The government's decision to embark on the long-term development plan was brought about by the dire economic circumstances resulting, among other things, from the political struggle that was being waged between the PAP's left-wing and the unions on the one side, and the PAP conservative technocrats in the government on the other. To understand this struggle we must pay attention to the merger issue and to education because the three elites engaged each other vehemently in these arenas.

From its founding in 1954 onwards the PAP had advocated independence through merger, but from 1954 to 1961 the Federation, and in particular

Prime Minister Tunku Abdul Rahman, opposed the idea for fear that Singapore's largely Chinese and left-wing oriented population would weaken the position of the Malay community.[39]

Improving trade ties with the People's Republic of China (PRC), which would constitute great opportunities for Singapore Chinese traders, was another touchy subject in the Singapore-Malaya relationship. The position of the PAP government was that trade ties with China were acceptable as long as it did not compromise or oppose the foreign policy of the Federation. The implications became clear when a group of Singapore businessmen organized a mission to China. In the course of the trip, Ko Teck Kin attended the 10th anniversary of the founding of the PRC in Beijing as the official guest of the Chinese government, accentuating the Chamber's strong ties with China.[40] This China-oriented behaviour and the emphasis on Chinese ethnicity was something the Singapore government observed with apprehension. It was hardly the image it wanted to present to the Tunku, who saw Chinese economic dominance as a problem and was constantly on guard against communist Chinese infiltration. Despite his continuing apprehension, the Tunku changed his tune, however, and on 27 May 1961, speaking at the Foreign Correspondents' Club in Singapore said that "sooner or later Malaya should have an understanding with Britain and the peoples of Singapore, North Borneo, Brunei and Sarawak".[41]

The issue of merger from then on dominated Singapore politics and eventually led to a crisis within the PAP. The left-wing of the PAP and the unions opposed the idea of Malaysia as a federation including the Borneo territories, Brunei and Singapore on ideological grounds. They, and also Indonesian President Sukarno, saw the whole plan as a neo-colonial invention of the British in order to retain influence in the region. As the technocratic wing of the PAP had merger as one of its priorities, an untenable political situation developed. From an economic and political point of view, the technocrats felt that Singapore as an independent unit would not be feasible. Lee Kuan Yew decided to bring the conflict into the open, and after a long debate on the issue in the Legislative Assembly a vote of confidence was called on 21 July 1961, in which all 13 left-wing PAP members abstained. With a narrow majority of 27 to 24, the conservative technocrat wing won.[42] The next day, the PAP Central Executive Committee, which Lee Kuan Yew controlled, expelled the left-wing and on 26 July, the breakaway faction set up a new party – the Barisan Sosialis.[43] After an uneasy cooperation of almost seven years, which had brought the PAP to power, its left-wing detached itself and became a strong oppositional force.

With the establishment of the Barisan Sosialis, an important political shift took place. It became clear the left-wing controlled the local party branches and the People's Association[44] and through it the grassroots links of the party with the community. The PAP was crippled because of the defection of the left-wing. Thirty-five of the 51 branch committees resigned, 19 of the 23 paid organizing secretaries defected, and only 20 per cent of the party's former members paid their subscriptions in 1962.[45] Therefore, when the Barisan was formed, it possessed some important political advantages. It had long focused its organizational efforts on politically-relevant secondary associations through persuasion and cooperation. These mainly consisted of non-English speaking Chinese organizations. The party could, therefore, rest on a sound organizational basis and had influential and charismatic leaders in its General Secretary Lim Chin Siong and Chairman Dr. Lee Siew Loh. Observers and academic analysts do not agree to what extent the Barisan was communist-controlled. Bellows expresses his doubts, in his thorough study on the Singapore political scene, and declines to affirm the party's communist-front status.[46]

Now that the left-wing was no longer restrained in a united front with the conservative technocrats, it immediately started a campaign to advertise its standpoints on education, internal security and the economy. At the same time, Lee Kuan Yew could attack the left-wing leaders now that they were no longer part of his party and government. The government used its powers to the limit. In Lee's own words, the labour unrest was the opportunity the government had sought to de-register the left-wing Trade Union Congress in November 1961.[47] His goal was to stop the Barisan from taking its struggle to the streets through strikes and, thereby, decrease its appeal to the working class.

Ko Teck Kin's savvy runs out: the 1962 Examination Boycott Commission

The dominance of the PAP government did not remove the political, social and cultural aspirations of the traditional multi-purpose elite. The Ambitious Chamber leaders continued an active role in political issues. One of these was education, that tinderbox of culture and politics, which had proved such a dangerous arena in the 1950s. As a stand on Chinese education was a statement on ethnicity and culture at a time when these issues were very sensitive in the Malayan context, Ko Teck Kin and his colleagues could have expected a strong government response. Still, the

Ambitious leaders felt they held a strong moral position and decided to involve themselves in the politics of education once again. The Barisan Sosialis also had considerable interest in education because it was an issue through which Chinese citizens could be coaxed into action. As it strongly influenced a number of student unions, it was an important actor in this arena.

The recent PAP party struggle had reinforced the government's opinion that the Barisan cleverly co-opted various groups by addressing them on issues close to their heart. During the mid-1950s, the left-wing had appropriated the Chamber's pro-Chinese education stand. The government and especially Lee Kuan Yew loathed the fact that the business leaders let themselves be used in this way, and Lee was looking for an opportunity to scare the tycoons straight. If we analyse the power politics of the day, he did not want an alternative power base to his own government to be formed through cooperation of the traditional and the ideological elite.

An opportunity presented itself during the autumn of 1961. In support of labour strikes, the left staged action by student organizations. On 27 and 28 November 1961, 300 Chinese Middle School students picketed the examination centres and formed human chains to prevent students from taking their exams. The issue at stake was a proposal by the Minister of Education to make the examinations uniform for all four language streams. Chinese pupils felt threatened by the change because the examination requirements included English language competency. Proponents of Chinese education saw this as an attack on the integrity of the Chinese stream.

However, instead of breaking up the pickets, the government told parents that their children would lose a full year if they did not take the examination. Under police protection, 60 per cent of students took their examination.[48] The government decided to present the whole affair as a communist plot through a public inquiry into the examination boycott. In this way, it wanted to chastise both the Barisan and Ko Teck Kin. Francis Seow was briefed by Lee Kuan Yew on the job of counsel in the inquiry. In the preparations, extensive use was made of the Special Branch information on alleged communist activity, and Lee was personally kept informed throughout the early stages.[49]

The Chamber as an organization had not been involved in the issue but its president and a number of Ambitious leaders took a position early on, protesting the changes and arguing that Chinese students would be adversely affected under the new system. A number of meetings were held at the Hokien Huay Kuan and the Ee Hoe Hean Club in August and

October respectively.[50] On 5 October, a delegation from the Singapore Chinese School Staff Committee Association headed by Ko Teck Kin saw the Minister of Education and drew up an agreement, which Ko Teck Kin signed.[51]

Seow recounted that Ko Teck Kin was a prime target but also that he was instructed about Ko's political utility to Lee Kuan Yew. This paradox exemplifies the inherent duality in the relationship between the state and the Chamber in this period. Ko was disciplined and courted at the same time.

> He was held in high esteem and regard in the world of business and commerce. A man of great pride, he radiated a powerful influence and authority over the Chinese populace. But Ko Teck Kin was, however, dabbling in national politics and, in the naive belief that he was helping to man the ramparts of Chinese language and culture, had lent his name and prestige to the agitation against the new education system. ... The government wanted to retain his goodwill because of his status with the Chinese commonalty but, at the same time, wanted to neutralize him, using the words in its best sense. ... The prime minister was keen that Ko should be exposed for dabbling in matters out of his depths; but was simultaneously anxious that he should not be so treated as to antagonize the Chinese community, for, to quote his words to me, 'He is worth at least 50,000 votes.'[52]

The Commission started its work on 2 May 1962, in the middle of the debate on merger, a point which will be highlighted in the next section. During these months the government used two parallel approaches towards the Chamber. While it sought its political support on merger, simultaneously it embarrassed its leader in public for political behaviour the government deemed dangerous. Lee Kuan Yew in his memoirs recounts only half the story when he describes Ko Teck Kin as apprehensive of the communists: "He had an economic stake in Malaya, where the rubber came from, and he was not going to side with the communists. After I got to know him better, I found him a sensible, reasonable man, deeply concerned about the future of the Chinese community in Singapore whose interests he felt it was his duty to protect".[53]

The report of the commission of inquiry is most revealing about the tactics used to expose Ko Teck Kin as a political amateur who had let himself be used by communists. Ko was made to wait to take the stand from the date originally scheduled (3 May) until 28 May. He was sent back by the commission each day with the excuse that not all the necessary preliminary information had been presented. Ko was required to appear in person at the proceedings on all the days the commission met in case it was ready to hear him. He was put on the stand in his numerous capacities in education: Chairman of Chung Cheng Management Committee and Chinese High School, and Chairman of the Singapore Chinese School Staff Committee Association (SCSSCA).[54] Seow immediately questioned Ko's competence.

> Seow: "Would it be fair to say that you are familiar with the education ordinance and the regulations made thereunder?"
>
> Ko Teck Kin: "Not very much."

Seow mentioned that the Singapore Chinese School Staff Committee Association did not object to the new system for two years.

> Seow: "Let us get it straight on record. Mr. Ko, you do not set yourself up as an educationalist?"
>
> Ko Teck Kin: "I am a businessman."
>
> Seow: "You are not an educationalist?"
>
> Ko Teck Kin: "No."
>
> Seow: "So that whether the 4/2 or the 3/3 is better [Seow is referring to the new and the old system respectively], one or the other is better, for Chinese education, you would not be in a position to say so?"
>
> Ko Teck Kin: "That might be so, but I signed on that day an agreement with the Minister of Education [Ko is referring to the 5 October meeting and agreement], so that there should not be any further criticism on this 4/2 system."[55]

This was the dominant theme that Seow continued to follow. Then after two days of restating the same question, Seow came to the point:

> Seow: "And yet Mr. Ko stood up at a public forum and you criticized the 4/2 system. The public forum at Nanyang University ... on 31st July 1961."
>
> Ko Teck Kin: "I don't remember."
>
> Seow: (curtly) "Yes, very well, we will refresh your memory. Before I hand up to you a newspaper report of your speech at that forum, I am suggesting to you, Mr. Ko, that that speech, which you made at that forum, was written for you by someone else."
>
> Ko Teck Kin: "Even if I did not write, those are still my views".[56]

Seow inferred that Ko Teck Kin was a mouthpiece for the Nanyang University Students' Union, an alleged communist front organization, referring to a *Nanyang Siangpau* report of 2 August 1961. Ko stated in defence of the speech that many rumours existed in those days that the government wanted to abolish the two years of Senior Middle school for Chinese schools altogether. When Seow once more said that Ko did not know what he was talking about, Ko Teck Kin snapped. Furiously Ko Teck Kin cried out, "That is an insult to my character. Don't you know that I am the president of the SCCC?" Seow responded, "I think I have had evidence on that earlier, but you don't have to tell me. We don't wish to engage in these fruitless exchanges."[57]

The interrogation turned again to the meeting on 5 October 1961 and Seow accused Ko of seeking a privileged position for Chinese education within the multi-ethnic system of Singapore. As more angry exchanges followed, Seow mentioned that some of Ko Teck Kin's children attended English language schools. This was a calculated blow to discredit Ko as half-hearted in his cultural cause for Chinese education, hedging his family's bets on the very system he was claiming to fight.

Even though Ko saw the 5 October agreement as a concession for Chinese education, the Nanyang University Students' Union and the left-wing Teachers' Union still opposed the new system. Their argument was that Chinese students could indeed finish their secondary education within their own stream. However, if they wanted to continue their education in a polytechnic, a teachers' college or another tertiary institute, they would still have to pass the other examinations. In their eyes, this constituted discrimination against the Chinese school stream and they proceeded to plan a boycott of the examinations in November 1961.

During his testimony, Ko dismissed criticisms from the left-wing, prompting Seow to mount an attack on Ko's capabilities as a leader.

> Seow: "That shows how irresponsible you can be. This is not a light matter. … Mr. Ko as community leader, as president of the SCCC, as president of the SCSSCA, you could have done an immense lot towards stopping the trouble in the schools that eventually flared up. … You just had to make a statement. People sought his advice and guidance, saw him as man of the hour. But he did not come through. In fact, you didn't rise to the occasion as a community leader, as the president of the SCCC, as the president of the SCSSCA."[58]

To understand the impact of this blow to Ko's status and "face", one must realize that newspaper coverage of the commission hearings was comprehensive and the general public devoured the reports. Lee Kuan Yew had humbled and humiliated the Chamber's president and cut the political aspiration of the SCCC down to size. The encounter exemplified the clash between the modern, authoritarian state elite and an alternative traditional power base. Disciplining Ko on the issue of education served the double purpose of the PAP technocrats of neutralizing this alternative power base while signalling to society at large the limits to political participation. Still, the PAP could not achieve one of its goals without assistance from the Chamber.

Lee Kuan Yew needs the Chamber: merger and Singapore politics

Immediately after the establishment of the Barisan Sosialis, caused by the vote on the merger issue, the PAP government had showed its teeth by openly opposing the Barisan, through deregistration of the trade unions and by going on the offensive regarding education. Still, Lee Kuan Yew felt reluctant to become openly anti-communist because he needed working class votes if merger were to be decided at the polls. British reports indicated that he thought he would carry the English-speaking Chinese, Indians and Malays (37 per cent of the population) but still needed 22 per cent of the Chinese-educated.[59] Lee went on the offensive on merger straightaway. In 36 radio broadcasts, 12 speeches in English, Mandarin and Malay each, between 13 September and 9 October 1961, he outlined the political development in Singapore and the PAP since 1954. These speeches focused on: why the PAP had decided upon the united front with the "communists"; why they had eventually split; and what they were fighting over in the merger debate. Most importantly, he wanted to get the point across that economically, socially and politically, Singapore and Malaya were inseparable.[60]

The local business community and the SCCC supported the economic logic of Lee's argument and the Chamber became a key factor in convincing the population of the political and social logic of the PAP arguments as well. The Singapore government presented its own strategy after negotiations with the Malayan side in a memorandum commonly known as the White Paper on Merger. The government agreed to Singapore's under-representation in the federal legislature in return for autonomy in education and labour policies. It also stressed that the free port status of Singapore would continue and that Singapore would retain a large proportion of its own revenue.

The role of the Chamber in the merger debate

The stakes of the merger debate were somewhat similar to those the Chamber and the Chinese community of Singapore had faced in the late 1940s and early 1950s. They lived and worked in a territory that would become part of a political entity of which they did not yet know the rules. Citizenship was again the key. This time the Chinese of Singapore were dependent on what the leaders of the Federation would decide. The PAP government had set out its position for which it needed broad domestic support if it wanted to impress the Federation government. The PAP had just lost its grassroots connections to the Barisan and now had to find a conduit to reach the Chinese-speaking part of the population. It looked to the Chamber because it still wielded great influence in the Chinese community through its domination of the pyramid of Chinese organizations. But if Lee Kuan Yew wanted to gain the Chamber's support, he would need to remove the lingering doubts of the Chinese community on its future status and political rights after merger. Despite his modernist image, Lee Kuan Yew had to depend on the traditional multi-purpose elite of the Chamber.

The passage of the White Paper that was to prove troublesome addressed the status of the Singapore citizens in the future federation. It stated "the 624,000 Singapore citizens will not lose the state citizenship rights they enjoy in Singapore. With merger they will automatically become nationals of the larger Federation and carry the same passport as other nationals of the larger Federation."[61] The sticking point was in the choice of terminology. Singapore citizens would become federation nationals, not federation citizens like the existing residents of Malaya. It was unclear what the repercussions of this difference might be, but it was feared that Singaporeans would hold second-class status in the Federation. The Ambitious leaders of the Chamber felt a responsibility to take up the matter. In order to preserve their status and influence with their constituency, they needed to be seen taking an active stance in safeguarding the interests of the Chinese community. This was enforced by their own role as businessmen with stakes in both the peninsular and the Singaporean economy. The Chamber decided to hold a public meeting to which *huiguan* and associations would be invited to advance their questions on citizenship, trade, education and language to the attending ministers.[62] Shortly after, when Lee Kuan Yew returned from a trip abroad, the SCCC hosted a welcome dinner. The speeches that night concentrated on the merger issue with Lee Kuan Yew praising the SCCC and Ko Teck Kin for their efforts to explain the issue to the general public.[63]

The forum was held on 13 January 1962 when more than a 1,000 delegates attended a meeting at Victoria Hall chaired by Ko Teck Kin. The turnout shows the continued strength of the communal network of the

Chamber leadership and gave Ko and his Ambitious colleagues a reason to feel empowered and central to political developments. In fact the Chamber President was convinced of the political strength of the Chamber and of the comparative weakness of the PAP government. He thought that the PAP was fighting a losing battle. On 1 December 1961, in a conversation with a British official in Borneo, Ko Teck Kin and Tan Eng Joo said that the present PAP leadership was totally discredited in Singapore. They observed the Barisan were gaining support and that strong right-wing leadership was lacking to counter this trend. They held that if Lee Kuan Yew were to hold a referendum on merger, he would certainly lose it.[64]

During the January meeting, Lee Kuan Yew and other ministers spoke at length on merger and their explanations were generally well received. Still, Lee Kuan Yew admitted later that he could not answer satisfactorily when a senior Chamber member asked him why all 600,000 Singapore citizens could not enjoy the same rights after joining Malaysia. Why was there a difference between national and citizen?[65] The question lingered and could only be answered by the Malaysian side, as others, such as David Marshall, pointed out. He predicted that ethnicity and political rights would eventually become the ruin of a Federation including Singapore.

The merger referendum

Since the Tunku was not forthcoming in dispelling the doubts that remained, the Barisan had a valid point with which to try and swing public opinion. It also meant that the Chamber and its Ambitious leadership continued to be in the limelight and were approached by both the technocratic PAP elite and the ideological Barisan elite for support. It had been decided that the merger issue would be put before the people of Singapore in a referendum. After much debate, the Legislative Assembly accepted the following wording for the referendum: "Do you want merger (A) in accordance with the White Paper, or (B) on the basis of Singapore as a constituent state of the Federation of Malaya, or (C) on terms no less favourable than those given to the three Borneo territories?" On 14 August, Lee Kuan Yew announced the referendum for 1 September, assuring all Singapore citizens they would automatically become Malaysian citizens. To prove his point, he read from a written agreement with the Tunku that he had obtained with the help of the British, thereby effectively demolishing the Barisan's objections to merger.

In an attempt to throw a last monkey wrench, the Barisan and Marshall's Workers' Party stepped up their campaign encouraging people to cast blank votes in protest. Lee decided to exert more pressure by unilaterally changing the rules, saying that blank votes would be interpreted as favouring "B" for complete and unconditional merger, which meant that all Singapore citizens not born in Singapore would lose their rights when Malaysia came into being. The tactic of changing the goalposts in the middle of a game would become a strategy more often used by the PAP in the future. The announcement indeed put the scare on the Chinese leaders. On 27 August, Ko Teck Kin led a delegation from the Chamber to the Prime Minister's office, seeking clarification of his statement on the interpretation of blank votes. When Lee reaffirmed his stand, Ko asked the opposition parties to categorically state their position if blank votes were to be counted as "B".[66]

In a Chamber meeting, Ko Teck Kin stressed that the Tunku had given the assurance that after merger, Singaporeans would automatically attain Malaysian citizenship and enjoy equal status. A choice for "A" would safeguard citizenship while "B" or "C" could result in the loss of citizenship. "A" would also ensure control over education, labour, social welfare and health care as well as the Singapore port's free trade status.[67] The MC decided unanimously that it would support "A" and placed ads in all the major newspapers on 30 August in which they appealed to "all public institutions, its affiliated trade associations and its members to awake their friends and relatives who possess the voting right to the duty of voting for Alternative "A" … and by dissuading voters from casting blank votes to the detriment of the rights and interests of the people of Singapore".[68] The merger referendum resulted in 70.8 per cent victory for the PAP.

The Chamber had done Lee Kuan Yew and the PAP a great favour. Aware of this, Lee, before going on his victory parade through Tanjong Pagar, met the Chamber leaders and thanked them for their support, reiterating that the clauses of the White Paper, especially those on education, labour, multi-lingualism, free port status and automatic citizenship would enter into the constitution of Malaysia.[69] The technocratic elite had needed the Chamber leaders in control of the traditional communal power structure to carry a victory in what they perceived to be their most important political battle.

4. Chamber utility and humiliation once again: political clashes

The year leading up to merger, which was to take place by mid-1963, proved to be tumultuous and the three contending elites in Singapore continued to test each other's strength. In the end, this process would result in the sidelining of the Barisan as an opposition party. The Chamber and its Ambitious leaders would be dealt a second blow by the PAP government when Tan Lark Sye was severely disciplined after he openly supported the Barisan. Again the motive for alignment with the Barisan ideological elite was the issue of ethnicity and culture through the politics of education. As before the PAP government drew its boundaries to political participation and came down hard on those who trespassed.

While merger was secured through the referendum victory, political trouble was by no means over. Indonesian President Sukarno started to add pressure to the situation on 20 January 1963, by declaring a policy of "*Konfrontasi*" against the planned Malaysia, which he called a neo-colonialist state. An economic boycott was the main weapon applied by the Indonesian side, which particularly hurt Singapore traders. The policy also included military action and terrorist bomb attacks as well as dropping agents in Singapore and Johor with the aim of destabilizing the basis for Malaysia.[70] A new factor entered the equation when a revolt broke out in Malaysian Borneo, staged by rebels calling themselves the North Borneo National Army. Lim Chin Siong, one of the Barisan leaders, had met the leader of the revolt a few days before and now the Barisan came out in support, hailing the revolt as an anti-colonial popular uprising. Backing for the uprising had come from Sukarno and a fiery war of words developed between Indonesia and Malaya. In the end, the tense situation brought together the members of the Internal Security Council in which the Singaporean government and the British had seats and the Federation government had the casting vote. On the night of 2 February 1963, a raid, called Operation Cold Store, was carried out in which 115 people were arrested in Singapore. The action removed some of the ablest and most experienced left-wing leaders, including Lim Chin Siong and 23 Barisan members from the scene.[71]

Meanwhile Singapore and the Federation were preparing for merger and were trying to secure as much power in the new constellation as possible. For the leaders of the Federation, this meant that they attempted to gain control over the budget of Singapore. A battle ensued between the PAP in Singapore and the Federation government over which departments and under which authority taxation would be organized and who would control revenues. Singapore had made it clear in earlier negotiations, and had received the Tunku's approval, that it wanted to remain in charge of its own finances. A just amount would then be forwarded to the Federal government. The Malayans now claimed 60 per cent of revenue and insisted that federal taxes had to be collected by federal departments. This provoked a strong reaction in Singapore. The Chamber was naturally concerned, because as businessmen, they were fiercely opposed to any measures that might interfere with the smooth running of their companies. In the context of merger, their whole logic for support was based on the economic rationale of a joint market enabling free-trade. Now they found themselves in need of a strong ally to keep the Federation government out of their business affairs.

From its side, the PAP, still trying to recover from the blow to its grassroots connections caused by the split with the Barisan, was still aware of the utility of the Chamber's influence over the Chinese community. The PAP needed support from the new roots in the Chinese community and Lee fell back on the traditional building blocks of Singapore society – the clan associations, the music and drama groups, the lending library associations, and the benevolent societies. In the six months leading up to the 1963 Singapore election, he toured every ward in Singapore to visit these organizations, gave speeches and held talks with the people to get their political support.[72] He was recognizing the power still encapsulated in the pyramid of Chinese organizations. On his tour of the Chinese community, he must have had many encounters with the top and secondary-level leaders of the Chamber who formed the leadership of the *huiguan*. The recognition of these organizations shows that the multi-purpose Chinese elite and the connection between economic, cultural, social and political affairs could substitute the PAP's failing formal political organization.

Lee Kuan Yew declared Singapore independent on 31 August 1963, the original day planned as Malaysia Day, the birth of post-merger Malaysia.[73] During the 15 days of full independence, Lee Kuan Yew called snap elections to renew the political mandate of the PAP. Campaigning for the 21 September 1963 polls developed into a pro- and contra-Malaysia fight between the PAP and the Barisan. Not sure of victory, the PAP fought the elections on the issue of its past record in economic and social policy, using every means to defeat its opponents. This included minimum lead time for calling the elections, excluding imprisoned Barisan leaders from standing for election, restricting campaign meetings, freezing funds of hostile unions, and withdrawing the registration of seven Barisan-dominated unions during the election campaign.[74] In the end, the PAP secured an absolute majority in the election. Ko, as Chamber president, welcomed the result.[75] Perhaps as a sign of thanks for his support to the merger efforts or as reconciliation after the humiliating experience in front of the commission of inquiry, Ko Teck Kin was appointed as one of the two Singapore members of the Senate of the Federation of Malaysia.

Tan Lark Sye and the 1963 elections

While Ko Teck Kin received a degree of compensation, another Chamber leader, Tan Lark Sye, was singled out to be disciplined over his role in the elections. To understand the development of this issue, we have to look at the history of Nanyang University and the role of Tan Lark Sye. Neither the British nor the Lim Yew Hock government had been very pleased that the Chinese-language university had been set up. Still, due to perseverance, private funding and the leadership of Tan Lark Sye, the university had been established. When the PAP came to power in 1959, Lee Kuan Yew knew he had a difficult job bringing Nanda under government control and reorganizing it in accordance with the education policy. He had been present at the official opening on 30 March 1958, and felt "the tremendous emotional commitment of our Chinese-speaking people to this project".[76] Because of this, Lee felt threatened by some of the prime movers behind Nanda. The combination of ethnicity, culture and politics, and the cooperation of the traditional Chinese and the ideological elite was too dangerous a threat to the PAP government to leave unanswered. In this case, the multi-purpose nature of the Chinese business elite, the central role of ethnicity, and the defence of Chinese culture in their legitimacy as community leaders proved incompatible with the de-ethnicizing of the PAP.

The government made its intentions for Nanda clear in the following months. On 28 October 1959, Lee Kuan Yew stated that:

> ... if Nantah becomes a symbol of Chinese excellence and of supremacy of Chinese scholarship and learning, then verily we will aggravate the position of the Overseas Chinese in all other places in Southeast Asia. ... Nantah graduates must demonstrate that they were graduates of a Malayan University which used the Chinese language as one of the media of instruction, not graduates of a Chinese university which, incidentally also taught the Malay language.[77]

A few months later, Tan Lark Sye announced that former Chung Cheng High School principal Chuang Chu-lin would be the next vice chancellor of Nanda. Chuang had been principal of Chung Cheng from its inception in 1939 until September 1957 when he was detained under the Preservation of Public Security Ordinance for his alleged role in the left-wing student actions. He was released in August 1958.[78] Lee Kuan Yew claims that the choice for Chuang was a show of defiance by Tan Lark Sye towards the government. Lee Kuan Yew writes: "We knew this would give the MCP greater freedom to use the university as a breeding ground, but we were not in a position to intervene without paying a high political price." He held Tan Lark Sye personally responsible and "made a mental note to deal with Tan at a later date".[79] The episode hardened the government stand on the status and role of Nanda. On 29 March 1960, it stated that:

> Under no circumstances should Nantah be regarded as a Chinese or Chinese-language university ... the original aim of Nantah is surely to found a Malayan university in Malaya to cater for the needs principally of the Chinese section of the population. But the ultimate aim must be a Malayan university to cater for all Malayans, Chinese or otherwise ...[80]

During the election campaign, the Barisan tried to capitalize on Tan Lark Sye's status, his activism in the struggle for Chinese education, and his antagonistic relationship with the PAP leadership. They asked Tan for financial support and later for a public endorsement of the Barisan candidates who were Nanda graduates or students. Tan did both, donating $20,000 towards the campaign cost of the 10 Nanda candidates while publicly urging Chinese voters to support them in the election.[81] His hope was that a Nanda graduate would become the Minister of Education in the Barisan government. Dr. Lee Siew Choh, the Barisan party chairman, later indicated that this would have been a natural choice.[82]

On 22 September, the day after the election, the Singapore government began legal proceedings to revoke the citizenship of Tan Lark Sye on the grounds that he had "collaborated with a group of communists at Nanda". Lee Kuan Yew wrote:

> We had decided to make an example of prominent figures who had acted as front men for the communists, believing that their wealth and standing in the Chinese-speaking community gave them immunity. Number one on the list was Tan Lark Sye, then honorary president of the Chinese Chamber of Commerce and the founder of Nanyang University.[83]

The official statement from the Prime Minister's Office read:

> The government has decided that no man, whatever his wealth, status and standing, shall with impunity play stooge to the communists and jeopardise the peace and prosperity of Singapore and the amity and unity of the races of Malaysia. ... He had openly and blatantly intervened in these elections by signing statements drafted by these communists standing as Barisan Sosialis candidates denouncing the government, using as cover his so-called protection of Chinese language, culture and education.[84]

The message was very clear. Chinese merchants who had ambitions to play the political game of education, Chinese culture and identity could expect harsh treatment. Larger ideological concerns and ethnic tensions at the heart of the feeble Federation of Malaysia caused these issues to be off limits. The PAP used this reasoning as a pretence to take out a strong leader with much clout among the Chinese electorate, eradicating a possible avenue for an alternative to its own power base. Tan Lark Sye could remain in Singapore only because he had gone through the process of British naturalization in the 1950s. Disgruntled, he later took some of his business ventures abroad after Singapore's expulsion from Malaysia. In Ipoh, Malaysia, he set up the Tasek Cement complex. At the launch of this industrial venture, he emphasized the considerable financial involvement of Taiwanese partners, defiantly asking the Singapore government why these fiercest of Chinese anti-communists would ever cooperate with him if he had really been a communist sympathizer. He had a point because as a businessman and a multi-millionaire he was not interested in a communist ideological line. He did think that Chinese language, culture and identity were important issues for the Chinese in Singapore. No doubt his view was strengthened by the fact that the Chinese social pyramid provided him with status and power; however, that did not make him a pro-communist.

The disciplining of Tan Lark Sye, and through him the Ambitious leaders of the SCCC, was another step in the process towards complete PAP control. The technocratic PAP government took full advantage of the opportunity to chastise a key member of an alternative elite. The scare of the Barisan running off with the party branch organizations had made the PAP aware that it needed to have much more direct contact with and control over the political grassroots. During the merger referendum campaign and the campaign for the general election, the PAP had been forced to turn to the Ambitious leaders of the SCCC and to the traditional civic organizations to reach the grassroots. Not wanting to rely on this elite and its middlemen organizations, the PAP decided to build a new system in which the state and party became integrated. After the PAP victory in 1963, Lee Kuan Yew announced plans for the establishment of Citizens' Consultative Committees (CCCs) in each of the 51 constituencies, all of which were operating by February 1965. Street Committees underneath them provided structural support.[85] Meanwhile, the Barisan decided to turn their back on the political system by boycotting parliament in 1965, thereby depriving the legislature of an opposition for the next decade and a half.[86] With the Barisan almost out of the equation and having recently chastised the two most senior leaders of the Chamber, the other elite that could be a contender to its power, the PAP must have thought that it had dealt sufficiently with its rivals. A new development, however, showed the power and the unifying qualities of the SCCC.

5. War debt movement

Few social groups or organizations undertook nationwide actions or initiatives that openly went against the government. However, issues left over from World War II would rekindle such an emotional political atmosphere that Chinese Singaporeans again gathered behind their traditional *huiguan* leaders in the SCCC to demand redress for events that had occurred 20 years earlier. Their leaders chose to act and did so even though their short-term economic situation might be adversely affected. They acted despite the diplomatic embarrassment their action caused the government. This showed the continued strength of the Chamber as a societal leader and a political force.

Ghosts from the past

In January 1962, when the first find of remains of war victims was reported at Pasir Ris, the Chamber MC asked three senior members to investigate. On 28 February, they reported that remains were also found at Siglap Road and Jurong and they proposed to set up a committee to investigate, dig up the remains, give them a proper burial, and erect a monument. Consequently, a 15-man committee was formed and the government was asked to make representations to the Japanese government for compensation. The Chamber also warned politicians that they should not exploit the situation for partisan gain.[87]

The role of the SCCC in the issue of the reburial of the victims of Japanese violence during the war and the campaign for a Japanese payment of financial reparation reveals much about the position, power and self-perceived mission of the Chamber in this period. Of course the nature of the issue did play a part in the resolve of the Chamber. The anti-Japanese struggle had been a defining episode for the Chamber in the 1930s and the same was true for its role in the civil defence of Singapore in 1941–1942. The emotional backlash from the rekindling of memories of the wartime atrocities was immense. The *Sook Ching*, the purge that the Japanese carried out in Singapore in February 1942, was devastating for the local Chinese community and the subsequent forced payment of $50 million by the Malayan Chinese community to the Japanese was seen as an additional act of cruelty.

Immediately after the war, the Chamber had already taken an active stand on the issue of Japanese atrocities. The SCCC opened offices all over the island to collect information and eyewitness accounts to help those who would otherwise not testify at the War Crimes Investigation team. Information would be collated by the Chamber and passed on to the Chinese Consul General.[88] Not all war crime cases were being treated in the same way. To the Chinese, it seemed that the British were only interested in securing justice for crimes committed against a handful of their own people and cared little for the much greater brutality inflicted on the countless thousands of Chinese. The Chinese Massacre trial in March 1947, conducted by the colonial court, was the last trial to be held. Men such as Tan Kah Kee and Tay Koh-yat had worked hard to collect testimonies but evidence of individual responsibility was deemed inconclusive. Only two officers were sentenced to death while five received a life sentence. The Chinese community was incensed at this leniency. The Singapore Chinese Massacre Appeal Committee, led by Colonel Chuang and Tay Koh-yat, petitioned the Governor to review the sentences, but in vain.[89]

A letter by the Appeal Committee dated 8 July 1947 requested that the government include the issue of the forced $50 million contribution in the war reparation talks with Japan while intentions to erect a memorial and to rebury victims of the World War II massacre were voiced in the letter by Tay Koh-yat to the government.[90] During a meeting held at the SCCC, the Appeal Committee decided to build a memorial at the 5th milestone along Thomson Road.[91] In the minutes of a Chinese Advisory Board (CAB) meeting of 9 December 1949, the plans of the Chinese Appeal Committee for a memorial at Thompson Road were mentioned again and the president said that he was sure that the Board would wish to take an active interest.[92] No action was taken, however, either by the colonial government on war reparation payments or by the CAB on the monument. With the signing of the San Francisco treaty between World War II allies and the Japanese in 1951, in which Britain signed for all its dominions and colonies, all possibilities for reparations seemed to be foreclosed.

Still, the issue surfaced again in 1962 in the middle of the Examination Boycott Commission and the merger debate. It is unthinkable that the *Sook Ching*, or any of the details surrounding it, would be forgotten in the decades after the war. The report of 1946 had listed the massacre and mass gravesites, and to say that these were now "discovered" in 1962 seems euphemistic. More likely, Ambitious forces in the Chamber decided that it would pay political dividend to revive the issue.

The collective experience during the World War II was an important marker for the local identity of the Chinese of Singapore. Lee Kuan Yew understood the sensitivity of the issue but while the PM expressed his gratitude and pledged his support to the Chamber for its initiative, the initial government reaction was guarded. It seems that its actions were restricted to asking the British government for the British Military Authority (BMA) files on the massacre. The fact that Lee was on a state visit to Japan reinforced the government's cautious approach to the matter. After his return, Lee received Ko Teck Kin, Yap Pheng Geck and Ng Aik Huan on 28 June 1962, a meeting at which the three leaders asked Lee again for his approval. He scoffed at their renewed request and told them that they were just creating confusion and problems. Despite Lee's harsh words, the Chamber received permission on 23 July to exhume the bodies and the government donated a plot of land for a memorial site, also promising to pay for the construction of a road to the tune of S$15,000.[93]

The Chamber achieved a degree of success in forcing the government to acknowledge the issue. The fact that the government felt obliged to cover part of the cost indicates that it was aware of the sensitive nature of the issue. More was required, however, before the government would put Singapore's relationship with Japan, an important source of much-needed investment, at risk. Chamber or government activity regarding either the exhumation or Japanese compensation was not reported in late 1962 and early 1963.

A new sense of urgency

The issue was not going to go away, and during the 9 March 1963 Chamber Annual General Meeting the major point discussed was compensation. In a rare show of member pressure on their leaders, the traditional constituency of the Chamber made clear that it expected decisive action. Members were in tears asking Japan for financial reparation, and there was talk of a boycott of Japanese goods. Tan Lark Sye gave a determined and combative speech after he was added to the existing nine-man committee. The Chamber had spoken with the Japanese Ambassador at this stage and Ko Teck Kin reported that he had expressed compensation was a possibility. While Ko expressed belief in the sincerity and goodwill of the Japanese, Tan talked about Japanese stalling and repeatedly revived the images of wartime atrocities.[94] It is unclear if Tan's addition to the committee was caused by MC and member frustration with the lack of progress and a sense that the Chamber needed to show its teeth. Some among the Ambitious might have been questioning Ko's credentials by now. They were questioning whether his beating at the hands of the government the year before had made him weak.

Just four days after the AGM, PM Lee released a statement saying that Japan was willing to compensate but that no amount had been set. Lee said he would meet the Japanese ambassador the following week, but did not reveal the government's intentions or goals.[95] Perhaps in an attempt to prevent the government from dampening the issue with a blanket of diplomacy, the Chamber set up its own meetings with the ambassador but, although lengthy discussions were held, no tangible results were achieved.[96] By pushing both the government and the Japanese, the Chamber made sure that the war reparation issue stayed in the papers and the public's attention. The record shows that the government tried to negotiate with the Japanese one-on-one.[97] The government was trying to deny the Chamber a role as a legitimate representative on the issue.

Whether inspired by strategic considerations to counter these government intentions or just acting on the wave of emotions, the Chamber announced it would now act on its existing plans to start a public campaign to raise money for a monument to commemorate the victims. It was estimated that S$375,000 would be needed. To kick-start the campaign, a fundraiser was organized for 21 April, which saw the participation of 609 organizations of all races.[98] While the government did not want the Chamber to be a party in the diplomatic sphere of the negotiations with the Japanese, it had to accept SCCC primacy in the public domain and agreed early on to help build the memorial park with a dollar-for-dollar subsidy. Lee Kuan Yew was present at the 21 April event. Reportedly, $133,768 was donated that day.[99] All these developments received much media attention, but no progress was made in the discussions with the Japanese, whether by the government or by the Chamber.

Added urgency resulted from developments in the regional and international sphere. With merger imminent, the British and most certainly the Malay government became part of the equation. Lee Kuan Yew affirmed that the SCCC stepped up the pressure on him to bring closure to the issue, apparently because it felt that the matter needed to be resolved before foreign affairs passed into the hands of a central government that was predominantly Malay – one that would presumably feel less strongly about the atrocities committed against the Chinese. Lee was not anxious to take up the issue but could not remain idle. In his own words: "The problem was not going to go away. The Chinese Chamber of Commerce had decided to bring the matter to a head, and as I was planning to hold elections just before Malaysia Day (31 August), I had to press its demands, whatever the consequences in terms of Japanese investment".[100] Because the Chamber had its finger on the button of a highly emotional social issue, the mishandling or evasion of which could have great electoral repercussions, it could dictate the government's foreign policy agenda.

The British were concerned about this development and there was quite a voluminous correspondence between British officials in Singapore and the British embassy in Tokyo. In June, Deputy High Commissioner Moore described and explained the pressures on Lee Kuan Yew, who was "compelled to keep step with the very strong demands of the SCCC (some of whose members become very emotional on the subject)".[101]

A stage had been reached at which amounts of compensation were being discussed. The Chamber was increasing the pressure by making a moral claim connected to the $50 million demanded from the Chinese during the war. To back this demand, its tone became even more determined and strong. In a meeting on 5 July between Tanaka, Ko Teck Kin and the SCCC leadership, Ko had voiced strong opinions to Tanaka, saying that if demands were not met "one could not tell how the Chinese would react".[102]

Making use of this influence on a key group of voters, the SCCC decided to increase pressure even more. Government negotiations with the Japanese failing to produce results, the Chamber decided to hold a mass meeting at the Padang on 25 August.[103] When plans became known, Lee Kuan Yew advised Tanaka to publish detailed ideas of a Japanese atonement package before the rally in order to make it obsolete, and thereby prevent an outburst of anti-Japanese feelings.[104]

Despite these attempts, as Lee said in his memoirs, the planning for the rally was coordinated with the government. PAP chairman Toh Chin Chye and Ko Teck Kin agreed on the resolutions that would be adopted a few days before. Ko had been his savvy self in realizing that the PAP government would be unhappy as long as the rally was going to be a purely Chinese issue and, therefore, had persuaded leaders of the other ethnic groups to join the rally. Lee decreed that existing Japanese projects would receive immunity, but ruled that no more visas would be issued to Japanese wanting to open new enterprises in Singapore until Tokyo atoned.[105] On 25 August, a crowd of 100,000 was reported and three resolutions were adopted: (1) To unite with Malaya, Sabah and Sarawak to make a joint claim, (2) To boycott Japanese goods, and (3) To ask the government to sever diplomatic relations if Japan would not pay.[106]

The British reacted with disappointment at the demands. They observed that it was obvious from Lee Kuan Yew's speech at the rally that the Singapore government had been forced to change its policy towards Japan. The Japanese had told British officials that, in their view, the agitation on atonement was communist inspired and exploited. Moreover, the Japanese accused Lee Kuan Yew of going back on the gentlemen's agreement twice.[107]

Ironically, the campaign that was fuelled by a sense of urgency to resolve the issue before Malaysia came into being ultimately resulted in demands that included consolidation of Singaporean and Malayan claims. Because the issue was not resolved before Malaysia Day on 16 September, the government in Kuala Lumpur became a central actor. A change in leverage on "the state" in its new form was visible immediately. The SCCC could not successfully pressure the central government as it had done with the Singapore government. The Japanese were acutely aware of this shift and when the Singapore government tried to get a high Japanese official and SCCC delegates together in Kuala Lumpur, the Japanese government was adamant that they would not discuss these matters with organizations like the SCCC anymore.[108] The SCCC continued to meet and discuss the subject but its tone had lost ferocity.[109] The Chamber leadership had also taken on new roles in Malaysia. Ko Teck Kin, now a senator, held talks with the Japanese; but he now formally represented the Malaysian government in the negotiations, not the Chinese of Singapore or Malaysia.[110] The Chamber would have to try to resolve the matter in the context of politics in Malaysia.

Attempts to revive the issue were made more than a year after Malaysia Day. Because of the political reality of Malaysia, however, the SCCC was not the Chinese representative to the central government. This role had fallen on a joint-action committee led by the Associated Chinese Chambers of Commerce of Malaya (ACCCM) but little progress was made. The SCCC did not back down and reiterated its claim of $50 million for Singapore and when the ACCCM met again, two points were forwarded by the Singaporean side: $180 million compensation for the whole of Malaysia and a leading role for the Tunku.[111] However, cooperation within the framework of Malaysia was far from ideal. It would take two more years for Singapore's exit from Malaysia before the issue was finally resolved. After Separation, the Chamber continued its initiatives and, in late 1966, the Japanese agreed to pay $50 million, half in compensation and half as a loan. A memorial was built at Beach Road and 15 February, the anniversary of the Japanese invasion in 1942, was picked by the Chamber as Memorial Day; every year since 1968 it has organized a solemn commemorative meeting on that date.[112]

6. Malaysia politics, 1963–1965

Ethnicity, economics and representation were at the heart of politics for two whole years from September 1963 until August 1965, during which Singapore was part of the Federation of Malaysia. At that time, it was not surprising that the Chamber was an active participant in this process. As traditional Chinese leaders in a new nation-state in which the Malays were the majority, they felt strongly about representing their ethnic group. As businessmen, they had supported the idea of merger, but soon the central government in Kuala Lumpur tried to impose a higher degree of control on their businesses than they were used to. Their strategic position in the political and economic arena meant, however, that the Chamber had a bargaining position in both the Singapore and Malaysian sides. Politically the Chamber controlled a voter base, while economically, Singapore Chinese businessmen were vital for the economic development of Malaysia. The tensions resulted in the Chamber becoming, at times, the ally of the Singapore government.

Growing apart: ethnic, political and economic tensions

The question of ethnicity was central to the political power struggle, the main issue being who would represent the Chinese of Malaysia. The government in Kuala Lumpur clearly did not want the PAP to enter the political fray in the peninsula. One academic observed that while it was not conclusively established that Lee Kuan Yew thought the PAP would be able to take the place of the Malayan Chinese Association (MCA) in the Alliance, he did make suggestions that the United Malays National Organisation (UMNO) might have to reconsider the legitimate leadership in the towns where the MCA would lose to the PAP.[113] The PAP decision to participate in the Federation elections proved to be a reason for great unease on the Malay side. The elections were held on 25 July 1964 and the PAP actively campaigned. Their rallies received good attendance but resulted in only one seat. While the election proved that the PAP could not take the place of the MCA, it had antagonized an important Malay-oriented faction of UMNO.

This faction engaged in a campaign to limit Singapore's influence on the central government, portraying Lee Kuan Yew and the PAP as anti-Malay. In articles in the Malay press, they made it seem that the PAP was out to destroy the special privileges of the Malays enshrined in the Federation constitution. Lee made the position of the Singapore state government clear when he said that every effort would be made to train Malays for top positions, but that preferential treatment by law was out of the question in Singapore. No quota system for employment opportunities for Malays was to be put in place and there would also be no special licences or land reservations for Malays.[114]

Racial tension came to a boil on 21 July 1964. A Malay/Muslim march in Singapore on the birthday of the Prophet Muhammad escalated into three days of riots, leaving 23 killed and 454 injured.[115] In this explosive situation, the Chamber took the initiative to calm down flared tempers. During the riots, Ko Teck Kin and Yap Pheng Geck returned from Kuala Lumpur and called a special meeting for 26 July at which the leaders of the various Chambers of Commerce discussed the issue. Prices, especially those of foodstuffs, had skyrocketed and the SCCC sent out a circular to all its retailers and organizational affiliates to ask them to refrain from price hikes.[116]

The riots had a profound effect on the leadership of the Chamber. It also made the Chinese community in general wonder whether being part of Malaysia was such a good idea. The ethnic and religious frenzy displayed in the riots had a clear connection to the political tension between the Singapore and the central governments. The whole issue sensitized Chinese Singaporeans to their Chinese identity. The leaders of the Chamber felt a strong responsibility for the well-being of their traditional constituency. Lee Kuan Yew recounts that Ko came to his residence one night "looking most worried. Having appealed to the Chinese-speaking to vote for alternative "A" in the referendum to join Malaysia, he felt keenly responsible for their present predicament, their helplessness when caught between Malay rioters and a Malay police force and army that were openly anti-Chinese. What could be done? Ko observed to Lee, "We cannot let down the Chinese people." Ko gave a clear signal in private that certain circles of the Chinese leadership were starting to think seriously about the desirability of an independent Singapore state. He told Lee, "You have good relations with the British Labour Party, can you not get them to help us out of this difficulty? Let us be on our own. It is terrible to live like this".[117] Of course this was, as yet, unspeakable in public. At the opening of the new Chamber building the week after, both Ko and Lee spoke confidently about the future of Malaysia and of Singapore's role in it.

On the 20 September official opening of the new Chamber building, Chinese organizations from all over the region were present, and Ko Teck Kin and others emphasized the role of Singapore in the new multi-racial Malaysia. Ko noted that "to establish Singapore as the New York of Malaysia we need two factors – co-operation, unity and harmony among the various races and co-ordination between the Central and State governments".[118] In the commemorative publication, the official Chamber line was reiterated: "Now the SCCC is neither an exclusive machinery of the Chinese merchants nor a racial organisation. It is now a unit of the Chinese citizens who are loyal to Malaysia and play their part in nation building".[119] Lee Kuan Yew also spoke, and his words were a shade more loaded: "After these ugly riots in July and again in September what of the future? Is there a future for

Ethnicity and modernity embodied in the new Chamber building, 1964.

Collection of Chinese Chamber of Commerce.
Courtesy of the National Archives of Singapore

and identity as the old building. It was still located close to the sources and symbols of state power – the Parliament House, the City Hall and the Supreme Court. However, the pure Chinese mansion evoking a traditional imagery of a connection with the motherland and a Chinese identity was replaced by a building that projected more messages. It was presented as a "splendid fusion between East and West" with the "outward appearance modelled after Chinese architectural design and the interior decoration following the Western pattern". With its 10 storeys, it was considered a modern skyscraper of sorts but it was topped by a Chinese-style roof and protected on the street-side by a nine-dragon wall and two large lion statues. Its interior celebrated utility, efficiency and modern management.

Architecturally and spatially, the new building was just as much a signboard of the Chamber's goals

Chinese in Malaysia? I confidently say yes, if they are Malaysians, and as long as there is a Malaysia".[120]

Politically speaking, the position of Singapore in the Federation looked untenable, not only from Singapore's point of view but from Kuala Lumpur as well. From December 1964 onwards, there was talk of constitutional rearrangements to the Singapore-Federation relation. Under pressure of Malay political forces and returning to his own previous doubts on the inclusion of Singapore in the Federation, the Tunku proposed a looser partnership with two independent states.

On the economic front, the common market had been a central issue for Singapore. During the finalization of the terms for merger in mid-July 1963, the two sides had reached an agreement. It included the establishment of a Customs Advisory Board and a gradual move towards a common market through a number of steps over 12 years with Singapore retaining its entrepot status.[121]

The mutual dependency of the Malayan and Singaporean economies had seen little change. Singapore's trade with Malaya amounted to roughly 20 per cent of its total and had a value of about S$2 billion in the early 1960s.[122] The purely economic logic of the symbiotic relationship of hinterland and entrepot remained. But the ethnic division between Malay agricultural producers and workers, on the one hand, and Chinese plantation owners, external financiers and traders, on the other, became much more contentious now that the political arenas of Singapore and Malaya were joined. The position of the Chamber within this ethnic divide was clearly on the side of the bosses, the financiers and plantation owners, and the free-trade supporters.

In the period just after merger, the Chamber had been positive about the economic possibilities and had tried to shape policy in favour of its interests. It projected the leading role Singapore entrepreneurs could play in Malaysia but soon, relations quickly became very tense politically and ethnically. Federal Finance Minister Tan Siew Sin fanned the flames with his budget speech on 25 November 1964, in which he announced tough new measures to increase revenue. These included a turnover tax and a payroll tax for all trading and business houses. Both were felt to affect Singapore and Chinese businesses disproportionately.[123]

The SCCC sent a memorandum to Tan Siew Sin saying that the taxes would strangle the diminishing trade and infant industries, as well as assist Indonesia in its *Konfrontasi* policy. Moreover, the memorandum argued that the turnover tax would lead to a rise in cost of living, while the payroll tax was expected to signal lay-offs and the shunning of investment in labour intensive industries.[124] From the point of view of the Singapore government, it felt as if Tan Siew Sin was out to block Singapore's economic progress.

The parting of ways

The political battle between the PAP and Malaysian UMNO was coming to a boil when the PAP decided that, in response to what it perceived as a Malay-dominated Malaysia, it would organize a united opposition in favour of a Malaysian Malaysia. To that end, the PAP took the initiative for the Malaysian Solidarity Convention in May 1965, together with other parties.[125] In the following months, parliamentary sessions in Kuala Lumpur were filled with abuse. Tan Siew Sin declared that it was impossible for Kuala Lumpur and Singapore to cooperate while Lee Kuan Yew remained PM, and UMNO extremists asked for Lee's arrest.

Political tension was again compounded by the decisions of the central government on economic policy and the two issues were becoming increasingly interconnected. Tan Siew Sin ordered the closure of the Bank of China (BOC) in Singapore, a bank important to its economy as it financed many small Chinese businessmen and also the important food trade from China.[126] The central government argued that the presence of the bank of the communist PRC posed a threat to the internal security of the Federation. It chose to take an essentially political look at the issue, which had immediate economic repercussions for the Chinese in Singapore. Because of this, the Chamber viewed the order not only as an economic setback but also as a repressive ethnic measure.[127]

Next, the central government announced a quota system for imports, a step that would again be detrimental to the Singaporean economy. The Chamber called a meeting with eight other commercial organizations and senior Trade Development Board (TDB) officials in Singapore.[128] While commercial organizations continued to communicate their problems and reservations on the BOC and tax issues to the central government, it seemed that Kuala Lumpur had no intention of changing its policy.[129] All these events took place while a break up of the Federation of Malaysia already seemed inevitable to many, and real solutions were no longer expected. Singapore was expelled from the Federation and was forced to declare its independence on 9 August 1965.

7. Chastised again: the case of the "Chinese chauvinists"

To understand the third instance in which top Chamber leaders, after Ko Teck Kin and Tan Lark Sye, were publicly chastised by the PAP government, we must first look at the election struggle inside the Chamber through which Soon Peng Yam, the last of the Ambitious presidents, came to power. After separation of Singapore from Malaysia, his views on the role of the Chamber and on the place of Chinese language and culture in the newly independent nation led to another showdown with the state. Traditional and communally-based leadership clashed again with the modern, technocratic and nationally-based leadership.

Competition over power in the Chamber

Ko Teck Kin had consolidated his hold on the presidency for an unprecedented three consecutive terms amounting to seven years (1958–1965). In the 1965 election, however, his succession was hotly contested in a showdown between Hokkien factions. Two issues were central in this battle of "old and established" against "young and dynamic": constitutional change

Soon Peng Yam: Chinese language champion.
Courtesy of the National Archives of Singapore

A Hokkien hailing from Tongan, Soon was born in 1912. He received primary education in China at Tan Kah Kee's Jimei School but soon immigrated to Singapore. He joined the Chamber leadership at 35 when he became a Council Member in 1947. He was an admirer and protégé of Tan Kah Kee, from whom he inherited a penchant for Chinese education. Eventually he would also take over one of Tan Kah Kee's power positions as President of the Ee Hoe Hean Club. Every week at the club, older members met to eat lunch in the manner Tan was said to have done: simple rice porridge and salt fish.[130]

Soon read a lot when working in one of his early jobs and, at that time, wrote short stories and satirical essays for a Chinese language publication. Later in life

and external strategy. These issues pitted Ko Teck Kin and his preferred successor Ng Aik Huan against Ko's former allies, Kheng Chin Hock and Soon Peng Yam.

Essentially, Soon presented himself in the 1965 election as a leader who would defend Chinese culture and the interest of the Chinese-speaking. Emphasizing his Tan Kah Kee heritage and his pedigree in culture and education, he implied that Ko could no longer lay claim to representing these interests. It seems that Soon was of the opinion that Ko had been in power for too long and that his independence of the state had slowly been compromised. He had helped the PAP to win the merger referendum, was greatly humiliated by the same, and then accepted a PAP government appointment as Malaysian Senator. Ko's independence had been compromised and, therefore, Soon wanted to take over the Chamber to safeguard the Chinese agenda.

Soon and Ko had been allies in the past, with Soon serving Ko as vice president from 1960 to 1962. Two theories exist for their falling out and the rift between Ko and Kheng. In the 1962 election, the Hokkien elected Ko unanimously. One source alleged that Ko's choice of vice presidents, in which he dropped Soon Peng Yam, caused the break up with Kheng.[133]

from about 1950–1954, he studied English with a personal English tutor. In an interview in 1980, he said that studying English was important because it was crucial for his later business.

Soon's core business was in the building industry through his Sim Lim Company which started out doing a lot of work for the British military bases. Later he diversified into finance, real estate and development. When industrialization became the focus of Singapore's economic development, he was involved in the initiative for an iron and steel plant and also participated in roof tile and Formica manufacturing. Later

he withdrew from the first venture while the two other businesses were unsuccessful.[131]

Soon was one of the Ambitious Chamber leaders, not only because he advocated an active role in politics for the SCCC but also because he was deeply involved in Chinese education and culture. For the Hokien Huay Kuan, in which he was an active member, he was in charge of the building of new premises for two of its schools.[132]

Other sources said that the reason for the disputes of Kheng and Soon with Ko lay in the controversy surrounding the naming of the big meeting hall of the new chamber building in 1964 with Soon and Kheng wanting to honour Tan Kah Kee, but Ko pushing for Tunku Abdul Rahman.

In the 1965 Chamber election campaign, the formation of power blocs within the Hokkien speech group and the securing of votes through the registration of new members was the main feature. The pattern was familiar considering the battle in 1958. Early on, the two Hokkien blocs put in their new membership applications. Reactions were not slow in coming. The smaller dialect groups, wary of being ground between two Hokkien millstones, had apparently logged many new applications as well. The Sanjiang and the Hakka, especially, had chosen this strategy to force the Hokkien to take them seriously.[134] It cannot be a coincidence that when the new Chamber officials were eventually installed, the Sanjiang were honoured through the appointment of a vice president from their speech group. This was the first and only time in Chamber history that this small minority group was included at the highest level.

One more controversy surrounded the election, breathing new life into the discussions about the large number of new membership applications, the control of voting blocks, and the need for constitutional change. Kheng revealed six addresses at which hundreds of members were registered and all six were connected to Ko, his businesses or his family members. The implication was clear. Kheng alleged that Ko was involved in vote-buying, meaning that he paid the membership fees, registered these members at addresses he owned or controlled and, thereby, was assured of votes in the election. The vote-buying allegations really sparked the election fracas.[135] Ko pushed Ng Aik Huan as his preferred replacement while Kheng backed Soon Peng Yam.

Ko, addressing the charges of vote-buying, claimed that the "rumours were a bad joke by Hokkien directors who were up to no good". Kheng then accused Ko of meddling and linked the huge Sanjiang increase in September 1964 to him. The *Nanyang Siangpau* wrote that it was unlikely "there was nobody buying votes with money" and warned that the Chamber's status and standing were at stake. After more controversy, the group around Ko and Ng Aik Huan withdrew from the election.[136] When the office bearers were chosen, Soon's victory was obvious. He was elected with a great majority, but in the election of the honorary presidents Ko Teck Kin was not chosen whereas all the other living ex-presidents were, indicating a slap in the face for Ko Teck Kin by the Soon-controlled MC.[137] More indications of continuing bad blood between Ko and Soon came at the installation on 15 March. Ko spoke only a few words before handing over the official "regalia" to Soon. He then left while the programme continued.[138]

The more cautious Ko, who had become more conservative in his view of how the Chamber should operate, was defeated by Soon who claimed he was the true defender of the interest of the Chinese community against the encroachment of the PAP government into Chinese culture. Ko had aligned himself consciously with the powers-that-be and his preference for the status quo within the Chamber was clear from his attempts to put his own candidate in the driving seat. This was exactly the point on which he was defeated by Kheng and Soon. Effectively they accused him of being fraudulent and implied that he had grown too fond of status and power, thereby losing his independence from the government. Soon especially was convinced that the Chamber still had a leading role as a social and political organization in Singapore, and even more so after separation from Malaysia.

Separation!

Soon Peng Yam was relieved that Singapore had exited Malaysia: "I felt that I was just like a daughter-in-law having to serve three mothers-in-law.

The central government of Malaysia, the Singapore government and the Chamber membership itself. After the separation, the Malaysian government was no longer a mother-in-law".[139] Most businessmen welcomed liberation from Kuala Lumpur's economic policy with unconcealed glee.

Lee Kuan Yew, appearing in tears on television when announcing separation, was devastated. His feelings strongly contrasted with what he pictured as the scenes in Chinatown. "They set off firecrackers to celebrate their liberation from communal rule by the Malays from Kuala Lumpur, carpeting the streets with red paper debris".[140] Most Singaporeans agreed with Soon and did not share the government's dismay. They were relieved to be spared further bouts of communal tension, which had caused the racial riots in 1964.

Lee's dismay was also not shared by the country's most prominent foreign advisor. Winsemius, the former leader of the UN development mission and now a regular consultant to the Singapore government, said in an interview in 1981 that

> ... to my amazement, a discussion had started: can Singapore survive? ... That is the only time I got angry in Singapore. I said: 'now you have your hands free – use them!' It was the best thing that happened during the whole period from 1960 till today.[141]

The Chamber welcomed a number of policies that resulted. It expressed relief and said that it was a very wise move of the Singapore government to abolish the turnover tax and to let the BOC open again.[142] The rejoicing businessmen remained convinced of one thing though: Singapore needed Malaysia's market, sources of capital and trade outlets.[143]

The Singapore Minister of Finance, Lim Kim San, met with the Chamber within days of separation to discuss the new national economic policy. He said the government would put equal emphasis on commerce and industry. He also said that close ties with Malaysia were to remain. Kheng Chin Hock in a statement approved of the government policy of trading with all nations. His implication was that trade with the PRC should be restored. He said Singapore should focus on China and India while maintaining good relations with the brother states of Malaysia, Sabah, Sarawak and Brunei. Soon Peng Yam proposed to Lim Kim San that the SCCC would organize a trade mission to China.[144] The *Nanyang Siangpau* reported that Foreign Minister Rajaratnam said relations with China needed to be maintained and consolidated. The Chamber, of course, supported this view wholeheartedly.[145]

Developing its vision for Singapore's future as a trading nation, the Chamber decided to go ahead with a trade delegation to China. Plans needed to be made quickly to be in time for the annual Canton trade fair in early October. Further ahead, the Chamber saw the need and its own task to organize delegations to countries in Southeast Asia, Europe, Africa, etc. It also advocated removing taxes and regulations that had been put in place when Singapore was part of Malaysia. The Chamber argued that deregulation was necessary to safeguard Singapore's role as an entrepot.[146] Soon reported to the MC on a meeting he had with Lim Kim San and Lee Kuan Yew. The ministers had told him that the four chambers of commerce would be invited on government trade delegations in the future. He said, however, that it looked as if the government did not appreciate the Chamber running away with the portfolio of foreign commercial affairs.[147]

The hammer comes down

Amidst the changes following separation from Malaysia, the SCCC saw opportunities to shape policies. The most controversial of these attempts was the question of Mandarin as a national language of Singapore. Of course, the Chamber leadership was still reeling from the two beatings it had received through Ko Teck Kin and Tan Lark Sye over the combustible combination of ethnicity, education and politics. In the minds of Soon and his closest ally Kheng, however, language was a marker of Chinese identity, dignity and pride. Now that the Malay majority in Kuala Lumpur was no longer calling the shots, they felt that the pendulum could swing back in favour of a logical and just place for the Chinese language and, therefore, education in Singapore.

During a Chamber MC meeting shortly after separation, amendments to the Singapore constitution were discussed. A number of members emphasized that "the status of the Chinese language should not be overlooked", and that, "if not spelled out in the constitution, the trend of English language suppressing Chinese language will continue and will lead to problems in society". Deputy Prime Minister Toh Chin Chye had said that great caution had to be exercised over the language issue and pointed out that the constitution already named all four languages as administrative languages, but some members of the Chamber doubted this statement.[148]

During the meeting Kheng pointed out that Mandarin was mentioned in the constitution as one of the four languages that could be used in parliament but that it was not stipulated as an official national language and proposed that this should be rectified. Kheng's motion was adopted and a memorandum was submitted to the government saying: "for more effective government, and for the sake of promoting greater goodwill and harmony between the Chinese community and the other communities, the Chinese language as one of the official languages must be written into the new constitution of our nation".[149]

Lee Kuan Yew reacted immediately and the Prime Minister's office released a statement the next day asserting that Malay, Mandarin, Tamil and English were all equal, official languages in Singapore, and that Malay would be the national language. The PM invited representatives from the four chambers so he could explain the language issue. Minister of Internal Affairs Inche Othman Wok warned the "language chauvinists" as well, saying that the government would not hesitate to take action against them.[150]

Lee Kuan Yew made his point in no mean terms: "I would like to hear the end of all this. Language, culture, religion: They are not political issues." He admonished the Chamber for this dangerous talk saying: "I had expected the old boys' associations – all these little boys who went to primary school and never went on to secondary school – to say this because they are of that kind of intellectual level." Even more scathingly and with more than a touch of sarcasm, he added: "I was deeply grieved when I saw that it was the intellectuals of the Chinese Chamber of Commerce – men responsible for the commerce and industry of our country, our nation – who have said these very unwise things." Singling out Soon Peng Yam in particular, Lee continued to explain that what had really "gotten under my skin" was that the Chamber should have known that there was no issue to begin with. Deputy Prime Minister Toh Chin Chye had assured Soon Peng Yam on a mutual flight that the status of the four languages would be enshrined in the new constitution. Soon still pushed the point and for that Lee Kuan Yew called him a "cowardly opportunist".[151]

Lee's attacks on the Chamber were not over. He summoned the leaders of the four chambers to his office again. Under the bright television lights, and in front of the cameras recording for a national broadcast the next day, he gave these powerful and rich men a lesson in politics. The report mentions him targeting Kheng for what amounted to nothing less than humiliation. Lee remarked sarcastically, "I am told the abacus is quite good … Mr. Kheng Chin Hock probably practices every day. So he can count." He also targeted Tan Lark Sye once more calling him "a mere tool of the communists" who "ate his own spittle", "a creeper and a crawler".[152] Six days later, the SCCC MC meeting dropped the petition on Chinese as an official language.[153]

After Ko Teck Kin and Tan Lark Sye, two more representatives of the Ambitious leaders had been chastised. The decisive action by the PAP government confirms again that it had firmly appropriated the right to govern without input or pressure from citizen groups. Soon and Kheng, acting upon their role as traditional Chinese community leaders, thought they could challenge, or at least influence, the state because they saw their representative role as defenders of Chinese interests as legitimate. The PAP made abundantly clear that such behaviour was unacceptable and would carry a price both institutionally and individually. The Chamber had learned its lesson. After Soon Peng Yam completed the habitual two terms as president, a new generation of Chamber leadership would take over from 1969.

Concluding remarks

The relationship between the SCCC and the state in this period was troubled with the contest over power and influence between three types of elites with three types of power bases lying at its heart: the Ambitious Chamber leaders grounded in traditional, communally-based power and wealth; the left-wing opposition of the Barisan with a foundation in ideological power; and the technocratic moderate wing of the PAP based on expertise. The contest was decided hands down in favour of the government. By the time Singapore was expelled from Malaysia, the PAP state had become an omni-present and dominant force. With "macho meritocracy",[154] the PAP governed the island and in the process eliminated all alternative bases of power. The left-wing had been instrumental in the PAP's rise to power but had turned into a liability and a threat to the technocrats in government. The union movement, on which the Barisan was based, was brought to heel and many union and Barisan leaders were incarcerated during Operation Cold Store. As a result, the ideological elite ceased to be an important factor in Singapore politics.

Grounded as it was in the Singapore Chinese community, the multi-purpose elite of the Chamber, whose orientation was pro-trade and pro-local Chinese, could not be so easily dismissed by the PAP. In the main political issues of the time, centred around joining and operating within Malaysia, economic development and the representation of the Chinese of Singapore, the Ambitious leadership of the SCCC had clear goals and strategies: Singapore's incorporation in Malaysia through a common market with the preservation of its trading entrepot status and maximum built-in security for the legal, social and cultural position of the Chinese population. These goals and ambitions led the Chamber to cooperate as well as compete with the PAP government.

Economically, the Chamber's advocacy of trade as the prime economic activity of Singapore was markedly different from the PAP technocrats' industrialization plans and, as a consequence, the SCCC lost influence on national economic policy. Politically, however, because the PAP had lost most of its grassroots connections to the Barisan, it needed the communal prestige and network of the Chamber to secure merger. Similarly, after having joined Malaysia, the Chamber could provide legitimacy for the PAP's claim of representing the Chinese of Malaysia and was, therefore, allied with the Singapore government against the central government in Kuala Lumpur. In these cases, the Chamber shared common interests and goals with the PAP. The SCCC leaders felt empowered and strengthened in their ambitions. They operated upon this strength in the case of the Japanese war reparation issue and, indeed, had the power and influence to force the PAP to deal with the matter on the Chamber's terms. To the PAP government, this strength of the Chamber posed a threat to its authority as the ruling elite, especially when the SCCC or its leaders acted in apparent cooperation with the ideological elite of the Barisan, as it did in a number of cases concerning Chinese identity and education. In doing so, the Chamber was an ethnically-defined and communally-based alternative elite to the technocratic elite of the PAP, and on many issues a conservative alternative to the Barisan.

The Chamber's utility and threat to the government were two sides of the same coin, originating in the nature of its power, the characteristics of its leadership, and the structure of its constituency. The power of the multi-purpose elite of the Chamber was based on the status and wealth of its leaders. Their domination of the pyramid of Chinese organizations meant that they wielded great influence over a large segment of the electorate. It also meant that their continued status depended on their representation of Chinese interests. Chinese culture and identity and, therefore, education and language were not just subjects of interest to the Chamber leaders; these issues were a vital, constituent part of their self-image, elite status and orientation.

To the government though, ethnically-based politics in Singapore was unacceptable because it would pose a serious challenge both to the legitimacy of the small, Western-educated elite and to its ability to govern efficiently and without dissent. Communally-based politics would enable alternative elites to pull strings, lay claims on national assets and influence policies. It was because of this that the issue of Chinese education and language was so contentious since the Barisan also continued to make it a vehicle to appeal to Chinese voters. The Chamber's involvement in these issues, therefore, amounted to a direct political threat to the PAP, which decided that the Chinese business leaders had to be taught who was boss. Humiliating Ko Teck Kin in public for his activities regarding education, stripping Tan Lark Sye of his citizenship on account of his support for the Barisan, and chastising Soon Peng Yam and Kheng Chin Hock because of their call for Mandarin as a national language, served to get the message across that the government was now responsible for and in complete control of economic, social, cultural and political issues.

CHAPTER FIVE

1966–1984
Differing worldviews of
Chamber and state:
Marginalization and uncertainty

... the real driving force behind the Chamber of the past was the fluid
and uncertain circumstances which so often required physical unity for
survival in the face of common threats. Now that there are no longer those
political undermining factors, there is no need either for the Chamber
to seek political stature to protect itself ... While many successful
Chinese entrepreneurs today may well continue to subscribe to the
SCCCI, this may be no more than symbolic and atavistic ritual ...[1]

AS SINGAPORE CAME TO TERMS with its expulsion from the Malaysian
Federation in 1965, it faced a number of challenges. Invoking an atmosphere
of continuous external ethnic threat, PAP leaders said apprehensively that
Chinese Singapore had to survive in a sea of Malays. Adding to these regional
tensions, the Cold War raged in Southeast Asia with the escalation of fighting
in Vietnam. Economically speaking, Singapore became involved in the New
International Division of Labour (NIDL), a pattern in which Western and
Japanese multinational companies (MNCs) were looking for cheap and
reliable locations to base production for exports to their home markets.

The government worldview was that of the developmental state.
Economic development and the creation of jobs, housing, infrastructure
and disposable income were crucial for the legitimacy of the PAP party/state,
and its chosen development strategy was rapid industrialization through
foreign direct investment (FDI). The PAP geared its socio-economic
policy towards pleasing foreign investors and it took an active part in the
economy through government-linked companies (GLCs). The technocratic
elite became the planner, facilitator and executor of economic and social
development. In order to ensure control and influence at the grassroots

level, the government established an intricate symbiosis of party and state, sidelining traditional social structures. The government was very successful in its endeavours because it secured robust economic growth, resulting in significant improvement in the population's standard of living.

This chapter analyses the Chamber's attempt and failure to comply with the dominant political and economic perspective of the PAP party/state or share the credit for national success. The relative importance of the Chamber in Singapore continued to decline because the Chamber continued to act upon its traders' worldview, based on trade, regional networks and small and medium-size family firms, that fundamentally differed from that of the state. With the experience of having seen the generation of their predecessors disciplined by the PAP over cultural and educational matters, the new leaders, who were more modern, better educated and were also much less ambitious in politics, are introduced as "the Pragmatists". This new elite was willing to partake in the state industrialization project in addition to their trading and services business, seizing opportunities in both spheres. But their constituency of traders, on whom they depended for their status, did not have this luxury of choice and, hence, forced the traders' worldview. This prevented the Chamber leadership from creating meaningful cooperation with the technocrats, needed to secure a significant role for Chinese business in Singapore's economic development.

The SCCC's activities concentrated on trade and trade promotion as it tried to carve out a role for itself through the organization of trade and friendship delegations. In another major project, the Chamber successfully tried to free Singapore traders from the monopolistic grip of the Western shipping conferences that dominated international transport. In both cases, the PAP turned out not to be a natural ally. Trade was peripheral to the state development plan and, therefore, received little attention or support. Where the traders' orientation interfered with the developmental state, the PAP actively pursued strategies that were diametrically opposed to the Chamber. Similarly, when state-run industrial and trading companies competed with local and, often Chinese, entrepreneurs, the PAP government invariably supported the state sector.

Concerning issues of values and culture in this period, in which nation and citizens were looking for identities, Chamber and state did not always find common ground when they were involved in activities and campaigns. While the SCCC continued to see culture and identity as almost absolute twinned entities that were steeped in tradition and rich in historical examples of their usefulness, the government was looking more for a tool to counter undesired behaviour and promote desired habits. While the government and the Chamber often used the same terminology – an indication that the latter was attempting to comply – they spoke a different language and operated from opposing worldviews.

When the first cracks were starting to show in the Singapore success model in the early 1980s, the government was grappling to find answers but failed to implement decisive changes in policy. The Chamber, likewise, struggled with its role and identity as it was increasingly marginalized.

1. The PAP state: economic development, political strategy and social control, 1966–1979

With the expulsion from Malaysia and the resulting establishment of the independent nation-state of Singapore, the Chamber found itself again in changing circumstances. As a period of consolidation of political power started, rapid economic development was the ultimate yardstick for the PAP government because it was the source of political legitimacy and, therefore, the PAP started to shape society in what it deemed to be the most rational and efficient way. The economic development plan necessitated new legislation to control labour and the efficient use of resources, while political continuity prompted the PAP to implement a new political representational structure from the grassroots to the government. The rationale of economic development permeated throughout Singapore society and bore testament to the technocratic orientation of the PAP elite. Chamber president Soon Peng Yam realized that the dominant factors in Singapore's social, political and economic issues had changed after separation. In a speech delivered at the New Year celebration in 1966, Soon spoke at length on capital sourcing, labour-capital relations and market expansion as well as, characteristically, on the question of how to continue trade development with an industry promotion policy.[2]

The Chamber diamond jubilee

Just months later, the Chamber had reason to celebrate, as it reached the venerable age of 60. No holds were barred to make this an occasion to remember and to create a stage where the Chamber could shine as one of the leading organizations of the young nation. Three full days of activities and events were planned and hundreds of guests from many countries in the region came to participate in the diamond jubilee, emphasizing the extensive regional trading network in which the Chamber performed a leading role. Central on the guest list were 365 representatives from the Chinese Chambers of Commerce, hailing from Hong Kong, Macao, the Philippines, Brunei and others, as well as various States of Malaysia including Sabah and Sarawak. The festivities were also attended by government ministers, MPs, members of the diplomatic corps, representatives from other chambers of commerce in Singapore and leading commercial and industrial personalities. Dragon and lion dances welcomed the guests as they gathered at the new Chamber building before a thunderous salvo of firecrackers signified the official start of the ceremonies. Over the three days, there were speeches, company visits, and plenty of joyful diversions. The showpiece event was the buffet dinner for 600 guests that was served at the Chamber building's roof-top garden, while an hour-long firework display, worth over $20,000, was set off from nearby Fort Canning Hill.[3] The Chamber was out to impress and its leadership had a point to make.

President Soon Peng Yam and Jubilee Committee Chairman Kheng Chin Hock were the two principal hosts and speakers for the Chamber during the festivities. From the point of view of the waxing and waning of different generations of leadership, the celebrations should be viewed as the last great public showcase of the Ambitious. A new generation would soon take over the helm. Enjoying his moment in the spotlight, Soon made it clear that he was still as ambitious as ever regarding the Chamber's role, declaring that:

> The future task of our Chamber is not only to mind our own business, but also reflect the views and aspirations of the people to the government. We will speak loud and clear what we know without reservations so that we may help the government to frame policies beneficial to the entire people and build our new born nation into a progressive, democratic and prosperous state where people of all races are equal.[4]

Finance Minister Lim Kim San was the guest of honour and the principal speaker from the Singapore government. He praised the Chamber for its commercial and civic contributions to the development of Singapore and stressed that it should now lead the search for new outlets of trade and markets for the nation's products. With more than a twist of irony Soon and Kheng were now on the receiving end of a glowing tribute from Lee Kuan Yew who, only months earlier, had called both men a danger to Singapore. Lee praised the Chamber, in an official written statement, for its role in helping to make the Republic "a vibrant, prosperous, tolerant and multi-racial nation".[5] The reality, however, was that the Chamber was not of central importance to the goals of the government.

Birth of the party-state: economic and political development

Already present in the political rhetoric previous to separation, the "survivalism" argument, the stressing of the vulnerability of Singapore and, therefore, the need for personal and collective sacrifice, permeated official speeches. In early 1966 Lee Kuan Yew anticipated British military withdrawal,[6] and in a statement that combined a number of elements that would become part of the government's staple communication diet, he said:

> Let us suppose the British decide to pull out from Southeast Asia and from Singapore ... What will happen to us then, with our present defence capacity? The Indonesians have an army of 400,000 and other neighbouring countries are much more powerful than us. We must calculate carefully, taking everything into consideration. All must understand that this is no longer a matter of survival of the individual, but a matter of the survival of a large group of people – of millions! What are the prospects of our survival? ... If you want a Chinese chauvinistic society, failure is assured. Singapore will surely be isolated ... We must firmly hold on to our corner of Southeast Asia. It is not negotiable. But we must also try our best to establish a model, multiracial society based on the principles of equality ... .[7]

This mantra-like emphasizing that the world was fraught with danger and filled with enemies threatening the survival of Singapore led some scholars to conclude that it aided the government in controlling and organizing society.[8]

If peace and tranquillity between the ethnic groups and with the regional neighbours were prerequisites, economic development was the main goal. Expelled from the Federation of Malaysia, Singapore had lost the market for selling the products its import substitution industrialization (ISI) strategy was to produce. The Singapore economy had to look farther afield for customers. A number of characteristics of the ISI plan based on the Winsemius report, however, were beneficial to this change or could be retained outright in an export oriented industrialization (EOI) strategy. Winsemius particularly favoured strong state action controlling labour, keeping wages down and realizing the plan through foreign direct investment (FDI). The EOI state development plan copied these points and stressed positive state intervention even more, with the state both kick-starting economic growth and taking a direct part in the process through GLCs.[9]

Singapore's decision to promote export oriented FDI came at the opportune moment of the development of the New International Division of Labour. This restructuring of the world's production and trading system was prompted by rising labour costs, high taxes, competition and other factors in industrialized countries, which forced companies from the West and Japan to developing countries. Success would depend on whether the government could make it more interesting and profitable for multinational companies (MNCs) to set up their production facilities in Singapore rather than in other developing nations. Under the guidance of the Economic Development Board (EDB),[10] Singapore marketed itself as the ideal location for internationally and regionally oriented industries and services. For manufacturing, export-processing zones offered tax incentives and other financially attractive terms to the MNCs.[11]

In order to provide a stable working environment for the foreign companies and a docile supply of cheap and relatively well-educated labour, the PAP government needed to bring the labour unions and the left-wing opposition under control. It did so through a number of legislative measures. The Trade Union Amendment Bill of 1966 was the first, followed by the Employment Act of 1968, and the Industrial Relations (Amendment) Act.[12] Explaining the need to change labour legislation, Lee Kuan Yew said that inflated union wishes and demands had arisen from the political reality of pre-independence days: "The legitimate trade unionism became a useful omnibus cover for the carrot you must offer the masses if you want them to join in driving the colonial power out ...". But the PAP government of independent Singapore could not offer workers "double and triple overtime and all the free days" because foreign investment would simply go elsewhere.[13]

The 1966 bill made it illegal for strikes and other industrial actions to be taken by any union without the consent of the majority of its members, and only to be obtained by secret ballot. On top of this, the 1968 acts "prohibited the unions from bargaining beyond the standards set by the Act during the first five years of operation of pioneer industries".[14] Lee made his intentions clear, drawing a comparison with British dockyard workers who staged a famous strike just after the war. He said, "Let me be frank. If that happens here at our harbour I will declare this high treason. I will move against the strike leaders. Charges can be brought in court later. I would get the port going straightaway."[15]

In order to make large infrastructural projects possible and to be able to greatly expand the government-subsidized public housing schemes, another legislative change was necessary. The Land Acquisition Act of 1966 made it possible for the government to acquire land at below market prices for projects benefiting the common good.[16] The Chamber expressed its very strong objection to the clause concerning compulsory acquisition of land needed "by persons or corporations" on the plea of public benefit, public utility or public interest. The Chamber argued that all these terms, unless properly defined, admitted room for a variety of interpretations under different circumstances. The Chamber stated that in cases of compulsory acquisition by a non-profit statutory board or by the government for any public purpose, it did not make any objections. It further expressed its concern over the power of the minister and the questionable opportunities for appeal concerning compulsory acquisition.[17] Of course, what the government wanted to establish with this Bill was precisely the flexibility that the Chamber feared.

Just as the logic of economic development had prompted legislative changes in order to secure a stable labour market and unhampered infrastructural improvement, it also, from the point of view of the PAP, necessitated changes to the political landscape and the structure of social and political representation. The Chamber was still the apex of the pyramid of Chinese organizations and its centrality to this structure had recently been impressed upon the PAP government during the merger issue. Although the SCCC helped the PAP to secure merger against the backdrop of Barisan opposition, it was also interpreted by Lee Kuan Yew as a threat. The PAP saw dependency on grassroots structures as a dangerous weakness and an obstacle to efficient government. Now it was time to remedy this weakness.

After 1965, Citizens' Consultative Committees (CCC), whose members were selected by the Member of Parliament (MP), were set up in every constituency. Having contact with the voters and being seen to act on their grievances and fears was an important signal the PAP wanted to send to the population. The system was later expanded with Residents' Committees, representing a number of housing blocks within the constituency. Furthermore, the People's Association reinforced the trend by expanding its network of Community Centres with the Management Committees comprising prominent members of the neighbourhood who played the role of intermediary between government and people. The People's Association and the Community Centres, officially state bodies, soon started to coordinate "meet the people" sessions for the MPs. This whole new pyramid of interactional and representational mechanisms between government and people stood under the control of the Board of Management of the People's Association headed by Lee Kuan Yew.[18] The crucial characteristic of this new representational structure was that it blurred the distinction between party and state. By late 1966, faced with this kind of competition, the Barisan decided to boycott the parliamentary system, thereby handing absolute domination of legislation and the state to its opponent. Since then the PAP has happily equated party and state because it serves to both legitimize its rule as well as to make it virtually impossible for opposition movements to challenge its domination.

This new representational structure competed directly with the existing dominant social structure and institutions. An example of the social implications of this political change is provided by Lam Thian, an SCCC and clan leader who observed:

> One of the clan functions was to act as a mediator in family, social and even business disputes. Though still influential today, the power of the clan leadership is waning. People are more legal minded these days. So, they do not depend so much on the clans. They do not respect the clan leaders as much as they used to do in the past.[19]

Lam's statement is an interesting indication of how the multi-purpose elite leadership of the clans and Chamber experienced state control. Having accepted and internalized the reality of the technocratic, modern, PAP orientation, the population increasingly looked towards the party/state to take care of its wants and needs. For Lam and his colleagues, this translated directly into a loss of "respect" by the people for the traditional leaders of the Chinese community who used to play this role. The rise of the modern state in Singapore signified the decline of the communally-based system. In independent Singapore, the "hegemony of the economic",[20] the total dominance of the creation of national and individual wealth, was directly connected to the worldview of the PAP and to a total package of social, cultural and political control by the party/state. The developmental state appropriated dominance over policy-making, and long term planning, and sidelined or usurped alternative power bases.

The new policies on industrial development and the regulation of labour led to an intensification of the politics of control. Corporatism, defined as the establishment of structures of selective and exclusive political representation, which affords the state an enhanced capacity to define social, political and economic goals, is a model that is often used to explain the political organization of Singapore society. In corporatism, state direction reconciled the interests of different groups and classes to the benefit of all.[21] The PAP government put in place state-initiated and state-endorsed channels of representation in the form of statutory boards designated to research, plan and implement government policies.

Chamber leaders were appointed or co-opted to fill positions in this corporatist structure, and served in institutions such as the Board of Commissioners of Currency, the Trade Development Board, the National

Wages Council (NWC), the Board of the National University of Singapore, the Port of Singapore Authority, the National Productivity Council and the Vocational and Industrial Training Board, to name just a few. Most of these boards were directly under the supervision of a government minister, and high-ranking officials had an important voice in them. The inclusion of Chamber leaders in this structure indicated that it was still accorded respect and status, although in the government's view the Chamber was not the only, sole and preferred, representative.

However, inclusion meant shared responsibility for policies that might not be favoured by the Chamber. A good example of this is the case of Ling Lee Hua, a senior Chamber leader, who recounted in an interview his stint as one of the employers' representative on the NWC in the 1980s. He said "he was condemned" because the representatives of government and the labour unions, who made up the other two-thirds of the NWC, could dominate the recommendations on wage levels. With the National Trades Union Congress (NTUC) under tight government supervision, the decision to raise wages in the "Second Industrial Revolution" was pushed through despite great concern and protest from the employers' side. Because the majority of the council supported the wage increases, the employers' representatives were forced to sign the recommendation. Ling recounts that he received many complaints from Chamber members who treated him as if he had "sold out" their interests and described the position he was in as a "lose-lose situation".[22]

The state's orientation and worldview on economic growth relied on FDI, the complete dominance of politics and impressive social control. In a pattern that would persist until 1985, the realities of Singapore's development would get the Chamber into trouble either with its membership or with the dominant PAP state.

2. The ambivalence of complying with the state: the case of economic development

Rather than attacking the government's dominant and interventionist position, the Chamber tried to earn a legitimate place and role in the new Singapore by complying with government plans. These attempts found expression in the promotion of trade and industry and in the replacement of the older Ambitious generation by younger leaders. The efforts of the SCCC were unsuccessful because of the traders' worldview that continued to dominate its actions and strategies. As a result, its attempts to comply failed and the SCCC did not become a central representative of local business.

Promotion of trade and industry

Minister Lim Kim San reminded the Chamber of what the government expected in his speech during the SCCC diamond jubilee festivities. He stressed that seeking new outlets for trade and securing new markets for industrial products was the top concern for Singapore.[23] In the eyes of the government, industrialization was the key word and the Chinese business sector would have to be forced to participate. The PAP considered the traders' orientation an old-fashioned, short-sighted outlook on economic development.

In a speech on the need for "forward-looking good management", Lee Kuan Yew stated that: "the old family business is one of the problems of Singapore. … One of the reasons for our floating an industrial development bank is because of the sluggishness with which people change habits. They are accustomed to buying and selling. And business is kept in the family. They have done this for hundreds of years. … Business management is a professional's job and we need professionals to run our business effectively".[24] Lee's disdain for the traditional Chinese family business is one-sided but does put into clear perspective what the PAP technocrats thought of the traders' worldview of the Chinese business community. Brushing aside a century and a half of the economic essence of Singapore as a trading and entrepot port, he equated modern with industrial and assumed the pre-eminence of the modern, Western management model.

Observations on this issue need to take into account the differences between a small percentage of elite family businesses engaged in both commercial and industrial activity and the greater part of the Chinese trade and commerce sector. The elite businesses and families, which provided the leadership of the Chamber, were more willing and able to comply with the government's industrialization policy. Soon Peng Yam was well aware of the hegemony of the economic and the government's interpretation of development since he was involved in industrial activities himself. However, the large majority of Chamber members were traders rather than industrialists.

The percentage distribution of business establishments by sector can be discerned from a Chamber survey of its members in 1971–1972. More than two-thirds of the 2,510 respondents were active in trade or services. "Foodstuffs", "Straits Produce" and "Banking, Finance and Insurance" were the three largest categories. Due to the categories used in the survey, it is doubtful if the companies not directly recognizable as active in trade or services all worked in industry. The categories of "Chemicals and

Pharmaceuticals" and "Engineering and Machinery" certainly included businesses trading in these products rather than producing them.[25]

These statistics help us to understand the prevailing outlook of the Chamber members and indicate a discrepancy in experience and business activity between the Chamber leaders and members. Chinese businessmen who wanted to be leaders of the Chamber had to represent the interests and the outlook of their constituency. They were aware that they owed their leadership positions to the mercantile orientation of the Chinese community but were also under direct pressure from individual and organizational members to impress upon the government the importance of trade for Singapore.

As a result, the Chamber as an organization focused more on trade promotion than local industrialization. Soon Peng Yam exemplified this position in a press report welcoming the resumption of trade and diplomatic ties with Indonesia, in which he stated that markets were a must for Singapore. He reminded the government that it was necessary to give "… equal importance to entrepot and industrialization because before full industrialization we'll have to depend on entrepot as the mainspring".[26]

New times, new leaders

The differences between the leaders and the led in the Chamber became clearer when a new generation of leaders came to power. This new generation, however, was just as much bound to the orientation of its constituency as the old generation. Hence, the problem of pleasing the government and representing the interests of the members remained.

Out with the old: the Bangpai incident

Before a new generation of leaders could rise to the top, the Chamber suffered the biggest internal conflict in its history. When under external pressure, internal fights often resulted and once again, the dispute formally was about the speech-group based election system and was couched in terms of "old" versus "new" and "traditional" versus "modern". Underneath, however, it was a fight over control of the Chamber leadership between the two main antagonists, Soon Peng Yam and Kheng Chin Hock, both belonging to the older generation. The conflict became known as the *Bangpai* incident because it centred on dialect group representation. The seeds for the Soon–Kheng disagreement were sown in the election of 1965, when Kheng supported Soon because the latter, as Kheng wrote in a letter to Soon dated 26 July 1968, had told him that "the existence of the *bang* in the Chamber is out of keeping with the times, therefore it should be abolished".[27] This modernist and strongly anti-communal stand challenged the logic of the power structure of the Chinese community. Consequently, the idea of scrapping the speech-group representation had very little chance from the outset. The leaders, who would have to decide to do so, had risen to the top through this system and would be seen as blocking the opportunity of those below them to do the same.

It was exactly for this reason that Kheng had long advocated terminating the system of *bang* representation, because he felt that it enabled the elites of each speech group to cling to status without giving any guarantee that these individuals would be willing to spend time and effort on the Chamber's causes. Furthermore, although a Hokkien himself, he thought it was a drawback that the system perpetuated Hokkien dominance of the Chamber. After the whole row was over, Kheng summed up his argument as follows. He contended that the election process was a two-tiered affair, which meant controlling the votes of members first and then the council members because the number of *bang* members decided the number of members on the management council. Kheng said that after the election of the council members, before they would take their positions, an arrangement was made behind closed doors to decide who would be president and vice president and who would head the committees.[28]

Although Kheng's observation and analysis of the power game was correct, he had used the very same clan and speech-group structure to propel Ko Teck Kin and himself first into the Hokien Huay Kuan and then to the top of the Chamber. The importance of his support for Soon Peng Yam in the 1965 election was similarly due to the fact that he could swing votes in the run up to the polls. Perhaps he was a truly principled modernist or a frustrated individual because a man of his comparatively limited wealth and at times undiplomatic character would never be acceptable as the ultimate leader of the Chamber.

At first, Soon, no doubt pressured by Kheng, seemed to tackle the issue. He included "abolishing the *bang* system" in the four new tasks of the 33rd management council that he outlined in his inaugural address on 15 March 1965.[29] From the beginning, however, Soon addressed the issue as a pragmatic political problem rather than as a matter of principle. He spoke about the need to streamline the organization to prevent "ambitious persons" from capturing it by "unethical means" and seemed to emphasize the technicalities within the constitution.[30] Soon's strategy was an example of the tendency of power to turn the power holder to conservatism. Immediately after attaining the presidency, Soon paid his dues to the system that got him there, incorporating the top leaders of the speech groups in the committee formed to study another amendment of the constitution.[31]

Principled opponents of the *bang* system rallied behind Kheng and talked in different terms. Strong support came from Colonel Chuang, who had been advocating a change of the election system since 1952. As often, he was most vocal, expressing, during the Annual General Meeting, his unhappiness over the fact that "... sixty year old ladies and dance hostess girls were members of the Chamber".[32] Although impossible to prove this intriguing statement, it has become enshrined in the unpublished collective memory of many Chamber members and leaders. A number of informants, always stressing confidentiality and insisting on anonymity, confirmed that there were strong rumours at the time about these practices. Some speech-group leaders put employees forward as Chamber members, paid the fees and, thus, increased the size of the voting bloc they controlled.[33] A fact that can be proven was the incidence of the registration of many individual and company members to one address. Scrutiny of the Chamber's 1964 membership list reveals that this phenomenon occurred especially within the Hakka and the Sanjiang community, although the Hokkien used this strategy as well in the 1958 election tussle. Among the 175 Hakka members, 44 were registered to one of three addresses of various branches of the Lam family. Among the Sanjiang, domination of the Shaw family was clear from the fact that 31 out of the 190 members were registered to the family's Robinson Road business address.[34]

Chuang pointed out that at a time of national solidarity and the need to overcome racial differences, it was unsuitable to maintain a speech-group based system. Furthermore, he called the practice of groups of members being registered at the address of one patron "member concentration camps".[35] He saw the whole system as a result of the British colonial divide and rule policy and called *bang* representation "an evil legacy of feudalism".[36] Others argued: "It is really a joke. On the map of Singapore, where is Fujian, where is Guangdong, and where is San Jiang? Don't we understand that we are already citizens of Singapore? We admit that we are Singaporeans while still thinking that we belong to certain factions. Isn't it a contradiction? Isn't it against the government's policy ...".[37]

Indeed, because of urban renewal and the development of suburban New Towns, speech-group specific areas and neighbourhoods diminished greatly or were torn down altogether. Hence, the geographical link between *bang* and location ceased to be an important identity marker in Singapore. What the argument of those opposed to *bang* representation overlooked completely is that the mental map of identity and power of members of the

Singapore Chinese community still very much included speech groups as a determining feature. This was exactly why the issue was so contentious and why most established leaders shied away from abolishing this time-tested way of defining power and hierarchy in the Chamber.

After the special committee had met a few times and made little progress, the issue was picked up again in 1968 after pressure by Kheng Chin Hock, who likened the leadership selection procedure to a process of "sharing the meat" between the most influential individuals and groups.[38] Two special general meetings were held in July of that year at which heated discussions pitted Soon as the "political pragmatist" who argued that the status quo was working against Kheng as the "principled reformer". Because Kheng only had a small group of supporters behind him who were willing to ruffle established feathers, and most of the members had a vested interest in the existing election procedure, the *bang* system remained. The changes that were proposed at the special general meeting were: (1) to abolish individual membership and only allow company or trade associations to join, (2) to increase the representation of the trade associations from six to 10 seats, thereby increasing the number of management council members from 51 to 55, and (3) to introduce the position of vice chairmen in the committees.[39] The significance of these changes lay in the fact that the second and third changes provided more positions to be distributed to keep all factions and speech groups happy. The changes, therefore, constituted a victory of conservative, pragmatic forces in the Chamber. Even the first change on the abolishment of individual membership was not significant because all existing members in that category were allowed to maintain their status. On 12 October, after three very tumultuous hours, the amendments were passed and the *bang* system remained.[40] In the eyes of one Chamber leader, the *Bangpai* incident of 1968 was a futile battle between "no change, and the Hokkien staying in control, and change, which meant that the Hokkien would be in control".[41]

With the completion of the second presidential term of Soon Peng Yam, the last representative of the generation of the Ambitious, politically active leaders left the stage. Although it is clear from the previous paragraphs that a continuity of the nature of power and the dominant orientation in the Chamber existed, new circumstances did demand a new type of leader. At this point in time, the change was necessitated by the fact that the previous generation had been actively discredited by the government and therefore could not provide the political access needed. After the leaders of the late 1940s, the 1950s and early 1960s, different attributes characterized the Chamber leaders of the next period.

In with the new!

Shortly after the constitutional amendments of 1968, in which the status quo of the power structure of the Chamber was preserved, it was time for the elections. Between 1969 and 1985 only three individuals held the presidency and with the addition of one more, they also held the majority of the vice presidencies for that period. The profiles of these four leaders, Wee Cho Yaw, Tan Keong Choon, Tan Eng Joo and Lim Kee Ming, show a number of shared characteristics.

All were sons or close relatives of first generation immigrants and business founders, receiving their business training in the family firm before taking the helm or venturing out. The level of education of this group was much higher than the previous generation, both in formal terms and additional skills acquired through self-study later in life. All four were, at some point in time, involved in industrial production, banking and real estate and, therefore, were in tune with the modern economy, while also having roots in the Chinese world of trade. Although not devoid of opinions concerning culture and politics, the activities and viewpoints of the new leaders were decidedly less confrontational than those of their predecessors. They accepted the primacy of the PAP state, and attempted to comply with the national developmental agenda by leading the Chamber back to business. They were pragmatists in their strategy for the Chamber, trying to capitalize on opportunities when they arose but never fundamentally going against government directives. Wee Cho Yaw, the first of these Pragmatist leaders, was elected Chamber president in 1969.

It is important to note that the characteristics presented for Wee Cho Yaw and the other Pragmatist leaders, as with previous generations, applied neither to the entire upper echelon of the Chamber, nor even remotely to its membership. As before, the Pragmatist leaders were an elite within the Chamber who were economic and socio-political brokers for external sources of money and wielders of power. In this capacity, they were familiar with the orientation of the PAP party/state and more willing to comply with the government's wishes. As the Chamber vanguard, Wee Cho Yaw, on the occasion of the swearing-in ceremony of 1969, made his view on the subordinate position of the Chamber clear when he said: "Our government has seen to it that there is the necessary political and labour stability as well as security, which is essential for economic growth and industrialization".[42] Minister Goh Keng Swee who officiated at the ceremony undoubtedly looked on with approval. The first official speech of the new leadership focused on the need to follow the lead of the government and to adhere to the modern orientation of the PAP party/state.

Wee Cho Yaw: Studied pragmatist.

Ministry of Information, Communications and the Arts. Courtesy of the National Archives of Singapore

Wee Cho Yaw was born in 1929 in Quemoy in Fujian province. Although his father, Wee Kheng Chiang, had been born in Kuching, Sarawak and had received an English education there, his second wife lived in China. The first eight years of Cho Yaw's life were spent in China until the Japanese invasion and the extended family was first united in Kuching before moving to Singapore. The Japanese invasion of Singapore disrupted Wee's education and after the war he spent time at both Chinese High School and Chung Cheng High School. Cho Yaw participated in the anti-colonial and anti-establishment activities in these schools in the late 1940s and his father pulled him out for fear of arrest. As a result, he never finished high school.[43] Still, a 1969 article, published at the time Wee became the Chamber's president for the first time, portrays him as intelligent, far-sighted and highly educated, dubbing him the "professor of the Chinese". In the article, Wee expounds his view on life laced with Chinese proverbs. "The richness of studying comes from the understanding of logic. … To be able to evolve ideas from logic one has to accept the good and discard the bad. Besides that, one needs determination. Thus, one should not give up until the aim is reached". His political strategy shines through in his philosophical guiding lights. "China's standard is based on '*Liyi*'. This is the only criterion. *Liyi* means to be upright in one's doings, and to follow the rules. One should think of society as a whole in one's doings, especially in the context of *Liyi*. Therefore, those who understand reason will be able to grasp the concept of *Liyi* and be able to serve the society".[44] For Wee, following the rules was not only a moral point, it was part of a pragmatic strategy to comply with the powers-

Wee was aware of the prevailing view in government circles that saw the Chinese business sector as old-fashioned and exclusively trade-oriented. Under his leadership, the Chamber began many activities to counter this image. Aided by other leaders and initiators such as Wee Mon Cheng and Ling Lee Hua, Chinese businessmen were told to "Go modern". In a series of talks, Wee Mon Cheng said Chinese entrepreneurs had to modernize and urged them to make use of available training programmes, and later focused that-be and to operate within the system rather than opposing it, a strategy that would characterize the new generation of Chamber leaders.

In a reflection on the generations of entrepreneurs in Singapore, Wee called Tan Lark Sye and Lee Kong Chian "real entrepreneurs" and called himself and his generation of founders' sons "managers".[45] His flagship company, United Overseas Bank (UOB), was founded by his father, uncle and five Hokkien partners as United Chinese Bank (UCB) in 1935. Before entering the family banking business, Wee was a commodity trader in his father's company from 1949 up to 1958, at which point he started working half days at the bank as the designated successor. Soon after he took over in 1960, *Konfrontasi* came. The early 1960s were a hard time.[46] Later, however, when Singapore did well, the bank did well too, and the 1970s was a decade of feverish acquisitions, mergers, diversification and international expansion for UOB. The company acquired substantial stakes in Haw Par, Sin Chew Jit Poh, Singapore Monitor/New Nation and, through a share swap, gained control of two bigger local Chinese banks – Chung Khiaw and Lee Wah. Expanding his business empire, UOB set up subsidiary

companies in finance, property and insurance, and entered into joint ventures with United Chase Merchant Bankers, Chase Manhattan Overseas and Nikko Securities to gain international experience. Wee proved to be a cunning businessman with a keen sense for opportunity. In a highly publicized tussle with the Hong Leong Finance group over rival take-over bids on Singapore Finance, UOB made an extra-ordinary profit of $11 million but the initiative somewhat soured the relationship with Hong Leong and its controlling Kwek family.[47] Over time, Wee developed into the most prominent Chinese business leader of his day. Although not easy to substantiate, his relations with the PAP government and the administrative elite are reported to be very close, an attribute that sometimes leads to covert criticism from some that he is too much of a "government man".[48] Wee was involved prominently in a number of other organizations. After Tan Lark Sye's death in 1972, he became the president of the Hokien Huay Kuan and was also the Chairman of Nanda's council during the tumultuous conversion of the Chinese language university into the fold of national tertiary education.[49]

on the need to modernize the Chinese family business and its "traditional business structures and practices". Chinese entrepreneurs needed to find new ways of financing their ventures: "Discard old ways of raising capital through friends and relatives if you want to modernize, industrialize".[50]

Throughout the 1970s, the government continued to press the Chinese business sector to move into industry and production and to "modernize". It did so because the traders' worldview prevailed among the members of the Chamber and few made the transition from trade to industry. As orientations continued to clash the government kept pushing its modernist perspective. At the 1975 swearing-in ceremony, for instance, Finance Minister Hon Sui Sen told the Chamber to "assess more objectively the world economic situation", saying that the SCCC's "... credibility will be immeasurably enhanced not only with its members but also with the government". He also urged the Chamber to set up a statistics department in order to be able to inform its members adequately for decision-making based on solid, empirical data.[51] Hon's unspoken message was that the Chamber was missing the boat and that its members conducted business on an old-fashioned, unreliable and unscientific basis.

As a result, alternative business organizations were taking the limelight in Singapore's representational landscape. The Singapore Manufacturers' Association (SMA) and the Singapore International Chamber of Commerce (SICC) were much more focused on industrial activities and worked much more closely with the state apparatus for economic development through the EDB, the Development Bank of Singapore (DBS) and various ministries. The establishment of a coordinating body for the four chambers of commerce and the SMA was advocated by government officials because they saw the racially-based chambers as archaic.[52]

The SMA took the initiative to establish a joint standing committee of business organizations, which the SCCC joined in 1974.[53] The government wanted developments to go a step further towards one Singapore Chamber or at least a federation. The Pragmatist leaders of the Chamber saw the writing on the wall and backed the plans. Eventually the Singapore Federation of Chambers of Commerce and Industry (SFCCI) was founded in 1978. It had an Executive Committee of 12 (4 from the SCCC, 2 each for the other members) and costs were roughly shared on a proportional basis.[54] Wee Cho Yaw was elected as its first president with Lim Kee Ming as vice president and KC Tan and Ling Lee Hua as board members.[55] The SFCCI proved to be an uneasy partnership and the institution remained less than central to the Singapore business world until the 1990s. It provided the image of a united front for the national and international purposes of the government but failed to address, at least in its early years, issues of substance. The SCCC's participation in it, therefore, did not lead to an improvement in its standing in the eyes of the government. Still, the Pragmatist leadership looked within the government-defined arena for roles the Chamber could fruitfully pursue. Mindful of the make-up of their constituency, they turned to issues that were close to the hearts of the Chinese businessmen and firmly anchored in the Chamber's history.

3. Chamber worldview and national foreign policy: trade and friendship missions

It was the role of regional trade representative of Singapore that the Chamber relished. At the swearing-in ceremony of 1973, Finance Minister Hon Sui Sen said that Chinese businessmen should be aggressive in the drive for increased exports. Newly-appointed President Tan Keong Choon replied that the Chamber was already preparing trade missions to a number of countries.[56] Before looking at the host of trade missions the Chamber organized in the mid and late 1970s, it is necessary to introduce a framework of the Chamber's way of looking at the world and Singapore's foreign relations.

The Chamber worldview

The Chamber worldview stemmed from its traders' outlook and was firmly rooted in the long history of Singapore as an important node in the Southeast Asian trading port network.[57] Having been thrust into nationhood unexpectedly in 1965, Singapore was ill-prepared in the field of foreign relations and first had to be put on the map internationally. In April 1966, Prime Minister Lee Kuan Yew went on an extensive tour of Asia, the Middle East and Eastern Europe, as well as visiting London.[58] Because Singapore faced a problem in recruiting and financing a diplomatic service, the government looked to the private sector for personnel. Interestingly, a number of old members of the Chamber leadership group of the 1940s and 1950s were appointed to diplomatic positions. Ko Teck Kin and Lien Ying Chow served as the first and second High Commissioner to Malaysia respectively and Tan Siak Kew was Singapore's first Ambassador Extraordinary to Thailand.[59] The Chamber as an institution was also recruited into national representational duties, forming two teams to boost trade. One represented Singapore at the Economic Commission for Africa and the Far East (ECAFE) conference in Bangkok in 1968 and another liaised with the SMA to promote Singapore export in general. The SCCC was also invited to join government missions, such as the 1967 government delegation to Russia and Eastern Europe.[60]

Although the Chamber must have been content with the role and participation it was extended by the government, the way in which it thought of the world was different from that of the PAP party/state. The Chamber's organizing principle for foreign relations can be visualized in a model of concentric circles. With Singapore at the centre, relations with

Malaysia were closest to its heart, followed by integration with Southeast Asia, Asia and the world at large. China occupied a more independent spot in the hearts of its leaders in their geography of relations and, therefore, ranked high on their list of foreign affairs priorities.

Malaysia: split and new relationship

Notwithstanding how important the two countries were to each other in economic terms, the Singapore-Malaysia relationship was tense and in a post-traumatic state in the first years after the 1965 separation, not least because of Lee Kuan Yew's personal sense of betrayal. The relationship entered a stand-off period, from 1968 to 1976, in which the two sides used each other as a whipping boy, but tempers did not flare too high. The Chamber had strong reasons for advocating cordial relations, in general, and close cooperation, in particular, on economic policy. Many Chinese businessmen in Singapore still carried out transactions in Malaysia or owned extensive business operations there.

Their main concern was that the establishment of two independent currencies would add to business costs and would make taxation and administration of business located in both countries concurrently more complex. The Chamber tried to drum up broad-based support in the business world in both countries and started a campaign to save the Malayan dollar as the joint currency for both Malaysia and Singapore. It tried to enlist the support of the SMA, the Association of Banks, the Shipping Association, Marine Assurance Association, among others, in Singapore and also contacted the ACCCM and the United Chambers of Commerce of Malaysia.[61]

A second hope was to convince the two governments of the need for extensive cooperation. In an attempt to promote economic ties, Soon Peng Yam proposed the establishment of a common market as a first step, a line that would be continued by the next generation of SCCC leaders.[62] Although Chinese cooperation continued across the border, the quest for a shared currency and a common market was unsuccessful. The ethnic and political issues, which had led to separation, equally prevented the two governments from considering cooperation in these fields. The joint airline was split in 1972, and the common currency arrangements and cooperation in the rubber and stock exchanges as well as the banking association were all ended in 1973.[63] Nevertheless, for the Chinese businessmen of Singapore, Malaysia remained the first economic partner and hinterland.

Southeast Asia

To the SCCC, Southeast Asia was the second ring of its regional order. The interest of the Chinese trading community in Southeast Asian relations of the young state of Singapore was understandable because a large amount of regional trade, to which Chinese networks were central, continued to take place. In a move exemplary of its worldview, the Chamber suggested the establishment of a trade research centre to cater to Southeast Asian businessmen. Regional chambers of commerce should take the initiative and pave the way, rather than having governments running this venture.[64] The Chamber's belief in regional opportunities is illustrated by its trade mission tour in March and April 1968 to Thailand, Cambodia, Burma, Hong Kong and Japan.[65]

With separation from Malaysia and *Konfrontasi* with Indonesia in the recent past, regional diplomatic policy was a sensitive issue to the Singapore government. A new development came when, in August 1967, the Association of Southeast Asian Nations (ASEAN) was created in Bangkok, with Indonesia, Malaysia, the Philippines, Singapore and Thailand as founding members. Singapore had its doubts because it thought the organization would benefit the weaker states. It was not until 1975–1976 that Singapore started to see and use ASEAN as an arena for positive action. Around this time, Lee Kuan Yew travelled to his ASEAN partners orchestrating a new prominence for the regional organization.

This new government stance towards regional cooperation was reflected in the activities of the Chamber. The SCCC attempted to connect and comply with government policy as a way of carving out a legitimate niche. The Chamber hopped enthusiastically on the ASEAN bandwagon stating that, with the common objectives, it would be easier for industrialists, bankers and other traders to cooperate and work towards the welfare of the region.[66] At the same time, Chinese businessmen tried to use examples and precedents in the region to push their own government towards the implementation of policies that would be beneficial to Chinese business. One SCCC leader called for a Singapore-Kuala Lumpur accord on tariffs and trade similar to a deal signed by Thailand and the Philippines.[67]

From the late 1970s, ASEAN started to encapsulate regional goals into an institutional framework, and a regional chamber of commerce, the ASEAN-CCI, was set up. Whereas the constituent members from all other ASEAN countries of this organization were state institutions, Singapore was represented by the newly established Singapore Federation of Chambers of Commerce and Industry through its president Wee Cho Yaw.[68] The forum was used to lobby for region-wide policy and institutions. It proposed, for instance, to set up a financial institution to fund joint projects. This initiative took the form of regional commodity clubs, which served to establish joint projects and buffer stocks to stabilize prices.

It was reported that Wee had a shot at becoming ASEAN-CCI president at the end of 1979, which perhaps fuelled the SCCCI initiative to create an investment group for ASEAN, open to businesses from all five-member nations, which would help to form joint ventures. A year and a half later in June 1981, the ASEAN Finance Corporation (AFC) was actually established with equity of US$100 million. SCCCI management council member Lim Ho Hup, President/Chief Executive of the AFC, said that the venture was expected to run as a merchant bank.[69] Lim Ho Hup had been the first director of the EDB in the 1960s. According to his own account, he was expressly brought into the Chamber to handle ASEAN-CCI matters. He was selected because of his vast experience, his good relations with the core of the economic policy machine of Singapore and his language skills.[70]

China

China was the third geographical element in the Chamber's worldview. Despite the turmoil of the Cultural Revolution in the PRC, Singapore's trade with China had continued and renewing formal relations was an important issue to the SCCC.[71] In the first years after separation, the Cultural Revolution in China made it virtually impossible to visit for any purpose but after Kissinger's ping-pong diplomacy, Chinese businessmen in Singapore were jumping for a chance to go as well, explicitly referring to the US reversal of diplomatic strategy, because "if Americans can go there, why can't we?" The Chamber made public plans for a trade mission to China in the fall of 1970.[72]

As Singapore had no diplomatic ties with the PRC at this time, the SCCC utilized its good connections with the Bank of China, which served as a go-between for the delivery of a letter requesting approval from the Beijing authorities for a visit.[73] Wee Cho Yaw was personally involved in preparations for the trip and even went to Hong Kong to contact Chinese officials through local channels there. Eventually, the mission visited Hong Kong as well as the famous Canton trade fair.[74]

From the inception of the Chamber, it had always been in good contact with whichever regime was in power in China. All these Chinese regimes, when looking for entries into Southeast Asia, first contacted the SCCC or similar organizations in the region. Apparently they thought that these Chinese organizations would either be more sympathetic to the goals of the motherland or could provide a smoother point of contact with the local government. The Chamber continued to be able to use this status in order to gain high-level access in Beijing. After the missions and delegations of the 1950s and the renewed contact of 1971, the Chamber kept the momentum going by organizing a 40-member trade and goodwill mission by the four Singapore chambers and the SMA.

Official endorsement, although sometimes hesitant, of the SCCC missions was an indication that the Singapore government saw the Chamber as an actor in business contacts with China.[75] The Singapore delegation met with a vice premier of the Hua Guofeng government, and as regimes changed in China, the Chamber maintained its status as the liaison. Tan Eng Joo led a mission of the Rubber Association of Singapore to Beijing shortly after Deng Xiaoping came to power. The delegation was already received by high-level officials of the post-Gang of Four regime.[76] The Chamber obviously had an important role and a central liaison position in Singapore's business contacts with China. However, trade with or investment in China was not high on the government priority list and would not be for another 10 years.

Trade missions

From both Chamber and newspaper sources, a long list of trade missions organized by the Chamber in this period can be compiled. It would be futile to trace all of them, but a few of their characteristics and reasons for their organization should be highlighted. First, they followed the pattern of the concentric circles of foreign interest of the Chamber described above, especially where they overlapped with stated government policy goals. Second, the Chamber viewed these activities in the light of a division of labour between the government and itself, and expected recognition and status in return for its efforts. The principal architect and executor of the boom in Chamber trade missions was Tan Keong Choon, the second of the Pragmatist leaders.

Under Tan's two presidencies from 1973 to 1977, the Chamber sent out many trade and friendship missions, especially to countries in Southeast Asia. Malaysia, Thailand, the Philippines, Indonesia and also Vietnam featured prominently. As was shown, these countries were all in the first and second circle of interest of the Chamber. The visits were used to cement ties between businessmen in the region, but often included meetings with top local political representatives. During the visit to the Philippines in 1973, for instance, the delegation discussed the subject of export processing zones with President Marcos.[77] Because of these contacts, the missions took on

Tan Keong Choon: Well-connected trader.
Courtesy of the National Archives of Singapore

Born in Tongan County, Fujian province in China in 1918, Tan Keong Choon was the son of Tan Kah Kee's brother. He attended primary and secondary school in China and studied history at his uncle's Xiamen University. On a break in 1937 visiting his uncle and other relatives, the Sino-Japanese war broke out, so he stayed in Singapore and studied English.

Tan started his own small import-export company in rubber, tea and textiles in 1940. Six years later he founded Nanya or Southseas Corporation, which dealt in rubber and timber, with a substantial investment from Lee Kong Chian. Between 1946 and 1948, Tan was very active in Shanghai where he had set up a Nanya office. Nanya business also brought him to Japan where he met and married his Japanese wife. In the early 1950s, he became involved in Nanyi or Southseas Commodities, another Lee Kong Chian company for which he dealt mostly in rubber and effected a few big deals with communist China.[78] In 1957 he was invited by the Lee Rubber Group, founded by Lee Kong Chian, to be Managing Director of Tropical Produce. He was an innovator in the rubber business, being the first producer to promote quality-graded standard rubber such as Standard Malaysian Rubber (SMR) and Standard Singapore Rubber (SSR). By developing the

a character that went beyond trade promotion. The link with the national agenda and the diplomatic element was clear as Chamber trade missions were sometimes briefed by senior officials. Before the trip to the Philippines, Minister Hon Sui Sen emphasized the ASEAN cooperation framework in which the trip took place.[82]

The missions to Indonesia were even more delicate in a political sense because relations between the two countries were hardly smooth. Bilateral trade was still excluded from Indonesian statistics, indicating the sensitivity of the issue of business relations with a Chinese-majority country. In order to break the ice, Tan Eng Joo suggested sending a culture and art group for a friendship tour to Indonesia. After consulting with Indonesian authorities, this format was found acceptable and the Singapore embassy in Jakarta extended an official invitation to the four Chambers and the SMA to organize such a mission.[83] The Chamber was seen as the organization machinery needed to produce rubber to set standards, he greatly improved the transparency of the rubber market. Through his efforts, SMR and SSR became household names in the natural rubber sector.

In the mid-1970s, he entered into property development when his flagship Nassim Mansion was built on a plot of land across from the Botanic Gardens where he had lived for 12 years in a colonial-style house.[79] His involvement in the financial sector was apparent in his directorships at Chung Khiaw Bank and Wee Cho Yaw's Overseas Union Bank. He also remained active in the property sector with a place on the board of Marco Polo Developments.[80]

Chinese education had his strong attention. He served Chinese High School, which was set up by his uncle, as Chairman of the board for many years, and was involved in many capacities in the Hokien Huay Kuan. Being a strong supporter of the Chinese education line of Tan Kah Kee and Tan Lark Sye, and

having been involved in Nanda, his views have not always been in line with the wishes of the PAP government in this field. A fiercely proud man, his strong personality sometimes landed him in contentious situations. When, in the mid-1990s, he felt that a group of men were trying to get into the board of the Chinese High School with ideas countering his own, he drummed up support and created a stand-off situation with two competing boards.[81] Still, throughout his private and public career, he was realistic about his role in the PAP state system, accepting many positions on government statutory boards and committees. Thereby, he acknowledged the leading role of the state, although he might have wished things to be different at times. He also strengthened his network with government circles, and was always on the alert for opportunities to further his private business interests as well as the interests of the SCCC.

with most historical ties with Indonesia and, therefore, the SCCC took up the organizational effort and collected donations from companies and trade organizations to finance the endeavour. Tan Keong Choon, the delegation leader, stressed that the visit would strengthen the spirit of fraternal cooperation among the ASEAN nations. The goodwill mission of 1974 had the intended effect, as the Chamber discussed possibilities for a real trade mission in response to the invitation of Air Marshall Suwoto Sukender, president of KADIN, the Indonesian national chamber of commerce and industry.[84]

Missions to countries outside of Southeast Asia were few and far between. Often, as in the case of a mission to the Middle East, representatives of the chambers and the SMA joined government delegations rather than organized their own visits.[85] Later in this period, the SCCC did send its own mission to Jeddah, Kuwait, Dubai, Teheran and Bahrain. This, however, was in direct response to Lee Kuan Yew's call to "get out, make contacts and sweat it out".[86]

The SCCC often consciously followed the government lead in its foreign endeavours and definitely aimed to comply with what it thought to be the expectations of the PAP on the Chamber's role as a Singapore representative abroad. It referred extensively to the national aims expressed within ASEAN, and also tried to excite its members into regional activities. Wee Cho Yaw, for instance, went on record saying that the opportunities in intra-regional ASEAN trade were not fully utilized.[87] The Chamber took advantage of its extensive network in Southeast Asia to get in touch with relevant local contacts. Of course there were the long-established ties with other Chinese chambers of commerce in the region, but personal business contacts were also used. Through these leads, meetings with local non-Chinese organizations and ministries were set up. At times, the government directly sought the views of the Chamber on how to find foreign markets. In response to this, the Chamber set up a sub-committee to prepare a memorandum. Predictably, in the light of the SCCC orientation, it produced recommendations to expand trade with ASEAN and China, as well as with other countries.[88]

An interview with Tan Keong Choon, conducted in 1996, illustrates how he viewed the Chamber's efforts in the mid-1970s. His statements reveal the expectation of an equal partnership in the representation of Singapore abroad: "So, we lead a lot of delegations to visit the ASEAN countries. ... It is a kind of cooperation between the government and the private sector." He also alludes to the fact that the Chamber did the government a great service by providing less formal channels for foreign relations in delicate times: "No, at that time the government was not so involved ... Because that time was a sensitive time. So, they let the business sector make their own contacts ... They (the government) just keep quiet, and allow you to do it. Anyway, if the private sector makes it a success or not a success, the government is not responsible. We paved the way for the government to go".[89]

Tan Keong Choon and other Chamber leaders were disappointed that these services did not lead to enhanced status for the Chamber as a dialogue partner on business issues and policies. The lack of government enthusiasm for the Chamber's efforts can be explained by referring to a number of central themes in the government programme for Singapore's development. First, trade was very subordinate to the efforts towards industrial development through the FDI strategy. The Chamber's efforts in trade promotion were always targeted at the periphery of the government's interests, as pressure from and limitations of the constituency of traders in the Chamber prevented it from achieving more results in the field of industrialization. Second, on the issue of trade, the government was much more interested in opening up new markets for Singapore than in improving trade with existing partners in the region. A statement by Minister Hon Sui Sen, calling on Chinese businessmen to move out of usual markets and combine available resources to conquer new global markets, is a clear illustration.[90] Again, the Chamber was fighting for the wrong cause. The third case, of trade with China, fell into this category as well. Controlling the sensitive ethnic balances in the region was an important tenet of the government's foreign policy. Openly courting the PRC, with many non-Chinese in the region still highly suspicious of that country's relationship with the Chinese diaspora, did not fit into the picture.

Although the Chamber leadership was trying to comply with what it thought the PAP government expected, it decided upon its strategies and activities based on its traders' worldview. It was not surprising that these efforts did not result in the intended increase of the Chamber's status. The government's relative autonomy vis-à-vis society in Singapore in general, and towards the Chinese business sector in particular, meant that it could easily make the interests of specific groups such as the Chamber subordinate to its broader development strategy. This pattern of power relations between the state and the Chamber was also apparent in the most extensive campaign of the Chamber in this period.

4. Attempting to fight for national interests: breaking the shipping conferences

The shipping sector was an important part of the trading economy of Singapore. The government planned to make Singapore Asia's second biggest shipping, ship-repairing and shipbuilding centre after Japan, in tandem with its infrastructural efforts to attract FDI. Towards this end, Singapore set up its own register of local ships in 1966, and two years later offered tax-free registration for foreign ships, creating the first "Asian flag of convenience". In 1968, it launched its own national shipping line, the Neptune Orient Line (NOL). To the Chinese traders who depended on marine transportation to move goods across the globe, shipping was a crucial enabling factor for their businesses. When problems arose concerning the near monopoly held by a small number of shipping conferences, the Chamber was eager to man the ramparts. It expected to find the government its natural ally in this struggle against the Western monopoly but, again, it was disappointed.

The shipping conferences were cartels of predominantly Western shipping lines that coordinated cargo allocation and freight prices on the main routes from the Far East to Europe and North America. The Far Eastern

Tan Eng Joo: MIT gentleman.

Ministry of Information, Communications and the Arts. Courtesy of the National Archives of Singapore

Born on 30 October 1919 in Singapore, Tan Eng Joo descended from immigrants from Chip Bee (Jimei) in Fujian province. His father and two uncles, one of them Tan Lark Sye, had moved to Singapore to work for Tan Kah Kee's rubber business. Later on in 1928, the family established Aik Hoe Rubber Company. Tan Eng Joo attended Anglo-Chinese School in Singapore after which he went to America to study. Through a New York business associate of Aik Hoe, Tan was introduced to MIT, where he pursued a building, engineering and construction major and an MA in structural engineering. After graduation, when the war had already broken out, he was recruited to work on ballistics in the National Defence Research Committee at Princeton.[91]

After the war, upon his return to Singapore, he was immediately recruited by his uncle Tan Lark Sye to help with the reconstruction of Aik Hoe. Tan Eng Joo would remain Director of the family rubber business until 1965.[92] His uncle and his Ambitious fellow leaders of the Chamber also involved Tan in the politics of decolonization when they made him president of the Democratic Party (DP). Eng Joo later admitted he was dumbfounded because he had no political aspirations at all, although he did agree with the DP platform. He felt forced by tradition to accept the position out of respect for his elders but was relieved not to be elected to parliament.

Freight Conference (FEFC), which dated back to 1897, for instance, was dominated by the old European, mainly British, shipping lines. Another conference of direct importance to business in Singapore was the Straits-New York Shipping Conference. The conference shipping lines attempted to create loyal customers by only offering rebates in conjunction with long-term contracts. The freight tariffs without the rebates were higher than the levels customary in worldwide shipping, but because the conferences monopolized the routes they plied, customers had little choice. For smaller customers with irregular cargoes, long-term contracts and, therefore, rebates were out of reach. Wee Cho Yaw, newly elected to the vice presidency in 1967, first raised the issue of the freight rates monopoly of the conferences and called it a leftover from colonialism. The SCCC was asked to look into the structure of the shipping conferences and especially into their tariffs and freight contracts by the Rubber Association of Singapore (RAS).[96]

While still working for Aik Hoe, Tan became involved in various manufacturing initiatives. One of these was a bottling franchise of Schweppes and Pepsi Cola called Union Limited, a venture in which he cooperated with Lien Ying Chow. In 1965, the year he left Aik Hoe, he became involved in Alliance Plastics, a company manufacturing lighting fixtures and illuminated signs, produced primarily for Philips. Later the company was renamed Amco Electrical Industries Ltd. and Eng Joo served as Chairman and MD.[93] Other business interests include directorates at Haw Par and Prima Flour Mill.[94]

Tan was involved in the sectoral representation of the rubber business at the national and international level. With independence, the colonial regulatory structure, organized through the Rubber Association of the Singapore Chamber of Commerce, was revised in 1964, with the Rubber Association of Singapore as a result. In 1967, the RAS was made a statutory board under government control and Tan Eng Joo was President of this important regulating body for its first 18 years.[95] Despite his family connection with Tan Lark Sye, he did not take over the latter's passion for Chinese education in the manner of the Ambitious Chamber leaders. He is seen by some in the Chamber as too much of a gentleman and not enough of a Chinese because of his English language education and personal taste for British style. Indeed, when I was invited to his house to interview him over tea and cakes, I was welcomed by Tan Eng Joo, nattily dressed in a tweed jacket, in affable Queen's English that nevertheless commanded attention. The house looked like an English stone country cottage and was furnished with the heavy furniture, paintings and other accessories befitting the style.

Similar to Tan Keong Choon, and very often operating as a dynamic duo, he sat on a host of government boards and committees, following the strategy of seeking and acknowledging active inclusion in the state representational system.

The pressure put on the Chamber by its trading constituency was clear. Chinese rubber producers and traders especially had an axe to grind because the two routes to the rubber market centres of New York and London, on which their export depended, were firmly in the hands of the conferences. After the devaluation of the pound sterling, the FEFC substantially increased its rates and started to demand payment in US dollars. The RAS and the Chamber organized a meeting on 8 April 1967, with Tan Eng Joo, the third of the Chamber's Pragmatist leadership generation and in his capacity of chairman of the RAS, presenting the case.[97]

The issue of the freight rates was presented as a matter of life and death, and the Chamber established a special committee, the members of which included all the Pragmatist leaders: Tan Eng Joo, Wee Cho Yaw, Tan Keong Choon, Lim Kee Meng, Ling Lee Hua and Wee Mon Cheng.[98] From the very beginning of the Chamber efforts in this matter, it was convinced that a wide base of support could be mobilized from among the national and regional commercial sector.

Expected support: appeals to the Singapore government

Local entrepreneurs viewed this problem as an expression of neo-colonial Western economic power over struggling young independent economies and they expected the government to come to their aid in condemning the monopolistic conference practices and in working constructively towards a solution favourable for local business. Throughout those years when the SCCC, in conjunction with many other organizations, tried to break the conference monopolies and provide an alternative freight channel, it would try to convince the government to support its efforts. In an early indication of what they could expect, the government showed its intentions even before the first general meeting on the issue was held. It redirected a three-man FEFC delegation, which had contacted the Ministry of Finance to discuss the issue, to the Chamber stating that this matter should be dealt with directly.[99] The implication was that the government did not see itself responsible for solving the problem.

Still, local traders continued to appeal to both the Singapore and Malaysian governments to act on the shipping fees issue. On 20 May, a broad representative base of the Singapore business world attended a Chamber-organized meeting to increase the pressure on the governments. Sixty-two trade associations sent 162 representatives, and an SMA delegation and a Malaysian MP were present.[100] A Working Committee was set up which was soon expanded to include one Indian and one Malay representative.

By early September, the first tangible strategies were discussed. At an extraordinary meeting of the ACCCM and the SCCC, Tan Eng Joo indicated two possibilities. His first and preferred scenario suggested that the Malaysian and Singapore governments should forbid the contract system in the spirit of the American anti-trust laws. A second alternative would be that all cargo owners or shippers would collectively opt out of their existing contracts with the various conferences. Cross-Straits cooperation was cemented in a joint committee of the SCCC and the ACCCM. While no official statement from the Singapore government was reported at this time, Malaysian officialdom, through Senator Gan Teck Yeow, also in his capacity as representative of the Malaysian Rubber Registration Board, voiced his support, highlighting the adverse effect of the monopoly on the local rubber sector.[101]

Formal organizations: local and regional

In the early months of the movement, and in keeping with the SCCC worldview, much of its attention focused on drumming up support in Malaysia. Assuming that trading houses in Singapore would transfer the increasing freight cost onto many of the producers, especially of rubber, in Malaysia, the Malaysian economy had as much if not more to fear from the shipping monopolies. As a result, official support followed from Inche Abu Bakar bin Pawanchee, Deputy Chairman of the Malaysian Rubber Exchange, who said that Malaysian rubber producers were "at the mercy of the shipping conferences".[102]

The anti-conference actions gained momentum when the FEFC announced a 12½ per cent increase in fees. This news prompted the Working Committee to send representatives to the Singaporean Minister of Finance Goh Keng Swee and make its point of view known in a public letter.[103] The Singapore government could ill afford to ignore the issue altogether and agreed to consider removing the shipping monopoly. Although Goh Keng Swee expressed support, he cautioned that the shipping conferences were not just commercial entities, but had a strong bond with Britain and the British government as well.[104] Renewed rate hikes also inspired higher levels of regional organization. The Working Committee sent information to concerned commercial parties in Thailand, the Philippines, Cambodia, Myanmar, Japan and Hong Kong, and received strong support from Thailand and the Philippines.[105] A collective solution was, however, not yet forthcoming on a regional basis. The first institutional arrangement to circumvent the conference monopoly was implemented by Singapore and Malaysia. As a result of the ACCCM's call on the SCCC to engage non-conference shipping lines, a Booking Centre was set up in Singapore to coordinate cargoes from local shippers to fill non-conference ships. The Booking Centre was housed in the building of the SCCC and a Kuala Lumpur office was to be set up as well. The two top rubber producers and traders in the Chamber, Tan Eng Joo and Tan Keong Choon, were elected president and vice president of the Booking Centre.[106]

Although the formation of a national body to represent shippers was one of the salient points of newly elected president Wee Cho Yaw's policy speech at the Chamber installation of 1969, little seemed to happen concerning this issue during the rest of that year and the better part of 1970. When Hong Kong shippers and industrialists revived the issue in October 1970 by raising commodity prices by 15 per cent and asserting that freight rates commanded this move, the Chamber responded by reactivating the dormant Working Committee. Tan Keong Choon was appointed to lead the revival of the Working Committee into a body comprising businessmen of all races.[107]

It seems plausible that the Chamber wanted a clearer signal of government support. Indeed when concrete plans were implemented, it was after a direct endorsement by the Finance Ministry. When Tan Keong Choon had advocated finally forming a national shippers' council, the government not only applauded the initiative but said it should be implemented as soon as possible. However, while saying they would support the establishment of such an organization, the government stressed that civic organizations should take the initiative. The government chose consistently to stay on the touchline and not get directly involved, an attitude that continued to frustrate the Chamber and the Working Committee.[108] The Working Committee was unanimously named to become the pro tem committee to establish the Singapore National Shippers' Council (SNSC) in September 1972, taking over the tasks of the Booking Centre on 1 January 1973.[109]

Playing the China card

Disappointed with its efforts at the national level and over the position taken by the Singapore government, the Chamber, rather than concentrating on the organization of the SNSC, decided to force its own solution by relying on the logic of its worldview. In an effort to break the FEFC monopoly, it turned to one of the strong nodes in its network and sent a team to the PRC to negotiate cheaper rates from mainland shipping lines. Wee Cho Yaw, leader of the mission, said that the step was taken because of continuing conference rate increases even though the FEFC was reported to have earned a 380 million sterling profit over 1970. The Chamber's status in China secured high-level access and the issue was discussed with Vice Minister Li Chiang and Vice Premier Li Xiannian and other officials. A few days after the mission, Wee disclosed that the PRC would send 10 ships per month to ply the Singapore-Europe line. Reportedly, this kind of volume would be sufficient to handle a third of the cargoes to European destinations.[110]

In December, the Chamber sent another mission to discuss the technical details of the offer. The small delegation of the Chamber led by Vice President Tan Keong Choon, the Booking Centre president Tan Eng Joo, and the managing director of the Booking Centre was extra motivated because four conferences, besides the FEFC, announced rate increases of 12½ to 15 per cent. A deal was made; Chinese ships would start to call on

Singapore regularly, but shippers were under no obligation to use them. The PRC state shipping line COSCO agreed to maintain or only slightly alter rates, at below conference levels, and bookings for the services of their ships could be made through the Booking Centre.[111] Reactions to the deal quickly followed. Pointedly, the FEFC stressed it was not worried by the competition of the Chinese ships, as it was confident of continued support from its member lines. This comment was especially relevant because NOL, Singapore's own state shipping line, had joined the FEFC.

Neptune Orient Lines said the new development did not worry them because if schedules or other issues with the Chinese vessels might clash, NOL could cooperate with the Booking Centre to work things out.[112] The Chamber tried to put moral pressure on the government through statements of its senior members incorrectly interpreting the NOL press release as an intention to get out of the FEFC. Vice President Tan Keong Choon said for instance that "we support the intention of NOL to terminate its membership of the FEFC". President Wee Cho Yaw asked local shippers to give support to and use the Chinese ships and the NOL because it would "only be a matter of time before the NOL would withdraw from FEFC".[113] This approach was based more on hope than on reality because the government and the NOL found themselves in a precarious situation, as the young line depended on the FEFC for its return cargoes from Europe.

Over the next few years, the Chamber continued to utilize its China connection with apparent success. Chinese ships and non-conference lines carried a significant amount of cargo and the conferences lowered their rates in certain parts of the market. Regionalization of shipping policy increased pressure on the conferences and eventually resulted in an ASEAN-based cooperation through its ASEAN-CCI. A regional Shippers' Council was set up, aggregating the efforts of the existing national bodies.[114]

Analyzing the dynamics of the interaction between the Chamber and the government in the case of breaking the shipping conferences, once again, it is clear the Chamber was fighting an issue that was not central to government policies and, therefore, did not receive the official support and recognition it felt it deserved. The Chamber's choice to play the China card to break the conferences further sensitized the issue as the Cultural Revolution raged in the PRC and many countries in the region were very apprehensive about the internal and external volatility of this communist powerhouse. Under these circumstances, although occasionally expressing support in principle, the government, out of consideration for the economic feasibility of its own shipping line NOL, left the initiative and implementation of shipping issues entirely to the private sector. In a number of other developments in trade, industry and finance issues, however, the competition between interests of the state and interests of the local business sector was much more outspoken.

5. Business competition between state and private sector

On a number of issues, the Chamber was disappointed that the government did not defend the interests of local businessmen. It felt that local private business deserved to be treated better than, or at least equal to, foreign private business. More importantly, the Chamber interpreted policies of the government as directly favouring public-sector enterprises over local private enterprises. Protests of the SCCC were vocal and almost continuous, but had little effect. The government was convinced of its economic development strategy to which the contribution of the local trading sector was far from crucial. The relative autonomy of the PAP state from the local business sector made it easy to ignore its protests. The prime reason for this lay in the developmental achievements of the state. Many economic and social indicators pointed to improving conditions. Between 1965 and 1970, GNP per capita doubled and GDP per capita grew annually by 10.7 per cent on average from 1965 to 1973. Availability of medical care markedly improved and infant mortality halved from 35 per thousand live births in 1960 to 14 in 1970. While primary school enrolment continued to be almost total, secondary school enrolment between 1960 and 1975 increased from 32 per cent to 53 per cent. The unemployment rate steadily declined from 8.9 per cent in 1966 to 3.9 per cent in 1974.[115]

This was the success story that the PAP could boast of when it called on local Singapore business to get with the programme. They emphasized their achievements even more when confronted with criticism and complaints from those same circles, stressing that sacrifice was necessary to reach success and that any lowering of standards or deviation from the path set out would jeopardize the best possible result. There were a number of cases in which the Chamber and the government clashed.

Financial policy and taxation

In the first case, an external development, the 15 per cent devaluation of the British pound sterling announced in November 1967, caused unease among local traders, who looked to the government for support and protection. Since the old Malaysian currency, which was tied to sterling, was still valid and the new Singapore currency was not yet in circulation, the Malaysian dollar was widely expected to depreciate as well. As a result of higher interest rates implemented by the Bank of England, rates in Singapore and Malaysia would feel strong upward pressure. The Chamber called on the government and expressed its hope that it would urge financial circles to be reasonable in their rate adjustment.[116] These hopes were proven illusory because within weeks interest rates had shot up to 8.5 per cent, prompting the Chamber to call on the Association of Banks in Malaysia to urge for a sector-wide reduction. The SCCC claimed that raising interest rates would gravely affect both commerce and industry in Singapore, noting in its letter that "disputes have arisen between local banks and import and export firms on the fixing of exchange rates as a result of the sterling devaluation".[117]

While the Chamber claimed that the banks were taking advantage of the situation, the banks said they were simply following the international trend. In an attempt to invoke government support for its position, the Chamber sent a memorandum with its arguments to Goh Keng Swee.[118] Soon after, Chamber president Soon Peng Yam sent a letter to the minister pressing for a cut in bank rates, which would, he argued "go a long way to help not only our industry and commerce but will also strengthen the national economy".[119] The government was unwilling to interfere and left the local business sector disappointed.

One sector in which local businessmen did receive preferential treatment was banking. The government had formulated a policy for the development of Singapore as a regional banking centre. In 1968 the government, after consultation with international banks, established the Asia Dollar Market as an international money and capital market where currency funds (in this case, US dollars) could be transacted. Bank of America was the first financial company to start an Asia Currency Unit in 1968 geared towards providing US dollars to locally-operating MNCs. Many other foreign banks followed and, by 1980, the Asia Dollar Market reached US$54.4 billion in turnover expanding to US$390.4 billion by 1990. This development, and the speed and efficiency with which the Singapore government implemented the legal and financial context necessary to establish this market, ensured that Singapore became the prime market for US dollars in Asia.[120]

In addition, the Monetary Authority of Singapore (MAS) had been set up as the regulatory body and central bank in 1971, as well as tasked to coordinate the policy of attracting foreign financial institutions. Local deposit banking was intentionally shielded from foreign competition through a system of off-shore licensing for foreign banks.[121] This government policy was welcomed by the local financial sector, which in this period was going through a process of consolidation and formalization. A number of takeovers and public listings occurred, resulting in a clear dominance of three banking groups: OCBC controlled by the sons of Lee Kong Chian and led by Tan Chin Tuan; UOB of Wee Cho Yaw and OUB of Lien Ying Chow. OCBC took over Four Seas Bank in 1973; UOB took over Chung Khiaw Bank in 1971, Lee Wah Bank in 1972, and International Bank of Singapore, established in 1974, by 1983. UOB Bank was publicly listed in 1970 and OUB in 1973.[122] The government policy of keeping foreign banks out of the local market definitely contributed to the ability of these three banks to secure a large enough home market to be able to venture out into the region later.

This did not mean, however, that relations between the financial sector and government were smooth from that time on. In 1974, in order to control rampant inflation resulting from the first oil crisis, the MAS ordered local banks to maintain a 9 per cent statutory deposit ratio. The Chamber argued that the MAS policy enhanced rather than quelled inflation because it caused bank rates to go up and negatively affected the Singapore stock exchange. Local merchants had to bear the burden of higher lending rates, which caused prices to increase. While the government indeed eased the measures, the Chamber maintained that the policy should be more lenient in order to let the economy grow.[123] A few years later, Chamber indignation was again fanned by a policy it felt put local traders at a disadvantage. When the government implemented a 20 per cent tax cut for businesses in five non-traditional trades and sectors for a period of five years, it asked that this measure be extended to the whole economy.[124] The government reaction was to be expected. It admonished the Chamber for making the request, saying that the traditional commodity trade was already strong, and did not need the incentive. "Local businessmen should try and venture into new business".[125]

Competition between the state and the Chamber constituency

The problem many local businessmen perceived was that, if they tried to venture into new business, they soon came up against both foreign firms, who operated from a position of experience and financial strength and sometimes operated under preferential taxation, as well as against an ever expanding public sector of government-linked companies (GLCs). The Chamber complained about unfair competition between the public and private sector and unsuccessfully tried to amend the situation.

Urban renewal

A perennial complaint of local entrepreneurs against the government was that the PAP did not use the opportunities in the national development plan to benefit local business. The way in which one of these complaints became a concern for the Chamber again highlights the pressure exerted by the constituency of the SCCC on its leadership. A number of trade associations from the building sector complained to the SCCC, of which they were all members, that the Urban Redevelopment Authority (URA) was only interested in big projects. In doing so, due to sheer size restrictions, the URA made it virtually impossible for (small) local companies to put in competitive bids against large foreign contractors. Four years later, little had changed as five trade associations reportedly asked the Minister of Law and National Development for local builder priority in tenders for urban renewal projects. The Chamber soon echoed this call, claiming that national interest was at stake. A fiery editorial in the *New Nation* was indicative of the government position in this matter. It argued that meritocracy was rightly a strong foundation for Singapore and that special privileges were dangerous. Tan Keong Choon's request for special treatment was falling on treacherous ground because it would raise building costs and blight the investment climate.[126] Nevertheless, the Chamber felt that the government did not try to benefit local business where it could have done so.

Intraco

Another complaint arose when local traders thought that the government was using a private company under its control to tax local traders. In May 1970, the government announced it would start levying a half per cent surcharge on the c.i.f. (cost, insurance and freight) value of imported goods from seven communist countries. Intraco, a government trading corporation set up in 1968 to enhance the bargaining position of Singapore towards socialist countries, would be collecting this tax. The Chamber argued that this was unfair and immediately dispatched a delegation to Goh Keng Swee to discuss the issue. It argued that as Intraco was officially a private company set up for the purpose of making profits from trading, it could not possibly collect surcharges. In the meeting, Goh Keng Swee agreed to lower the levy significantly, while pledging that the remaining taxes collected would be used for local education at Nanyang University and Ngee Ann Polytechnic.[127]

A few weeks later, however, it was announced that the tax would remain and Intraco would be in charge of collection. This decision was made after

Goh Keng Swee and Wee Cho Yaw had a meeting in late June. Wee later explained at the Chamber monthly meeting that the government gave two reasons for its change of heart. It was not prepared to reduce the levy significantly but was also of the opinion that a small reduction would be meaningless and, therefore, decided to stick to the original plan. It did reaffirm that the levy would not benefit Intraco but would indeed be used for local education.[128] It has been difficult to find out whether the government originally planned to use the revenue for local education or had planned to just add it to the general tax income. Likewise, it has been difficult to ascertain from the sources whether the Chamber was unjustly paranoid about the issue because Intraco was merely a coordinating umbrella organization for trade relations rather than a competitor to local traders. The fact remained that the Chamber, and many local Chinese traders, perceived their worst fears to be true.

Chamber actions on the public versus private business debate

At the end of the 1970s, the issue had dissipated little, and a further confrontation between government and Chamber and the public and the private sphere ensued. In the 1970s, the state took an extensive role in commercial enterprise through shareholding and representation on boards of directors. It operated businesses through three fully government-owned holding companies: Temasek, Sheng-Li and MND. Because of these business holdings and the extensive state apparatus of ministries, departments and statutory boards, the government was also the largest employer, which further allowed it to control macro-economic development through wage policy.[129] By 1974, it had direct or indirect participation in 124 firms including vital industries such as iron and steel, shipbuilding and shipping.[130] Dependency on MNCs was high with the possibility of problems for the future in technology and skills transfer. Breaking away from MNC dominance would necessitate a strong government role but, at the same time, would benefit GLCs more than private local industry.[131]

In 1977, when Wee Cho Yaw was again elected president, he asked the government to be clear about the distinction between a private and a public sphere in business so that entrepreneurs could "take functional risks without reservations". His answer to the prevailing lack of clarity was to propose a revision of the tax structure to favour local business and to implement more direct forms of communication, urging the establishment of a liaison body between government and private sector.[132] Wee's call was flatly rejected by the government. Goh Keng Swee commented that the government engaged in business: "not for fun but to fulfil new needs, not by taking over existing business but through establishing new ones. Government enterprises do not get preferential treatment, concealed subsidies or monopolistic rights. ... there is no book of principles which demarcates the respective spheres of private and public enterprise and it is fruitless to argue about where the limit should lie ...".[133]

After this ministerial admonishment, the SCCC Commercial sub-committee went to work to discern specific difficulties in public-private sector demarcation. Housing developers, who were hit the hardest, were heard first behind closed doors. Interviews with representatives of retailing, industry and the import-export sector were also conducted. After a number of these sessions, newspapers reported that the Chamber had presented its views to the government in a memo that was particularly critical of the lack of regulation to prevent encroachment by Japanese companies on the local building and contracting market. The Chamber denied these reports and said its memo would focus on the role of private and public companies rather than on specific encroachments by foreign companies.[134] When the memo was presented, the government reaction was slow in coming. The Ministry of Finance did not discuss the Chamber complaints until seven months later.[135] The tardy response indicates that the government was not taking the Chamber's complaints or its report very seriously. Indeed, the following year, the government continued to push its plans for the national economy on the local business sector without consultation.

In the midst of this discord, a Chamber election was due and the top job was up for grabs. Lim Kee Ming was tipped for the job straight away and was reported to have the blessing of the Hokkien.[136] For the first time in 21 years, a Teochew was elected to the presidency of the Chamber. Lim Kee Ming completed the quartet of Pragmatist leaders.

As the picture book "modern" Chinese businessman, Lim displayed his Pragmatist credentials right away, calling for industrialization, greater efficiency and the creation of large private conglomerates. He recounted that a previous president had mentioned the need to be industrialists as well as traders, that a knife could not be sharp on both sides. In his inaugural speech, Lim countered by asserting it could be done because the Chinese business sector was not a knife but a sword.[137]

However, he inherited some sticky issues that were pressurising the business sector as a whole and had the strongest effect on small- and medium-size Chinese companies. The NWC guidelines for 1979 came in conjunction with a policy on skills upgrading of industry. In practical terms, this development resulted in a triple burden on employers. First, wages were raised to force businesses towards higher labour productivity

Lim Kee Ming: Teochew cosmopolitan.

Ministry of Information, Communications and the Arts. Courtesy of the National Archives of Singapore

A Teochew born in 1927, Lim was well-educated. After primary education in Chinese, he eventually obtained a B.Sc. in Economics from New York University, and an MBA from Columbia. He also studied economics in Chinese at Lingnan University in Canton. His children attended the American School in Singapore and all had tertiary education in the US. At home, however, he made them speak Teochew and Mandarin. While his work ethic and eating habits were described as being "very Chinese", everything else about him, his wife and his family was portrayed in the press as "modern". He even looked a bit like a dandy posing with his cars for

and higher value-added production. Second, the mandatory employer contribution to the Central Provident Fund was raised. Third, to generate revenue for educational initiatives and retraining schemes, a new levy, withholding a percentage of gross wages for the Skills Development Fund (SDF), was introduced. The SCCCI declared it could understand the logic of this approach but voiced its concern that small and medium enterprises (SMEs) would suffer and proposed a number of adaptations.[138] Lim Kee Ming advocated that the SDF levy be waived for smaller firms not operating in manufacturing. This was, of course, a rather naive point of view as the aim of the government was to push the Singapore economy from low-tech commerce to high-tech manufacturing. Still, the Chamber called on all its trade association members for comments and installed sector-specific review panels for construction, building materials, hardware and machinery, and trading to discuss the NWC recommendations.[139]

In the following years, the Chamber continued to emphasize that the policy of wage increases and business taxation was hurting local companies. In memoranda to the NWC and the SDF Council, it asked for temperance on the general principle of increases or, at least, for measures to cushion their impact on local SME companies.[140] In order to produce some supporting data for these pleas, the SCCCI in 1981executed a survey into a picture illustrating a feature article, summing up which of them he used for which occasion.

The family business, "Lim Teck Lee", which concentrated on import and export, was made big by his father, Lim Cher Min, who had been an MC member of the SCCC, just like Kee Ming's uncle. Lim Kee Ming took over responsibility for the family business but also ran a large number of other firms, including Lee Wah Bank, the Nissan car dealership and Federal Paints. He entered into industrial production and joint ventures with foreign companies and acted as local agent for other foreign firms. Some of his brothers worked in the family business and the eldest served as Singapore's senior commissioner of trade to Hong Kong in the early 1970s.

Similar to the other three Pragmatist leaders, Lim sought and accepted a host of official positions. In 1961 and 1963, he was adviser to the Singapore ECAFE delegation and served as deputy leader for the 1966 mission. He played an influential role when EDB was first established in 1963 and served in a number of other representative institutions of Singapore's corporatist structure. He was a Rotarian and a close friend of Wee Cho Yaw.[141]

the effects of the wage policy, mechanization and productivity drives, and the like. The survey among the Chamber's members concentrated on the behaviour of workers and on employer-employee relations.[142] The most striking outcome was that the survey showed that Chinese companies generally did not follow NWC guidelines at all. Still, they were concerned about the goals the government expressed through them, because they expected that existing and prospective employees would be drawn to other sectors of the economy. They also feared that they would be forced to change their management practices and, thereby, would lose control over their businesses. A case in point was that the NWC wanted to abolish the system of giving bonuses to employees in the form of "*hongbao*". These "red packets" with money were handed out to employees at Chinese New Year and were based on company profits and the employee's performance over the last year. Many Chinese businessmen feared that their employees might falsely assume that the NWC set wages, thus alienating them from the employer. Sia Yong, a senior Chamber member, captured the prevailing mood among Chinese SME employers by noting that they did not want the government to interfere with their business. He commented that the traditional bonus system was effective, although a bit old-fashioned, and made "the bosses feel in control".[143]

The wage increase policy and tax increases brought the question of modernization and upgrading right into the small traditional Chinese companies. They felt forced to join the march into unfamiliar territory without yet seeing government policies specifically targeting their sector with aid and guidance. By concentrating on opposing the general policy and by asking for specific exemptions for their sector, the traditional SMEs and the Chamber as their representative were fighting a losing battle.

The sentiment among the members of the Chamber was clear throughout this period. They perceived the government to be encroaching on what they considered the legitimate territory of private business. They pressured the Chamber leadership to conduct research on the issue and to confront the government on a number of specific issues. As a result, the state continued to see the Chamber's constituency of local Chinese business as an old-fashioned sector stubbornly resisting the logic of economic development.

6. Cultural confusion and Confucian culture: education, national campaigns, and Asian values

Continuing to aspire to play more than an economic role in Singapore, the Chamber tried to participate in the building of a modern nation through initiatives and activities in the realm of education and culture. This was a clear indication that the Chamber leaders wanted to continue the multi-purpose elite tradition of their predecessors. However, under its new Pragmatist leadership, the SCCC redirected its efforts in the contentious arena of education away from Chinese-language schooling to vocational initiatives and aimed to improve its image by actively supporting various government campaigns. Although at times acknowledged by the state for these efforts, the Chamber always remained a small cog in the extensive corporatist government machinery. The Chamber leaders saw an opportunity to influence national education policy when the government first introduced the concepts of Asian values and Asian culture as a counter balance against Westernization. The PAP government realized that changing the economic and industrial structure would necessitate a continuing rise of the education level of Singapore citizens. Pulling together the country through "nation building", and the inculcation of "useful" values in tandem with the quashing of traits and tendencies perceived to be "harmful", were central to government's developmental approach. Inevitably, the government's view of what was "useful" or "harmful" concerning culture was destined to clash with the views of the Chamber, which, despite the disciplining it had received from the government on culture, still saw itself as an essentially "Chinese" organization and, therefore, felt entitled to a role in the national discussions. While the government saw ethnicity and culture as instruments to be controlled through corporatist management, these two concepts remained crucial markers of identity and heritage to the Chamber. Still, the Pragmatist leaders of the Chamber tried to work within the parameters of the government system in order to improve its image.

Educational activities of the Chamber

Cautious because of the manner in which Ko Teck Kin and Tan Lark Sye were disciplined by the government for their Ambitious involvement in Chinese-language education, the Pragmatists moved away from that contentious area. They concentrated on promoting science and technology, as well as vocational and other forms of adult education in line with the national requirements identified by the PAP.

The main vehicle for the new Chamber education strategy was its SCCC Foundation, which was established in 1966. The goal of the foundation was to provide scholarships and bursaries and make donations to charity and social work. Among the recipients in 1970 was Lee Kuan Yew's son Lee Hsien Loong, one among six students awarded $500 for excellent marks in attaining their Higher School Certificates. The Chamber tried to present a multi-ethnic image in 1971 when a young Malay woman received $2,000 to further her studies.[144]

Wee Cho Yaw initiated upgrading the financial basis of the Foundation, and after he was first elected president in 1969, he added new goals to its agenda. The promotion of education in science and technology was a project financed by the fund, in addition to the scholarship programme. Wee supported the government's modernization efforts and this project allowed the Chamber to develop a more modern image and allowed the Pragmatists to present themselves as new, different and modern leaders. The three newly elected Chamber chiefs, President Wee Cho Yaw and Vice Presidents Tan Keong Choon and Teo Soo Chuan together donated $430,000 to the fund.[145]

In making their large donations, the three leaders followed the old financial tradition of the Chamber that top leaders would set the example to be followed by the membership. Over the preceding decades, a number of the wealthiest families had already set up charitable organizations themselves and now they contributed handsomely to the Chamber foundation. The Lee Foundation, set up by Lee Kong Chian, contributed $200,000, and $150,000 was donated by the Shaw Foundation. By the end of the year, virtually all big business names and families had donated and the target of $2 million was reached. The Chamber donated $1 million to science promotion projects, and invited representatives from the National Science Council and the Ministry of Education to advise the Chamber on suitable causes. Over the next years, the money was used to purchase science equipment for schools and for the construction of science labs for the students.[146]

A second programme organized industrial training and job orientation for undergraduates. Businessmen, university dons and scientists provided the expertise for the programme. Headed again by Wee Cho Yaw, and financed by a grant of $40,000 from the foundation, the "earn-and-learn" plan aimed for 500 places in the first year. The program received official support from the government through Science and Technology Minister Toh Chin Chye's call on Singapore firms to open their doors to the students, saying that the initiative would provide insight for the participants into what makes Singapore tick.[147]

A third field of education into which the Chamber ventured was that of training specifically targeted at companies. It had, in the past, organized public seminars and talks, and new government policies and regulations were often the topics of these meetings. Now, the Chamber developed specific courses benefiting the day-to-day operation of businesses. At first, courses concentrated on language and covered subjects such as Chinese-English translation and Malay correspondence.[148] The SCCC Education committee was put in charge of developing a plan for what were called "commercial improvement classes".[149] In the first few years the courses focused on explaining the existing opportunities and regulations in the Singapore business environment, with others focused on income tax structures and business taxation. In the early 1970s, management-consulting courses were introduced and the whole curriculum of courses on management and administration were developed in conjunction with Nanyang University. In the late 1970s, the Chamber successfully organized accounting and marketing courses leading to London Chamber of Commerce and Pitman certificates.[150]

Finally, the Chamber started targeting language courses for adults. "Mandarin is tailored for business", stated a "beaming" Lim Kee Ming, when he announced special Mandarin classes for dialect-speaking businessmen at the Chamber. In 1982, the SCCCI set up a $100,000 language lab to teach Mandarin. Among the first courses offered was a Mandarin for Beginners class, which was so popular that an extra class followed shortly after. Another course guaranteed mastery of 1,200 characters, training students to read

90 per cent of newspaper content.[151] When asked about their motivation in joining the courses, students replied that: "the government is promoting Mandarin now and I don't want to lose out".[152] The government approved of the Chamber initiatives concerning adult language education and, subsequently, the press paid quite some attention to the fact that the wife of cabinet minister Jayakumar enrolled in a newspaper reading course.[153]

At the time the Chamber was redirecting its educational activities towards vocational, science and business studies, Nanyang University, the flagship of Chinese education, was slowly being integrated into the national tertiary education structure. Wee Cho Yaw, in his capacity as chairman of the Nanda board, took on this responsibility, an activity for which he did not receive applause in some Chinese education circles. In the process, Nanda lost much of its original zeal and structure, not to mention that its Chinese character was dispensed with. Wee's willingness to oversee the process, and take the blame for squandering the proud Nanda tradition, shows the length to which the Pragmatists would go in order to please the government.

National campaigns

The Chamber equally cooperated with the government in national campaigns. From its rise to power, the PAP government had utilized the "national campaign" as an instrument to disseminate information and organize society. These national campaigns were instruments of public mobilization with the purpose of changing collective behaviour. The campaigns, 66 of them between 1958 and 1982, were initiated by the Prime Minister's office and were all aimed at creating a more disciplined and rational society.[154] The form most often chosen was an annually returning period of attention to a well-defined topic and message. High-level officials would make numerous speeches and the associated events would receive blanket coverage in the media. Societal organizations would be involved to stage meetings, or even at times to take on the running of the entire campaign. The SCCC was often involved, an indication that the government still considered the Chamber as an organization with a significant constituency and a channel through which the population could be reached.

As the PAP party/state became more entrenched, it increased the use of this tool. The Chamber supported many of these endeavours and often appointed one or more of its directors to sit on the organizing committees. It did so when its objectives and perspectives coincided with those of the government but the added effect for the Chamber was that it could publicly align itself with the government to improve its image in the eyes of the PAP party/state. The Chamber could present itself as a modern organization aware of the changes necessary to make Singapore successful. Inferring that pragmatic arguments were the only reason for the Chamber to support these efforts would do injustice to the civic pride and genuine feelings of national development that were present among the Chinese business elite.[155] Tan Keong Choon had become personally involved in a campaign aimed at cleaning up and beautifying Singapore. The Chamber became deeply involved, organizing a drive among its members to whitewash and repaint their shophouses, a lucky draw, and the construction of illuminations throughout the city. Tan also claimed that he was the one who coined the slogan "Singapore, Garden City".[156]

Two campaigns – one on courtesy and one on punctuality – out of the wide array, show how the government connected these campaigns to propagating desired behaviour and values, as well as how existent and desired behaviour were portrayed. Both campaigns promoted values in line with the behaviour desired of a docile hard-working industrial labour force. They were presented as "modern" and "Western" and contrasted with prevailing "bad habits" portrayed as old-fashioned and "Asian". Run by the National Trades Union Council, the Courtesy Campaign, launched in 1979, was part of a larger government strategy to re-educate the population. Newspapers paid attention to a Chamber event supporting the issue, and which was held on the eve of the official launch of the campaign by Lee Kuan Yew. One article centred on an example given by an unnamed Chamber council member about an older member who did not acknowledge him when greeted. By implying that the older member did not return the greeting because he was older and, therefore, considered himself superior in the hierarchy of the Chamber, the article equated "not gracious" with traditional and "old-fashioned". The choice and presentation of this story were full of morally-charged assumptions about the traditional social ways. Assuming that "traditional" Chinese society was ruled by hierarchy and face and automatically resulted in discourteous behaviour, the story implied that these ways and values were unsuited for a "modern" society.[157]

Similar assumptions and moralizations were prominent in another important campaign at the time. The Punctuality Campaign had been ongoing since 1968 and had been run by the People's Association. In 1981, the Chamber started sharing the responsibility of running the campaign in order to contribute to raising productivity, efficiency and team spirit. In a number of seminars and public discussions, the question why the Chinese were so notoriously late was answered by referring to lifestyles and value systems. One speaker held that because the Chinese were brought up in an agricultural society, they were more relaxed and less rigid in keeping time. In the modern society of Singapore, this had developed into a bad habit. Lim Kee Ming subscribed to this point of view when he presented plans to promote the "Drive to save money and time". He stressed that leisurely *kampong*-style agricultural life was not suitable anymore.[158] The media was positive about the fact that the Chamber and a number of other organizations had taken the initiative to put their shoulders under the campaign, but did not share Lim Kee Ming's conviction that persuasion would be effective. The *Business Times* commented gloomily that chances were bad because it was no longer a government campaign. "… Singaporeans must always be led, told or forced to do things. One wonders whether the soft approach will ever work in the city state".[159] Both these campaigns had a negative judgement of "traditional values", and especially Chinese values, as a strong undercurrent. In the eyes of the government, some of the traits of Chinese behaviour were not in line with the requirements of a modern society and, therefore, had to be changed.

The uncertainty of culture and values

Culture was an important concept in the government's orientation and in the implementation of its plans for economic and social development. Because it assumed that culture was a system of human behaviour, the PAP had to pay attention to culture if it wanted to shape and re-shape society. Two government discourses on Chineseness, Asianness or culture are distinguishable in Singapore in this period. One stressed the negative aspects of the Asian identity, while the other sought to select the positive aspects. The first, dominant discourse was that of modernity, meritocracy and efficiency, in which Singaporeans were categorized as being different, and indeed needing to be different from other Chinese or Asians. Lee Kuan Yew made two revealing statements on this subject. "We look Chinese. We speak Chinese. But if a man from China speaks to a Singapore Chinese, he will discover that the Singaporean is already a distinct different type[160] … when you have left the ancestral home and are no longer governed by mandarins trained in the Analects, but by British administrators trained on General Orders which enjoin them to hold the ring fairly and honestly for all who live under their dispensation, it is that much easier to break out of the barren confines of the past".[161]

For the sake of economic development, the government felt strongly that certain family-oriented values and institutional arrangements in business were detrimental and should be changed. Hon Sui Sen told the Chamber that Chinese businessmen should drop the bad habit of nepotism and adopt a new outlook and approach to business. He questioned if the old patterns could withstand the rigours of the modern economy.[162]

Alternatively at various times and for various reasons, the government did invoke a second discourse on the positive role of Asian culture and Confucian values. Goh Keng Swee, for instance, said that traditional virtues of Singaporeans, such as self-reliance, were the key that turned an island-swamp into a thriving metropolis.[163] In this discourse, language was a central marker and vehicle for cultural values that needed to contribute to Singapore's welfare and development. In the early 1970s, the government started to worry that the swing in education towards English could also have undesired results. Lee Kuan Yew said: "If we become like some societies speaking pidgin English, mindlessly aping the American or British with no basic values or culture of their own then, frankly, I do not believe this is a society worth building, let alone defending".[164] Later Lee Chiaw Meng, a former minister of education, said: "Proficiency in the mother tongue – Chinese, Malay or Tamil – is needed to ensure the preservation of our moral values and cultural heritage".[165]

Speak Mandarin Campaign

The promotion of Chinese language and education had always been a focal point to the Chamber, and especially its Ambitious leaders. Well before the government became involved, when Soon Peng Yam was president from 1965 until 1969, the Chamber promoted the use of Chinese quite vigorously. Soon inaugurated an education month during which, in 1966 and 1967, the use of Mandarin as well as dialects was promoted.[166] In the following years the campaign dwindled as the Chamber under the new Pragmatist leadership focused its educational attention on vocational activities. When members, at the Annual General Meeting in 1971, tried to put some constituency pressure on their leaders and urged for new action to defend Chinese education, the browbeaten reply was that this matter depended on the choice of parents.[167] The shift towards education in English with Mandarin, Tamil or Malay as a second language in the curriculum had been significant. Enrolment in these English-stream schools rose from 60.3 per cent in 1966 to 86.1 per cent in 1976, while enrolment in Chinese-stream schools, which taught all subjects in Mandarin except for second language classes, dropped from 32.8 per cent to 13.8 per cent. As a result, English became the lingua franca among school children by the 1970s.[168]

These statistics are a stark contrast to numbers on the dominant language of households, which indicate that as late as 1980, 76 per cent of Chinese households used a Chinese sub-ethnic language such as Hokkien, Teochew or Cantonese in their home.[169]

When the government started to stress the importance of the mother tongue in 1974, the Chamber could not resist hopping onto the bandwagon of Chinese language and education once more. In an echo to imperial China at the time of the "Hundred Days Reform" in 1899, Tan Keong Choon expressed support for Lee Kuan Yew's call for mother tongue studies. Tan emphasized the importance of the mother tongue for cultural identity, saying that people should have "Chinese for culture and morals and English for science".[170] In a televised discussion on the government policy of bilingualism, Lee Kuan Yew stated he was looking forward to the day when 80 per cent of the people would be bilingual, but claimed that there were 12 or 15 years more to go.[171] One sticking point in the government promotion of the 'mother tongue' was that the policy considered Mandarin to be the common shared version of Chinese, when in fact, as argued by a number of Nanda students during the discussion, Mandarin was "not part of our heritage" as many Chinese learned to speak another dialect as their first language.[172]

At this point in time, the Chamber implemented two symbolic and important changes. Both were examples of how the Pragmatists tried to please the government and show its intentions of being part of the modern, developmental orientation of the PAP party/state. The first change pertained to amending its name to Singapore Chinese Chamber of Commerce *and Industry* (italics by author), and it was re-registered at the Registry of Societies. Obviously, the change was made so as to represent "industry" as well as "commerce".[173] The SCCCI felt that the government stereotype of the Chamber as an organization of old-fashioned traders was undeserved and untrue. However, only the English language version of the Chamber's name was adapted; the Chinese name remained as it was. The second change the Chamber implemented under government pressure was that it changed its language of operation from Hokkien to Mandarin. Wee Cho Yaw was in favour of Mandarin but Tan Keong Choon was quoted as saying that it would be a great loss and that it would hinder the Chamber in its activities and many other leaders agreed with Tan.[174]

With the election of Lim Kee Ming in 1979 heralded as a "minor landmark", editorials emphasized the significance of this new, modern leader for progress in the Chamber's old-fashioned organization. The *Straits Times* connected the two issues saying that now that the Hokkien hold over the presidency was broken, Mandarin could be adopted as the official Chamber language.[175] Given the pedigree of the Pragmatists, it was inevitable that the Chamber's official line would follow the government policy, even though many members might not concur. Many still considered the various Chinese languages as valid means of communication. Still, the government announced, through Parliamentary Secretary Ow Chin Hock, that it expected Mandarin to become the common language within the next 10 or 20 years. Strong reservations were reported from clan and *bang* associations, citing the case of the Hokien Huay Kuan. How could an organization expressly based on a shared language and a shared place of origin be expected to decree that its members could not speak their own mother tongue in their own association?[176]

The same argument did not, of course, hold true for the Chamber, which as an inter-*bang* organization was home to many Chinese languages. Still, Hokkien, as the language of the dominant majority had the status of lingua franca. However, the Chinese community at large, due to education in English and Mandarin, was turning to those languages as a means of common communication. Therefore, with younger members joining the Chamber, the need for Hokkien as a lingua franca diminished and Mandarin was chosen to replace it. The express government wish made it a pragmatic choice for the Chamber to change its ways. Older members with weaker Mandarin skills were openly invited by the Chamber leadership to continue to use their dialect and the dominant languages used in the Chamber meetings only slowly changed from dialect and Mandarin to Mandarin and English over the years.[177]

After more pressure from the government, the Chamber, with a number of other organizations, formed a Speak Mandarin Committee, with the slogan "More Mandarin, less dialect". This development went in tandem with the government launch of a "Use Mandarin" campaign. Through this campaign, the government urged everyone, including government clerks, hawkers, bus conductors and taxi drivers, to use Mandarin instead of dialect.[178] The authorities announced that the Chamber-led Speak Mandarin Committee would organize the activities and explained that the central rationale behind the whole endeavour was that dialect hampered the bilingual education policy and thereby stood in the way of the country's economic prosperity.[179]

There were serious reservations among older Chamber members. An anonymous contemporary leader described the mood of this group and said they felt that the government was insincere and half-hearted about the Chinese language. By implementing a "speak" Mandarin campaign instead of a "learn" Mandarin or a "read" Mandarin campaign, the government made clear that the written language, the carrier of history and culture, was left out if not forced out.[180]

Despite these misgivings, the Pragmatist leaders went along with the government's views on language and organized a mass meeting of clan, trade and civic organizations on the use of Mandarin. Leaders of the seven largest *bang* urged all Chinese to learn Mandarin "for greater self-respect, stronger unity and spreading of cultural values". In a notable turn-around, Tan Keong Choon now said that Mandarin represented "the strong character of the Chinese people and the cream of a few thousand years of Chinese history". The response from a thousand representatives of four hundred clan, trade and civic organizations during the mass meeting was overwhelming, and a motion supporting the use of Mandarin was passed with widespread support. Lim Kee Ming said that he had expected some opposition but was happy that it did not materialize.[181] Perhaps the fact that TV cameras were present for the live vote encouraged the nigh absolute endorsement of the Mandarin cause.

Thus, the Chamber became the standard bearer for a government campaign. Every year from 1979 onwards, during one month, it would organize all kinds of activities connected to the use of Mandarin, such as speech contests, courses, singing, story telling, and the like. In the Chamber's own words, it assumed a "very active role in encouraging a wider use of Mandarin among the Chinese community".[182] The Chamber was aware that the government was testing its usefulness as a social organization. The implied message was that the Chamber would have to play an active part in the campaign if it wanted to be taken seriously as a junior partner in the cultural part of the government's corporatist structure.[183]

The accounting of Asian values

On the subject of Asian values, the Chamber was faced with a similar dilemma. On the one hand, it felt it had a legitimate say in the discussion and could speak with authority. On the other, it felt forced to adhere to the PAP version of Asian values. But a significant part of the Chamber membership and leadership was of the opinion that the essence of their Asian value system lay in a number of traditions and institutional arrangements which had been actively discouraged or destroyed by the government. As one observer put it, there was resentment over the lack of acknowledgement for the entrepreneurial skills and the personal networks of the Chinese business sector. Chinese businessmen felt strongly that the institutional structures of family, clan and company brought significant stability to the nation. "Resentment had accumulated at being ruled by one Lee Kuan Yew who did not have a feel for times past or who did not know in himself what it is to be Chinese".[184] When the government started adding Asian values to its repertoire of tools to keep economy and society in check, the Chinese of Singapore and the Chinese business leaders must have thought that new opportunities for their language, culture and way of life lay ahead.

The government perceived threat of, what it called, Westernization and deculturalization was to be countered by Asian values. Asian values were needed to counter "morally dubious" social values of the West, and the academic and media explanation that the economic success of postwar Asian capitalism was due to the special traits of Confucianism further promoted that value system as a way of life for the Chinese of Singapore. Education was to be the cornerstone in achieving the reversal of Westernization. A clear policy signal of this view came in 1978, when the Ministry of Education (MOE) initiated a move to preserve the best nine Chinese stream schools under the Special Assistance Plan. In the 1980s, religious ethics were deemed to be a useful vehicle to convey cultural and moral values. At first, when religious knowledge was included in the school curriculum in 1982, Confucianism was not included as Buddhism was chosen to represent the religious life of the Chinese community. However, Lee Kuan Yew soon made it known that he thought that Chinese parents would probably rather have Confucianism than Buddhism. Harvard professor Tu Wei-ming was brought in and, in 1983, the Institute of East Asian Philosophies was founded to guide the process. Eventually, however, the religious knowledge programme was discontinued in 1989.[185]

With the entrance of Asian values into the socio-political arena and the related attention for Confucianism in education, the Chamber was eager to take up an active role, and portrayed itself as the prime example of a Chinese institution steeped in tradition, Confucianism and Asian values. However, both in language policy and in the values campaign, Chamber and government continued to have quite different views of what language and culture meant and what purpose these two should serve.

Still, the SCCCI pronounced at its 75th anniversary that "Asian Values are the guiding philosophy of the Chamber".[186] Wanting to heighten its profile as a leader in Chinese culture and values, the Chamber language centre produced a series of audiotapes on the essence of Confucius' thought.[187] In addition, as a first in a series of festive occasions, the Chamber organized a Mid-Autumn Festival dinner celebrating the richness of Chinese culture. It invited members of other trade bodies and government departments to partake in the festivities. The SCCCI had always held a Chinese New Year celebration for its members, and now the Chinese festival series was organized for 200 officials from other chambers, business councils and government departments as well. Directly linking old traditions with modern political goals, Tan Keong Choon pointed out, during the Duanwu (Dragon Boat) Festival celebration at the Chamber, that Duanwu embodied loyalty to one's country.[188]

On a number of occasions, the Chamber sought to introduce Asian values arguments into discussions on political issues. The discussion surrounding the preference of Chinese companies to give *hongbao* bonuses instead of structural wage increases was one example. Another Chamber attempt to link its view on traditional values to social policy came when it opposed a law compelling children to take care of their aged parents and a law linking the licensing of religious activities with the compulsory establishment of old age homes. In the course of the discussions on these two pieces of legislation, the Chamber gave its recommendations to the government Committee on Problems of the Aged.[189] It argued that friends, good health and job security were what old people needed most to bring meaning to their lives. Aside from emphasizing the need for filial piety and respect for the aged, the SCCCI advocated the creation of a part-time employment market and the setting up of a fund with 6 per cent of the contributions to the Skills Development Fund and payroll tax. This fund should then be used to finance retirement benefits, to keep the aged up to date on medical health and nutrition, and to allow community centres to set up more health, educational and recreational activities. The Chamber also advised implementing tax relief for young people taking care of the older family members.[190] None of the Chamber's suggestions were taken up.

There was a clear distance between the views of the Chamber and the government on the meaning of Asian values and to what end they should be promoted. The Chamber perceived much ambivalence in the government's use of tradition and culture. On the one hand, the clan and the Chinese family business, two bases of institutional structure of the Chinese community, were under constant criticism as being outdated. The government often reiterated the need to move with the times and portrayed the family business as a problem. On the other hand, senior government officials emphasized that Asian values were crucial to the survival and the continued success of the nation. Obviously, the government version of Asian values differed from what many Chinese considered them to be. The government tried a number of types, versions and vehicles, as was shown by the inclusion of moral ethics and later Confucianism in the secondary school curriculum. The eventual removal of these subjects indicated that the government had not figured out how the values they preferred could be packaged and communicated as Asian values. Both language and religion were discarded as too dangerous to be the vehicle of choice.

In the meantime, Chinese groups concerned about preserving their form of Asian values received some food for thought from Second Deputy Prime Minister Ong Teng Cheong. In a clear example of the way the government viewed culture as a pragmatic and malleable category, he told the Chinese of Singapore to "take a good look at those cultural values worth preserving, and simplify or improve on those that are outmoded". He urged Chinese to "be bold and make radical changes" to "bad practices". These included "extravagant celebrations on happy occasions, the growing habit of gambling and the many unnecessary ceremonies at weddings and funerals." He observed that there would be "problems if different dialect groups observed different practices in a small place like Singapore".[191]

With this kind of government attitude towards culture, and with the uncertainty surrounding the values and vehicles it would promote and condone, it was no surprise that the Chamber was wary of taking too bold a position on the issue, especially when the Singapore success story was starting to show some serious cracks.

7. The makings of a crisis: 1979–1984

The period 1979–1984 was a transitional one for Singapore in its economy as well as in politics. Forced to deal with the economic problems and attempting to introduce a second generation of leaders, the PAP had trouble finding and implementing successful solutions to the country's development problems and in fulfilling the high expectations of the population. The resulting success, albeit limited, of opposition parties at the polls meant the feeble beginnings of the reintroduction of politics as an arena of contest and competition. For the Chamber, the period was characterized by uncertainty, as the state did not offer a strong lead. This exacerbated the identity crisis in the Chamber about which roles to aspire to and what external strategy to pursue.

Restructuring the economy

The oil crises of the early 1970s and the resulting worldwide recession and restructuring had a great impact on Singapore. Having barely come to terms with the military pullback of the British, this new development posed a challenge to the PAP party/state. Although the Singapore economy did not go into recession until 1985, economic problems and serious challenges to the government's development policy prompted the PAP party/state to take action.

In the years 1973 to 1979, real GDP growth per capita had been wiped out completely by growing inflation. Despite government efforts to change the economy from trade based to manufacturing and industrial production, there was little change in the dominant pattern. The share of manufacturing in the country's GDP rose only by one per cent, while the share of commerce dropped slightly.[192] Furthermore, a number of developments in the late 1970s resulted in a net loss of international competitiveness for Singapore. Other developing countries started to compete with Singapore in attracting MNCs because of the adverse effect of rising wages in Singapore and falling wages in Western countries eating into Singapore's comparative advantage.[193] With a growing population and the need for continued national investment in education and infrastructure, these developments were a severe threat to Singapore's economic future.

The government's economic recovery strategy after 1974–1975 had been geared towards improving comparative attractiveness to foreign capital compared to other Newly Industrializing Countries (NICs). Labour was forced to accept even lower wages and fewer rights. A bounce-back did occur but despite this growth in higher value-added goods, an even larger increase in low value-added manufacturing goods exported to the US and the European Economic Community under the Generalized System of Preferences (GSP)[194] trading scheme was starting to irritate the manufacturers in those markets. As a result, lobbies were started and some increased tariffs on Singapore exports were implemented by the EEC as early as 1976.[195]

The PAP strategy of attracting even more MNCs meant that their relative importance in Singapore manufacturing grew. Statistics for 1982 indicated that these companies shipped 72 per cent of Singapore's direct exports and generated 70 per cent of its pre-tax profits. MNCs, however, were in specific sectors and indigenous manufacturing had managed to carve out niches for itself. Sectors dominated by local capital included transport equipment (shipbuilding and repair), food industry, and textiles and clothing, and were mostly low value-added and low technology in nature. As early as the mid-1970s, the government tried to provide incentives to indigenous firms to upgrade.[196]

By 1979, the PAP government decided to forcibly change the markets of labour and production. Goh Keng Swee and Lee Kuan Yew followed the advice of Dutch economic advisor Winsemius to move Singapore upmarket.[197] Labour shortage, the strength of the Singapore dollar, the impending loss of comparative competitiveness and the danger of losing GSP pushed the PAP to change its strategy and develop the Second Industrial Revolution Plan. This plan consisted of a number of years of government-set wage increases, vast investment in infrastructural improvement, new limits on imported labour, tax incentives for investment, and industry-based organization of labour. Mechanization, automation and computerization were to be encouraged. By bearing a lot of the costs, the government aimed to create a comparative advantage in higher value-added production while simultaneously introducing labour-replacing technology and stimulating on-going education of the workforce. The plan represented a major attempt at state intervention in and control of the process of industrial upgrading within the NIDL.[198]

Despite a degree of success, in an oversimplified sense, the effect of this big intervention was that it put great pressure on the local low-tech production sector, and also on the trade sector, which was equally forced to follow the wage increases. It was described above how these developments affected the Chinese business sector and how the SCCCI reacted. Despite the obvious problems with the upgrading approach, the government focus remained on industrial production within the NIDL. Only during and after the 1984–1985 crisis did it realize the limitations of this model.[199]

While corporatism was the government's model to deal with representation in business, social and educational spheres, it had equally tried to set up a structure of specific representational channels to deal with political representation in a more controlled manner. Party/state organizations were built up from the grassroots to the highest levels of government. Still, some political developments started to worry the PAP. The 30 per cent opposition vote in the 1972 general election, for instance, was interpreted by the PAP as a protest. It viewed it as a containable phenomenon, and as a pre-emptive measure started bringing in new and younger leadership to the higher echelons of party and state.[200] Of the new faces introduced at this time, three would prove to stand out in the decades to come: Goh Chok Tong, Tony Tan and Ong Teng Cheong. They were given positions in the cabinet and/or in the PAP central executive committee. While all three had experience in business management, Tan, with his background in banking at OCBC, was one of the few members of the de facto business aristocracy to come forward in politics.[201] Goh and Ong had been scouted early and nurtured as talented potential party men through scholarships and a carefully planned business career in several

GLCs. Goh started with the most high-profile jobs, presenting the 1979 budget, running a by-election campaign for the PAP and being the man in charge of the campaign on "total defence".

Still, leadership renewal proved to be insufficient to continue the PAP's 100 per cent control of the country's legislature. A 1981 by-election in the Anson constituency was won by opposition candidate J. B. Jeyaratnam of the Workers' Party. He was the first non-PAP member of parliament since 1968. Developments concerning housing and the economy were seen as the reasons for the large opposition vote. By the time of the Second Industrial Revolution Plan, 80 per cent of the population was housed in government-controlled Housing Development Board (HDB) flats. The success of this government-subsidized housing programme, however, was a problem too. The enormous powers of social control it resulted in became the focus of non-cooperation and dissent and ultimately new political opposition. Family budgets were strained when HDB apartment rents rose sharply.[202] After the Anson by-election, there was a backlash of government intervention. A stranglehold monopoly was enforced on the press through Singapore Press Holdings.[203] Even though one seat in parliament was never going to give the opposition any influence over legislation, the PAP was very concerned with the show of public dissent. In a speech in February 1982, cabinet minister Rajaratnam said: "the role of an opposition is to ensure bad government". The PAP saw Jeyaratnam's election as the first step on the road to Singapore's economic ruin.[204] In the following years, the PAP would throw all its political, legal and judiciary might at the opposition and at Jeyaratnam in particular, attempting and eventually succeeding in ousting him from politics.[205]

In light of the electoral disquiet, legislative steps were taken to prevent the mood spreading and resulting in disruptive claims by the labour force. The 1982 Trade Unions (Amendments) Bill further emphasized cooperative industrial relations by specifically defining union activities as promoting "good" industrial relations, improving work conditions, and helping to increase productivity. Even the *Straits Times* observed: "the amendments are a systematic attempt to remove any legal obstacles in the way of the nation's objectives".[206] Societal dissent and political opposition remained prominent, causing the government to look into constitutional reforms in order to pre-empt a further electoral slide. In August 1984, the non-constituency Member of Parliament proposal was pushed through parliament in order to guarantee that at least three seats would be held by non-PAP members. The PAP rationale for the move was that in this manner, the people did not have to actually vote for the opposition in order to get a token opposition voice in parliament, but voting patterns changed little.[207]

Further economic problems in the mid-1980s continued to damage the government image as efficient leader of the country's economic development. The economic recession and the domestic socio-political developments forced the government to overhaul its economic and political plans. From 1978 until late 1984, the PAP government implemented a number of economic and political plans that were not sufficiently effective to take away the sense of uncertainty on the part of the people and the government alike. The mounting identity problems of the SCCCI need to be viewed in this national context.

Crisis in the Chamber

Ever since the PAP won the 1959 election, the relative power and influence of the Chamber had diminished as the party/state had grown stronger. With the PAP's legitimacy dented on the economic as well as the political fronts, the SCCCI could conceivably have seized the opportunity to regain some lost ground. This short period of relative weakness of the state was not enough to lift the Chamber because it was relatively weak itself and, therefore, indecisive about its external strategies. The prime reason for this was that the Chamber did not have a clear, well-defined role that gave it some clout and independence. While most of its membership still came from traditional and small family enterprises, the SCCCI leaders were increasingly involved in the modern service sectors of banking, finance and real estate. Internal developments illustrate some of the choices and problems faced by the SCCCI.

The SCCCI and government economic policy

Initiatives by the Chamber leadership illustrate the continuation of its willingness to comply with government policy. It focused on a few areas of active state initiative and policy: modernization, industrialization and regionalization. In his inauguration speech in 1979, Lim Kee Ming called on local trading firms to merge and aim for conglomerate trading companies such as existed in Korea and Japan. He also contended that the same could be attempted in banking, shipping and manufacturing, sectors in which similar advantages of economies of scale would apply. The Chamber's own role in this development could be to broker in these mergers and partnerships.[208] Apart from size, efficiency and productivity concerns, Lim's proposal supported the government idea that Singapore companies could gain access to advanced technology through cooperation with foreign companies. His statement that SCCCI member companies should consider foreign and local non-Chinese partners in these efforts was perhaps the most noteworthy aspect of his proposal. Membership of the Chamber was, after all, still restricted to majority Chinese-owned companies.[209]

Later in the year, in a keynote speech at the 19th graduation ceremony of Singapore Polytechnic, Lim Kee Ming told the graduates to pitch their expertise to local companies. In his view, young technical talent was not reaching the world of local business and he proposed that the Chamber would take the initiative in matchmaking graduates and companies.[210] Talent was flowing to GLCs or foreign firms. Lim's underlying message was that Singapore companies should follow government policy and get involved in industrial production and higher technology. Only in this manner could Singaporeans "be at the vanguard of the 2nd industrial revolution".[211] The plan was generally well received and one editorial called it "a breath of fresh air".[212] But by the next year, however, the initiative had turned completely sour.[213]

In a familiar pattern, while the intention of the Chamber leadership to continue to comply with government policies was evident, the Chamber membership forced the leadership to voice concern about undue pressure on local business, especially on the small and medium enterprise (SME) sector. In the early 1980s the perennial business sector concern over government interference with, and taxation of, entrepreneurial endeavours that would result in higher cost of doing business united SME members in the SCCCI. Their apprehension was exacerbated by the pressure to modernize and by the competition with both local GLCs and MNCs.

Power to the small

In this period of economic difficulty for SMEs, a movement from among the rank and file of the Chamber started demanding more structural arrangements to ensure the adequate representation of their interests and needs. The 110 trade association members of the SCCCI were the driving force behind this development. Together they represented an estimated 8,000 to 10,000 companies, predominantly those of smaller scale. At the AGM of 1981, six trade association (TA) members[214] tabled a proposal to double the amount of seats for trade associations under the Chamber constitution from 10 to 20. Effectively, the proposal would give smaller companies a larger say in the Chamber.[215]

Ling Lee Hua, a respected Chamber leader and a rubber and pepper trader, put his weight behind the cause, asserting that greater contact between Chamber and the trade associations was necessary.[216] Ling had organized a get-together to establish a better rapport and bridge the communication gap between the Secretariat and Commerce Sub-Committee members of the Chamber and their counterparts in the affiliated trade associations. He said that this gap prevented the Chamber from fully and effectively reflecting the views of the trade associations on policy changes to the relevant authorities.[217] Of course, the Secretariat was directly under the control of the top leadership; so this statement can be interpreted as criticism that the leadership had allowed a gap to form. With so much momentum behind the proposal, the official changes to the constitution were a mere formality.[218] In 1983, the trade association members chose their 20 council members from amongst themselves with the customary eye for the representation of the various dialect groups.[219] The membership had scored a victory over the leadership.

In a further development that showed the majority of the Chamber had strong feelings about the tradition and identity of their organization, the membership application of Metal Box Singapore Ltd. presented the Chamber with some degree of trouble. According to the requirements for membership under its constitution, any aspiring corporate member needed to prove that its equity was 51 per cent Chinese owned, and furthermore had to declare a dialect group to which it belonged. The ownership structure of Metal Box Singapore was complicated to say the least. The largest part of its shares, totalling 41 per cent, was held by its British mother company Metal Box (UK) Plc. A further 34 per cent of shares were held by Fraser and Neave and Malayan Breweries Ltd (MBL). In both these companies, OCBC, the banking firm controlled by the Lee family of the late Lee Kong Chian, had a large stake, thus providing a strong Singapore Chinese element. Heineken from the Netherlands owned 40 per cent of MBL, however, and thereby diminished the Chinese character of Metal Box Singapore. The remaining 25 per cent of the company's shares were traded on the Singapore stock exchange. As it was impossible for the firm to prove its Chinese ownership, Metal Box withdrew its application, after having been made aware of the detailed requirements.[220]

A scathing editorial highlighted the folly of calculating the "Chineseness" of a publicly-listed company and reiterated that the Chamber's "racial barriers are anachronistic". The editorial drew a direct comparison with the SMA which, it emphasized, was open to all and urged the SCCCI to change its rules.[221] In a quick and unequivocal response, President Tan Keong Choon stated that the Chamber would not relax its entry rules.[222]

Split personality leads to identity crisis

The pressure by the government on the Chamber had been mounting for decades and the organization was starting to show the strain. Newspapers regularly pointed out that new generations of entrepreneurs failed to see any use in joining the SCCC. On the election of 1975, one report stated that "... young Singaporeans are more interested in joining the SMA, Rotary or Lions". It continued with the observation that the "Chamber might have become an anachronism in modern multi-racial Singapore. With an independent Singapore government the need for a liaison body has lessened".[223]

An embarrassing deadlock during the 1977 election only worsened this image of being an outdated institution. The Hokkien tried to have the Teochew forward a presidential candidate, but internal competition resulted in the stalling of the whole election process. The ensuing haggling over the leadership positions reinforced the idea that the Chamber was a playground for rich Chinese merchants rather than an organization that could be a constructive part of Singapore society. The Chamber received a clear warning from high government circles when a *Business Times* article said that the SCCC had become too conservative, entrenched in old roles, and was not revamping itself nor re-orienting the organization away from the prevailing clannishness. The *Straits Times* echoed this point of view observing that "with Singapore independence, the Chamber must co-operate with the government and promote national instead of sectoral interests".[224]

In a long critical article a year later, the *Business Times* called on the Chamber to drop the use of dialect and the *bang* election system, and referred directly to the internal factional strife among the Teochew which had prevented the SCCC from smoothly appointing a president. The paper held that the whole organizational structure and culture of the Chamber blocked the inflow of young leaders. This badly needed new blood preferred to join the SMA because they deemed it to be more active and functional while perceiving that the political and commercial influence of the SCCC had eroded. In the eyes of the *Business Times*, the Chamber had become an atavistic and symbolic institution.[225]

Things did not change when Lim Kee Ming was elected in 1979, despite him stressing immediately that economic growth and maintaining political stability were to be the core tasks for the years to come.[226] Shortly after Lim's ascent to power, the *Far Eastern Economic Review (FEER)* published an obvious "double bill" spread on leadership renewal in Singapore. The articles made a causal connection between Chamber and government efforts to introduce new faces, asserting that: "Lim's election came close on the heels of the setting up of a new Ministry of Trade and Industry in Singapore, headed by Goh Chok Tong." The election of Lim was described as "an attempt by a venerable but declining organisation to modernise itself to meet the demands of a changing society." The article noted Lim was a "manufacturer, as well as a banker and trader". Fittingly, Goh Chok Tong's first official function as Minister of Trade and Industry was that of guest of honour at the swearing-in ceremony of Lim and the new MC. On that occasion, Goh stated that the recent inclusion of "Industry" in the official name of the Chamber was "a refreshing change" which "reflected the Chamber's recognition of the importance of industry in our economy". Lim was aware, though, that a significant number of Chamber members felt that the government policy of attracting and accommodating foreign investors had been to the detriment of indigenous trade and industry. Caught sitting on the fence between his constituency and the needs of the national economy, Lim had to acknowledge, however, that "given the scarcity of national resources and the relative small size of the population, it is obvious that the government must adopt such a policy".[227]

This indecision, or to put it more fairly, this inability to chose between its traditional power base and the new political reality, was the reason for the Chamber's decline when it slowly relinquished its position as the pillar of the Chinese community. The *FEER* article points out that this was almost inevitable because the Chamber, in championing Chinese language, education and culture, had come into direct conflict with the government, which was pushing for national integration aimed at transcending the various ethnic groups within Singapore. This government push was also sensitive to the economic and security issues of the region and, specifically, of Singapore's hinterland of Malaysia and Indonesia. Even in the field of economics, the Chamber had failed to become part of the so-called "developmental elites" of the new Singapore nation. With a degree of understatement, it noted that some observers were saying that the SMA was "beginning to overshadow the Chamber".[228] This process had been underway since 1959 and the government clearly favoured other channels to reach the local business world and to get feedback on its policies.[229]

The occasion of the Chamber's 75th anniversary presented an opportunity to discern how the role of the SCCCI was seen by the government as well as by itself. The dominant self-image that was projected through historical overviews and statements by its own leaders was that of the Chamber as a bridge between the government and society, and as a venerable organization with "a long history, firm foundation and undying zeal".[230] Lim Kee Ming, in his anniversary speech, emphasized the history and the "groundedness" of the Chamber and of the local enterprises it represented. He made a direct appeal to the government to "bolster firms with roots", because only these would weather the economic crises that foreign companies would not.[231] Environment Minister Ong Pang Boon, the keynote speaker for the government at the festivities, painted quite a different picture. Rather than seeing the history and tradition of the Chamber as a positive quality, he asked the question that given "the present divisive clan system, how can the Chamber fight for national interest and protect its members all the way through and enable them to compete with foreigners here and abroad".[232] Counter to the image that the Chamber was important because of it rootedness and national conviction, Ong highlighted that protectionism, called for by the Chamber in a number of developments, would destroy Singapore's economic foundation. He pictured the Chamber as a "stymied and conservative organization" which should "learn from Japanese management as well as from their spirit of patriotism, nationalism and togetherness".[233]

The inevitable conclusion from these divergent perceptions of the role of the Chamber has to be that the Chamber and the government still represented two different worldviews. Their premises of change, development and social responsibility were grounded in opposing ways of understanding the world. The persisting economic and budding political problems, which failed to result in clear government policies, did not help to unite the two orientations. The continuing Chamber attempts to show sensitivity towards the government's wishes and to comply with its core policy goals equally failed to convince the PAP party/state. In short, the insecurity and uncertainty of the government in this period strengthened the inherent schizophrenic tendency of the Chamber along the lines of the needs and goals of its membership and those of its leadership.

Concluding remarks

A number of internal and external factors diminished the status and power of the Chamber vis-à-vis the state. Internal factors originated in the relation between leadership and membership. Attempts by the SCCC's new, younger and better-educated leadership of the Pragmatists to reposition the organization within independent Singapore and to comply with the policies and expectations of the PAP party/state failed. The principal reason for the failure was that, in contrast with the "big business" background of the Chamber leaders, the majority of the membership was still involved in small and medium commercial ventures and their operations, strategies and actions were framed by their traders' worldview. The new leadership could not ignore or cast off this traders' outlook. Chamber leaders were not just individual businessmen who had done better than others. Their position at the top of the SCCC required that they represent the economic and social interests of their trader constituency – a constituency which in turn would confer status and power on its leaders through the integrated socio-political system of the *huiguan*, *bang*, trade associations and, ultimately, the Chamber. This symbiosis of power, status and representation meant that in its external strategies, the Chamber remained loyal to its traders' worldview, despite its attempts to comply with the logic of the government development plan. It sought to help its constituents fit into modern Singapore, without abandoning their core business or beliefs, but was faced with a determined state.

The external reasons for the loss of status and power of the Chamber were defined by the government's worldview. Leading a now fully independent nation, the PAP government set up a strong party/state apparatus that was built on and legitimized by meritocracy and successful economic development. The chosen strategy was industrialization through FDI and the placement of Singapore as a base for production of multinational companies within the NIDL. This strategy effectively ignored the local merchant sector and, thereby, eroded the Chamber's status. The SCCC missed the mark with the government by picking issues that were either not central to the PAP development plan, such as trade promotion, or even went against the PAP's larger global economic logic such as in the case of the fight against the Western shipping monopolies and complaints over undue competition of the public sector with local private enterprise. The Chamber struggled at the fringes of the PAP grand plan, not at its heart.

The Chamber also lost its prominence in socio-political and cultural matters. As the SCCC(I) was expressly founded on an ethnic and not a national basis, its role as a political force was downgraded from being a crucial representative of the major ethnic group during decolonization and the period of independence within Malaysia to being the voice of what the PAP saw as a suspect sub-group of cultural and class interests. This process was reinforced by the introduction of a complete new system of social representational structures by the PAP party/state, which effectively sidelined the traditional structure of clan and speech group associations of the Chinese community.

For a period of time, it seemed that there was a possibility of cooperation between state and Chamber over values and culture. Having identified "Westernization" as a negative influence on Singapore society, the government experimented with the introduction of campaigns and education based on the merit of Asian tradition and practices. As the PAP tried different definitions, modes and forms of Asian values, the Chamber participated enthusiastically, propagating what it thought were the central tenets of Chinese culture. It also accepted the lead in the Speak Mandarin Campaign despite opposition from inside and outside the Chamber. Over the years, it often found itself using a different yardstick by which to measure culture and values; its worldview and that of the PAP party/state continued to differ. As a result, the Chamber was cautious in pursuing its own interpretation of Asian values without some indication of government approval.

When the Singapore success story began to show its first cracks, uncertainty was caused by the fact that, for the first time since the PAP came to power, social and economic policies were not showing the customary efficient results. The PAP was forced to develop its Second Industrial Revolution programme, but the programme weighed heavily on the local business sector and failed to be successful. In the corporatist complex of government-sanctioned and government-controlled channels of communication and representation, the Chamber leadership was co-opted into economic, financial and cultural boards and committees. The Chamber was faced with a familiar choice. Would it be an ally of the state in pressing for modernization, industrialization, education and the government version of social campaigns, culture and values? Or, alternatively, would it speak for the economic interests of SMEs and be the champion of a different interpretation of what Chinese language and culture meant to local people? The Pragmatists continued to attempt to do both but the double bind of leadership and constituency remained. Membership was, after all, still largely made up of SMEs, traditional trading companies and labour intensive manufacturing. Furthermore, a large part of the Chinese community was still dialect speaking and saw their Chineseness as a real identity marker.

The internal and external pressures on the Chamber led to an identity crisis. Internally, tensions between leadership and membership were played out in the successful dash for power by the trade association members, which indicated that the traditional base could counter the cosmopolitan elite of the Chamber. Externally, the government continued not only to see the SCCCI as non-essential, but referred to it as old-fashioned, traditional and hampered by the constraints of family and culture.

Constitution Exposition, 1959.

Courtesy of the National Archives of Singapore

David Marshall at a Merdeka rally.

Ministry of Information, Communications and the Arts. Courtesy of the National Archives of Singapore

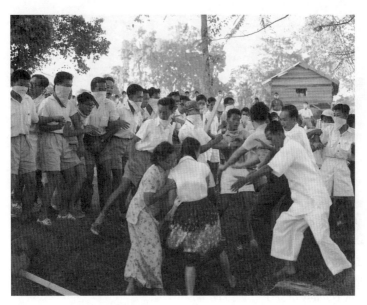

1961 examination boycott.

Photograph by courtesy of SPH – The Straits Times

Merger referendum voters at Tongan Huiguan, 1962.

Ministry of Information, Communications and the Arts. Courtesy of the National Archives of Singapore

PM Lee Kuan Yew meets with Ko Teck Kin and other SCCC leaders just before the 1962 merger referendum.

Photograph by courtesy of SPH – The Straits Times

The Civilian War Memorial at Beach Road built in 1964.

Ministry of Communication and the Arts. Courtesy of the National Archives of Singapore

The Merlion: image of a nation.

Copyright Sikko Visscher

The state housing the nation: Toa Payoh New Town, 1967.

Courtesy of the National Archives of Singapore

Jurong Industrial Park, 1967.

Courtesy of the National Archives of Singapore

CHAPTER SIX

1985–1997
Change of fortune: Chamber reforms and state reorientation

Please be mentally prepared for what must be changed. [1]

BETWEEN 1985 AND 1997, THE CHAMBER experienced an enormous change of fortune. It revamped itself drastically through a number of internal reforms, culminating in a constitutional change in 1993 that abolished the *bang* based election system. It also turned around the decades of trouble with its image and status in the national business arena and its relationship with the PAP state. From the identity crisis of 1984 it slowly emerged as a confident business organization with an increasingly close relationship with the government, and receiving more and more praise for the role it played. This chapter will relate how this amazing change of fortune for the Chamber came about.

First of all, it needed the toughest economic ordeal the young nation had encountered when a recession hit Singapore hard in 1985. For the first time since decolonization, its economy contracted and government reaction was needed. It overhauled the economy and formulated plans that included more emphasis on the tertiary sector, trade and a comprehensive initiative towards the development of local small and medium enterprises (SMEs). These measures proved to present significant opportunities for the SCCCI in arenas in which it felt confident. The worldview of the Chamber and its members had always been closely linked with the local SME sector, as well as with trade and services in the region. The Chamber was eager to take part in the government master plan for SMEs and implemented hands-on programmes directly benefiting this sector. The SCCCI further cooperated with the government by helping to expand trade in old and new guises and promoting the policy of increased ethnic cooperation in business. The opening up of China, and its subsequent economic rise, was the other change of fortune that greatly affected the SCCCI's position. With the government eager to benefit from the worldwide fixation on China, the Chamber used, and greatly expanded, its activities in Chinese networking and China brokering.

After the initial hardship, this period saw the Chamber forging ahead with a new élan. Internal reforms brought leadership rejuvenation, the rise of a new generation of "Reformer" leaders, and a professionalization of the Chamber's activities, in both form and content. The SCCCI established a more professional, modern image, so it could become a viable dialogue partner for the government. It was ready to acknowledge the primacy of the state and wanted to cooperate with it to establish a meaningful niche in the representational structure of Singapore.

In the process of adapting itself to the state's wishes, the Chamber lost the social and cultural roles it had called its own for 80 years. Bowing to the wishes of the state, the responsibilities for the social and cultural welfare of the Chinese community were officially handed over to new, state endorsed institutions. Having been a multi-purpose institution since its inception, the Chamber came to grips with the fact that in modern Singapore it can only claim a successful role as a commercial organization.

In the following sections the pivotal reform of the Chamber will be introduced before the explanation and analysis of how the SCCCI could make such a remarkable turnaround from the throes of an identity crisis to lobbying success.

1. The great reform of 1993: ending the *bang* system

On Saturday 21 August 1993, members and leaders of the Chamber started streaming into its premises at 47 Hill Street. The car park attendants were out in force to valet the many cars, most large, some small, in the most efficient manner. Soon the meeting hall was filled and there was a buzz of excitement in the air. This was the day the venerably aged institution was to make official its largest reform ever. Attempts had been made from as early as 1929 to do away with the election system based on the proportional representation of the various dialect groups or *bang*. Those gathered were acutely aware that major leaders of the Singapore Chinese community, such as Tan Kah Kee and Lee Kong Chian, had failed to achieve what was about to be enshrined in the SCCCI's constitution. In the 1950s and 1960s, members had almost come to blows over the issue in heated and emotional meetings, some of which had taken place in the very same hall where the Extraordinary General Meeting had now gathered. The man responsible for this revolution was Kwek Leng Joo, a young man at 40, bespectacled and impeccably dressed.

While the task of seeing through the momentous reform had been left to the younger generation, it would of course be impossible to accomplish anything without the tacit approval of the elders behind the scenes. A core group of leaders served as an acting and controlling group, especially during election time, and in 1993, the outgoing president Tan Eng Joo was its spokesman. A division of labour between the status of the old generation and the knowledge and image appeal of the younger generation was necessary. The election of the council in 1993 proved to be the watershed event. A new generation of "Reformers" was given the task that the Pragmatists of the previous generation were unwilling, or unable, to perform. Section 2 will show how initiatives by the transitional figure of Linn In Hua had been important in paving the way, but for abolishing the *bang* system, a new breed of leader was needed.

Tan Eng Joo, a good friend of Leng Joo's father, had followed Leng Joo's progress and had short-listed him as his possible successor at the beginning of his second term as president. During talks between Tan and Kwek Leng Joo in January, the elder convinced the younger to take the job. In those talks the issue of reform of the *bang* election system was addressed with Tan impressing on Kwek the importance of abolishing the dialect group system. Tan remembers that he gave Kwek the assurance: "If you are able to do that, you are doing better than ... the previous term council. All the more power to you, do it and you will get my full support. If I can, I will try to persuade the support of others".[2] Kwek Leng Joo needed little convincing or reassuring because he also felt the need for change. In his activities on statutory boards and in other public organizations, he had realized that the image of the Chamber was a problem and that reform was needed if it wanted to be a viable actor in the Singapore representational system.[3]

With general consent, Kwek Leng Joo was elected as the second youngest president ever of the SCCCI. He wasted no time and immediately announced plans for radical reform, revising the dialect-group based election system, in order to "rebuild the SCCCI to keep with modern times and to meet new challenges". Providing an indication of the pre-arranged

Kwek Leng Joo: Focused reformer.
Courtesy of SCCCI

School and obtained diplomas in hotel management from New York University and from Takushoku University in Tokyo.

After the death of Kwek Hong Png, the eldest son Kwek Leng Beng firmly took charge of Hong Leong but Leng Joo was actively involved in many of the businesses. A division of labour was established with Leng Beng in charge of the business side, while Leng Joo would be the conglomerate's face to the outside world, fulfilling the representational jobs, the public relations and most socio-cultural activities. In this light, it was not surprising that he, rather than his older brother, became Chamber president. Hong Leong had developed into a major conglomerate, which included property development activities through City Development Limited, financing activities through Hong Leong Finance and Singapore

Kwek was born in Singapore in 1953 into a well-known business family. His father, Kwek Hong Png, who hailed from Tongan County in Fujian province, was one of the founders of the extensive Singapore/Malaysian business conglomerate of Hong Leong. Leng Joo attended the Anglo-Chinese School and Maris Stella High

nature of the election and of the pre-planned character of the reforms, Kwek also announced that the advertisements for new staff to strengthen the Secretariat had already been sent to the local newspapers.[4]

He did not lack confidence; he claimed the role of saviour of the Chamber during his first press conference and vowed to restore the Chamber to its "former prominence". Kwek's statement on the *bang* election system was startling and bordered on the arrogant. He said that there existed a "groundswell ... which feels the Chamber should do away with the unnecessary trappings and get on with important things such as helping its members to establish better business ties with China". In conclusion he claimed that he would need four to six weeks to "put [the] Chamber in order".[5]

The confident tone never left Kwek, who announced that a special

Finance, and worldwide partnership and ownership of hotels through CDL Hotels. By the 1980s and 1990s the Hong Leong empire had established good connections with the PAP party/state, counting former government ministers Dr. Goh Keng Swee and Ong Pang Boon among its directors and senior advisors.

In accepting the responsibilities of president of the SCCCI, Kwek fulfilled a wish expressed by his father towards the end of his life. Kwek Hong Png had told Leng Joo that he regretted being less active in the Chamber and had asked him to make amends. When the opportunity presented itself, Kwek Leng Joo obliged. He served one term as vice-chairman of the General Affairs Committee before becoming a candidate for the presidency.

Kwek held many other posts, not only in Chinese circles but also in wider arenas. Among these were the vice-presidency of the Tung Ann association, the presidency of the Real Estate Developers' Association of Singapore (REDAS), and the chairmanship of the Singapore professional soccer league and the National Youth Achievement Award Council's Board of Trustees, as well as positions in the Chinese Heritage Centre (Board of Governors), the National Wages Council, the National Arts Council and the Nanyang Technological University's Board of Advisors.

As an avid photographer Leng Joo has exhibited work on Jiangsu Province.[6]

review committee would soon be formed, "to transform the Chamber into a modern, efficient and professional trade organization in the shortest possible time".[7] Perhaps wanting to create a clean break with the past image and practices of the Chamber, Kwek delivered a "hard-hitting" acceptance speech. The terminology and imagery he used to expound on the "poor public image" was revealing. He claimed that the young talented individuals of the Chinese community had loathed serving in the Chamber "fearing that their valuable time and energy might be dispensed in solving meaningless clan matters". Now, the time had come to "break the clan stranglehold", because "abolishing the clan system [would be] pivotal in attaining long-term growth and development for the Chamber".[8]

Despite all the tough talk, delivery on all these promises depended on a lot of diplomatic skill and compromise. Kwek approached the *bang* leaders

Tay Beng Chuan: Rebel turned leader.
Courtesy of SCCCI

After spending a short time in Longxi County in China, Tay defied his father's orders and returned to Singapore for his education. He attended Yock Eng School, which in the 1950s was the third Chinese language high school involved in student political activity. Tay had strong anti-colonial feelings, which made him rebel and boycott English class. He was quite active in the student movement, which had Lee Kuan Yew as its legal advisor, as a secondary leader but was expelled around 1956/57. Afraid of arrest and deportation because he was a stateless resident, he fled to Malaysia, where he obtained Malaysian citizenship, and later to Australia where he finished high school and obtained a Diploma of Commerce from Geelong Golden University. He did not obtain his Singapore citizenship until the 1970s, after three rejections of his applications.

Tay Beng Chuan was born in Palembang, Sumatra in 1939. The family business, Kee Hock, in which his father, uncle and grandfather participated, evolved from fishing to inter-island shipping and provided the family with the opportunity to move to Singapore after the war. While the men of the older generation stayed in Singapore, Tay's father sent his wife and children to China. His mother was eventually elected representative of the region and pictures of her with Mao Zedong exist.

After his uncle had been an MC member for two terms, Beng Chuan joined the Chamber Council in 1977. Tay was a very active member and leader of the Singapore Shipowners' Association in the 1960s and 1970s but never took much interest in *huiguan* or *bang* affairs.[9]

with respect, showing them the necessity of reform by emphasizing the big picture. He also stressed the importance of improving the image of the Chamber in the eyes of the government. Credit for the reform would be taken collectively but in private he confronted the individual *bang* leaders with a yes-or-no choice and told them he would resign immediately if the reforms failed.[10] The task of bringing the minds of council members and clan leaders together to establish a new system fell on a special committee, headed by General Affairs Committee Chairman Tay Beng Chuan, which was given six months to draw up a proposal.[11] Tay was the second of the Reformer leaders, and faced a tough challenge.

Upon his appointment as the head of the constitutional change committee, Tay said he believed that the "spirit of change was present" but also that "tedious negotiations" awaited.[12] In Tay's own words "it took more than ten preparatory meetings and many get-togethers with the honorary presidents" before his committee managed to produce an acceptable proposal.[13] The process of convincing was supported by meticulously prepared briefs of the Secretariat, which spelled out the point-by-point changes to the old constitution, the proposed change and the rationale.[14] By now the abrasive and combative tone of the first speeches had stopped and the new system was couched in inclusive language stressing the need for the Chamber to strengthen its relations with the private sector, as well as with social and cultural organizations and to keep its spirit and tradition alive. After three hours of deliberations behind closed doors, the council accepted the proposal in principle.[15]

The Extraordinary General Meeting of 21 August 1993 was called to endorse the proposed changes and amend the SCCCI's constitution. Talking to journalists before the vote, Kwek was confident and said he did not expect much opposition. "If there is any opposition at all, it will be from the older groups".[16] Indeed, not all old members had reacted enthusiastically to Kwek's plans. One senior member's initial reaction was, "Does Kwek want to chase us out, or what?"[17]

When it was time to count the votes, however, 377 ayes dwarfed the two nays and the abolishment of the *bang* system became a fact.[18] Tan Eng Joo proudly recounted, "You know, when it came to abolish this, I think it was 99.7 per cent supported. … A total success! Glad for that."[19] In this manner, the Chamber, after 87 years, ended the principle of elections based on *bang* representation. This was the most important step the Chamber could make, both dramatically and practically, to reinforce its image in the eyes of the government. Throughout its history, the issue of *bang* representation had surfaced, caused competition, disruption and outright conflict but was always summarily left unsolved.

Not long before the constitutional change, the Minister of State (Trade and Industry and Defence) Brigadier-General (Reserves) Lee Hsien Loong[20] had said "to remain relevant today, the Chamber should … strive to ensure that its representation reflects the fastest growing sectors and industries in the economy rather than the traditional clan and dialect groups".[21] Now that the Chamber had finally taken the initiative, the government enthusiastically backed the Chamber's reforms.

2. Politics and economy of Singapore: recipe against recession, 1985

How can the momentous turnaround of the Chamber, in the throes of an identity crisis in 1984 and bearing the image of an outdated institution, to being applauded by the government for its significant reform, be explained? In many ways, the recession that hit in 1985 provided the catalyst. It forced the government to re-evaluate its economic policies and thereby gave the Chamber the opportunity to become more closely involved in finding solutions for the nation's economic predicament. The resultant national change opened up new avenues for the Chamber in old and familiar topics.

The 1985 crisis

In a gloomy speech at the Chamber's Chinese New Year celebration of 1985, Tan Keong Choon said he expected a contraction of the Singapore economy by three to four per cent. He vowed that the SCCCI would do its best to help all sectors deal with the bad economy and stressed that the government should consider helping SMEs.[22] Tan said that the Chamber would help traders hit by hard times and would discuss with the government ways to reduce the cost of business. He reiterated that local Chinese businessmen could not continue to pay high overheads and argued that high rental cost, increased Skills Development Fund (SDF) and Central Provident Fund (CPF) contributions and payroll tax would have to be lowered.[23] The three operative issues in Tan's statement were: SMEs, traders and cost of business. Over the years the government had raised the cost of business in an attempt to change Singapore's economic and industrial structure through technological upgrading. However, the taxes, levies and mandatory contributions through which this plan was enforced weighed heavily on the local SME industries and traders.

Tan's prediction came true and 1985 was an exceptional year in the history of the independent state of Singapore. For the first time, the economy experienced a recession as its real gross domestic product (GDP) per capita fell by 3.4 per cent.[24] The downturn in 1985 was not an isolated incident because the economy had been under pressure, arguably from as far back as the oil crises of the mid-1970s. The causes for this economic setback lay both at home and abroad. Global recession had meant a reassessment of the New International Division of Labour (NIDL), the system from which Singapore had benefited so much. Robotics and computerization were reducing labour costs in the West and combined with rising wages in Singapore over the previous years had resulted in a loss of comparative advantage.[25] This loss was exacerbated by the fact that Singapore was steadily losing its protected status under the Generalized System of Preferences (GSP) structure of international trade. Local industries were struggling with the dual challenges of technological upgrading and industrial innovation on the one hand and with high business overheads on the other.

The SCCCI had indicated the problems resulting from the rise in the cost of business for a number of years and blamed the forced wage rises, the new levies for the SDF, and the payroll tax for the economic problems. Naturally therefore, the Chamber saw economic relief measures for local business in the form of a policy of business cost reduction as an absolute necessity for recovery. Early in 1985, the Chamber stated its case in a memorandum, which listed all increases of business overheads in the previous 10 years, with the obvious aim of convincing the government to roll back or revoke some of these pressures. In a statement exemplary of the Chamber attitude towards the authorities at the time, Tan Keong Choon said that the memorandum needed to be general in order to avoid conflict. The Chamber did not want to imply that it would prescribe policy to the government, or infringe upon its responsibilities; it would suffice just to indicate problems, so the "government would know how to tide over businessmen". He added most emphatically that the "Chamber ha[d] no intention of becoming an opposition party".[26]

Inclusive policies, concerted efforts

In a display of unity and cooperation, business leaders and the government wanted to create circumstances conducive to economic improvement. When the government presented its budget for 1985, industry leaders applauded its intentions. An article summing up the reactions of the Singapore Federation of Chambers of Commerce and Industry (SFCCI), the Singapore Manufacturers' Association (SMA), the Singapore International Chamber of Commerce (SICC) and the SCCCI showed that they considered the economic framework presented as a "businessmen's budget" but still had suggestions for further cuts.[27] At the swearing-in ceremony of the Chamber that year, the man responsible for the national budget, Finance Minister Richard Hu, was fittingly the guest of honour. In the speeches delivered that day the diplomatic tone of mutual acknowledgement and carefully worded suggestion was prevalent. On behalf of the Chamber, Tan Keong Choon extended the government a helping hand, saying that it would set up a sub-committee on the economic situation to study the slump and make recommendations. He said that policy makers could benefit as the "government [wa]s often slow in recognizing" specific sectoral problems. Of all the speeches, that of former president Soon Peng Yam alone had a distinctly combative tone as it addressed SME problems. Soon stated that these problems were "partially due to the measures taken by the government in the past. It neglected grooming local capital by emphasizing importation of foreign capital." On top of that he bemoaned the government's penetration of the private sector where it competed with its own citizens.[28] In his speech Dr. Hu said "we know what is going on" and pointed out that external factors beyond the control of the government were the main reason for the economic troubles.[29] While stopping well short of taking any blame, Hu did unveil government plans that answered the core of the criticisms of both Tan and Soon. He said that small industry and the service sector were targeted for government support, and added that the whole package of business costs would be looked at as well. Opening up of new export markets and specific SME promotion would be included in the government agenda.[30] Forced by economic recession and changes in the world economy, the PAP, after more than 20 years, returned to the logic of local business: small and medium enterprises and trade.

Enthusiastic reactions were kindled when the government presented its recession-fighting strategy. The bosses of the major business organizations endorsed the economic plan to pull Singapore out of the slump. Lee Kuan Yew called for two to three years of wage restraint during which wages and CPF contributions would not be changed. Another widely-welcomed move was the announcement by Deputy Prime Minister (DPM) Goh Chok Tong that a Small Enterprise Development Bureau would be established. The Chamber immediately offered help to formulate a framework and a set of rules and emphasized that eligibility should not be too restricted.[31]

In order to provide information, the Chamber sought feedback from its constituency and organized a discussion in cooperation with seven of its trade association members. One of the suggestions was emphasis on promoting entrepot trade.[32] This reaction shows that many still retained the "trader" worldview. Historically, the entrepot trade within a *laissez-faire* context had been the mainstay of Singapore up to the late 1950s and trade and commerce remained important to its economy. In 1985, commerce was still responsible for 23.4 per cent of Singapore's GDP with financial and business services at 23.2 per cent, transportation and communication at 22.3 per cent, and manufacturing at 19 per cent.

In what was called a "degree of consultation with the local private sector ... unprecedented in the post-1959 Singapore public policy process", the government reached out for feedback.[33] The consultation process centred on the "Economic Committee", under the leadership of BG Lee.[34] The Economic Committee was given the brief to inventory the strengths and weaknesses of the various sectors of the Singapore economy, to analyze the internal and external causes of the recession and to produce policy recommendations to put the economy back on track. Eight sectoral sub-committees with representatives from local and international business and from some key statutory boards were set up to cover manufacturing, services, banking and financial services, international trade, local businesses, entrepreneurship development, fiscal and financial policy, and manpower.

The SCCCI was represented on all, sometimes through member companies and sometimes through senior leaders. In the "local business" sub-committee especially, the Chamber not only counted three of its senior leaders (Lim Kee Ming, Linn In Hua and Teo Soo Chuan) among a total of eight members, it also was responsible for submitting four specific studies on the import/export, construction and property development, and the transportation, motor vehicles and shipping sectors as well as on the roles of the public and the private sector. The Economic Committee had to propose a viable new framework that would bring business costs down.[35]

When the committee's report came out it declared that comparative costs in Singapore would not be higher than in Taiwan, South Korea or Hong Kong. The report indicated four crucial fields where business costs would be controlled: CPF contributions, taxes, wages and investments. Business and employer organizations came out with a ringing endorsement when the government decided to implement the essence of the Economic Committee recommendations and take swift action.[36] The government underscored its shift in priorities towards local business when it donated $1 million to the SFCCI. The five SFCCI member organizations were handed this sum to promote export and services. The reaction was that of disbelief and spokesmen for the organizations said "We were stunned, it is not everyday that the government gives out money voluntarily".[37]

In the following years, the attitude of constructive cooperation between government and private sector prevailed as Singapore came to terms with the recession. While the PAP party/state elite remained firmly in control of national strategy and policy decisions, they took the expressions of societal and sectoral needs seriously enough to set up an elaborate feedback system.[38] When the Chamber announced it would set up an economic department dedicated to collecting relevant economic data past, present and future, the government applauded the initiative.[39] At the Chamber swearing-in ceremony of 1987, BG Lee said that the Chamber was well positioned to provide broad-based data; because it was home to representatives from "all sectors" it could offer the government an overview of the state of the economy.[40]

The improvement of the Singapore economy was hardly due exclusively to the efforts of the government or the private sector. A number of external factors were instrumental in the quick turnaround of the country's economic fortunes. The world economy rebounded, restoring economic growth and consumer spending in Singapore's primary export markets. As a result of increased economic activity and world interest in the Asian economy, the country's service sector was able to grow quickly to become a decisive third pillar of the national economy along with trade and industry.

3. The Chamber in post-recession Singapore: familiar themes, new roles

After 1985, the Chamber went through a series of important internal changes and successfully engaged in a number of roles in the economy. Changes in the environment in which the Chamber operated had often led to internal changes and adaptations. However, the internal reform and reinvention of the SCCCI that took place between 1985 and 1997 was one of the most thorough and significant in its history. These changes led to the intake of a new group of leaders and the streamlining of the secretariat, paving the way for Kwek Leng Joo's reform in 1993. Internal reform went hand in hand with external opportunities that the Chamber seized upon with confidence in the wake of post-recession economic policy that heralded roles close to the Chamber's heart and tradition. After discussing the internal reforms, three roles will be highlighted to illustrate the Chamber's new profile in the economic sphere: representation of the SME sector, trade promotion activities, and cross-ethnic business cooperation.

Internal developments in the Chamber

The elections of 1985 provided the first development in this trajectory of internal change and yielded a new cohort of leaders. Two years earlier, the Chamber had already professed that it was looking for new council members with a tertiary education, who were effectively bilingual and around 45 years old.[41] A large intake of new leaders in 1985 was made possible due to the creation of a new official position in the SCCCI: the Honorary Council Member. At an extraordinary annual general meeting in 1983, the Chamber had established this position in order to allow old and distinguished members their commensurate status while opening up de facto leadership positions for younger members wanting to get involved in the day-to-day running of the Chamber.[42] In the 1985 election seven new members were elected to the council. Notably, the rejuvenation took place without competition or inter-*bang* rivalry as all 45 candidates of the various dialect groups were returned unopposed.

The Chamber prided itself on the new council members and pointed out their educational level in its press releases. Among others, a computer scientist with Ph.D. qualification, a real estate developer with a first class degree in building science, and a lawyer were presented.[43] Still, the changes did not yet affect the composition of the top leadership, as almost the entire incumbent team of office bearers was returned to power. Tan Keong Choon, the re-elected president, pointed out it was "no use to change horses halfway at a critical time".[44]

In the meantime, the necessity of financial and organizational reform was brought home by Vice President Linn In Hua's revelation that the Chamber had accumulated a S$600,000 deficit. The main reason for this was the significant drop in rental income from its own premises. As a first measure to rebalance the financial situation, Linn announced stricter controls on spending.[45] A year later in 1986, as a result of its financial troubles, the Chamber celebrated its 80th birthday in modest fashion.

Still, 300 guests joined the SCCCI's 80th birthday, which was acknowledged by the government through the presence of Singapore President Wee Kim Wee as the guest of honour at the reception and Minister of Education Tony Tan at the anniversary dinner.[46] As recently as five years earlier, the government image of the Chamber had been quite different from the self-image projected by the SCCCI. Now, it seemed that with the Chamber starting to accept the state's views and expectations, the government acknowledged that some of the Chamber causes should be endorsed. President Wee said, "the Chamber had developed into an organization that can represent the country's interests" and mentioned the importance of Asian values to the Chamber's and Singapore's success.[47] President Tan Keong Choon stated that although the SCCCI might have less direct influence on the government than before, this loss could be compensated by better and more effective communication.[48] The statement reveals a lot about the Chamber's changed relationship with the state since the war. For much of the 1940s and 1950s the Chamber wielded real influence and was an important political force. In the 1960s and 1970s the Chamber had felt that it should have influence but was denied by the PAP party/state. The admission that, by the 1980s, the Chamber could do no more than "communicate" the interests and worries of its members to the government reflected the power reality of independent Singapore.

Two editorials illustrate the official and popular view of the Chamber attempts at "staying relevant". *The Straits Times* pointed out that in keeping with the changes in education and language use, the SCCCI would inevitably become more English-speaking and that *bang* division would as a result be steadily less relevant. Its main message of continuity and change to the Chamber was to "include English speakers and retain tradition".[49] A Chinese language editorial emphasized that the "Chamber still has [a] heavy responsibility to shoulder". It outlined the historical significance of the organization not only in trade and commerce but also in leading the Chinese community on citizenship and other issues. However, it pointed out that, under the new socio-political constellation of Singapore, "the Chamber [could] no longer be the representative of the people" and "the Chamber should enlarge its membership, change its image, and revamp its structure and electoral system".[50]

The Chamber proved sensitive to the need for such change. Therefore, the main internal discussion surrounding the 80th anniversary festivities did not dwell on past glory or on the wish to regain the primacy of old. Rather, leaders focused on the problem of attracting young, talented and dedicated individuals to lead the Chamber to a constructive role and new significance in the future. However, it proved difficult to find new leaders. Despite the leadership renewal taking place, the "new" cooperative relationship with the state had not yet proven effective enough to attract large numbers of younger new members. The Chamber still held the image of having been in a troubled relationship and competition with the government in the recent past. What the Chamber was left holding then, was, as one of the newspapers put it, a large sign saying "Wanted: young people to help Chamber change its old image".[51] One week later, the same paper continued its pithy analysis of the Chamber's dilemma, headlining, "Image or generation gap, Chamber must decide".

The 1987 election of Linn In Hua

The elections of 1987 constituted a step towards pulling in new faces. Eleven old guard members stepping down provided room for new entrants to the council. The new blood amounted to 13 and included, as in 1985, a number of better-educated individuals with experience outside the Chinese business sector. Hwang Soo Jin, the Managing Director of United Overseas Insurance and Director of United Overseas Finance, was a former deputy speaker of Parliament. Dr. Gwee Yee Hean, the Chief Executive

Linn In Hua: Initiator and organizer.

Courtesy of SCCCI

Linn In Hua was born in 1924 on Quemoy, the same island close to Xiamen from which Wee Cho Yaw hailed. In 1936, Linn and his family immigrated to Penang where he attended the famous Chinese-language Chungling High School. His father became the managing director of the local branch of Lee Kong Chian's Lee Rubber Company. The family moved to Kuala Lumpur in 1946 and set up the company "South Engineers", which operated as agent for manufacturers of large engines and other machinery such as MAN and Deutsche Traktor.

Later in life, after turning 30, Linn did his English-language O- and A-levels in order to be able to study physics at London University. In 1966, Linn let himself be bought out of the Malaysian

operations of South Engineers and moved to Singapore. There he developed the independent Singapore part of the company under the name "East Machinery", initially concentrating on the pre-existing connections he had with the PRC machine tool branch for which he operated as agent and distributor.

Sia Yong, who was his classmate at Chungling, introduced him to the Chamber management council in 1971. When Wee Cho Yaw was forced to serve a third term as president from 1977–1979, Linn was his Chairman of the General Affairs Committee and took on all the secretarial tasks normally performed by the president. In this way he saved Wee time while gaining valuable insight and experience "in the seat". From 1983 until 1987 he was vice president to Tan Keong Choon. In newspaper articles published at the time of his election to the presidency, he was described as totally fluent in English and at home with new technology, but also as a "typical Chinaman". It was highlighted that his given name, In Hua, meant "to protect the Chinese" and he was portrayed as outspoken, sometimes causing a stir with his direct approach. He described himself as "by nature and interest an organizer" and thought that because of this trait he was "the right man for the job at the time".[52]

Director of Industrial and Commercial Bank, held a Ph.D. in educational science and had worked as an academic at Nanda.[53] The companies these men represented were owned or controlled by Wee Cho Yaw, indicating a new trend that the big business families were content to have professional managers looking after their business as well as their representational affairs.[54] The big business families had been reorganizing their company structures since the early 1970s into holding companies that controlled listed businesses. This split of control and professional expertise allowed the inclusion and use of professional management expertise without losing a tight grip on the business as a whole.

The same principle could be seen in the "business of representation". The self-renewal of the Chamber was shaping up in 1987 with 20 per cent new faces on its Council, and 48 per cent of the Standing Committee under 49 years of age. Also, with 57 per cent of those Standing Committee members holding tertiary education degrees, it looked like the younger and professional Chinese would have a greater influence on the Chamber. The traditional "kingmakers" of the various dialect groups, such as Wee Cho Yaw for the Hokkien and Teo Soo Chuan and Lien Ying Chow for the Teochew, remained further in the background.[55] However, they exercised considerable control behind the scenes and must have endorsed and promoted the leadership renewal. One reformer president explained that a core group made up of the honorary presidents and a select few of the senior and experienced members served as an "acting and controlling" force, especially during elections.[56] As with their companies the "kingmakers" could continue to control the Chamber while simultaneously benefiting from the expertise and the image factors provided by the inflow of new members. The rejuvenation of the Chamber council through the elections of 1985 and 1987 had taken place under the stewardship of VP Linn In Hua, who went one step higher in the SCCCI hierarchy when he was elected president. He had backing from the Lee family, known for its reform agenda, as well as from the core leadership group.

Linn's agenda for the SCCCI was to modernize and rejuvenate as well as to educate and train. His goal for the Chamber was to expand Singapore's economy in line with government economic policy. He would strive for a closer relationship with the government and other business organizations, thereby fostering the Chamber's influence. In an extensive newspaper interview shortly after his election, Linn put a great premium on the Chamber-state relation, saying that the role of the SCCCI as a link between government and society needed to be cherished and extended. In order to stay abreast of developments in the national policy environment, Linn planned to establish study groups on company law, taxation, productivity and wages to tap existing expertise.[57] In his opinion, which belied the traders' worldview, one important avenue for growth lay in increasing the country's trade volume and to this end the Chamber members should develop their

ASEAN network, and should also target new markets such as the Asia-Pacific, Europe and the United States. The Chamber should take greater responsibility for the economic and social well-being of the other racial groups of Singapore.[58] In short, he promised to be a "work-horse" president, trying to get the SCCCI to move on all of these different issues.[59]

That work was still needed was indicated by an editorial entitled "Chinese Chamber – old values, new goals", which highlighted Linn In Hua's agenda in positive terms. On the performance of the Chamber in the recent past, however, the editorial was scathing in its criticism. It said that as a lobby group the Chamber had been overshadowed by the SMA. During the economic crisis of 1985–1986 the Chamber "floundered along with its members failing to provide directions and [had] hardly [been] able to influence government policy for the benefit of its members." It was this helplessness that had inspired some new leaders to run for election and that had enabled Linn to bring a "sense of purpose in the once sleepy Chamber".[60] On one issue, Linn, otherwise the very embodiment of change and renewal, held on firmly to tradition. He went on record that instead of wanting to get rid of the *bang* structure, he understood its advantages and wanted to maintain its practice.[61] He recalled later that he said: "If there is a better system, let's go, but if not better, keep quiet".[62]

One way "Linn the organizer" tried to instil a sense of purpose was to professionalize the administrative and organizational procedures of the Chamber. He scouted around for talent and strengthened the secretariat. One of these people remembered that a handbook with standardized protocols for Chamber functions and an employee-training manual were compiled. More secretarial backup was necessary and the number of employees in this section of the Chamber rose steadily.[63]

During the next election of 1989, Linn successfully continued his strategy of bringing in younger and better educated council members. He emphasized that youth was not necessarily the ultimate goal. He said that those over-60 years old would provide backbone. Members between 45 and 60, who were established and experienced, would contribute their time and expertise, while those between 30 and 45 would provide youth and flexibility.[64] The balance between continuity and change needed to be maintained, and the status, connections, support and donations of the wealthy old members were as important to his reforms as the professional expertise, education level and youth of the new council members.

In a dramatic turn of events, acute problems due to heart disease forced Linn to step down in October 1989. Tan Eng Joo, being the next in line in the Chamber hierarchy, was elected to the presidency and he committed himself to the goals of rejuvenation and professionalization set by Linn.[65]

One of the new aspects that he added entailed the recruitment of a relatively new category of members: women. President Wee Kim Wee triggered the change when he asked about female directors at Chamber. At the time, the Chamber lacked any female leaders and women were also grossly under-represented in its membership. Therefore, it started a recruitment drive with the very ambitious aim of enlisting 1,200 new female members in one year. While that figure was not reached, a significant number of women started joining. In May 1990 for example, 20 of the 119 new members sworn in were female, and a new woman member led them in taking the membership pledge.[66]

In the years after the 1985 crisis, the Chamber, under the leadership of Linn In Hua, was changing recruitment patterns and internal organization. While this was a slow process, external opportunities presented themselves to give the SCCCI a much-needed boost to its relevance and status. In the following sections three developments will be highlighted.

Skills development, business education and the SME programme

While the government had stated periodically that local business was important too, little was done before 1985 to structurally lift the SME sector. Existing policies and programmes were targeted at industry only. In 1981, in a telling example, Lim Kee Ming said that he welcomed consultation but stressed that it should not be a one-way flow of ideas from policy makers to the business sector. He complained diplomatically "all too often governments tend to adopt the narrower definition of consultation".[67] What he meant was that the PAP government tended to tell local business what was going to happen rather than listen to its needs. The needs the Chamber communicated over the following years were clear enough: provide aid to the small, specifically to small and medium, enterprises that were willing to face the difficulties of upgrading. However, Lim's message of small being beautiful and "traditional [being] modern" would only receive full government support after the 1985 recession and in the 1986 SME master plan.[68]

Pre-recession activities

In the years before 1985, the Chamber was involved in a number of initiatives that would stand it in good stead when policy changes were made. From as far back as 1979, when the government introduced the SDF levy, the Chamber had been carving out a niche in skills development and business education in cooperation with the government. Importantly, the issues of the upgrading of traditional companies connected to the interests and needs of the main constituency of the Chamber, the small Chinese family business. The government intended to work with and through local organizations to set up plans, to survey needs and to come to practical implementation of the plan meant to benefit all Singaporean companies. The Chamber carried out feasibility studies, conducted surveys to gauge the needs and interests of members, ran some pilot projects with SDF money, and in 1984 sent to the SDF council plans for a $2 million skills centre at the Chamber. The economic crisis provided the big boost for the skills programme, both on the government and the Chamber side. In 1985, the council committed to paying 90 per cent of a series of training programmes amounting to $2 million over the initial three years, which would be executed and administered by the SCCCI. Through the programme, the Chamber became a partner of the government in an area of policy central to the PAP line.[69]

Computerization was another field of great significance and possibilities for the SCCCI and its members. With some help of the SDF the Chamber ventured to enter the computer age. A small inventory of members' needs indicated that interest was great and a computer-training centre was installed at the Chamber. Soon computer courses were offered in all kinds of varieties and suited to specific needs. The Chamber, aware of the need to upgrade, decided to move towards the computer to handle its own activities, investing $100,000 to go on-line.[70] To further the cause of computerization the SCCCI's newly elected council member Ker Sin Tze, a former NUS senior lecturer in economics, organized a four-day computer hardware and software show, which showed microcomputers capable of working with Chinese characters. Promoting the use of modern technology in smaller companies, the Chamber organized an industrial robotics show in November 1983, which coincided with the national Productivity Week. More of its members were interested in the Economic Development Board (EDB) grants offered for SME conversion to mechanized production.[71]

The SCCCI was successful in opening up new areas of educational activities. Almost all courses focused on running an efficient and successful company. An indication of the variety on offer: cargo and airfreight, the property market and its potential, bookkeeping, shipping goods, and the new Uniform Customs Practice Code. With the upgrading of SMEs, the SDF council discussed the possibility of the Chamber organizing Training Within Industry programmes for its members, and incorporating the courses into its existing array.[72]

In the pre-recession years, the Chamber built up its confidence in vocational training and skills development. After recession struck, the implementation of a clear government policy and ample funding from the national budget aided the Chamber in developing an even higher profile.

The Chamber as SME champion after 1985

The realization on the government's part that appeasing local business and providing them with a fighting chance in the Singapore business arena would be an important political, if not economic, weapon in fighting the recession, led to an SME support policy. Linn In Hua recalled that the Economic Committee of 1985–1986 had created the political room for these initiatives. This development also boosted the importance of the trade associations within the Chamber, as they were the representatives of SME business. During weekly lunches at the Chamber, trade association members would present their sector, its problems and specific needs.[73] Much work still needed to be done to help the local SME sector to become competitive. In an attempt to fathom the training needs of its members and to gauge the demand for its courses, the SCCCI conducted a survey among its members. Not surprisingly, the results indicated that most Chinese firms did not have any training resources and that more than half of SMEs lacked basic in-house training. From the results, the Chamber concluded that the Training Centre would rapidly need to triple its capacity.[74]

In September 1985, the Chamber organized a seminar for SME firms that would set the tone for its strategy. Specialists from the National University of Singapore were invited to speak on the subjects of "modernizing traditional business", "overcoming operational difficulties of SME's" and "R&D for SME's".[75] As had been successfully achieved in the SDF training courses, cooperation with professional and government institutions became the dominant Chamber mode of operation.

In 1986, the Chamber and the government combined forces and planned to help 5,000 enterprises through a training programme conducted by the Chamber. After the SMA and the Singapore Indian Chamber of Commerce, the SCCCI was the third organization to launch such a programme. The Chamber was also planning to start up its own Business Development course. To make it possible for more companies to benefit from the Small Enterprise Bureau (SEB) and Chamber courses, during the financially difficult times, a 70 per cent rebate on course fees was offered in 1986. The programmes proved very successful and soon the Chamber felt obliged, due to popular demand, to offer a second and then a third business programme on SME business planning, while permanently cutting fees.[76]

EDB workshops brought together government officials, entrepreneurs, bankers and prominent businessmen for the first time on such a broad scale. The biggest problem identified by all sides in the discussion was the lack of financing for the various promotion schemes.[77]

As practically oriented courses and seminars continued, attempts were made to serve a larger client base. At first the operating language of all meetings was English, although Chamber leaders urged Chinese SMEs to attend as well. The logical development was the SCCCI organizing a Meet the Client workshop for SMEs entirely run in Mandarin. This first such workshop, organized in cooperation with the National Computer Board and the Economic Development Board, focused on inducing SMEs to "innovate and grow".[78] The meeting attracted 300 Chinese-speaking Chamber members, and this success prompted the Singapore Malay Chamber of Commerce to plan a Malay version of the workshop series.[79]

In its own efforts to help small firms to innovate, the Chamber set up task forces on general business guidance and legal advice. It also established a business competition through the Young Entrepreneur of the Year awards. Finally, by publishing a Trade and Services directory and by including more Mandarin material in its resource library, the Chamber aimed to lower the information threshold for small companies. The Chamber was not alone in these endeavours as five other government agencies worked in close cooperation with the EDB: the National Computer Board, the National Productivity Board, the Trade Development Board, and the SME division of EDB. The Chamber became a formal constituent part of this large SME support network through its five-man liaison team working with the EDB SME division. Linn In Hua emphasized that SCCCI activities in this field would not just be targeted at its own members but would be available for other SMEs as well.[80]

Close cooperation with the government did not mean that the Chamber was not critical of official policy or the perceived lack thereof. In 1989, Linn In Hua described Finance Minister Hu's budget as containing "no special provisions whatsoever" for small business. Linn complained that too few small businesses had benefited from the programmes designed for them. He called for a progressive income tax for corporations or for exempting companies with less than 10 employees from paying SDF levies.[81] Most of the time, however, cooperation between government and Chamber was rather smoother. The government combined its various approaches and policies in a "SME Masterplan" for retailers, of which the EDB and the SCCCI jointly produced a Chinese-language version.[82]

The Chamber further developed its computerization assistance programme. One of the Chamber members involved recounted that the first implementation of this model took place in the early 1990s when a number of spare part companies were aided in setting up a computerized stock management system. Similar implementations were conducted with furniture, hardware and timber associations, and, a few years later, with associations and companies in the textile sector.[83]

The government's retreat from its 20-year policy of favouring big business, foreign as well as government-linked companies (GLCs), in its economic policies, and its renewed attention for local SMEs meant that the Chamber could capitalize on its longstanding pedigree. Now that the needs of the majority of members, many of them SMEs, no longer clashed with national economic policy, Chamber leaders could develop programmes and successfully cooperate with the government to enhance the Chamber's status.

Trade and regional cooperation

Similar to the case of SME support, the government, due to the 1985 crisis, moved towards the Chamber point of view concerning trade. Although some changes had already been set in motion before 1985, the recession was the catalyst for government re-evaluation on trade and thereby presented the Chamber with a further opportunity to shine: unleashing the power of its traders' worldview came naturally.

The first signs of a government move favouring trade came with the appointment of Minister of Trade and Industry Goh Chok Tong, who acknowledged the traditional role of the Chamber in trade. At the swearing-in ceremony in 1979, he told SCCCI members to use the new concessionary income tax rate for exports and to open up new markets in West Asia, China and Latin America.[84] However, as the *FEER* reported, the "official government position was that while there was a need for local manufacturers to improve their export performance, this was seen principally as a matter of individual effort". In a reversal of this position, the government decided to implement, by early 1983, what the private sector had long lobbied for: the Trade Development Board (TDB). The government's decision was seen by some private-sector sources as an indication of the different approaches to economic management taken by Goh and his successor, Tony Tan.[85] Chamber leaders reacted enthusiastically, and Tan Keong Choon said that the issue of new markets would be discussed and that trade missions would be planned. The Chamber would conduct surveys of non-traditional markets to look for opportunities, and work with the TDB. The efforts resulted in a number of missions to unknown markets in Eastern Europe.[86] These small missions did not have a marked effect on the national trade statistics, and it took the shock of recession to stir government and Chamber into real action.

The trade fair of 1985

In response to the economic troubles, the Chamber played an active role in opening up trading avenues that would help Singapore return to its prosperous pre-1985 record. International trade and transhipment was still the backbone of the economy, and, reconfirming the longstanding logic of the regional trading system and the worldview of many of the Chinese traders in the Chamber, Southeast Asia was still Singapore's main trading partner accounting for 29 per cent of its trade in 1984. Half of this ASEAN trade (or 15 per cent of total trade) was with the traditional partner Malaysia and another third (or 10 per cent of total trade) with Indonesia.[87] Organizing trade fairs and trade missions to expand these traditional markets and explore new ones were the SCCCI ventures to increase trade. As in the case of the SME sector, the Chamber cooperated closely with the government to achieve results.

Aware of the economic problems ahead, Tan Keong Choon had taken the initiative in 1984 to organize the promotion of local products through a fair to be held in July 1985. It was not the first time the Chamber had staged such an event. It had done so during the 1930s and in 1959, when it proudly put Singapore on the map as a territory under self-rule. The commercial exhibition focused on ASEAN and the Asia Pacific and had 30,000 square metres available for producers. International and local response to the Chamber's call was very good with 80 per cent of stalls booked two months before opening. In the end 250 companies from 13 nations filled a near capacity 550 stalls, with the PRC taking up a tenth of available space. In addition, 14 trade delegations from countries as far afield as Hungary and Japan visited Singapore to attend the fair, which was officially supported by the TDB and the Singapore Tourist Promotion Board.[88] Chandra Das, the highest official of the TDB who was the patron of the fair, hailed the Chamber initiative as the biggest such event in 26 years.

Regional trade missions and initiatives

Many trade missions organized by the SCCCI in these years had regional destinations. Building on existing ties, which had traditionally been the strong suit of the Chinese business sector, the Chamber also utilized the opportunities presented by its presence in the ASEAN-CCI. Another feature of the trade promotion activities was that more often than not, they would be embedded in an SFCCI context or otherwise conducted in cooperation with the other leading business organizations of Singapore. Also, missions were timed to coincide with official diplomatic exchanges or government-to-government contacts. A good example of this pattern is provided by a Chamber delegation to the Philippines, deliberately planned to take place one week after President Corazon Aquino's state visit to Singapore.[89] In the case of the 1988 Chamber visit to Taiwan, the timing of its trip was also clearly in tandem with state activities. With the market situation in Taiwan changing as a result of economic liberalization, three other missions from Singapore visited the island within one month.[90]

Apart from the region, the Chamber was involved in trade promotion to other parts of the globe as well. Multiple trips to both the USSR and South Korea indicated the Chamber's wider interest.[91] Japan was another area targeted, as was India, seen by the Chamber and the government alike as a country of great opportunities.[92] The Chamber used the ASEAN-CCI for contacts beyond the five member states and was instrumental in the establishment of a number of new structured business dialogues such as the ASEAN-US business council, the ASEAN-Australia business council and the ASEAN-Japan business council.[93]

Entering the European market

Even greater promise lay in Europe, considering its conversion to a single market. Therefore, Europe was an obvious target for diversification and the Chamber pursued two approaches to gain access. The first plan of attack involved the clever use of a loophole that would make it possible to avoid import tax. Exporting Singapore goods to Europe through the former French colonies of Mauritius and Reunion meant that they could enter the European market tariff-free.[94] The second avenue for increasing exports to the EU was to establish a permanent venue in Europe itself to showcase Singapore products. The "organizer", Linn In Hua was again the instigator and driving force behind the plan, which he first floated for the local furniture-producing sector. Figures indicated that in 1987, 150 Singapore companies exported furniture to Europe worth $263 million. Linn argued that this figure should make the sector set up a permanent display centre to service the European market.[95]

In 1989, on the eve of a trade mission to Europe, the Chamber announced that it considered Rotterdam an attractive site as this city had already attracted commitments from South Korea and Taiwan to open similar trade centres. The cost of a similar Singapore venture, estimated at $3.6 million, would be shared by the SCCCI, Dutch investors and a subsidy from the Rotterdam city government. The mission proved to be the start of cooperation with the Dutch, and thereby an example of a successful response to the government's call to open new markets.[96] Seven Chamber members confirmed their participation, putting total private sector investment in the venture at $1.4 million. The Rotterdam Centre was seen as an important opportunity for smaller companies to spread their wings.[97]

Trade fair 1989

Four years after the successful trade fair of 1985, the Chamber capitalized on the experience gained. The Asia Pacific was again a main target region for trade promotion, and a forum on technology transfer was included.[98] The Chamber also looked eagerly at new markets in Yugoslavia, the Soviet Union and other Eastern European nations that were undergoing major changes, while Reunion also featured prominently. The PRC was the juggernaut and the centre of attention at the fair, giving credence to Singapore's claim that it could be a bridge between the steadily expanding Chinese market and the rest of the world. A quarter of the booths available at the fair were occupied by the 350-strong delegation from the PRC. Their visit was a success as the Chinese exhibitors secured $70 million worth in contracts.[99]

Capitalizing on its traders' worldview, the Chamber had little trouble taking the limelight in the promotion of trade. Its traditional strengths in the regional networks and in connections with China were complemented with initiatives targeting new markets. It allowed the Chamber to make significant contributions to the national goal of increasing trade.

Ethnic co-operation

The government's approach to nation building and its concept of national values hinged on the idea of a two-tier system. The premise was that each ethnic group in Singapore would retain its identity and value system. Superimposed on this ethnic landscape would be the national identity and the "shared values" tying society closer together and giving it a common purpose. Placing national interest before the interests of the ethnic community was a central tenet to this approach to the nation. This interpretation presented the Chamber with a dilemma. It was obviously a Chinese organization, had an extensive regional network with similar Chinese bodies, as well as a traditional link with the PRC. Still, it was expected to act within Singapore on a multi-ethnic principle. Through the years the Chamber occasionally made token gestures of good faith to show that it could act beyond ethnic boundaries, awarding scholarships to non-Chinese students.[100] In general, though, these examples remained token gestures until 1987.

When Linn In Hua became president, he said that the Chamber should take care of all racial groups. Acknowledging the reality of the ethnic mosaic in Singapore and conscious of the need for cooperation, he stated that other racial groups should be integrated in Chamber activities. Wasting no time, Linn announced that the Chamber would forge links with the Singapore Malay Chamber of Commerce (SMCC) through a 10-member joint working committee.[101] Malay companies would get access to education and training facilities and programmes while SCCCI members could extend their networks. More initiatives followed and during a lunch with the Singapore Indian Chamber of Commerce (SICC) Linn said that the Chamber sought cooperation with industrial, commercial, cultural and educational organizations in order to create more mutual links.[102]

The Chamber would achieve these lofty goals through the promotion of "Eastern philosophy".[103] Linn avoided using the term "Confucian values" because of its ethnic definition. The multi-cultural approach was continued over the ensuing months as the Chamber forged closer ties with the SICC.[104] Cultural and social events concerning sports, education and cultural values would provide the initial agenda while at a later stage the SICC could help the Chamber with contacts in Middle Eastern and African markets.[105] Linn's intention was to create an environment of mutual acquaintance and trust between the leaders of the assorted Chambers. This spirit of cooperation and togetherness was vividly illustrated when the four Chamber presidents joined hands and laid a wreath at the War Memorial during the annual ceremony organized by the SCCCI.[106]

Combined activities entered the realm of business through IT seminars, reciprocal admission to courses and joint trade missions.[107] Business ties between the SCCCI and the SMCC were eventually formalized when a joint venture holding company was established. The company was owned equally by the SCCCI and the SMCC and initially aspired to be active in food and beverage exports. Proudly, the two Chambers invited BG Lee to be the guest of honour at the official announcement of this business endeavour. While the initiative was meant to promote multi-ethnic cooperation, its backers were eager to point out that the Malay-Chinese venture had sound business underpinning and market access.[108]

Cooperation was further enhanced when Malay businessmen seized opportunities in new markets. The SMCC promoted international exposure and decided to appoint a nine-man team to join an SCCCI mission coinciding with Lee Kuan Yew's 1988 trip to the PRC.[109] On the itinerary of the mission, a visit to some of the "Muslim areas" of the PRC figured prominently.[110] One significant result of this joint trip was that it gave SCCCI and SMCC leaders the confidence to take the existing Sino-Malay holding company and jolt it into some serious entrepreneurial action. Among the projects considered were Chinese-Muslim restaurants, trading activities with China and the Middle East, a travel business, a chain store franchise, and investment in PRC based handicraft centres. Meanwhile, the financial side of the business was taken care off through a construction of non-transferable A and B shares for Chinese and Malay investors respectively.[111] The holding company ventured into a number of areas and eventually teamed up with provincial authorities in China through the Ningxia International Chamber of Commerce to set up Sing-Hui Enterprises, a business exporting *halal* meat products from China to Southeast Asia.[112]

Linn's initiatives for more cooperation between the ethnic Chambers seem to have borne fruit when organized through chamber-to-chamber exchanges and projects. Yet these successes were balanced by the internal competition between the various business organizations in the SFCCI arena, a tale told in the next section.

SFCCI

The fact that all this inter-Chamber activity took place while a separate, formal vehicle of cooperation existed in the form of the SFCCI begs the question why Linn put so much effort in alternative, and less formal, channels of cooperation. The explanation lay in the internal politics of the SFCCI. In 1988 and again in 1990–1991, major internal conflicts marred the image and efficiency of the SFCCI. The issue was one of status rather than of domination or control. Two of the leaders most involved in the controversy, Tan Keong Choon and Tan Eng Joo, were convinced that the SCCCI deserved a special position in the SFCCI. They argued that its membership of more than 5,000, combined with the more than 100 trade association members, meant that the Chamber was five times larger than the SMA, which had around 1,000 members in 1985.[113] They also felt that as an independent vehicle of local business, the Chamber had the moral right to claim prominence over the Singapore International Chamber of Commerce and the SMA, which they regarded as remnants of colonial times. This position not only directly countered the wishes of the government, it also hampered cooperation with these two important business organizations to further develop the multi-ethnic initiatives started by Linn In Hua.

The first flare-up occurred in 1988 when events left the SFCCI without a president. Closed-door sessions were held to reach consensus on a unanimous presidential candidate. One such meeting ended unsuccessfully when the sitting president Mr. Ramachandran of the Indian Chamber gave three options, proposing to stay on himself, to appoint Robert Chua of the SMA, or to appoint Linn In Hua.[114] Two weeks later another meeting ended in disarray when Robert Chua walked out angrily. A *Straits Times* editorial tried to analyze the row and said that its sources indicated that the Indian Chamber and the SMA wanted the incumbent Ramachandran to stay on while the SCCCI, the Malay and the International Chamber preferred a Chinese candidate. However, because the SCCCI had held the presidency from the inception of the SFCCI in 1978 until 1986, this Chinese candidate would preferably not be a member of the Chinese Chamber. Robert Chua of the SMA then pushed himself forward as a compromise candidate but failed to get SCCCI support, walked out and threatened to pull the SMA out of the SFCCI.[115] Tan Keong Choon was the SCCCI representative in the SFCCI board at the time, and flatly rejected Chua as a candidate, displaying what the other parties interpreted as arrogance.

The SFCCI was under a considerable amount of pressure to resolve the row because the AGM, which would appoint the president, would have to be held by the end of November 1988. Also the SFCCI was supposed to host a Philippines delegation headed by that country's Minister of Trade.[116] The image and relevancy of the SFCCI was at stake.

The diplomatic way out of the power struggle was to save the faces of all the contending parties. To this end an alphabetic rotation system was proposed under which all five organizations would in turn provide the president of the SFCCI. The SCCCI would be the first in line.[117] Eventually, the five organizations reached an accord and Linn In Hua was appointed as the new president while the rotation principle was adopted as the rule for future succession. No formal changes were made to the constitution, however, because the compromise was seen as a gentlemen's agreement. Next to Linn In Hua as president, five vice presidents, one from each member organization, were appointed. In the wake of the row, BG Lee said that the admirable new SCCCI culture of collaboration should spread to the SFCCI as well. He was quoted as saying that the "success of the SFCCI will be a measure of the priority that its members have placed on the goals of national economic development".[118]

The success of the SFCCI must not have been the priority of its members as another stormy episode unfolded in 1990–1991. After the election in 1990 of Mr. Ramachandran of the Singapore Indian Chamber of Commerce as SFCCI president, the Federation cancelled two scheduled meetings. Reportedly this was due to the fact that the SCCCI refused to acknowledge Ramachandran as president.[119] BG Lee linked the SFCCI troubles directly to the SCCCI, and urged the Chamber to set aside ethnic sentiments and focus on cooperating for the common good, noting that:

> increasingly, when businessmen meet one another, they are more concerned to find out which industry the other person is in, rather than which village in China his ancestors came from. To remain relevant today, the Chamber should therefore strive to ensure that its representation reflects the fastest growing sectors and industries in the economy rather than the traditional clan and dialect groups. There is a need for a strong national body and the SFCCI can and should be close.[120]

Despite this government admonishment, bickering continued when the SFCCI met behind closed doors for the first time in six months in April 1991. The conflict escalated further when the Chinese and Malay Chambers voiced their non-support for SFCCI president Ramachandran in a joint declaration of Tan Eng Joo and SMCC president Haji Jalil. They hastened to say that their stance would not hinder cooperation in the federation itself because their opposition was directed against the person and not against the Indian Chamber.[121] Tan Eng Joo blamed Ramachandran personally for the problems with the SFCCI's publication "Singapore Exporter".[122] Tan further fanned the flames of conflict when he reiterated the SCCCI desire that the SFCCI president should be a Singapore citizen. However, implementation of such a rule would exclude many Singapore International Chamber of Commerce members as well as various SMA leaders. Tan Eng Joo said that companies which were majority foreign owned would not stick it out with the true blue Singaporeans if business interests were at stake.[123] The acrimonious atmosphere continued and left the Federation ineffective. In the words of a senior executive of the Singapore International Chamber of Commerce, the Federation's only real task is to be a front office for Singapore in international affairs, especially as the country's representative in the ASEAN-CCI. Apart from that it was a "PO box ... pretty empty and devoid of substance".[124] The ethnic Chambers were there to stay and chose other channels than the SFCCI to explore cooperation within Singapore and international networks.

Summing up the implications of the internal and external changes for the Chamber, the substantial rejuvenation and intake of higher educated council members was a major development. Carried by broad based support within the Chamber and from the *bang* organizations, the rejuvenation combined continuing influence and status for the older generation with the tapping of professional experience and the public relations value of the younger generation. Furthermore, in post-recession Singapore, the Chamber could further the interests of a substantial part of its membership by its role in promoting and representing SMEs and helping this sector to implement modern management practices. Accepting its role as a constituent part of the multi-ethnic business landscape, the SCCCI initiated some cooperation with other organizations. In the framework of the SFCCI, however, this cooperation did not take shape. The SCCCI was still looking for another anchor in Singapore's representational system besides its SME supporting role. The advent of the PRC in the regional and world economy provided just that.

4. China: the Chamber's new genie

If the Chamber had been granted two wishes on its role in the Singapore economy, it would probably have (1) asked for an important role in an economic policy field that was central to the government's overall vision for the country, and (2) wished that this role would allow the Chamber to marry its historical identity and worldview with a new, modern face. When Deng Xiaoping started rubbing the lamp of China's economy in earnest, the genie that appeared promised the Chamber developments beyond its wildest dreams. It was ready to fulfil the role the government desired: putting Singapore on the map as the partner, advisor and facilitator of economic exchange between the PRC and the rest of the world. Early on, the Chamber's activities focused on trade promotion and two-way communication with China. Later, as markets and opportunities expanded further, it was instrumental in the World Chinese Entrepreneurs Convention initiative, which aimed at developing the role of the ethnic Chinese diaspora in the Chinese economy.

Trade missions and brokerage

The opening up of the PRC economy started in December 1978 with the implementation of the Four Modernizations policy by the Deng Xiaoping government. Still, pulling the country out of so many years of planned economy, not to mention the devastating years of the Cultural Revolution, proved difficult. A further wave of reforms in 1984–1985 heralded a new phase for overseas business participation in the PRC. The trade fair organized by the Chamber in 1985 seemed to be well timed to accommodate the PRC's eagerness to venture out and meet the international business community. The success of the Chamber in attracting Mainland Chinese exemplifies one strong card it could play in its China strategy: its existing network of good relations with Chinese authorities and various government-owned and new private companies.

Another characteristic of the SCCCI's China strategy was to broker this access to, and knowledge of, the PRC to other, non-Chinese, parties. An example of this second approach was the intensification of existing cooperation with the Associated Chambers of Commerce and Industry of Malaysia in the exploration of investment opportunities and markets in China.[125] The third major Chamber approach was linking up with government initiatives. To guide its economy to greater heights, the PRC enlisted a number of former senior Singapore officials. Retired former minister Dr. Goh Keng Swee became an economic advisor in 1985, and Fong Sip Chee, MP and former Minister of State, accepted a similar position.[126] While economic ties did develop, a nagging realization that Singapore was not doing as much, or as well, as investors from Hong Kong made government and entrepreneurs aware that more coordinated initiatives were needed. Linn In Hua put developments in perspective when he gave a guest lecture at the NUS MBA programme. He stressed that more effort was needed as Hong Kong developed links with China at a much faster rate than Singapore. Export figures supported his view: in 1978, Singapore exported US$60.4 million and Hong Kong US$63 million, while in 1984 Singapore exported only US$238.4 against Hong Kong's US$5,032.9 million.[127]

Singapore's response came in the form of an extensive government-to-government initiative. During a state visit to the PRC, Lee Kuan Yew, Minister of Trade and Industry Tony Tan, and Finance Minister Richard Hu held two days of closed-door meetings on trade and investment with top Chinese officials. The talks resulted in a number of deals but were mainly important because both sides could explain their aims and ambitions. Singapore was trying to cash in on the China card and its immigrant connection was highlighted by the delegation's visit to Xiamen in Fujian province. Due to this link Singapore was "the second gateway to China after Hong Kong". Instead of the traditional trade relationship, what was now marketed was Singapore's special merits in development expertise. The cultural and linguistic affinity of Singapore companies could aid China in its development.[128] Leadership and initiatives of the Singapore government on China were needed and expected by local business. In a report on SCCCI plans for joint activities in China with Malaysian counterparts, for instance, it was expressly mentioned that the two would "explore [opportunities in] China after the government had paved the way".[129] In short the three approaches of the Chamber towards China from the early 1980s were: "use the network", "be the broker" and "follow the government".

To reinforce its three strategic avenues, the Chamber set up a China research desk to collect data. It also stepped up its cooperative efforts with PRC organizations to heighten its profile as a valuable partner for Mainland parties. In 1986, Guangxi province was the first of many Chinese provinces to hold a trade fair in Singapore, and the SCCCI and the Chinese Merchandise Import-Export Association jointly sponsored this event. Linn In Hua said that intensified SCCCI involvement in similar events would help Singapore become a middleman for trade with, and investment in, the PRC. In the same year, the Chamber's ties with China allowed its members to capitalize on real business opportunities. A delegation from the Singapore construction and real estate sectors led by Tan Keong Choon went to China to explore the situation. Encouraged by the Singaporean interest, the Chinese side subsequently sent a 30-member delegation to pitch a number of real estate projects in and around Shanghai.[130]

Still, independent observers reported on Singapore's efforts in a different vein. Dr. Khaw Wei-kang argued that "despite its modest successes in trading with China, Singapore hasn't formulated a coherent policy that will in the long run give it a permanent competitive edge". He saw a number of basic shortcomings of Singapore in comparison with its competitors from Hong Kong and Taiwan. The geographical disadvantage would be nearly impossible to remedy, but more importantly the "so-called cultural and linguistic affinity between China and Singapore cannot be taken for granted ...".[131] However, voices such as Khaw's were rare in this period when possibilities in China were heralded with unbridled optimism.

The Chamber was among the optimists and further developed its activities in line with the government policy to increase Singapore's middleman role. It also expanded its brokerage role to Western organizations by cooperating with the French Chamber of Commerce in Singapore in a France-China Council. On the China side of the equation, as more Chinese provinces asked the SCCCI to sponsor their promotion exhibitions, it strengthened its relations with important organizations such as the China International Trade and Investment Corporation.[132]

Linn In Hua, after being elected president, proved to be an active proponent of the Chamber's strategy towards the PRC. He envisioned the traders of Singapore as matchmakers for foreign investors to explore markets, transfer technology and invest in international trade in the region and firmly included the PRC. During a seminar organized by the Chamber to discuss the use of Chinese language, most of the local and foreign academics and professionals on the panel agreed that the language was potentially very valuable in the realm of business. Not long after, therefore, Linn presented his vision concerning the PRC at a dinner in honour of a delegation from the China Council for the Promotion of International Trade (CCPIT), maintaining that Singapore could be a gateway for China's trade benefiting both Mainland businessmen and investors from abroad.[133]

Over time, the "use the network" and the "follow the government" approaches started to coincide more frequently. A clear example of this development came in 1988, when 17 Beijing companies held a week-long trade fair in Singapore. The Singapore TDB had actively promoted the event, which was sponsored by the SCCCI and the Chinese Merchandise Import-Export Association, and similar events with other cities followed. Overall trade figures with China were encouraging with two-way trade over 1987 amounting to $4.5 billion. The balance of trade, which had been in favour of the Mainland, started to take on a healthier outlook as well, with Singapore exports to China increasing by 60 per cent in the first quarter of 1988.[134] The SCCCI's successful strategy towards China found its apex in a mission in September 1988. With the participation of SMCC members and coinciding with a TDB delegation and an official Lee Kuan Yew visit, the trip exemplified the three strategies set out above.[135]

Not all aspects of the encounter with the awakening economic giant were plain sailing though. An economic law expert of Beijing University advised Chamber members to avoid joint ventures and run their own business in China because the lack of a clear legal system would make cooperation with a Mainland partner too risky.[136] The whole world was soon reminded through the Tiananmen incident of 4 June 1989 that China might be opening economically, but that the CCP would vehemently oppose political reform. The Chamber called the use of tanks and firepower on unarmed students "inhumane" and declared that it was "shocked and horrified". It also said the brute use of force had impeded the close business relations and had stalled the Chamber's carefully nurtured trade ties.[137] The Chamber, and the Singapore business community, did not lose too much time rekindling the fire of the profitable trade relations. With Sino-Singapore trade in 1988 exceeding $5.7 billion the stakes of the game were just too high. Barely two months after 4 June, 25 per cent of the booths at the Chamber's trade fair were occupied by businesses and organizations from the PRC, who in total won $70 million worth of contracts.[138] China's highest official to visit Singapore during the fair was Commerce Minister

Hu Ping. He spoke at a Chamber seminar on the "latest situation in China". He went to great lengths to emphasize the economic opportunities and euphemistically added that the country had "returned to normal". China was very focused on boosting tourism and promoting multilateral trade. Hu Ping met with the top brass of Singapore trade and industry and disclosed that Beijing was ready to consider a dedicated investment zone for Singaporeans, if Singapore so desired.[139]

World Chinese Economic Convention

In the course of the 1980s, boosted by the opening up of the PRC and fed by academic and journalistic explanations of the success of Asia's Tiger Economies, interest in the Chinese diaspora increased enormously. Confucian values were seen as one aspect of the success of the Chinese minorities worldwide, while the informal networks tying these Chinese groups together were seen as a special conduit of market information, capitalization, risk avoidance and, most of all, profit. As a result of both this positive attention and as an expression of a successful identity, Chinese the world over started to take their local and national *huiguan* to a next level, establishing regional and worldwide organizations based on shared ancestry or a shared place of origin in China. Singapore organizations headed by Chamber leaders were also involved in these activities and the Chamber soon unfolded plans to take an active part in the diaspora endeavour.

The first initiative was taken in 1988 by Linn In Hua who carried a proposal through the council to establish "sister Chamber relations" with the Filipino-Chinese Chamber of Commerce and with Kadin, the Indonesian national chamber of commerce.[140] Ambitions to develop the Chamber's connections into a close network with Chinese communities around the world were first voiced in early 1989. Tan Eng Joo, who took over the presidency and inherited the plans, developed the ideas into a World Chinese Entrepreneurs Convention (WCEC).[141] Of course, the initiative fell in line with the government's vision of making Singapore the bridge between the Chinese economy and the rest of the world. Tan had no trouble, therefore, securing not only extensive government endorsement, but also an impressive level of active participation from the highest officials. This clear gesture was important because it constituted an official endorsement of the utility of a certain type of Chineseness. Tan explained later:

> I was able to get for the convention, Lee Kuan Yew, [Minister for Information and the Arts] Brig.-Gen. Yeo, [and] our [Singapore] president

Wee Kim Wee to give a garden party ... for all the delegates from all over the world. And then to have our Deputy Prime Minister Ong Teng Cheong to officially close the convention. I don't think in history, you are going to find another convention with this kind of support from the government. Because this [was the] first time, never before in the world. And in a very, very sensitive spot. I want to make absolutely certain that we have that support. To dispel any fear that this is a political convention or in any way racist.[142]

When Senior Minister[143] Lee Kuan Yew opened the convention, 800 delegates from 75 cities in 30 countries had gathered. In his keynote speech, Lee concentrated very much on the experience of Singapore Chinese, stressing they had changed because of multi-culturalism, multi-racialism and multi-lingualism. This confronted them with an environment in which it was "necessary to make special efforts to pass on core cultural values, those dynamic parts of Confucian culture which if lost will lower our performance". He added that with the pressing Singapore need to go international, Chinese entrepreneurs overseas would be valuable contacts because, as he put it "ethnic and cultural empathy facilitates rapport and trust". The same primordial links would present great advantages to ethnic Chinese businessmen returning to China.[144]

In his opening remarks, Tan Eng Joo emphasized that

... the globalization of the ethnic Chinese is a historical fact. What we have in mind is to reinforce our commonality, our shared heritage. Through our commonality, we share and appreciate some indisputably ethnic qualities. Among these, that extra ingredient that makes us risk-takers and business-oriented. Grit and determination aside, it is that extra factor, the fourth factor of production – entrepreneurship – that gives life to business.[145]

Tan in the same speech suggested that an international network of Chinese business communities, irrespective of nationality, could be woven. The central messages in these two speeches, business advantage through cultural affinity and the opportunity of being a bridge to the PRC economy, set the tone for the remainder of the convention.

Many stressed the indivisible nature of the relationship between Chinese business and culture. One editorial in favour of this view wrote "the performance of the 'four Dragons of Asia' has confirmed that Chinese culture is the main driving force in Asian economic development".[146]

One of the speakers, Singapore Minister for Information and the Arts, George Yeo drew a picture of the old heartland of China and the advanced and modern periphery of the Chinese diaspora. China did not have the monopoly of wisdom on Confucianism anymore, he argued. "It is the periphery which first absorbs outside influences and which then transmits these influences into the centre ... The centre, which is China, needs the periphery to help it achieve its great transformation".[147] Ethnicity and migrant identity were crucial for the periphery's success. "To put it in a crude way", Yeo said, "if these Asian migrants were to become white in everything but skin, their dynamism [would] surely be affected".[148] From the PRC side, Rong Yiren, the head of CITIC, expressed the hope that ethnic Chinese entrepreneurs would show more interest in following China's development and promoting economic and technological cooperation between their countries of residence and China.[149]

During the closing dinner, Singapore's Deputy Prime Minister, Ong Teng Cheong, returned to the issue of learning and speaking the mother tongue. He argued that language acted as a strong unifier to the Chinese diaspora, because it conveyed ideas and values forming the culture of a community. Confucianism, a value system he commended for its dynamic application of values, would be transmitted through Mandarin. Armed with this cultural and linguistic skill, the ethnic Chinese would be in a position to cash in on the opportunities in the Mainland Chinese economy.[150]

The convention was deemed a great success and immediately plans were made to organize similar gatherings every two years.[151] The SCCCI had used its status to put itself at the vanguard of the ethnic Chinese network at a time when the entire economic and political world was looking for ways to benefit from the economic opening up of the PRC. The fact that the Chamber did so with not only the backing, but the full policy support, of the Singapore government only strengthened this position. The three strategies overlapped. Because the Chamber had the network, which the PAP government dearly wanted and needed, it could be the broker following, and protected by, the government's diplomatic and political endeavours.

The China network expands but culture is tested

For the SCCCI, the prime mover behind the WCEC, the positive effects and the tangible returns of the convention were apparent very soon. The Chamber's standing in the eyes of PRC officialdom had risen to greater heights and in 1992, a staggering 130 delegations from China visited the SCCCI office. This was twice the number of the previous year and 75 per cent of all incoming delegations the Chamber received that year.

Apart from strengthening its network, the Chamber also heightened its profile as a place of training and education for Mainland leaders. In 1992, the SCCCI hosted 270 senior managers from China who attended nine tailor-made courses at the Chamber training centre, compared to only two in 1991.[152]

The next step in the Chamber's network strategy was helping its members to establish better business ties in the PRC. In 1993, this translated into close cooperation with the Chinese embassy and two trade missions. There were also plans for a SCCCI-led investment company, which would draw together potential investors from other Chinese Chambers in countries like Malaysia, Indonesia, Thailand, Hong Kong and Taiwan, to penetrate the Chinese market.[153]

Of the three China strategies of the Chamber, outlined earlier in this section, the "use the network" approach was the most successful. This success seemed to indicate that the assumption of cultural affinity leading to better business was indeed true. However, of the other two strategies, "be the broker" and "follow the government", the latter inherently indicated the inability or unwillingness of Singapore Chinese entrepreneurs to go it alone in China. In the remainder of this section, the validity of the approaches will be analyzed and the assumption of cultural advantage will be scrutinized.

Linn In Hua's warning that Hong Kong had capitalized on the opportunities in China was already quoted above. Although total Singapore investment in China did rise dramatically, so did that of Hong Kong and Taiwan. Apparently, the pressure caused by investors from these two countries forced their Singapore competitors to move deeper into China. Of the 15 Singapore business projects announced in 1993, 10 were outside of Fujian and Guangdong, compared to half of the projects going there in 1992. The superior market penetration and presence of Hong Kong and Taiwan investors were given as the main reasons for Singapore ventures moving inland.[154]

In 1993, during Prime Minister Goh Chok Tong's official visit, the Chinese Minister of Foreign Trade and Economic Cooperation said that Singapore investors did not have the guts to invest in large-scale projects. There was some truth to his observation, as some of the apprehension and difficulties of Singapore investors in China became apparent. Macroeconomic factors had wiped out profits for many joint ventures and foreign enterprises in China. Although opportunities were present, investors rightfully worried about devaluation, inflation and an overheating PRC economy. Lack of clear legislation and enforcement added to investor worries and the much-heralded tax incentives proved complex and difficult to realize. These findings did not constitute a ringing endorsement for the assumption that all ethnic Chinese investors would be successful in the PRC.[155]

Despite the active role of the SCCCI, individual entrepreneurs and companies were indeed not going to the PRC in the expected numbers. Also, in the eyes of the government, doing business only on the bases of *guanxi* connections and along kinship lines was judged to be too sporadic, ad hoc and small scale. Therefore in 1993, in characteristic PAP style, government policy and economic initiatives were presented as the desirable method for getting the ball rolling. Peh Chin Hua, a PAP Member of Parliament, understood why Singaporeans were afraid to take the plunge, saying "the fear came from being used to Singapore's regulated business environment and being unused to operating in China, where relationships, rather than regulations, count".[156] While trying to assuage this fear through its business initiatives, the government also increased its efforts to further improve its direct business, planning and policy exchanges with the Chinese central government. China was keen to partner Singapore in business projects in third countries, as the PRC minister of foreign trade and economic co-operation (Moftec) indicated during a visit to Singapore. The investment road show he led drummed up $1 billion in potential deals in China. Singapore and China also set up a high-level joint committee on bilateral trade and economic co-operation.[157]

The Singapore top brass was very interested in pitching their formula of state-led growth combined with political and social stability to the PRC, with Lee Kuan Yew and Goh Keng Swee as the driving force behind Singapore's contacts with China. The establishment of the joint committee indicated that the new generation of Singapore leaders under Prime Minister Goh Chok Tong had also succeeded in convincing China that Singapore could provide the PRC with the knowledge, experience and "software" of the implementation of state-led growth.[158] The SCCCI stepped up its education role towards China in this process, and launched a three-week training scheme for 28 provincial and municipal leaders to help them understand how Singapore's economy and urban planning worked.[159]

As examples of how government initiative and leadership led to increase in private investment, the cases of Shandong and Suzhou are fitting. In the course of 1993, both Lee Kuan Yew and Goh Chok Tong during separate trips to China visited Shandong province with large business delegations in tow. Partly as a result of these delegations a number of business projects started to get off the ground and private Singapore investment in Shandong rose significantly.

In 1993, a team led by Lee Kuan Yew was gathering information on which location in China would be most suitable as a site for the transfer of Singapore's experience in township planning and development.[160] It is informative to look at why Suzhou was eventually picked. While the government continued to sing the praises of the advantage of culture, language and network connections, the reality seemed somewhat different. Located in Jiangsu province in the hinterland of Shanghai, Suzhou was not a hometown to ethnic Chinese businessmen in Singapore. Rather, Singapore had been actively sought out by Jiangsu's governor who had asked the General Manager of the Bank of China in Singapore to put him in touch with local big businesses. A number of Singapore tycoons reacted to these advances and visited Jiangsu. Lee Kuan Yew and Ong Teng Cheong heightened the province's profile in 1993 through visits. It was argued that, while Singapore business was squeezed out of Guangdong by the Hong Kong investors and out of Fujian by the Taiwanese, they could compete on par with other investors in Jiangsu. In one article it was billed as an advantage that "*guanxi*, or connections, matter less here [in Jiangsu] and business is conducted in a more clear-cut way than in some other parts of China". One investor said that in Jiangsu "negotiators behave more professionally, and many of them have been educated in the West. Details are thrashed out point by point and the agreement is then drawn up in black and white to ensure there is no misunderstanding".[161]

Slowly, and not without frequent problems with the local and provincial authorities, work on the Suzhou Industrial Park, Singapore's largest investment in China, proceeded. Inaugurated in February 1994, the 70 square kilometres of industrial park, housing and infrastructure were planned to cater to both Singaporean and foreign tenants. As these companies were "using the Singapore bridge", an important aim of this government-to-government project was to transfer Singapore expertise on building and running such a venture to the Chinese counterparts. Some voices from business circles, however, complained that the Suzhou project was too much geared towards good relations and too little to business sense.[162] Eventually, cultural differences, political miscalculations and a lack of competitiveness, led to the disengagement of the Singapore government from the project.[163]

In contrast to the government-led initiatives in China, some observers pointed out that there was a different category of Singapore businessmen in China. One article argued that while talk on business in China was abundant, actual Singapore penetration was less than optimal. The author reminded readers that a group existed which had already been doing business in China long before the big government push. Their characteristics: "They read, speak and write Chinese effectively, and if bilingual they prefer Chinese; they are almost entirely Chinese-educated and saw doors of MNC's and government jobs [in Singapore] remain shut; they are familiar with Chinese history, geography, customs and culture and feel at ease in China; they are at home in Chinese style interpersonal interactions and are effective in building up relationships with their partners." The group in question was, of course, the Chinese-educated, many of them Nanda graduates. A significant number of members of the SCCCI fell into this category and this fact explained why the Chamber could be so successful with its "use the network" strategy. The language skills and genuine cultural understanding of its members provided a real bridge to Chinese counterparts. In contrast, as the author pointed out, Singapore's bilingual policy had failed to produce for younger generations the level of Chinese language and cultural understanding necessary to have an edge in China.[164]

In conclusion, the question of the actual results of Singapore's business ventures into China hardly mattered to the effects that all the attention for China brought the Chamber. As the success of its "use the network" approach indicated, it was able to activate connections with and networks in China to its advantage, thereby strengthening its claim to the government that it could be a valuable bridge. The successful organization of the WCEC further enhanced the Chamber's stature. In the final analysis, the opening up of the Chinese economy and the resulting ambition of the Singapore government to put Singapore on the map as a business interface presented the Chamber with the opportunity to convert its cultural and network capital into improvement of its image in the eyes of the government. It enabled the Chamber to again occupy a position of importance in the Singapore socio-political system.

5. Representation of Chinese values and education

While the Chamber was gaining status and influence in the realms of SME promotion and China connections, it was stripped of a number of roles in the arena of culture. The Chamber was closely involved in the government policy to introduce a system of three separate channels of representation for cultural, social and educational, and economic affairs. Traditionally, the SCCCI had been at the apex in all three of these fields but from 1985 onward, two of these three roles were stripped away and transferred to new organizations. On the one hand, this diminished the status of the Chamber and showed that it had to bow to the wishes of the government in these matters. On the other hand, however, having been stripped of its cultural roles, which had so often landed it in trouble with the PAP party/state, the Chamber gained stature in the eyes of the government. It had to sacrifice some roles to shine more in others.

A trinity of organizations

The Singapore Federation of Chinese Clan Associations (SFCCA)

The tasks of preservation and propagation of Chinese culture were bestowed by the government upon the SFCCA, an organization that was specifically established to fulfil this government-initiated and government-defined role. This official mandate meant that it was clear from the outset that the SFCCA would not have a completely free hand in defining what Chinese culture was and how it would be promoted. It should be remembered that the government official responsible for the initiative, Deputy Prime Minister Ong Teng Cheong, had only recently warned the Chinese of Singapore to abandon those parts of their cultural tradition that had become "bad habits". Now Ong was the guest of honour at the inaugural dinner of the SFCCA, which had been formally established on 27 January 1986. Ong told those present that the Chinese clans could do more together and that the Federation could play a major role for the government aim of promoting Confucian philosophy.[165] One newspaper described the "consolidation of the clans" as a reflection of the change in social relations in the Chinese community by which the focus was shifting from clan to community.[166] It would be more true to say that after many years of dwindling and weakening, the clans had chosen to accept the reality of the representational structure of Singapore. By cooperating in a government-endorsed umbrella organization, they accepted responsibility for the implementation of certain state views and policies in return for a legitimate stake in the system and a much better chance of survival of their form and function.

The executive board of the SFCCA was set up to reflect the diversity of the Chinese community. The seven organizations that established the SFCCA were: the Singapore Hokien Huay Kuan, the Teochew Poit Ip Huay Kuan, the Singapore Kwang Tung Hui Kuan, the Nanyang Khek Community Guild, the Singapore Kiung Chow Hwee Kuan, the Sam Kiang Huay Kwan and the Singapore Foochow Association. The men who took up positions on the board were predominantly the older generation clan leaders who had already retired from active duty in the Chamber but were almost all honorary presidents or honorary council members. The job of chairman was given to the familiar and obvious figure of Wee Cho

Yaw. As the president of the Hokien Huay Kuan, and as the most powerful and influential of the elders of the Chinese community, he was a natural choice, more so because he was an acceptable candidate in the eyes of the government. The Federation found its first home on the premises of the Hokien Huay Kuan.

As the appointed guardian of Chinese culture and with its officials drawn from the generation of the Chinese educated, it is no surprise that the SFCCA soon voiced its concern over the decline in the standard of Chinese education in Singapore. During the first annual general meeting in 1986, Wee Cho Yaw called on the government to review its Chinese language policies and cited China's economic open-door policy as an added reason.[167] Rather than announcing increased attention, however, the government called on the SFCCA and the SCCCI to take more initiatives to promote the use of Chinese.[168] They did, and over the years they introduced a range of projects and events for this purpose, mostly within the framework of the annual Speak Mandarin Campaign.

While the Federation was still trying to coax the government into increasing its budgetary spending and policy initiatives on Chinese language education, the tone and angle it used was quite different from the approach taken by the Chamber or groups of its members in the past. It conformed to government policy as it spoke with a less than independent voice. Activities the Federation developed included a resource centre, scholarship and bursary schemes for students, and even a kindergarten. It published a number of books on the history and the customs of the Chinese of Singapore and organized various exhibitions on these issues. The annual highlight, from 1991 onwards, was the traditional Chinese River Hongbao fair co-organized by the SFCCA to celebrate the Chinese New Year.[169]

Government praise for these initiatives was often forthcoming. At the opening of an exhibition on Confucius, Ong Teng Cheong praised the SFCCA and the SCCCI for their efforts.[170] The status and importance of the SFCCA as a social and cultural organization was confirmed a few years later when Goh Chok Tong chose a dinner hosted by the Federation and the Chamber in his honour as the venue for his first full-length speech as Prime Minister.[171] As part of the transfer of power from Lee Kuan Yew to Goh Chok Tong, the SFCCA paid a glowing tribute to Lee. Wee Cho Yaw observed that "Mr. Lee is English-educated but he never forgot his Chinese heritage and worked hard to preserve Chinese values and culture in Singapore". As a gift, a collection of Lee's speeches on education, culture and language was presented to the out-going prime minister.[172] The event illustrates the acceptance of the division of power between the government and the Chinese representational organizations. The historical record, partly illustrated in the previous chapters, would have warranted a more critical view of Lee Kuan Yew's actions towards the *huiguan* as well as his views and policies concerning language, education and culture. The leaders of the Chinese community chose, however, to commend Lee for his achievements rather than to criticize him for what they might consider his shortcomings.

The SFCCA remained, in the first decade of its existence, firmly led by the older generation. The seven founding organizations appointed very senior, if not the most senior, leaders to the SFCCA. They were most often men retired from active Chamber duty during the rejuvenation campaign of the late 1980s. The enshrinement of an older generation of Chamber leaders in the SFCCA was an illustration of their acceptance of government control over the representational structure as well as a sign of government respect.[173]

Chinese Development Assistance Council (CDAC)

With culture and tradition allotted to the SFCCA, the social and welfare activities of the Chinese community were by 1991, according to the government, in need of a coordinating body. Both the Malay and the Indian community had already established such organizations: Mendaki was established in 1981 for the Malay community, and Sinda in 1989 for the Indian community.

To complete the representational structure, Goh Chok Tong first mooted the idea for a Chinese equivalent in July 1991, and the CDAC was indeed formed in April 1992.[174] With a mission statement to help the poorer members of the Chinese community, the Council was adamant from the outset that this goal should be achieved through education and training, not through handouts. The SFCCA and the SCCCI were given the task of getting the CDAC off the ground and they set up the initial educational programmes through the clans and connected the CDAC to the state-run community centres. The Council had a board of directors of English- and Chinese-educated members and a board of trustees with an advisory role. At first the offices of the CDAC were on the Hill Street premises of the SCCCI, before it moved to its own building. Wee Cho Yaw was appointed first chairman of the board of trustees, confirming his central position in the troika of representational organizations of the Chinese community.[175]

Funding of the Council was to be drawn from the community. Two approaches were followed to secure a steady flow. On the one hand, an endowment fund was set up in which gifts and grants would be pooled. At the outset, Wee Cho Yaw and Lien Ying Chow led the CDAC endowment-fund charity drive. The Hokien Huay Kuan contributed $1 million, which was to be spread out over 10 years. Members of the fundraising committee included Robert Chua of the SMA, and Chamber leaders such as Chua Gim Siong, Teo Chiang Long, Tan Eng Joo, Shaw Vee Meng and Tan Keong Choon.[176] The other stream of income was generated through Central Provident Fund contributions. Every working Chinese citizen could indicate that, as he or she paid the mandatory CPF fees, an extra amount would be taken and transferred to the CDAC. The proceeds of this check-off scheme were estimated to amount to $5.7 million a year.

Commenting on target groups and goals, BG Lee said that the CDAC should be active in vocational skills training in Chinese while simultaneously stressing the importance of learning English. He also suggested that the clan associations could help the CDAC to reach out to the underprivileged. This way they could carve out a new role by providing volunteers and tutors while facilitating the CDAC with inroads into the target communities.[177]

Prime Minister Goh was abundantly clear that he wanted the CDAC to concentrate on vocational and educational programmes. True to the PAP principle of meritocracy, he emphasized that the CDAC was set up to "help poorer Chinese escape the under-achievement trap through self-help programmes such as extra classes and worker training ...".[178] In the ensuing years, the CDAC ran a well-funded and extensive Skills Training Awards programme and was also involved in making modern educational infrastructure, such as personal computers and internet access, available to those who could not afford them.[179]

With the trinity of Chinese representational bodies in place, the government made sure that their role and position were understood within the larger setting of national identity and shared values. For the Chinese community it meant that the three organizations looking after its commercial, cultural and social interests, the SCCCI, the SFCCA and the CDAC, would be subordinate to the PAP state, which remained in charge of defining and safeguarding the national interest.

Shared values and education

One of the government initiatives regarding national interest was a renewed effort to construct a Singapore identity through a set of national, shared values. If pulling the nation together was one aim of this endeavour, creating a cultural antidote to the perceived dangers of modernization and Westernization was the other. Emphasis on the conservative and "traditional" elements of the nation's Asian heritage was central to the government's approach. In the previous chapter, it was shown that the propagation of traditional values alone harboured the danger of being interpreted by the different ethnic communities as liberty to give their respective communal cultures pride of place. On the other hand, elevation of the values of one of these communal cultures to the level of national culture, as was attempted in the Confucian values campaigns, risked the anger and frustration of the other ethnic communities. Therefore the government introduced the concept of shared national values as an umbrella over the various sets of communal values.

The Chamber understood that the shared values would have a firm base in the conservative elements of Confucianism so well suited for economic development and national stability. It rightly felt that if hard work, respect for and obedience to hierarchy and authority, and the subjugation of the individual to the collective good were to be elevated to the level of national values, the Chamber could use its image to good advantage. Many of the older generation of leaders believed strongly in these values, especially diligence, thrift, and filial piety, and saw them as the bases for the success of the proverbial self-made, rags to riches tycoon. They had felt all along that loss of these values would mean the impoverishment of Singapore society. The Chamber presented itself as a force in the retention and propagation of these values.[180]

Among the Chamber leaders, Linn In Hua was especially sensitive that there would be no room for Chinese cultural muscle flexing.[181] Linn seldom talked about "Chinese values" but pushed more inclusive terminology to ensure that all the various ethnic constituents of Singapore would stay securely on board. In his speech at the first monthly meeting of his presidency he said the Chamber would promote "Eastern philosophy".[182] In a newspaper interview he used the term "Eastern values"[183] and later he spoke of the nation's "fine oriental cultural heritage".[184] Under Linn's guidance the Chamber positioned itself firmly behind the government's umbrella approach to the issue of national values.

Education efforts

The activities of the SCCCI in the field of education continued to reflect a division of labour between the nation's two value systems. "Western knowledge" for the brain and "Eastern knowledge" for the heart and soul. Business training had become the mainstay of the SCCCI educational activities, but on the Asian heart and soul, the Chamber's education line was less clear. While the SCCCI continued to occasionally lament the decline in standard of Chinese language education, its efforts lacked the ideological and emotional edge of the 1950s and 1960s. Still, Linn In Hua made upgrading of the level of Chinese education one of his points of action, and he led a delegation to the National University of Singapore, the National Institute of Education and the Singapore Science Council to discuss the subject.[185] Also, through its involvement in the annual Speak Mandarin Campaign, the Chamber advocated the need for more formal education of Chinese for children, written as well as spoken.[186] However, when the SCCCI was asked to set up Chinese language schools together with the clans, it declined the honour. Not eager to re-enter the potentially contentious arena of undergraduate education, it chose to focus on adult education and continued to provide Mandarin courses with a business angle at its training centre. Both the Chamber and participants alike cited China's open door policy as the main reason to study the language.[187]

There was increasing demand for English courses as more Chinese executives and traders wanted to learn or improve their English for an edge in business. The SCCCI English courses were especially popular among the 30 to 40 year age bracket and attracted mostly Chinese educated, sole proprietor and SME participants.[188] While the Chamber might have still aspired to a role in Chinese language education, this intent failed to find expression in its actual activities. With the SFCCA responsible for imparting knowledge about Chinese culture, the SCCCI, unwilling to be involved directly in Chinese language schools, had become an organization supporting, rather than initiating, efforts in Chinese language education.

More values

In his first speech as Prime Minister in February 1991, Goh Chok Tong set out the ideas of the government on national values. He emphasized that Singapore should have shared values, identifiable to all. Apart from these, different people or groups could practise their own values, but only as long as these communal values did not clash with national values.[189] Under Goh's personal guidance, five values central to the nation and the national identity of its citizens were formulated. They were defined as: placing community above the self, upholding the family as the basic building block of society, resolving major issues through consensus instead of contention, stressing racial and religious tolerance and harmony, and regard and community support for the individual.[190] At the presentation of these values, Goh Chok Tong indicated that the government saw the SFCCA and the SCCCI as two organizations that could help preserve the essence of culture both on the communal as well as on the national level.[191] It is perhaps curious to see that the government continued to include the Chamber in these matters, even though it had itself divided the activities of the Chinese community over the Chamber, the CDAC, and the SFCCA. The official separation of the tasks of the three institutions must be analyzed in tandem with continuity in personnel. The top brass of the Chinese community, with Wee Cho Yaw as the prime example, was involved in the running of all three organizations. Still, the fact that the SFCCA and the CDAC were set up constituted a significant change for the Chamber. Since its inception, its multi-purpose elite role meant that it acted in the social, cultural, political as well as economic arena. The Chamber's Chinese language and educational ambitions had often brought it into conflict with the state. Now that it had bowed to the state and its cultural and social roles had been taken away, the SCCCI had become a more acceptable partner to the government and could cash in on its internal changes and relish its remaining external roles.

6. Legitimate roles

The 1993 reform of the SCCCI *bang* structure was an important factor in gaining legitimacy in the eyes of the government, and the Chamber continued to implement internal changes to further build up its image as a crucial business organization in the national and international arena.

Continuing internal reform

The new election system introduced in 1993 was a shining example of the ability of, but also of the necessity for, the SCCCI to combine continuity with change. Indeed, as important as doing away with the system of *bang* representation was the need to keep the various *bang*, the trade associations and the corporate and individual members satisfied with the power structure of the Chamber. From the 1995 election, therefore, the procedure for selecting the council of the Chamber would be a four-stage affair. During the first stage, the out-going council would elect from its midst 15 incumbents to sit on the new council. During the second stage, all eligible members would elect 26 new council members in a free election. During the third stage, the trade associations would elect 17 council members. Finally, during the fourth stage, the seven *bang* organizations, not surprisingly the same seven that were the founding members of the

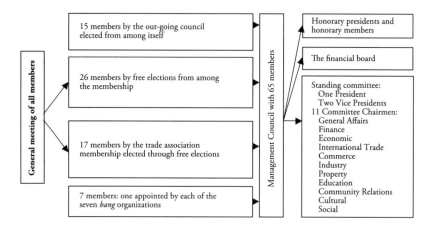

Figure 3: Organizational diagram of the SCCCI after the 1993 constitution

SFCCA, each would appoint one member to complete the new council. In a new requirement intended to allay fears of the Chamber losing its roots, the new constitution stipulated that every future president had to be able to speak Mandarin.[192]

The new system did not, however, fully exclude possibilities of wheeling and dealing about seats between different factions, *bang* or otherwise. Only stages two and three were based on free elections, and the practice of no-contest appointment to the council remained if the number of candidates in these stages was equal to the number of seats. In the 1997 election, this led to a group of Nanda graduates, which had forwarded a 24th candidate for stage two, receiving a quiet word from some high Chamber officials. They were advised to recall their candidate so as to prevent a voting round with possible embarrassing results.[193] Teething problems were to be expected, however, as Kwek Leng Joo indicated when he said it would probably take two or three elections before the overhaul would filter through.[194]

During the next two elections, two trends were noticeable as a result from the reform and from the efforts of Kwek to attract new blood from leading local businesses and government-linked companies. Government-linked and stock-market listed companies had, in the past, faced the problem of having to choose a dialect group to fall under, which was one reason for these companies refusing to join. More importantly, many of these businesses had not wanted to be part of the Chamber as long as it had an old-fashioned air around it, and had failed to come to terms with the realities of the Singapore power balance. Now changes had been made, the

Chamber could welcome new members such as the Development Bank of Singapore, Pidemco Land and Neptune Orient Lines. The second trend of a new generation entering the council was continued by the likes of Wee Ee Cheong, son of Wee Cho Yaw and Philip Ng Chee Tat, son of property development tycoon Ng Teng Fong.[195]

Kwek had identified two more types of members as targets for growth: women and professionals. A recruitment drive for women members had already been undertaken in 1990, but after Kwek made recruitment of women a priority, 400 to 500 newcomers joined.[196] It was not until the 1995 election that Gan See Khem and Claire Chiang became the first two women to be elected to the council.[197] Two years later, the Standing Committee included Gan and Chiang as the first female committee chairpersons for education and community relations respectively.[198]

The admission of professionals, as opposed to businessmen, into the ranks of SCCCI members was a trickier issue. Allowing these professionals to join as individuals rather than as representatives of a company meant the reinstatement of individual membership, which was abolished in 1968 because of allegations of vote-buying and admission of the infamous "dance girls". Therefore, when the Indian Chamber opened its doors to professionals in 1991, Chamber president Tan Eng Joo did not see any need to follow suit.[199] That attitude was reversed by his successor who very much wanted to welcome lawyers, accountants, business consultants and the like. Before the end of Kwek's second term he had secured acceptance of additional constitutional changes. First of all the problem of individual membership was solved by the "associate member". Associate members would not have voting rights but would otherwise enjoy all rights and opportunities of full members. This new category opened the door for professionals to join the Chamber. Kwek also introduced a new position, the Immediate Past President, to the standing committee. Without serving more than the permitted two terms as president, the out-going top man could make sure his legacy would be well preserved.[200]

The road ahead

A number of activities the Chamber undertook since 1993 indicated the new direction in which the organization wanted to develop. Having secured a positive image through the election reform and the inclusion of women, professionals and non-Chinese members, the Chamber now needed to build on its past track record to show it could make relevant contributions to Singapore society. The SCCCI drew on its recent strengths in the diaspora network and China brokerage on the business side of things but also managed to invoke achievements of a more distant past in a contemporary manner through publications and events. The relationship with the government, meanwhile, seemed to.be positively affected by all these developments, as the Chamber cemented a relevant and legitimate role for itself in the mainstream of the business world, the representational structure and Singapore society at large.

World Chinese Business Network

It is not surprising that the Chamber wanted to build on the success of the WCEC, putting itself on the map as a leading organization in the Chinese diaspora. Of course, the support of the Singapore government before and during the event and the praise it bestowed on the Chamber after its successful conclusion had been a boost to the SCCCI. The initiative for the World Chinese Business Network (WCBN), a direct extension of the WCEC, soon proved to be in synch with government expectations. Not aware that the SCCCI was planning to set up an electronic database on the internet linking ethnic Chinese businessmen the world over, Lee Kuan Yew, during the second WCEC meeting held in Hong Kong in 1993, propounded exactly the same idea. Arguing to the crowd of ethnic Chinese businessmen that their networking efforts could be more efficient, he advised them to compile directories listing names, biographies and business backgrounds, as well as character and credit references, and to make this information available electronically.[201] Kwek eagerly informed the press that he was pleasantly surprised at Lee's call and that it would mean a boost for the existing SCCCI project to link up Chinese chambers of commerce and ethnic Chinese businesses on a global scale.[202]

The site (http://www.wcbn.com.sg/, 1 February 2007) was launched two years later in December 1995 and was met with much national and international media attention. "New web site provides link to the Chinese diaspora", was the headline with which the *Asian Wall Street Journal* heralded the news of the WCBN, noting that the site would give people a chance to peek into the realm of the Chinese business network. The Chamber declared that the main purpose of the network was "to create more business opportunities for the Chinese businessman". With information available in English as well as traditional and simplified characters, the site and its bulletin board were accessible to all entrepreneurs, Chinese as well as non-Chinese, looking for business opportunities.[203] The WCBN, apart from expanding the bridge function between the PRC and the rest of the world, also coincided with another major government strategy. One of the PAP slogans was to make Singapore an "intelligent island", thereby putting the island's economy on a firm base of state-of-the-art information technology infrastructure. Priding itself on being ahead of the technological game, the government recognized the commercial potential of the internet, and its future as a business tool. WCBN was seen as a powerful indication of the information age.[204]

"Historic past, bright future"

Contrary to the subdued celebrations on the occasion of its 80th anniversary, the Chamber's 90th birthday was celebrated in grand fashion. A number of initiatives were undertaken and various special events were staged throughout 1996. The highlight of the year was the gala dinner for 2,000 guests held in November, with Prime Minister Goh Chok Tong as the guest of honour. Goh emphasized the value of the Chamber for the nation's regionalization and globalization efforts with a plaque bearing the inscription "Fang Yan Si Hai", a Chinese phrase that translates to "Let's cast our eyes on the four seas".[205] Proud of the Prime Minister's praise and acknowledgement, the Chamber put the inscription prominently on the cover of its anniversary publication. Confident of the role of the organization he was leading, Kwek Leng Joo declared that the Chamber was "still playing [a] pivotal role in bridging the government and the Chinese community, and will continue to do so".[206]

The respect and acknowledgement that now started to show through in the attitude of the government towards the Chamber gave it the confidence to invoke the proud imagery of past achievement. In 1998, on the occasion of the annual commemoration of World War II victims, the Chamber organized an exhibition on the Japanese occupation that was a direct spin-off of the book, *The Price of Peace*, written and published in English and Chinese under the auspices of the SCCCI. Through the exhibition, in which the local Chinese anti-Japanese movement and the Chinese contribution to Singapore's civil defence received due attention, the Chamber highlighted the role it had played in the past. It also, if indirectly, referred to the last time it had been able to force the government to do what the Chamber wanted, during the blood debt movement in the 1960s. Indeed the commemoration and the exhibition were staged at the memorial site built with the money raised through the Chamber's efforts at that time.

While there was room and opportunity for the Chamber to take the limelight in certain fields, others were acknowledged as being out of bounds and firmly outside of the ambitions of the SCCCI. The national election of 1997 provided a clear example that a role in national politics was no longer a goal. The government had called early elections and as usual precious little time was available for an election campaign. In a surprising move, the largest opposition party, the Workers' Party (WP) of veteran J. B. Jeyaratnam, pulled in Tang Liang Hong to help it challenge the PAP in the group representation constituency (GRC) of Cheng San.[207] Tang, a Nanda graduate, former head of the Nanyang Fine Arts Academy and a known advocate of Chinese language and culture, attracted much attention in Cheng San, a part of Singapore with lower than average income and education levels, as well as a high percentage of Chinese-educated and dialect-speaking Chinese. Tang and the WP team tried to exploit these demographics and voter polls indicated that they might have a chance of claiming the first ever opposition victory in a GRC. Without expanding on the intricacies of the campaign, the main issue proved to be Chinese identity. After some statements by Tang on the issue of a perceived rift between the English-educated and the Chinese-educated, the PAP top brass stepped in. In a direct reference to 1965, Lee Kuan Yew and Goh Chok Tong called Tang a "Chinese chauvinist" and conjured up images of national ethnic breakdown if the WP would succeed. The significance of the use of the term "Chinese chauvinist" and the direct link with Tan Lark Sye and his alleged involvement in left-wing politics in 1962 was lost on many of the younger generation. The older Chamber leaders I spoke with after the election were all keenly aware of the ill-concealed threat to anyone who considered connecting the issues of ethnicity and class in Singapore politics.[208] The PAP reshuffled the pack and Prime Minister Goh himself stepped in as candidate in Cheng San. Due to intense rhetoric and electoral pressure, the PAP managed to hold on to Cheng San, but only with a small margin.[209]

Since Chinese identity and the government policy on language and culture were so central to this tempestuous election campaign, the reaction of the SCCCI was indicative of its stance towards the government on an issue it had claimed as its own in the past. This time however, the Chamber steered well clear of the campaign. Only after the PAP won the elections did it release a press statement. "It [the Cheng San victory] shows that the majority of Singaporeans value and cherish racial and religious harmony and do not take the slightest chance of allowing racial and religious politics in parliament. They are in consensus with the government in maintaining the time-tested policy of a multi-racial, multi-religious and multi-lingual society with English as the common language. This policy must be upheld by all Singaporeans as a prerequisite to sustaining our economic progress".[210] A clearer endorsement of the complete government dominance of the political sphere could hardly have been given. The Chamber equally clearly distanced itself from its past claims of autonomous authority on ethnic, education and language policy.

Not long after, the SCCCI chose a new council. Tay Beng Chuan, the man who had successfully completed the constitutional negotiations, was rewarded with the presidency. Leadership renewal, constitutional reform, incorporation of women and professionals, and a clear political indication by the Chamber that it understood its role in modern Singapore led to an unprecedented level of government recognition. Among the government appointees for Nominated Member of Parliament were two Chamber leaders. Tay Beng Chuan received his inclusion into the country's legislature because of his presidency of the Chamber.[211] While Claire Chiang as women and family rights campaigner was not selected directly because of her Chamber affiliation, the significance remained. The new generation of Reformer leaders were seen by the government as valuable representatives on the national level.

Concluding remarks

Between 1985 and 1997, the outlook of the Chamber was drastically altered as it experienced and realized a momentous change of fortune. From being threatened to become the ugly duckling of the Singapore business scene, it emerged as a confident player in a number of arenas crucial to the nation's economic welfare. The crisis of 1985 proved to be a major turning point for Singapore, as it forced the government to evaluate its policies. Through the changes first indicated by the Economic Committee, the government made a significant return to a number of characteristics of the Chamber's worldview: local business, trade and Chinese identity.

This allowed the Chamber to successfully fulfil three roles: nurturing and training the nation's SMEs, promoting Singapore as a regional hub and a global trading centre, and building bridges to the China economy. The small family firm, the quintessential Chinese shop and trading house, had continued to make up an important part of the Chamber's membership. The role in SME promotion and upgrading, therefore, reflected the socio-economic organizational base of the SCCCI. Its commercial pedigree and its networks in the region had been the bedrock on which the organization was built, while the utility of the Chamber's Chineseness in Singapore's strategy towards the PRC had its roots in another essential feature of the organization: the fact that it was, and always had been, a representative of Chinese business.

These achievements were facilitated by a change of the guard in the Chamber leadership. A younger and reform-minded generation took the helm, led and encouraged by the pivotal figure of Linn In Hua, the Organizer, who set many wheels in motion. The two other Reformers, Kwek Leng Joo and Tay Beng Chuan, continued to reinvent the Chamber. Changes in organizational structure and in the identification of goals and roles led to a gradual increase in government praise for the Chamber's endeavours. In return for its acknowledgement of the primacy of the state and by accepting that its roles in social and cultural affairs were taken away, the Chamber secured for itself a viable future as the representative of Chinese business in Singapore.

Conclusion

ONE CENTURY OF THE CHINESE CHAMBER, going on two centuries of modern Singapore and 40 years of independence for this young nation. Reflection should encompass all times, but round numbers seem to give us more room to reminisce and analyze. In the preceding chapters the history of the centenarian SCCC(I) has taken centre stage, but the review also provided an opportunity to look at Singapore history from a different angle than the customary focus on the PAP state. There were 140 years of modern Singapore history before the PAP came to power and this book argues that a number of the defining characteristics of the island and its people, formed in that period, constituted a lasting legacy of which the Chamber was and is a prime agent.

Modern Singapore was founded as the quintessential trading port and immediately became part of the network of goods, people and finance of Southeast Asia and beyond. The logic of this network would prove to be an enduring worldview for the territory. For 50 years Singapore was a Far East Wild West; young men flocked there in pursuit of money. The colonial system of *laissez-faire* and indirect rule was formalized in the mid-19th century, with the leaders of the various ethnic groups more or less responsible for their own community. The Chinese, by far the largest of these migrant groups, were led by successful merchants who were in charge of the *huiguan* and *bang* organizations that formed the backbone of the Chinese community in Singapore. They were the ones who were selected by the British to represent the Chinese on the colonial councils and the Chinese Advisory Board.

Spurred on partly by initiatives from a disintegrating late-imperial China, these Chinese leaders decided they wanted a more independent body to represent the interests of the Chinese of Singapore towards the British and towards China. Therefore, in 1906, the Singapore Chinese Chamber of Commerce was established. That its headquarters was a traditional Chinese mansion, but was located in the heart of the colonial seat of power, signified its representational roles. In the decades before the Pacific War, the Chamber proved the prime force organizing and representing the Chinese. It kept abreast of, and exerted its influence on, commercial and social policy, and became part of the rise of Chinese nationalism through the activities of its members in Mainland Chinese political parties, and the protest against the Japanese incursion into the Motherland.

Immediately after the war, from 1945 to 1950, rebuilding the island and the beginning of a journey towards self-government resulted in a process of localization of the Chinese. With new in-migration slowing to a trickle and return to China blocked by first the civil war and later the deterrent of a communist regime, the sense of Singapore as home was further strengthened. Unexpectedly, the Japanese occupation put question marks behind the legitimacy of colonial power and opened the door to empowerment of local populations. Given the lack of a party political system and the general lack of political organizations, the Chamber was well-positioned to fill the representational void. Despite the dented status of the colonial overlords, the British still called the shots and determined the rules of the budding political system after the war, and the Chamber chose its leadership to suit this reality. The work-with-the-British leaders of the Chamber were selected for their English language ability, and their status in the eyes of, and access to, the late colonial system. However, the issues they chose to fight over – the introduction of income tax and the question of who was to have political rights in Singapore – indicate that they were willing to petition the British and even oppose colonial policy.

In the following years from 1951 to 1958, the political awakening continued as the basic questions of citizenship, enfranchisement and the cultural identity of the local population were decided. The Chamber played a deciding role in putting and keeping these issues on the political agenda while continuing to fill the political void. The political arena changed when a host of political parties and unions entered the fray. Politics slowly evolved from ethnically-based elitist to non-communal populist and the Chamber oscillated between a less or more politically active role in this new system. On one hand, Ambiguous leaders wanted to stay out of party politics and tried to safeguard the status the Chamber enjoyed in the old elite-based system. They feared the left-wing attempts to use the Chamber as a vehicle for ideological, anti-colonial action over the issues of language and education. The Ambitious, on the other hand, were inspired by the vision of independence and wanted to ensure that Chinese economic and social interests would be well-represented, and thought active political involvement was the best strategy. After trading control of the Chamber a few times throughout the 1950s, the Ambitious eventually won the internal contest in 1958. However, by then the Ambitious had already learned that relying on the traditional organizing principles of the Chinese community to muster support for their political vehicle, the Democratic Party, did not work. From their own campaigning, the Ambitious had achieved a significant expansion of the electorate with a large percentage of working class Chinese. Ideological awakening, the organizational activity of left-wing parties and unions, and difficult economic times led to a vibrant political atmosphere. The social democrat parties reaped the reward of these circumstances and were voted into power: the Labour Front in 1955 and the PAP in 1959.

On the bumpy road to the birth of independent Singapore, from 1959 to 1966, the Chamber was paradoxically disciplined as well as courted by the nascent state. Three groups with distinct styles, backgrounds and constituencies competed for power: the technocratic elite of the conservative wing of the PAP, based on knowledge and efficiency; the traditional multi-purpose elite of the SCCC, based on wealth and status; and an oppositional, ideological elite of the PAP left-wing and later the Barisan Sosialis, based on class. Ethnicity, language and education constituted the flash points of this competition. The crucial context of independence through merger into Malaysia played an important part because it infused the question of ethnicity with more, and potentially contentious, dimensions. After the technocratic elite of the PAP, led by Lee Kuan Yew, expelled the party's left-wing, it needed ways of rallying support for securing victory in the merger referendum. Having lost its grass-roots organizations to the Barisan, the PAP courted the Chamber and received its backing. However, when the Chamber came out in support of Chinese education and identity, fighting alongside the Barisan, the government severely disciplined the Chamber leaders responsible and the Chamber paid the price of ambition. It is little wonder that in this period of competition over and reshaping of power, the

Chamber chose to build a new headquarters. Still undoubtedly Chinese but also pointedly modern, the building was ready for Singapore's role as the New York of Southeast Asia. Due to political change and the assertive role of the state, the power of the Ambitious, multi-purpose elite had been diminished and a new relationship with the state would emerge.

Between 1966 and 1984, the ever more powerful PAP state and the Chamber both held defined views on the world and on their desired future for Singapore. The developmental state was pitted against the traders' worldview as the PAP chose export industrialization and reliance on FDI for its plans while the Chamber leadership, partly under pressure from its constituency of small traders and entrepreneurs, clung to its traditional focus and strength: SMEs, regional networks, and trade and services. The Pragmatic leaders who had taken the reigns of the Chamber attempted to comply with state policy but failed to get government support for their causes. First of all, trade and commerce was no longer the cornerstone of economic policy. In the fight against the shipping conferences the government was too entangled in the international system to join the Chamber, and was too focused on diplomatic repercussions to openly support a solution including the PRC. Concerning Confucian and Asian values, the Chamber's emotive definition proved to differ fundamentally from the PAP's pragmatic understanding. Finally, the perceived unfair competition between the public and private sector was not acknowledged as a problem by the state. As a result the Chamber lost power and influence, and found itself marginalized.

In its all-encompassing approach to society, economics, politics and culture, the PAP state overplayed its hand and, from the late 1970s, the success story of Singapore, impressive though it surely was, started to show some cracks. Changes in economic flows, world recession due to the oil crises, and socio-political unease at home necessitated a government reaction. Some of these policy changes were less than successful and up to 1985 no decisive new course was mapped out. This led to uncertainty in Singapore at large but also fuelled a crisis of identity in the SCCCI.

During the years 1985 to 1997 in the wake of state reorientation and internal Chamber reforms, a change of fortune developed for the SCCCI, as it was transformed from an ailing organization in crisis to a vibrant part of the Singapore representational landscape. The 1985 economic recession proved to be the catalyst for a number of fundamental changes in PAP policy. Realizing that dependency on MNCs and FDI had become too high, it turned back to some of the traditional strengths of Singapore: its local entrepreneurial sector, made up in large part of SMEs; its central location in Southeast Asia and the trade and services hub function for the region;

and its possibilities as a bridge to China. All these policy changes, plus the government's invitation to local business to be part of the feedback and policy-making circle, presented opportunities for the SCCCI to shine in traditional areas of strength and expertise. It heightened its profile as the champion, organizer and coordinator of the SME cause, it enthusiastically pursued trade promotion with renewed vigour, and it capitalized on its strong China network.

In tandem with this, a new generation of Reformers took the helm. They realized that internal reform, rejuvenation and professionalization were needed if the Chamber was to benefit to the utmost from the government's reorientation and gain for itself a place of renewed centrality and influence. The *bang* election system was scrapped in 1993 and membership drives brought in young, new members, women entrepreneurs and GLCs. While enhancing its economic role, the Chamber had to relinquish two of its other foci as a multi-purpose elite: its cultural and social programmes and leadership. The government took away Chamber primacy on these issues by establishing the SFCCA and the CDAC respectively, signalling its own dominance. By succumbing to state pressure and endorsing the new institutional arrangements, the Chamber gained state praise and cemented its position as prime business lobby organization.

Looking back on the Chamber's first 100 years, what constituted its defining characteristics? First, it was, since its founding and by its own choice, a Singaporean organization. Even before the Pacific War, local issues were an important focus and the process of localization brought Singapore, its politics and social development even more to the centre of the Chamber. From then on, despite interests in China and the region, and through merger with, and separation from, Malaysia, Singapore provided the geographical, operational and emotional bases from which the Chamber worked. Second, it was an ethnic organization, representing the interests of the Chinese. It stood at the apex of the pyramid of Chinese organizations and for 87 years its leadership election system was based on sub-ethnic Chinese identities. In colonial times, when racial categories were seen as natural ordering principles, the Chamber's Chinese identity was the inherent logic of its very existence. Later, as ethnicity became intertwined with class and politics, its Chinesesness brought the Chamber into competition with other political actors, most prominently the state. However, with the opening up of China and the worldwide fascination with the awakening giant, the Chamber fruitfully cashed in on its networks with China, as well as with ethnic Chinese the world over, to profile itself as an ethnic intermediary for all who want to profit from the PRC boom. Third, the Chamber has always been a business organization centred on trade and services. It was a home for the Chinese shopkeepers, traders and craftsmen as well as a vehicle for status and power to their leaders, the rubber barons, the banking tycoons and the trading *towkays*. Since the latter were also the community's social, cultural and political leaders, and because their status and power was based on wealth and business success, the Chamber was always more than only a commercial organization.

It was the most significant ethnic representative during the colonial days and played a crucial role during decolonization and the formative years of the political arena of independent Singapore. It gained and lost influence and power over time because of changes in the nature of politics and power. Through the process of nation building the SCCCI had to partly succumb to the rising power of the PAP state. However, the underlying logic of Singapore's economic, regional existence remained strong, causing the state, since 1985, to revert back to local business, trade and services and a regional outlook which included India and China. The staying power of the logic of this traders' worldview and the embeddedness of Singapore in a regional network of economic and ethnic roles has played into the Chamber's strengths. It embodies Singapore through its SME membership, its regional networks of trade, information and services, as well as its links with China and the ethnic Chinese the world over; exactly what modern Singapore has been about ever since 1819.

When analyzed in this historical context, the 25 years of the Singapore Miracle based on PAP government planning, FDI and MNCs was shown to be a temporary diversion from a more enduring and deeper pattern. Within this dynamic, the Chamber is one of the very few remaining organizations from pre-PAP days that survived and consistently stood for an alternative direction and perspective for Singapore. This stand meant that it competed with the PAP developmental state, which actively eliminated alternative power bases in the Singapore political and social arena. The Chamber was disciplined and marginalized but still survived.

On one hand, the subjugation of the Chamber by the PAP party/state symbolizes the road taken by many young nations in pursuit of economic development and modernity through the initiative and coordination of a strong state; a story of formalization and professionalization. On the other hand, the Chamber's continued existence and regained importance signals that Singapore's identity as a centre for trade and services, tied to the region through various networks and flows of money, goods and services, is an enduring characteristic. The SCCCI embodies the traders' worldview that remains the heartbeat of Singapore.

President Wee Kim Wee arriving at the SCCCI 80th anniversary celebrations, 1986.

Ministry of Information, Communications and the Arts.
Courtesy of the National Archives of Singapore

Celebrating Chinese New Year at the River Hong Bao, 1993.

Ministry of Information, Communications and the Arts. Courtesy of the National Archives of Singapore

Official recognition: President S.R. Nathan presenting the instruments of Nominated Member of Parliament to Tay Beng Chuan.

Ministry of Information, Communications and the Arts. Courtesy of the National Archives of Singapore

President S.R. Nathan and Mrs Nathan attending the Mid Autumn Festival at the SCCC, 1999.

Ministry of Information, Communications and the Arts. Courtesy of the National Archives of Singapore

The family of Lee Kong Chian making its mark on the Central Business District with the construction of the OCBC building in 1979.

Courtesy of the National Archives of Singapore

Lien Ying Chow adding OUB, the "tallest building in Southeast Asia", to the Central Business District skyline in 1986.

Courtesy of the National Archives of Singapore

Wee Cho Yaw's UOB joins
OCBC and OUB in 1992.

*Ministry of Communication and
the Arts. Courtesy of the National
Archives of Singapore*

Singapore skyline 2006;
Republic Plaza (left) of the
Kwek family added in 1996
and the SCCCI office building
nestled in between the four
Chinese family financial
towers.

Copyright Sikko Visscher

1998–2005
Epilogue

THE LAST RESEARCH VISIT TO Singapore necessary to finish my dissertation was made in 1999 and that scholarly exercise covered the history of the Chamber up to 1997. With the 100th anniversary of the Chamber in 2006, it would have been silly not to try to bring the reader up to speed on the full first century of the SCCC(I). However, my visits since 1999 have been too infrequent and too short to enable me to include a real chapter on 1998–2005 with anywhere near the same quality of analysis or depth of sources. A short epilogue will have to suffice to sketch the developments.

In these seven years nothing has happened that would contradict the main themes of the narrative and analysis of the chapters or the salient points presented in the conclusion. In many ways, continuity was the order of the day in the internal operations and external focus of the Chamber. We must conclude that the Reformers provided this continuity. Tay Beng Chuan became president replacing Kwek Leng Joo, serving from 1997 to 2001, only to be succeeded by a returning Kwek from 2001 to 2005.

In tandem, the two ensured that the Chamber stayed the course laid out by the Reformers from as far back as 1985. Upholding the image of the SCCCI as a modern business organization working for the common good of the whole of Singapore, Kwek and Tay attracted increasing numbers of

GLCs through the improved relations with the government. An indication of the newfound accolades the Chamber was receiving can be found on the website of the President of the Republic, S.R. Nathan. In a 2001 speech at the SCCCI Chinese New Year celebration, he commended the Chamber for its positive contribution to fostering racial harmony and social stability, as well as promoting inter-ethnic understanding and cross-cultural appreciation. He was heartened that the SCCCI fully appreciated the realities of Singapore's multi-racial make-up.[1]

The government equally acknowledged the position of the Chamber as a Chinese institution, and as a home for many Chinese-educated Chinese. In a speech at the SCCCI's 95th anniversary, BG George Yeo, then Minister of Trade and Industry, reminded his audience that after the Pacific War the split between the Chinese-educated and the English-educated reflected two different views on Singapore's destiny and connected this with views on, and ties with, Mainland China. Admitting that both Tan Kah Kee and Tan Lark Sye had suffered the consequences of their views, he said that both were now honoured and their place in Singapore history respected. Although his analysis is not entirely historically sound and downplays the role of the PAP government, it is an indirect admission that the "alternative view" on Singapore's destiny, which was so closely connected with the Ambitious Chamber leaders and their worldview, had legitimacy despite the PAP marginalizing and disciplining of the Chamber through the years.[2]

This re-evaluation of history allowed the SCCCI to act upon its image and status as a Chinese organization. The main expression of this action was the restoration of Wang Qing Yuan, formerly the headquarters of the Tongmenhui and the villa where Sun Yat Sen stayed, into the Sun Yat Sen Nanyang Memorial Hall. The building houses a museum concentrating on the history of the Chinese revolution in the Nanyang, the ethnic Chinese initiatives towards the Motherland in the interwar years and the plight of the local Chinese during the Japanese occupation.

In the economic arena, the Reformer presidents continued to profile the Chamber as the largest and most versatile broker between different types of business. To that end professionals were encouraged to become members under the Associate Membership category. In a further expansion of the variety of the membership, foreign companies were also allowed to join. Imagine my surprise when, not yet aware of this change, upon checking the SCCCI website and online directory I found that the very Dutch ABN/AMRO Bank had become a member of the Chinese Chamber in Singapore. This is a clear sign that inclusiveness within Singapore and internationalization are key items on the Chamber agenda.

Another area of continuity is the profiling as an ideal broker for information on, and contact with, China. During these years, the Chamber further developed its role as founder of the WCEC by taking on a six-year term as WCEC Secretariat from 1999 onward. Meanwhile the WCBN website is maintained and seminars on the business context of the PRC are conducted regularly. Chinese delegations still comprise the majority of foreign visiting groups, and the PRC also remains a prime destination for delegations that the SCCCI organizes itself or is a constituent part of.

Still, the Southeast Asia region remains an important focus especially in its relationship with its two largest neighbours, China and India. The Chamber is once again providing the ASEAN-CCI President through one of its own vice presidents, thereby embodying its regional networks. In addition to continuing the age-old tradition of Singapore as regional trading hub and connecting point to India and China, the SCCCI is also acting upon the regionalization policy of the government.

The buildings of the Chamber have played a symbolic role throughout its history and it is no surprise that the Reformers have taken initiatives in this field as well. With extensive upgrading to its Hill Street home, the SCCCI looks set to remain at that location for some time to come. Another Chamber building has been constructed at a significant spot, however. On the corner of Telok Ayer Street and Church Street a modern office was built together with a number of partners. The purpose of the development is to generate income through rental, thereby putting the Chamber on a financially sound footing.

In 2005, the last year of its first century, the Chamber membership once again had the opportunity to select a new leadership. Apart from selecting 12 fresh faces to the MC, a new president, Chua Thian Poh, took the helm.

So does the election of Chua mark a change or will the path opened by the Reformers be followed? His rise to prominence can be seen as a return to the self-made entrepreneur, an individual who is street-smart rather than book-smart. His personal experience also harks back to the regionally oriented, self-made man rather than the sons of arrived business families.

These factors might indicate the staying power of the migrant experience and the regional worldview through Chua, but his policies do not only point in that direction. While he emphasizes that the Chamber not only looks after the interests of the "big boys" and should equally focus on the traditional constituency of the SMEs, his flagship project is the new Chamber Enterprise Development and Services Centre, which will especially focus on newer, modern enterprises. Also, while he draws on the

Chua Thian Poh: Chip off the old block.
Courtesy of SCCCI

Chua Thian Poh is the seventh of 14 children in what he describes himself as "a traditional Chinese family". His father ran a lighterage firm and also built *tongkangs*, enterprises the son joined at 16 with only his O-level qualifications.

Soon Chua struck out on his own, making his first millions by 21 through manufacturing equipment for the logging industry. However, just a year later, timber prices fell and his business went deep into debt. Rebounding, he entered the import-export business in Indonesia but suffered millions in losses again after the 1978 devaluation of the rupiah. Falling and rebuilding a few more times, he has become a significant player in real estate development through his Ho Bee Group with projects and assets in Singapore, London and Shanghai.

Chua professed not to be interested in politics but is Chairman of the Bishan East Citizens' Consultative Committee, is a council member on the National Arts Council and the Singapore Sports Council, and is Deputy President of the HHK. He serves on these and other bodies out of a sense of duty and tradition springing from his family background, using the oft-heard phrase "when you make it you have to give back to society".[3]

traditional values of shared responsibility, he chose to take his newly elected MC on a two-day retreat to Bintan to brainstorm.[4]

Therefore, characteristic elements from the Chamber's 100-year history seem to be mixed with and applied to the needs of modern-day Singapore. Time will tell whether this continuity of tradition and its application to modernity will enable the Chamber to retain a position of distinction and importance.

SCCCI office building in the CBD, 2006.
Copyright Sikko Visscher

Making its mark on the edge of Chinatown, its constituency's traditional base, and the Central Business District, the seat of the modern businesses of the Chamber leaders and international companies, the latest Chamber building gives physical form to the symbolic bridge it maintains between these two arenas.

Appendix: Presidents and Vice Presidents of the SCCCI, 1906–2007

Dialect group
H = Hokkien
T = Teochew
C = Cantonese
Hak = Hakka

1906	Goh Siew Tin, **Director** (Chao'an, H)
	Tan Hoon Chew, **Deputy Director** (?)
1907	Chua Chu Yong, **Director** (T)
	Goh Koon Siew, **Deputy Director** (?)
1908	Goh Siew Tin, **Director** (H)
	Chua Chu Yong, **Deputy Director** (T)
1909	Lim Wee Fang (Lam Wai Fong), **Director** (C)
	Teo Sian Keng, **Deputy Director** (H)
1910	Teo Sian Keng, **Director** (H)
	Liau Chia Heng, **Deputy Director** (T)
1911	Liau Chia Heng, **Director** (T)
	Teo Sian Keng, **Deputy Director** (H)
1912	Liau Chia Heng, **Director** (T)
	Tan Sian Cheng, **Deputy Director** (H)
1913	Lim Peng Siang, **Director** (H)
	Liau Chia Heng, **Deputy Director** (T)
1914	Liau Chia Heng, **Director** (T)
	Lim Peng Siang, **Deputy Director** (H)
1915–1917	Lim Peng Siang, **President** (H)
	Tan Teck Joon (Tan Jeck Joon), **Vice President** (T)
1917–1919	Tan Teck Joon (Tan Jeck Joon), **President** (T)
	Tan Sian Cheng, **Vice President** (H)

1919–1921	See Teong Wah, **President** (H)
	Tan Jiak Yue (Tan Jiak Ngoh), **Vice President** (T)
1921–1923	Lim Nee Soon, **President** (T)
	Lim Twee Chien (Lim Chwee Chiang), **Vice President** (H)
1923–1925	Lim Twee Chien (Lim Cwee Chiang), **President** (H)
	(died Feb. 1923)
	See Teong Wah, **President** (H)
	Tan Keng Tong, **Vice President** (T)
1925–1927	Lim Nee Soon, **President** (T)
	Seet Boo Ee, **Vice President** (H)
1927–1929	Seet Boo Ee, **President** (H)
	Lee Wee Nam, **Vice President** (T)
1929–1931	Lee Wee Nam, **President** (T)
	Seet Boo Ee, **Vice President** (H)
1931–1933	Lee Choon Seng, **President** (H)
	Yeo Chan Boon, **Vice President** (T)
1933–1935	Lum Mun Tin, **President** (C)
	Lim Kheng Lian, **Vice President** (H)
1935–1937	Lim Kheng Lian, **President** (H)
	Lum Mun Tin, **Vice President** (C)
1937–1939	Tan Chin Hean, **President** (T)
	Lim Kheng Lian, **Vice President** (H)
1939–1941	Lee Kong Chian, **President** (H)
	Lum Mun Tin, **Vice President** (C)
1941–1946	Lien Ying Chow, (term aborted by war, Dec. 8, 1941,
	resumed Sept. 1, 1945), **President** (T)
	Tan Lark Sye, **Vice President** (H)
1946–1947	Lee Kong Chian, **President** (H)
	Yong Yit Lin, **Vice President** (Hak)
1948–1950	Yong Yit Lin, **President** (Hak)
	Tan Chin Tuan, **Vice President** (H)
1950–1952	Tan Lark Sye, **President** (H)
	Tan Siak Kew, **Vice President** (T)
1952–1954	Tan Siak Kew, **President** (T)
	Ko Teck Kin, **Vice President** (H)
1954–1956	Ko Teck Kin, **President** (H)
	Yap Pheng Geck, **Vice President** (T, straits)
1956–1958	Tan Siak Kew, **President** (T)
	Ng Quee Lam, **Vice President** (H)
1958–1960	Ko Teck Kin, **President** (H)
	Yap Pheng Geck, **Vice President** (T, straits)
1960–1962	Ko Teck Kin, **President** (H)
	Yap Pheng Geck, **Vice President** (T, straits)
	Soon Peng Yam, **Vice President** (H)
1962–1965	Ko Teck Kin, (term extended by one year), **President** (H)

	Yap Pheng Geck, **Vice President** (T, straits)
	Teo Hang Sam, **Vice President** (T)
1965–1967	Soon Peng Yam, **President** (H)
	Lim Kee Meng, **Vice President** (T)
	Tong Ching Hsien, **Vice President** (Sanjiang)
1967–1969	Soon Peng Yam, **President** (H)
	Lim Kee Meng, **Vice President** (T)
	Wee Cho Yaw, **Vice President** (H)
1969–1971	Wee Cho Yaw, **President** (H)
	Teo Soo Chuan, **Vice President** (T)
	Tan Keong Choon, **Vice President** (H)
1971–1973	Wee Cho Yaw, **President** (H)
	Teo Soo Chuan, **Vice President** (T)
	Tan Keong Choon, **Vice President** (H)
1973–1975	Tan Keong Choon, **President** (H)
	Chew Teng How, **Vice President** (T)
	Tan Eng Joo, **Vice President** (H)
1975–1977	Tan Keong Choon, **President** (H)
	Chew Teng How, **Vice President** (T)
	Tan Eng Joo, **Vice President** (H)
1977–1979	Wee Cho Yaw, **President** (H)
	Lim Kee Meng, **Vice President** (T)
	Teo Soo Chuan, **Vice President** (T)
1979–1981	Lim Kee Meng, **President** (T)
	Tan Eng Joo, **Vice President** (H)
	Tan Keong Choon, **Vice President** (H)
1981–1983	Lim Kee Meng, **President** (T)
	Tan Eng Joo, **Vice President** (H)
	Tan Keong Choon, **Vice President** (H)
1983–1985	Tan Keong Choon, **President** (H)
	Chng Tok Ngam, **Vice President** (T) (Died Jan 84)
	Lim Tow Yong, **Vice President** (T) (from 28 Feb 84)
	Linn In Hua, **Vice President** (H)
1985–1987	Tan Keong Choon, **President** (H)
	Lim Tow Yong, **Vice President** (T)
	Linn In Hua, **Vice President** (H)
1987–1989	Linn In Hua, **President** (H)
	Tan Eng Joo, **Vice President** (H)
	Leong Heng Keng, **Vice President** (C)
1989–1991	Linn In Hua, **President** (March 1989 until 31 Oct 1989), **President** (H)
	Tan Eng Joo, **President** (from 31 Oct 1989), P. (H)
	Leong Heng Keng, **Vice President** (C)
	Lin Chai Chin, **Vice President** (T)
1991–1993	Tan Eng Joo, **President** (H)

	Lin Chai Chin, **Vice President** (T)
	Cheong Wing, **Vice President** (C)
1993–1995	Kwek Leng Joo, **President** (H)
	Freddy Lam Fong Loi, **Vice President** (Hak)
	Teo Chiang Long, **Vice President** (T)
1995–1997	Kwek Leng Joo, **President**
	Freddy Lam Fong Loi, **Vice President**
	Teo Chiang Long, **Vice President**
	Tay Beng Chuan, **Vice President**
1997–1999	Tay Beng Chuan, **President**
	Freddy Lam Fong Loi, **Vice President**
	Teo Chiang Long, **Vice President**
	Chia Ban Seng, **Vice President**
1999–2001	Tay Beng Chuan, **President**
	Freddy Lam, **Vice President**
	Peter Seah, **Vice President**
	Chia Ban Seng, **Vice President**
2001–2003	Kwek Leng Joo, **President**
	Freddy Lam, **Vice President**
	Peter Seah, **Vice President**
	Chia Ban Seng, **Vice President**
2003–2005	Kwek Leng Joo, **President**
	Freddy Lam Fong Loi, **Vice President**
	Peter Seah Lim Huat, **Vice President**
	Chua Thian Poh, **Vice President**
2005–2007	Chua Thian Poh, **President**
	Freddy Lam Fong Loi, **Vice President**
	Peter Seah Lim Huat, **Vice President**
	Chia Ban Seng, **Vice President**
	Thomas Chua Kee Seng, **Vice President**
	Bobby Chin Yoke Choong, **Vice President**

Notes

Introduction

[1] The odd-looking parentheses in this abbreviation are mine. Established in 1906 as the Singapore General Association for Chinese Commercial Affairs, the Chamber took on the name Singapore Chinese Chamber of Commerce (SCCC) in 1921. In 1978 the organization added the word "Industry" to its English name and in abbreviated form became known as the SCCCI. I will use the term "Chamber" throughout the text and will use "SCCC" or "SCCCI" in discussing events before or after 1978 respectively. In the introduction and conclusion I will use SCCC(I) to refer to the Chamber in its entire history of 100 years.

[2] Accounts on the SCCC(I) are included in a number of broader studies on the Chinese elite of Singapore in the late 19th and early 20th century. See for instance: Lee Poh Ping, and Godley 1981, and the works of Yen, and Yong. Lim Choo Hoon, Huang, and Yeo 1973b are notable articles on the political orientation, the business concerns, and the political campaigns of the Chamber in the immediate postwar years. A number of other studies, some of which extend beyond the 1950s, notably Suyama, Lim How Seng, Cheng 1985, Ng, Hsieh, Thomas Tan Tsu-wee 1983, and Liu and Wong focus on the structure of Chinese society and address the Chamber only as a constituent part of that system. A few former Chamber leaders briefly address the organization and its role in their memoirs. These works include Wee, Ward, Chu and Salaff, Yap, and Lien and Kraar. The Chamber itself provides the only integrated accounts of the Chamber's history. See Singapore Chinese Chamber of Commerce 1964, Singapore Chinese Chamber of Commerce and Industry 1981 and 1996, but these are limited in scope and lack critical analysis. The only sizeable academic monograph on a Southeast Asian organization similar to the Chamber is a study of the Federation of Filipino-Chinese Chambers of Commerce and Industry by Chong Carino.

[3] The organization was founded by 500 individuals and company members, and by 1909 its ranks had swelled to 2,000. For the postwar period membership has stood around 5,000. It should be realized that a growing number of associations, each with its own larger or smaller membership, had joined the Chamber over time, thus extending its representational base.

[4] McVey 1995, pp. 2–5.

Chapter 1

1   The founding of modern Singapore by Raffles, and the early history of the British settlement is discussed in Chew and Lee, and Turnbull.
2   See Wolters.
3   Dick, p. 5.
4   Reid 1988 gives an excellent account of regional developments. For specific cities and regions, see Sutherland for Makassar; Low for Penang; Willmott for Semarang; Sandhu and Sandhu and Wheatley for Malacca; Cushman, and Wu for Penang, Kedah and South Thailand; Trocki 1979 for Johor, and Lee Kam Hing for Aceh. Hyde provides an analysis of the colonial influence on the trading system while Purcell, Wang Gungwu 1990, 1998 and Reid 1996 tackle early Chinese contacts with the region.
5   Reid 1993, pp. 13–32.
6   Dick 1993, p. 5.
7   See Reid 1993, Campo 1993 and Wong Lin Ken, p. 123.
8   Credit links, often between merchant minorities and local producers, predate the European presence in Southeast Asia. See also Wong Lin Ken, pp. 160–3.
9   Turnbull, p. 68.
10 See Wong Lin Ken.
11 For the first 50 years of colonial Singapore the sex ratio for Chinese was around 10 males to 1 female with peaks to 14 to 1 in the late 1830s and early 1860s (Lee Poh Ping 1978, p. 39). Due to continued inward migration predominantly by males, the sex ratio remained distorted well into the late 1930s.
12 By 1836 the Chinese were the largest ethnic group and by 1849 they made up more than half of the population (Singapore Blue Book material collated and quoted in Chiew 1995, p. 43). Early Singapore was also home to Malays, Bugis, Orang Laut, Parsees, Arabs, Baghdad Jews, Chettiars, Armenians and many others from Asia and Europe interested in making money.
13 *Singapore Free Press,* henceforth SFP, 1857, quoted in Turnbull, p. 36
14 See Trocki 1979, pp. 20, and Song, pp. 14–5.
15 Trocki 1979, pp. 208–9.
16 See Ownby and Somers Heidhues, especially the introduction by Ownby and Somers Heidhues and the epilogue by DeBernardi.
17 For information on secret societies, see Freedman, pp. 65–74, Vaughan, pp. 95–125, Jackson, Comber, Blythe, and Mak.
18 Trocki 1979, pp. 90–1 and pp. 103–7.
19 See also Trocki 1990, and Butcher and Dick.
20 Rajeswary Brown, pp. 78–82.
21 Trocki 1990, p. 5, pp. 70–1 and p. 222.
22 Ibid., p. 5.
23 See Lee Poh Ping 1978.
24 Lee Poh Ping 1978, Chapter V.
25 The first Chinese man to be appointed on the Legislative Council was Hoo Ah Kay in 1869. Hoo Ah Kay, better known as Whampoa, was born in China and

came to Singapore with his father around 1830 from Canton. He spoke excellent English and socialized extensively with the British colonial elite. The family entered the ship chandelling business and owned plantations. Later, he would be appointed extraordinary Executive Council member. In 1883, Seah Liang Seah was appointed to the Legislative Council followed by Tan Jiak Kim 1889 (Song, p. 55, p. 194 and p. 213). Turnbull provides more detail on the precise composition and functions of the two councils (Turnbull, pp. 78–82).

26   See Edwin Lee.

27   See Lee Poh Ping 1978, pp. 90–1, Edwin Lee, Chapter 6, and Turnbull, pp. 87–8.

28   Huff, pp. 86–9, and Lee Poh Ping 1978.

29   See Andaya and Andaya, pp. 210–1 and Somers.

30   Hyde, pp. 118–9.

31   See Drabble, pp. 19–21 and Song, p. 294.

32   Hyde, pp. 126–7.

33   See Campo 1992, Twang, and Touwen.

34   Cheng Lim Keak 1985, pp. 4 and 7 and Lee Poh Ping, p. 86.

35   For more information on migration, see Reid 1996 and Wickberg.

36   See Hsieh, Jiann 1977, Wang Gungwu 1981, and Spence.

37   The Hokkien form the largest dialect group growing from just under 30 per cent in 1881 to just over 40 per cent in 1911, a percentage they have maintained ever since. The Teochew percentage shrank from 26 per cent in 1881 to around 17 per cent for the first two decades of the 20th century and stabilized at around 22 per cent after World War II. The Cantonese grew from 17 per cent in 1881 to a high of 25 per cent in 1921 before slowly dropping back to around 17 per cent after the war. The Hainanese and the Hakka were significantly smaller and each constituted about 5 per cent to 7 per cent of the Chinese population. The Fuzhou, the Sanjiang, the Henghua and the Hokchia, hovered around 1 per cent to 2 per cent each to complement the picture (statistics compiled by Cheng 1985 from various sources and tabulated on p. 14).

38   Cheng 1985, p. xvi.

39   According to the Executive Secretary of the Hokien Huay Kuan, the fact that the official name of the organization is erroneously spelled with only one "k" is due to an administrative mistake at the Registrar of Societies office during one of the occasions when it had to register or re-register. When this event occurred was not known to him (interview with Kua Soon Khe, 26 October 1996).

40   For discussion on the Singapore *huiguan*, see Hsieh, Cheng Lim Keak 1985, Mak, and Ng.

41   Hamilton, pp. 74–81.

42   Ng, pp. 484–5. For postwar developments of the *huiguan*, see Brøgger.

43   See Wang Gungwu 1981 and Reid 1996.

44   See also Clammer, and Chia.

45   See Visscher 2002b.

46   Cheng 1985, p. 14.

47   Ng, p. 488.

[48]   Huff, pp. 233–5.

[49]   Ibid., pp. 80–8 and p. 208.

[50]   The Cantonese were the first when they set up the Kwong Yik Bank in 1903; the Teochew dominated when Sze Hai Tong Bank followed in 1906; Hokkien initiatives resulted in three banks, the Chinese Commercial Bank (1912), the Ho Hong Bank (1917) and the Overseas-Chinese Bank (1919). The three latter banks would later amalgamate and form the Overseas Chinese Banking Corporation in 1932. In a complementary development, the first Chinese insurance company, Great Eastern, was established in 1908 (Yong 1994, p. 50).

[51]   For tables, see Yong 1994, pp. 64–5 and Lee Poh Ping 1978, pp. 101–6.

[52]   Turnbull, p. 128.

[53]   The term "Chop", originally meaning "stamp" or "seal" is equivalent to "business" or "company".

[54]   Between 1906 and 1921, the organization bore the name Singapore General Association for Chinese Commercial Affairs. In 1921, the name was changed to Singapore Chinese Chamber of Commerce. For the sake of clarity I will refer to the early organization also as "the Chamber" or "SCCC".

[55]   The Chinese hailing from Fujian province initially formed one block and were all Hokkien. The Guangdong Chinese were subdivided into the different dialect groups: Cantonese, Hakka, Teochew and Hainanese.

[56]   Yong 1994, p. 27.

[57]   See the appendix for a complete list of Chamber presidents.

[58]   Yong 1994, p. 27.

[59]   Ibid., pp. 23–46.

[60]   Ibid., pp. 387–90.

[61]   Song, pp. 387–90.

[62]   Shanghai had the *primeur* in 1902 (see Rhoads). Overseas Chinese merchants were following the pattern in Manila (1904), Batavia, Penang (1907) and Bangkok (1908). See Godley 1975 and Skinner, p. 170.

[63]   Yen 1995b, p. 137.

[64]   Godley 1981, pp. 369–70.

[65]   Yong 1994, p. 26.

[66]   Goh Siew Tin, who became the first President of the Chamber, was an old friend of Chang and had been close to the Qing bureaucracy, holding a title (Yen 1995a, p. 142).

[67]   Huff, p. 106.

[68]   The Produce Exchange was located in the commercial heart of the city at Raffles Place, right between the Western banks and trading houses and very close to the Chinese godowns and shops along Boat Quay.

[69]   Huff, p. 45.

[70]   Trocki 1990, p. 238.

[71]   Fong, p. 51.

[72]   Wang 1981, pp. 130–3.

[73]   Chiew 1995, pp. 46–8.

[74]   These developments forced upon the Qing court the realization that it needed a

foreign affairs ministry; the *Zongli Yamen* was established in 1861.

75 See note 30 above. Whampoa was the consul for Russia and Japan in the Straits Settlements as well (Song, pp. 52–4).

76 Yen 1995b, pp. 201–5.

77 Ibid., pp. 205–7.

78 At the elite level cooperation between the Straits-born and the China-born was not uncommon at all. Individuals active in the SCBA and the SCCC in the early part of the 20th century were Lim Boon Keng and his son, as well as S.Q. Wong, and Tay Lian Teck. Sir Lim Han Hoe was part of a number of special committees of the SCCC in 1939 and 1941 by invitation. Lim Peng Siang and See Teong Wah, both at past presidents of the SCCC, met with their SCBA colleagues often in their capacity as CAB member and Municipal Commissioner respectively (Yong 1994, pp. 70–4).

79 See Yen 1995b.

80 SCCCI 1986, pp. 92–3.

81 For more information and analysis on Chinese political nationalism in Singapore and Malaya, see Akashi, Leong, Chui and Hara, Yong 1994, and Chui 1996.

82 Colonial Office Files 273: Original correspondence between the Colonial Office and the Foreign Office relating to the Straits Settlements and the Federated Malay States, 1838–1939. *CO 273/571/13, Monthly Report by Chinese Secretariat for Mar. 1931* and *CO 273/586/1, for Aug. 1933*

83 Spence, pp. 300–60.

84 See Leong, Chui and Hara and Yong 1994.

85 SCCCI, *80th Anniversary Publication,* pp. 86–125; Ward, Chu and Salaff 1994, Yong 1994, p. 131 and *CO 273/586/1 and 606/1, Monthly report by Chinese Secretariat, Oct. 1933 and July 1935.*

86 See Akashi.

87 This biographical sketch was based on: Tan Kah Kee's memoirs (Ward, Chu, and Salaff 1994, Yong 1994 (Chapters 6 and 7), and interviews with his nephew Tan Keong Choon and his son Tan Kok Kheng for the "Pioneers of Singapore" collection of the Oral History Department of the National Archives of Singapore (1984).

88 See Yen 1995b, pp. 308–9. For a discussion of the aftermath of the Jinan incident in Singapore, see Akashi, Chui 1977, and Yen 1995b.

89 Lim Choo Hoon, p. 19.

90 Yong 1994, p. 144, Turnbull, pp. 146–8, Pang, Leong, and Chui and Hara.

91 Yong 1994, p. 99.

92 By the end of the 1930s, the leading *bang* organizations were: the Hokien Huay Kuan for the Hokkien; the Teochew Poit Ip Huay Kuan for the Teochew; the Singapore Kwang Tung Hui Kuan for the Cantonese; the Nanyang Khek Community Guild for the Hakka; the Singapore Kiung Chow Hwee Kuan for the Hainanese, and the Sam Kiang Huay Kuan for the Sanjiang.

93 Rudolph, pp. 161–3.

94 Turnbull, pp. 172–185, Donnison, pp. 378–9, Ward, Chu and Salaff, pp. 153–7, Lien and Kraar, pp. 72–3. For interviews with survivors of the battle of Singapore,

see Singapore Chinese Chamber of Commerce and Industry 1995, pp. 216–34 and pp. 249–307.

95 Cheah, pp. 23–4, Rudolph, pp. 158–65 and Turnbull, p. 190.

96 I experienced how strong feelings were 53 years after the events when I lived at Dempsey Road in one of the buildings that were once part of the English Army Camp on the hill next to Holland Road. The Japanese had used this facility during the *Sook Ching* as a screening facility and reportedly executions had taken place there. At night young Chinese cab drivers refused to deliver me to my door further up the hill. Chapter 4 will explore the 1960s "war debt" issue.

97 See Singapore Chinese Chamber of Commerce and Industry 1995, pp. 235–48 for personal accounts.

98 Hicks, and Shimizu and Hirakawa, pp. 140–1.

99 Lim Boon Keng was made OCA Chairman, and S.Q. Wong, Tan Ean Khiam, Lee Wee Nam, Yeo Chan Boon, Lee Choon Seng, Tan Lark Sye and the Shaw brothers were forced to serve as board members. In total about 250 Chinese leaders were gathered and held hostage at the Goh Loo Club.

100 For a detailed contemporary account, see the article by the OCA Secretary Y.S. Tan, *Straits Times* (henceforth *ST*), 12 and 13 June 1947. The *ST* was established as a weekly in 1845 and became a daily newspaper in 1858. Soon after its inception and throughout colonial times it was the leading English language newspaper. During the Pacific War the paper appeared under the banner of *Syonan Times* and later *Syonan Shimbun*. After the war it picked up its role as the main colonial paper reporting on the British-endorsed decolonization developments but giving little attention to the viewpoints and activities of more anti-colonial forces. In independent Singapore, the press would come to be closely monitored, and the *Straits Times* would remain the largest English-language daily and the paper closest to the government. For additional information, see Rudolph, 166–73, Cheah, pp. 24–5 and 46–7, Turnbull, pp. 195–7.

101 The five were Lee Wah, Ban Hin Lee, Sze Hai Tong, United Chinese, and OCBC.

102 This Japanese currency was nicknamed "banana money" because of the illustration on the bills.

103 See Shimizu and Hirakawa, pp. 114–7, Wilson, pp. 56–60, Cheah, pp. 36–7, Rudolph, pp. 166–72, and Turnbull, pp. 199–201.

104 Twang, pp. 91–5.

105 See also Huff, pp. 277–8.

Chapter 2

1 Yap, p. 105.

2 See Donnison, pp. 160–2. For an overview of the Malayan economy for 1946, see Turnbull, p. 220, Donnison, pp. 225–6 and p. 262, and *Far Eastern Economic Review*, henceforth *FEER*, 14 May 1947.

3 *ST*, 7 Sept. 1945.

4   Wong Siu-lun 1995, pp. 6–9.
5   For more information on the labour movement and the MCP activity in Singapore, see Clutterbuck Chapters 2 and 3, and Bloodworth 1986, Parts 1 and 2.
6   *Minutes of the Public Sessions of the Singapore Advisory Council,* 6 Feb. 1947 and various dates.
7   The Hokien Huay Kuan for the Hokkien, the Teochew Poit Ip Huay Kuan for the Teochew, the Singapore Kwang Tung Hui Kuan for the Cantonese, the Nanyang Khek Community Guild for the Hakka, the Singapore Kiung Chow Hwee Kuan for the Hainanese, and the Sam Kiang Huay Kuan for the Sanjiang. For the percentages of the various dialect groups, see note 37 in Chapter 1.
8   *Minutes of the Singapore Advisory Council,* 5 Dec. 1946.
9   *ST,* 13 Dec. 1946.
10   *ST,* 18 Aug. 1947.
11   *ST,* 20 Aug. 1947.
12   Huff, p. 221.
13   *ST,* 30 Sept. 1947.
14   This biographical sketch of Lee Kong Chian is also based on: interview with his son Lee Seng Gee for the Pioneers of Singapore project, 20 Aug. 1980, Melanie Chew, pp. 24–8, Kua, p. 43, Tan Ee-Leong, Wilson, pp. 40–2, *New Nation,* 16–17 Aug. 1971, *Singapore,* May 1990, pp. 23–4.
15   Prominent Straits Chinese C.C. Tan formed the party with fellow lawyers John Laycock and N.A. Mallal, attracting many from the upper social strata of the Straits Chinese.
16   *ST,* 3 Sept. 1947.
17   *ST,* 9 Aug. 1947.
18   ST, 24 Nov. 1947.
19   Yap, p. 104.
20   This biographical sketch of Yap Pheng Geck is also based on: Yap, Kua, p. 14 and Colonial Office file 1030: *Original correspondence of the Far Eastern Department relating to the Federation of Malaya and Singapore, 1954–1960, CO 1030/259.*
21   *Minutes of the Singapore Advisory Council,* 27 Nov. 1947.
22   *ST,* 28 Nov. and 8 Dec. 1947.
23   *Insight,* Jan. 1979, p. 15.
24   This biographical sketch of Tan Chin Tuan was based on: Lee Su Yin, Melanie Chew, pp. 215–8, *ST,* 2 May 1971, *Insight,* Jan. 1979, pp. 8–18, *The Star,* 3 Sept. 1979, *New Straits Times,* 10 May 1983 and *ST,* 24 May 1992.
25   *ST,* 19 Dec. 1947.
26   SCCCI 1964, pp. 117–9.
27   *ST,* 31 Dec. 1947.
28   *ST,* 4 Apr. 1946.
29   Lim Choo Hoon, p. 35.
30   See, for instance, Colonial Office file 537: *Colonies general supplementary original correspondence, 1759–1955. CO 537/2137* for May to Sept. 1947.
31   *Minutes of the Singapore Advisory Council,* 3 July 1947.

[32] *ST*, 8 Sept. 1947.

[33] Lien and Kraar, p. 35.

[34] Among the people who used to meet at Lien's house were Tunku Abdul Rahman and Tan Cheng Lock, and he sometimes went to the Tanjong Rhu Club to discuss matters with Tan Lark Sye and Lee Kong Chian.

[35] For more information, see Secretariat of Chinese Affairs, National Archives of Singapore, reel 6 folio 0102, and *ST*, 10 July 1947.

[36] See Lien and Kraar, p. 88. This biographical sketch of Lien Ying Chow is based on: Lien and Kraar, *ST*, 18 Oct. 1978, 20 Sept. 1981 and 1 Sept. 1992.

[37] *ST*, 17 Jan. 1948.

[38] *ST*, 5 Feb. 1948.

[39] Yong 1985, p. 55.

[40] *ST*, 7 Jan. 1948.

[41] Turnbull, p. 231, and *ST*, 31 Mar. 1948.

[42] *ST*, 10 and 11 Sept. 1947.

[43] See for instance Yeo and Lau, pp. 118–20, and Turnbull, pp. 223–4.

[44] Drysdale, p. 38.

[45] *ST*, 4 July 1947.

[46] Lim Choo Hoon, p. 43.

[47] Yong 1985, p. 52.

[48] See SCCC, *Fifty-eight Years of Enterprise*, p. 115. Of the 30 members of the Chamber's 1941 council, 21 were left and an election was held to fill the quota (SCCCI, *80th Anniversary publication*, p. 341).

[49] Sng Choon Yee, interview, 5 Mar. 1981, in *Pioneers of Singapore* A64/48 pp. 342–54.

[50] *ST*, 11 and 27 Sept. 1945.

[51] *ST*, 8 Oct. 1945.

[52] *ST*, 6 Apr., 1 June and 29 Aug. 1946.

[53] Minutes of meetings of the CAB of 15 July, 5 Sept. and 9 Dec. 1949. In Secretariat of Chinese Affairs, No. 163–49, Enclosures 8, 25 and 39.

[54] Rudolph, pp. 172–3.

[55] In 1947 the general literacy rate was 374 per 1,000 and only about two-thirds of children between the ages of six and 12 attended school (Huff, p. 277).

[56] See Doraisamy, pp. 47–50, and Gwee, pp. 111–4.

[57] *Supplement to the Ten-Year Programme*, pp. 108–9.

[58] Lim Choo Hoon, pp. 25–30, Yeo 1973a, pp. 43–8 and *ST*, 20 Jan. 1948.

[59] *ST*, 8 Oct. 1945.

[60] *ST* 10 Oct. and 11 Oct. 1945.

[61] SCCCI, *80th Anniversary publication*, pp. 343–4, *ST*, 2 Oct. 1946 and 16 Mar. 1948.

[62] For more on the CDL and the KMT, see Chui 1985, pp. 1–9 and Chui and Hara, pp. 9–12.

[63] Chui 1985, p. 49.

[64] Chui and Hara, p. 12.

[65] These five were Tay Koh-yat, Quek Sin, Lee Chin-tian, Chew Hean-swee and Chuang Hui Chuan.

[66] *ST*, 25 Sept. 1946 and interview with Dr. Chui Kwei-qiang, 11 June 1996.

[67] Interview with Chwee Meng Chong, Spring 1999.

[68] *Nanyang Siangpau*, henceforth *NYSP*, 29 Jan. and 9 Feb. 1948. The *Nanyang Siangpau* was established by Tan Kah Kee in 1923, with the express purpose of promoting his own manufactured goods and products. Because it published reliable data daily on the price of rubber and other key commodities, the paper soon became popular in Chinese business circles. In 1937 the paper changed hands, although it stayed in the family. George Lee, younger brother of Tan's son-in-law Lee Kong Chian, acquired the paper and the Lee family would remain in control of it until the government forced it to divest in 1977. Although the postwar ownership of the paper was moderate and included a number of KMT leaders, its editorial staff was allowed to display leftist and anti-colonial leanings (Interview with former journalist, January 1997). See also Chui and Hara, pp. 50–1.

[69] *ST*, 26 Sept. 1946, Chui and Hara, p. 48.

[70] *NYSP*, 20 Sept. 1946.

[71] Chui and Hara, p. 80.

[72] Chui 1977, pp. 82–6. Chui and Hara, pp. 14–20 and Turnbull, p. 240.

[73] Cheah, pp. 4–5.

[74] Drysdale, pp. 6–7.

[75] Turnbull, p. 225.

[76] Drysdale, pp. 6–8.

[77] *ST*, 5 July 1946.

[78] Lim Choo Hoon, p. 27.

[79] *ST*, 3 Dec. 1946.

[80] *ST*, 4 Mar. 1947, Heng and Sieh Lee, Mei Ling, p. 130.

[81] Lau 1991, pp. 212–23 and *ST*, 1 Jan. 194.

[82] *ST*, 9 Jan. 1947.

[83] Lim Choo Hoon, p. 28.

[84] *ST*, 3 Apr. 1947.

[85] Lim Choo Hoon, p. 28.

[86] Turnbull, pp. 226–7.

[87] Lim Choo Hoon, p. 29, Yong 1994, p. 277.

[88] *ST*, 20 Jan. 1948.

[89] Yeo 1973a, pp. 41–2 and Drysdale, p. 26.

[90] Turnbull, p. 227.

[91] Heng and Sieh Lee, p. 199, Yeo 1973a, pp. 48–51, Lim Choo Hoon, p. 30.

[92] *ST*, 1 Feb. 1948.

[93] Turnbull, p. 221.

[94] *ST*, 27 Sept. 1945.

[95] *ST*, 15 June 1946.

[96] *ST*, 26 Sept. 1945 and 9 and 13 Sept. 1946.

[97] Of importance to the smuggling trade between the Netherlands East Indies and

Singapore was the Singapore Overseas Chinese Import and Export Association, established on 15 Jan. 1946, in which Palembang Chinese who had fled to Singapore played a crucial role (Twang, pp. 205–7).
98 *ST*, 15 June 1946.
99 Huang Jianli, pp. 170–4.
100 Twang, pp. 94–5.
101 Huang, p. 176.
102 Ibid., p. 178.
103 Ibid., pp. 179–80.

Chapter 3

1 Singapore political report for February 1952 by Local Intelligence Committee, Colonial Office file *CO1022/206*.
2 *Singapore Free Press*, henceforth *SFP*, 17 May 1949.
3 Speech by H.E. the Governor, Sir Franklin Gimson to the CAB, 15 July 1949, *Public Relations, Singapore Press Release no. JL.49/96*. In: Secretariat of Chinese Affairs.
4 *CO 1022/207*.
5 Lim Choo Hoon, pp. 35–6.
6 *ST*, 30 Nov. 1950.
7 *ST*, 28 Feb. 1951.
8 *ST*, 30 Nov. 1950.
9 *SFP*, 4 Jan. 1951.
10 *ST*, 28 Feb. 1951.
11 *ST*, 6 Jan. 1951.
12 *CO 1030/259*.
13 Chew, Melanie, p. 42.
14 Kua, p. 43.
15 Chew, Melanie, p. 48.
16 *Singapore Chinese Chamber of Commerce minutes of the monthly meetings, 1906 to 1971*, National Archive of Singapore, 19 Feb. 1951.
17 *CO 1022/173 Extract from PMR 1/1952*.
18 Yeo 1973b, p. 145.
19 Nanda Graduates Friendly Association, pp. 37–41.
20 Chew, Melanie, p. 20.
21 *ST*, 16 Oct. 1954.
22 Wilson, p. 118 and Nanda Graduates Friendly Association, pp. 46–9.
23 Chew, Melanie, p. 25.
24 This biographical sketch of Tan Lark Sye is also based on: *CO 1030/259* and Kua, pp. 38–40.
25 For more information on the politics of merger, see Lau 1998.
26 *ST*, 16 Mar. 1952.
27 *CO 1022/206*, Mar. 1952.
28 *ST*, 29 Mar. 1952.

29 *CO 1022/206*, Apr. 1952.
30 Tan Ee Leong interview for *Pioneers of Singapore*, 28 May 1981, p. 165 and Chew, Melanie, pp. 29–33.
31 See Tan Ee Leong interview for *Pioneers of Singapore*, 28 May 1981, pp. 166–8. Tan's account does not give a clear date when these developments occurred. Interviews with other prominent Chamber members from that era corroborate his story and confirm it took place in 1953.
32 Interview with contemporary of Ko, 10 Jan. 1997.
33 Data provided by Lim Hup Choon trading company, interview with Ling Lee Hua, 3 Feb. 1997.
34 This biographical sketch of Ng Aik Huan was based on: Kua, p. 75, interview with Ng Aik Huan for *Pioneers of Singapore*, 3 Apr. 1981, Chui and Hara, p. 73, Yong 1994, pp. 278–81.
35 *Xinjiapo Zhonghua Zongshanghui bangpai lunzheng lai long qu mai* (The Singapore Chinese Chamber of Commerce, the origin and development of the dialect group controversy) (1969), pp. 54–7.
36 SCCC, *80th Anniversary publication*, p. 349.
37 This biographical sketch of Chuang Hui Tsuan was based on: Ban and Yap, Tan Chong Tee, Gough, Cheah, p. 73, *ST*, 3 Feb. 1955, *CO 1030/259*, and Kua, p. 10.
38 *CO 1022/173 Extract from PMR 1/1952*.
39 Lien and Kraar, p. 86 and *Nanfang Evening Post editorial*, 6 Sept. 1952, in *Weekly Digest of the Malay, Chinese and Tamil Press*, Singapore National Library, NL10987–8.
40 *Sin Chew Jit Poh*, henceforth *SCJP*, editorial, 13 Sept. 1952, in *Weekly Digest*.
41 *SCJP*, 30 Sept. 1952.
42 *SFP*, 28 Oct. 1952.
43 *ST*, 24 Dec. 1952.
44 Ibid., and *ST*, 25 Dec. 1952.
45 *ST*, 2 Nov. 1954.
46 *ST*, 3 Nov. 1954.
47 SCCC, *Minutes of meetings*, 22 Dec. 1954 and *ST*, 22 Dec. 1954.
48 *ST*, 29 Dec. 1954.
49 *ST*, 24 Jan. 1955.
50 *ST*, 28 Jan. 1955.
51 *ST*, 29 Jan. 1955.
52 *ST*, 4 Feb. 1955.
53 The number of unions increased from 91 with 48,595 members in 1950 to 187 with 139,317 members in 1955 (Gamer, p. 201). In 1955, 946,354 and in 1956 454,455 man-days were lost due to 29 strikes (Huff, p. 295).
54 See Harper 2001.
55 See Department of Education, Colony of Singapore 1953, pp. 108–9.
56 *Colonial Secretary to Director of Education, 22 Oct. 1954*, in *History of negotiations with the SCCC of the Ministry of Education*, National Archives of Singapore, ME3971, p. 1.

57 *Note on conversation between Lee Kong Chian and Mr. Blythe, 15 Apr. 1953*, in ibid., p. 55.

58 *Young to Blythe*, 2 July 1953, in ibid.

59 This was not the first time that plans for a Chinese language university were brought up. In 1946, Tan Lark Sye, Ng Aik Huan and Lee Kong Chian proposed setting up such an institution. They consulted Tan Kah Kee, founder of Xiamen University, who advocated a regional Chinese Teachers' Training College rather than a full-scale university. The plan did not receive enough financial and popular support to be pursued (Yong 1994, p. 281).

60 Lind, p. 103.

61 *CO 1022/346*, 19 May 1953.

62 While the history of Nanyang University is, no doubt, an important mirror of the socio-political developments of the time, and while the development of this institution is closely linked to individuals in the Chamber, it is too daunting a task to weave this whole complicated story into the present study. Surely the history of Nanda deserves a large volume of its own.

63 *Blythe to Young, ME3971*, p. 3, 22 Oct. 1954. In: *History of negotiations with the SCCC of the Ministry of Education.*

64 *SCJP*, 12 Jan. 1954.

65 *SCJP*, 4 and 23 Mar. 1954.

66 Bloodworth, p. 61.

67 Yeo and Lau, p. 130.

68 Arumugam, p. 61 and Drysdale, pp. 74–5.

69 SCCC, *Fifty-eight years of enterprise*, pp. 125–6 and Bloodworth, p. 63.

70 Yeo 1973b, p. 191 and SCCC, *Minutes of meetings*, 30 May 1952.

71 Sweeney, p. 266.

72 Bloodworth, pp. 63–5.

73 Drysdale, p. 80.

74 Bloodworth, p. 66.

75 *Report of the Constitutional Commission, 1954* and Yeo 1973b, p. 255.

76 Turnbull, p. 251.

77 See Bellows 1968, Chapters 1–3 and 1970.

78 See Chapter 6 of Clutterbuck, Fong, Bloodworth and Drysdale. For a different perspective on Lim Chin Siong, see Tan and Jomo.

79 SCCC, *Fifty-eight years of enterprise*, p. 128.

80 *ST*, 16 Mar. 1954.

81 *ST*, 14 Jan. 1955.

82 *NYSP*, 5 Feb. 1955.

83 *NYSP*, 7 Feb. 1955.

84 *ST*, 8 Feb. 1955 and *NYSP*, 7 Feb. 1955.

85 *ST*, 1 Mar. 1955.

86 Ibid.

87 *ST*, 8 Feb. 1955.

88 *ST*, 11 Feb. 1955.

89 *ST*, 12 Feb. 1955.

90 *ST*, 1 Mar. 1955.
91 Interview with Lim Cher Kheng, 5 July 1996.
92 Sweeney, p. 216.
93 Ibid., interview with Nicoll on p. 295.
94 Ibid., interview with Rajah on p. 295.
95 *SFP*, 22 Mar. 1955.
96 Bellows 1968, p. 128.
97 Pugalenthi, pp. 11–2.
98 Sweeney, p. 292 quoting Elegant, p. 164.
99 *ST,* 2 Apr. 1955.
100 Peritz, p. 111, interview with Tan Eng Joo, Sept. 1962.
101 Yeo 1973b, pp. 268–70.
102 *SFP*, 18 Mar. 1955.
103 Radio Malaya transcript quoted in Pugalenthi, p. 14.
104 *ST*, 4 Apr. 1955.
105 Gamer 1972, pp. 21–2.
106 Singapore, following the Westminster tradition of the British, had a constituency-based election system in which the "first-past-the-post" principle was applied.
107 Yeo and Lau, p. 134.
108 *ST*, 26 May 1955 and *NYSP*, 27 May 1955.
109 Gamer 1972, pp. 23–4.
110 Yeo 1973b, p. 134.
111 Gopinathan, pp. 71–2.
112 Although a Teochew, Lim was never much involved in Teochew organizations. He was closer to the Hokkien and was friends with Tan Lark Sye and Soon Peng Yam. Being very vocal and having a somewhat combative nature, he clashed on numerous occasions with the old KMT supporters in the Chamber. Among his most important achievements as Legislative Assembly member from 1955 to 1959 he lists Chinese education, regulations on anti-corruption and compulsory voting (interviews with Lim Cher Kheng, 5 July 1996 and 17 Feb. 1998).
113 Yeo 1973b, p. 168.
114 *NYSP*, 8 and 9 June 1955.
115 *SCJP*, 5 July 1955.
116 All-Party Committee of the Singapore Legislative Assembly (1956): *Report on Chinese Education*. Government Printing Office, Singapore.
117 Yeo 1973b, pp. 148–9.
118 SCCC, *Minutes of meetings*, 22 Dec. 1954 and *Zhongxing Ribao*, 19 Aug. 1955.
119 *NYSP*, 2 Mar. 1956 and 5 Mar. 1956.
120 Yeo 1973b, p. 149.
121 *SCJP*, 4 Oct. 1955.
122 *NYSP*, 8 Oct. 1955.
123 Yeo 1973b, pp. 151–2.
124 *NYSP*, 18 Apr. 1956.
125 Interview with Linn In Hua, 25 Mar. 1997.

126 Information on the internal nomination system was only related to me for the Hokkien, and it has been suggested that the smaller *bang* in particular would follow more autocratic patterns whereby the dominant leader would personally nominate the candidates. However, the possibility for independent candidates to put themselves forward through forcing an election round in the Chamber was open to all dialect groups.

127 Interview with Tan Keong Choon 1980, p. 133.

128 *ST*, 26 Jan. 1958.

129 See Tan Chong Tee, Cheah and Gough.

130 *ST*, 27 Sept. 1986.

131 Chui and Hara, p. 68.

132 *NYSP*, 12 Apr. 1957.

133 *ST*, 26 Jan. 1958.

134 The Hokkien received 16 seats, the Teochew six seats, the Hakka from Dapu three seats, the Cantonese two seats, the Sanjiang two seats, the Hainanese one seat and the Hakka from Meixian one seat. One seat was allocated to the trade associations (*NYSP*, 10 Feb. 1958).

135 *NYSP*, 3 Feb. 1958.

136 *NYSP*, 6 Feb. 1958.

137 *NYSP*, 7 Feb. 1958.

138 *NYSP*, 10 Feb. 1958.

139 *NYSP*, 1 Mar. 1958.

140 *NYSP* and *SCJP*, 2 Mar. 1958.

141 *NYSP*, 15 and 29 Mar. 1958, *NYSP*, 1 Jan. 1959 and Pek Cheng Chuan interview 1980.

142 Yeo 1973b, p. 172.

Chapter 4

1 Lee Kuan Yew in *ST*, 6 Oct. 1965.

2 *Singapore Chinese Chamber of Commerce and Singapore, Department of Information 1959*, pp. 55–7.

3 Ibid.

4 Ibid.

5 SCCCI, *80th Anniversary publication*, p. 366.

6 Interview with Ling Lee Hua, 6 Jan. 1997.

7 *Sunday Times*, 9 Aug. 1959.

8 Turnbull, p. 268.

9 *NYSP*, 9 Aug. 1959.

10 Barr, chapter 9. See also Bloodworth, Drysdale, Josey, George, and Minchin.

11 See Vennewald.

12 Interview with contemporary Chamber leader, 10 Jan. 1997.

13 Interview with contemporary Chamber leader, 14 Nov. 1996.

14 See Plato.

15 Ibid., p. xlviii, my italics.
16 *ST*, 10 Nov. 1959.
17 *NYSP*, 2 Apr. 1959 and *Xinjiapo*, pp. 57–60.
18 *NYSP*, 1 Apr. 1959.
19 *NYSP*, 22 and 26 Apr. 1959.
20 *SCJP*, 29 Apr. 1959.
21 *NYSP*, 20 June 1959.
22 *SFP*, 1 Aug. 1959.
23 *SFP*, 9 Dec. 1959.
24 *NYSP*, 25 Feb. 1960.
25 *Sunday Mail*, 1 May 1960 and *SCJP*, 23 Mar. 1961.
26 See Huff, p. 360. In the period under analysis in this chapter, the proportional contribution to GDP of manufacturing and construction rose from 16.6 per cent to 20.5 per cent and from 5.3 per cent to 8.6 per cent respectively. The contribution of commerce over the same period dropped slightly from 24.6 per cent to 23.6 per cent (Huff, p. 303).
27 The alternative business organizations were the Singapore Chamber of Commerce (SCC, established 1837), the Singapore Indian Chamber of Commerce (SICC, established 1924), and the Singapore Manufacturers' Association (SMA, established 1932), while the ethnic representational model had recently been completed with the establishment of the Singapore Malay Chamber of Commerce (SMCC) in 1956. The Malay and the Indian chambers had a membership of around 100 to 200. Although the SCC shared the SCCC's trade orientation, its membership of around 500 or 600 was comprised of Western businesses. The SMA had been started by a handful of manufacturers during the Depression. Although its late 1950s membership of around 400 to 500 was a mix of foreign and locally-owned enterprises, its leadership was dominated by foreigners, which changed only in 1963.
28 Most probably Ko referred to non-manufactured goods and goods manufactured outside of Singapore and their percentage of total imports and exports. An indication of the continued importance of commerce to Singapore in 1960 is that it was the largest sector with 24.6 per cent of GDP. Social services was 19.6 per cent, manufacturing 16.6 per cent, financial and business services 14 per cent, transport and communications 8.8 per cent, construction 5.3 per cent, agriculture and fishing 3.6 per cent, electricity, gas and water 1.7 per cent, and quarrying 0.2 per cent (Singapore national accounts, quoted in Huff, p. 303).
29 Unidentified newspaper, 30 June 1959. A copy of this article is in the possession of the author. Due to the relocation of the newspaper collection of the National Library of Singapore at the time of rewriting, it was not possible to ascertain in which newspaper this article appeared.
30 *Sunday Times*, 20 Mar. 1960.
31 SCCC, *Fifty-eight years of enterprise*, p. 132.
32 The PAP envisioned a park, developed by the government, to attract investors. Jurong Town Corporation would in time become an important model. Lee Kuan Yew, p. 347.

33 Winsemius said that the fact that he had made his mark in administration as well as in business was an important factor to the PAP government. Others had been proposed but the Singapore government preferred Winsemius (interview with Dr. Winsemius, The Hague, 1995).

34 United Nations Industrial Survey Mission, pp. 195–201.

35 Interview with Dr. Winsemius in Drysdale, p. 252.

36 Interview with Dr. Winsemius, The Hague, 1995.

37 Interview with Dr. Goh Keng Swee, 24 Jan. 1997.

38 *Sunday Times* and *Sunday Mail*, 18 Mar. 1962.

39 Yeo and Lau, p. 139.

40 FO 1091: *File of the Office of the Commissioner General for the United Kingdom of Southeast Asia, 1955–1962. FO 1091/107, Special Branch report to Singapore Intelligence Committee, 24 Sept. 1959 to 14 Oct. 1959.*

41 Sopiee, pp. 125–7.

42 Yeo and Lau, pp. 141–2.

43 Clutterbuck, p. 154.

44 The People's Association ran community centres where some recreational facilities were combined with channels to disseminate information to citizens through radio, government brochures, etc.

45 Turnbull, p. 272 and Bloodworth, Chapter 28.

46 Bellows 1970, p. 76.

47 Lee Kuan Yew, pp. 387–9.

48 Ibid., pp. 408–9.

49 See Seow 1994, pp. 33–4.

50 Tan Lark Sye was in charge of the Hokien Huay Kuan and Ko was the President of the Ee Hoe Hean Club. For a list of meetings, see *Commission of Inquiry, Vol. 1., 21 May 1961*, p. E4 and *Vol. 1., 23 May 61*, p. D4.

51 Ibid., *Vol. 1., 23 May 61*, p. E4.

52 Seow 1994, pp. 36–7.

53 Lee Kuan Yew, p. 414.

54 *Commission of Inquiry, Vol. 2., 28 May 62*, p. E5.

55 Ibid., *Vol. 2., 28 May 62*, pp. E6–E7.

56 Ibid., *Vol. 2., 29 May 1962*, p. A5.

57 Ibid., *Vol. 2., 29 May 1962*, p. C1.

58 Ibid., *Vol. 2., 29 May 1962*, p. E2–E4.

59 DO 169: Singapore and Malaysia political affairs. Letter from O'Brien to R.C. Ormerod, dated 26 Sept. 1961, in *DO169/246*.

60 See Lee Kuan Yew, pp. 395–401. The government was greatly aided by the erratic political course the Barisan took on merger. Having split over their opposition to merger, they now advocated that merger could only take place satisfactorily if Singapore became one of the founding states. It has been suggested that the Barisan expected that this would prove unacceptable to Kuala Lumpur. They opted to sell this strategy to the Singapore population and then blame the Malayans when they barred Singapore from merging with the Federation.

61 *Memorandum setting out heads of agreement for a merger between the Federation of Malaya and Singapore.*

62 *SCJP*, 1 Dec. 1961.

63 *NYSP*, 4 Jan. 1962.

64 *CO 1030/996.*

65 Lee Kuan Yew, pp. 414–5.

66 *SCJP*, 28 Aug. 1962.

67 SCCC, *Minutes of meetings*, 28 Aug. 1962.

68 *ST*, 30 Aug. 1962.

69 *ST*, 6 Sept. 1962.

70 Bloodworth, p. 273.

71 Yeo and Lau, p. 143.

72 Bloodworth, p. 279.

73 The Tunku had delayed the ceremonies for a last minute United Nations survey to confirm that the people of the North Borneo territories were indeed in favour of merger.

74 Turnbull, p. 277.

75 Drysdale, p. 339.

76 Lee Kuan Yew, p. 333.

77 *Singapore Government Press statement, BYC/Infs OC. 91/59*, p. 3.

78 *NYSP*, 12 Jan. 1960.

79 Lee Kuan Yew, p. 332.

80 *Singapore Government Press statement, JK/MC.MA 93/60*, p. 4.

81 *NYSP*, 14 and 15 Sept. 1963.

82 Bloodworth, p. 283.

83 Lee Kuan Yew, p. 511.

84 Ibid.

85 See Chan 1996 for a detailed analysis.

86 Bellows 1968, pp. 341–49 and Gamer 1969, p. 204.

87 SCCCI, *80th Anniversary publication*, p. 382 and *SFP*, 1 Feb. 1962.

88 *ST*, 8 June 1946.

89 Turnbull, pp. 222–3.

90 *Secretary of Chinese Affairs, National Archives of Singapore file SCA 6, folio 0495 and 1139.*

91 Ibid., *File SCA 6, folio 1077.*

92 *Minutes of Meeting of the Chinese Advisory Board, 9 Dec. 1949. In: Secretariat of Chinese Affairs, No. 163-49, Enclosure 39.*

93 SCCC, *80th Anniversary publication*, pp. 382–6.

94 *NYSP*, 10 Mar. 1963.

95 *NYSP*, 14 Mar. 1963.

96 *NYSP*, 28 Mar. 1963.

97 *NYSP*, 5 Apr. 1963.

98 *NYSP*, 29 Mar. 1963.

99 *NYSP*, 14 Mar. 1963 and SCCCI, *80th Anniversary publication*, p. 387.

100 Lee Kuan Yew, p. 495.

[101] Letter from Moore to Trench, Embassy Tokyo dated 6 June 1963, in *DO 169/193*.
[102] Letter from UK High Commissioner to Hammer, Colonial Office dated 11 July 1963, in *DO 169/193*.
[103] SCCCI, *80th Anniversary publication*, p. 387.
[104] Letter from Ward, Singapore High Commission to Hammer, Colonial Office dated 22 Aug. 1963, *in DO 169/193*.
[105] Bloodworth, pp. 281–2.
[106] SCCCI, *80th Anniversary publication*, p. 387
[107] Inward telegram from Earl Selkirk to Secretary of State for the Colonies dated 26 Aug. 1963 in *DO 169/193* and Correspondence from the British Embassy in Tokyo to the Foreign Office, dated 29 Aug. 1963 in *DO 169/193*.
[108] See Telegram from Singapore to Commonwealth Office dated 20 Sept. 1963 in *DO 169/193*.
[109] *NYSP*, 26 Oct. 1963.
[110] *Malay Mail*, 30 Oct. 1963.
[111] *NYSP*, 31 Oct. 1964, *SCJP, Malay Mail*, 31 Oct. 1964, 5 Apr. 1965 and SCCCI, *80th Anniversary publication*, pp. 392–3.
[112] SCCC, *Minutes of meetings*, 31 Oct. 1966 and *ST*, 26 and 27 Oct. 1966.
[113] Andersen, p. 79.
[114] Drysdale, p. 361.
[115] Fong, p. 151.
[116] SCCCI, *80th Anniversary publication*, p. 368 and *Sunday Mail*, 26 July 1964.
[117] Lee Kuan Yew, p. 575.
[118] SCCC, *Fifty-eight Years of Enterprise*, p. 9.
[119] Ibid., p. 19.
[120] Ibid., p. 22.
[121] SCCCI, *80th Anniversary publication*, pp. 384–5.
[122] Regnier, p. 29.
[123] Lau 1998, pp. 214–5.
[124] *ST*, 2 Dec. 1964 and *Malay Mail*, 3 Dec. 1964.
[125] *ST*, 22 June 1965.
[126] Turnbull, pp. 284–5.
[127] *NYSP*, 30 June 1965.
[128] *NYSP*, 6 July 1965.
[129] SCCC, *Minutes of meetings*, 31 July 1965. *Malay Mail*, 28 and 29 July 1965.
[130] Interview and lunch with Soon Peng Yam, 26 June 1996.
[131] Interview with Soon Peng Yam, *Pioneers of Singapore*.
[132] Additional source, *Singapore Monitor*, 10 Sept. 1984.
[133] *Xinjiapo*, pp. 24–9 and *SCJP*, 6 Jan. 1962.
[134] *ST*, 16 Sept. 1964, *SCJP*, 18 Sept. 1964 and *SCJP*, 27 Sept. 1964.
[135] *NYSP*, 30 and 31 Jan. 1965.
[136] *NYSP*, 1 Feb. and 12 Feb. 1965.
[137] *NYSP*, 9 March 1965 and *Xinjiapo*, pp. 24–9.
[138] *Sunday Times*, 15 Feb. and *NYSP*, 16 Mar. 1965.

[139] Interview with Soon Peng Yam, *Pioneers of Singapore*, p. 57 and p. 61.
[140] Lee Kuan Yew, pp. 17–8.
[141] Winsemius, quoted in Drysdale, p. 404.
[142] *NYSP*, 10 Aug. 1965.
[143] Interview with Soon Peng Yam, quoted in Liu, p. 587.
[144] *NYSP*, 13 Aug. 1965 and SCCC, *Minutes of meetings*, 31 Aug. 1965.
[145] *NYSP*, 22 Aug. 1965.
[146] SCCC, *Minutes of meetings*, 31 Aug. 1965 and *NYSP*, 2 Sept. 1965.
[147] *NYSP*, 3 Sept. 1965.
[148] SCCC, *Minutes of meetings*, 30 Sept. 1965.
[149] *NYSP*, 1 Oct. 1965.
[150] *NYSP*, 2 Oct. 1965 and *Malay Mail*, 2 Oct. 1965.
[151] *ST*, 6 Oct. 1965.
[152] *Sunday Times*, 24 Oct. 1965.
[153] SCCC, *Minutes of meetings*, 29 Oct. 1965 and *SCJP*, 30 Oct. 1965.
[154] Vogel, p. 1049.

Chapter 5

[1] *Business Times*, henceforth *BT,* 20 Jan. 1978.
[2] *NYSP*, 1 Jan. 1966.
[3] *Malay Mail*, 3 Mar. and various articles in the *ST*, 15 Mar. 1966.
[4] *ST*, 15 Mar. 1966.
[5] *ST*, 15 Mar. 1966.
[6] Withdrawal of the British military presence from Singapore was not just a matter of defending the nation, it had profound economic implications as well. The contribution of the bases was estimated to be responsible for 20 per cent to 25 per cent of Singapore's GNP in 1966. In 1968, when withdrawal became official British policy, the effect on the labour market was expected to be a doubling of true unemployment by 100,000 (*FEER*, 17 Feb. 1966 and 18 Feb. and 24 Feb. 1968).
[7] Lee Kuan Yew quoted in Josey, pp. 307–8.
[8] See for instance Rodan 1989, pp. 88–91, Chan Heng Chee 1971, Hill and Lian, Chapter 1, David Brown, pp. 20–1 and Regnier, pp. 229–32.
[9] Rodan, 1989, p. 64.
[10] The Economic Development Board was established in 1961. After reorganization in July 1968 when the Development Bank of Singapore was set up and made responsible for development financing operations, the EDB concentrated on planning and integration of national economic development. The statutory board, a category of which the EDB is an example, is a characteristic tool of the technocratic state-led nation. PAP Singapore has put many of the state's policy, service and regulatory functions in the hands of statutory boards. This exemplifies the stress on efficient, knowledge-based governing. The boards have a high degree of relative autonomy from parliament but perform their tasks in a conceptually integrated fashion. This keeps political interference to a minimum.

11 Mirza, pp. 85–91.
12 Rodan 1989, pp. 91–2.
13 Lee Kuan Yew quoted in Josey, pp. 353–5.
14 Chua, p. 61.
15 Lee Kuan Yew quoted in Josey, p. 429.
16 Clutterbuck, pp. 342–3.
17 Letter of SCCC to Select Committee dated 11 July 1966. In: *Report of the Select Committee on the Land Acquisition Bill, pp. B12–B14.*
18 Clutterbuck, pp. 323–4, Tremewan, pp. 48–9, Chan Heng Chee 1978, and 1996, pp. 161–70, Cheng Lim Keak 1985, pp. 137–9, and Quah, Chan and Seah.
19 Lam Thian quoted in *ST*, 8 Oct. 1972.
20 Chua, p. 172.
21 Rodan 1989, p. 30.
22 Interview with Ling Lee Hua, 3 Feb. 1997.
23 *ST*, 16 Mar. 1966.
24 Lee Kuan Yew quoted in Josey, p. 442.
25 Cheng Lim Keak 1985, pp. 99–101.
26 See *ST*, 8 June 1966.
27 *Kheng Chin Hock, Press release, Nov. 1968.* In: Straits Times Clippings Archive.
28 Ibid. See Chapter 2, Section 5 for more on the election process.
29 *Xinjiapo*, pp. 11–19.
30 *ST*, 9 Mar. 1965 and *SCJP*, 28 Apr. 1965.
31 *NYSP*, 1 Apr. 1965.
32 *NYSP*, 7 Mar. 1965.
33 Interview with contemporary leader, 12 Oct. 1996, interview with contemporary Council Member, 5 July 1996.
34 SCCC, *Fifty-eight Years of Enterprise*, pp. 189–217.
35 *Xinjiapo*, pp. 60–72.
36 Ibid., pp. 96–109.
37 Ibid., pp. 72–88.
38 *Xinjiapo*, pp. 11–19.
39 *NYSP*, 7 Aug. 1968.
40 *Xinjiapo*, pp. 11–19.
41 Interview with Ling Lee Hua, 6 Jan. 1997.
42 This biographical sketch was also based on: Melanie Chew, pp. 220–4, Tee, pp. 26–32, *Sunday Mail*, 13 and 27 June 1971, *Singapore Business*, Oct. 1978, *Insight*, May 1980.
43 Melanie Chew, pp. 220–1.
44 *Minbao*, 10 Apr. 1969.
45 *ST*, 23 July 1995.
46 Melanie Chew, pp. 221–2.
47 *FEER*, 20 Aug. 1982.
48 Interview with veteran journalist of Chamber affairs, 8 Jan. 1997, interview with Nanda graduate Chamber member, 26 Nov. 1996.
49 *Sunday Times*, 16 Mar. 1969.

50 *ST,* 20 and 27 Nov. 1972.
51 *New Nation,* 17 Mar. 1975.
52 *New Nation,* 1 Feb. 1971.
53 *ST,* 2 Feb. 1974.
54 *ST,* 1 July 1977.
55 *NYSP,* 29 Apr. 1978.
56 *ST,* 16 Mar. 1973.
57 See Chapter 1, Section 1.
58 Josey, p. 313.
59 See Melanie Chew, Lien and Kraar, and *Singapore Government Press Statement MC.AP.8/66(FOR.) 6 Apr. 1966.*
60 *ST,* 3 Oct.1966 and *NYSP,* 2 Aug. 1967.
61 *ST,* 24 Aug. and 6 Sept. 1966.
62 *Eastern Sun,* 9 Dec. 1968.
63 Turnbull, p. 315.
64 *ST,* 18 Mar. 1966.
65 *ST,* 2 Feb. 1968.
66 *New Nation,* 28 Feb. 1977.
67 *ST,* 12 Mar. 1977.
68 Interview with Lim Ho Hup, 5 Feb. 1997.
69 *ST,* 19 Nov. 1979 and SCCCI, *Annual Report 1982,* p. 73.
70 Interview with Lim Ho Hup, 5 Feb. 1997.
71 The PRC was not a major trading partner of Singapore: in 1960 2.5 per cent of Singapore exports went to China, in 1970 1.4 per cent. Of Singapore's imports 3.4 per cent originated in China in 1960 and 4.8 per cent in 1970 (Krause, Koh and Lee, pp. 32–4).
72 *ST,* 30 Apr. 1971.
73 *New Nation,* 7 July 1971.
74 *ST,* 24 Aug. 1971 and *New Nation,* 3 Sept. 1971.
75 *ST,* 2 Sept. 1976.
76 *ST,* 21 Oct. 1977.
77 *ST,* 19 Sept. 1973.
78 Interview with Tan Keong Choon, *Pioneers of Singapore,* pp. 46–56.
79 *Sunday Times,* 20 Mar. 1983.
80 *ST,* 28 Jan. 1993.
81 *ST,* 14 Nov. 1996 and 6 Feb. 1997.
82 *Sunday Times,* 16 Sept. 1973.
83 *SCJP,* 1 Nov. 1973 and 1 Feb. 1974.
84 *ST,* 10 Jan. 1975.
85 *ST,* 30 Mar. 1974.
86 *BT,* 1 Sept. 1977.
87 *ST,* 17 Mar. 1977.
88 *ST,* 2 May 1975.
89 Interview with Tan Keong Choon, 29 July 1996.
90 *ST,* 17 Mar. 1977.

91 Interview with Tan Eng Joo, *Pioneers of Singapore*, pp. 3–7.
92 Interview with Tan Eng Joo, 5 Aug. 1996.
93 Interview with Tan Eng Joo, *Pioneers of Singapore*, p. 50 and pp. 56–7.
94 *BT*, 1 Nov. 1989.
95 Interview with Tan Eng Joo, 5 Aug. 1996.
96 *ST*, 16 Mar. 1967 and SCCC, *Minutes of meetings*, 31 Mar. 1967.
97 Interview with Tan Eng Joo, *Pioneers of Singapore*, p. 22 and *NYSP*, 2 Apr. 1967.
98 SCCC, *Minutes of meetings*, 31 Mar. 1967 and *NYSP*, 2 Apr. 1967.
99 *NYSP*, 29 Apr. 1967.
100 See *Sunday Times*, 21 May 1967, *NYSP*, 21 May 1967 and SCCC, *Minutes of meetings*, 31 May 1967.
101 *ST*, 5 Sept. 1967, *Malay Mail*, 5 Sept. 1967 and SCCC, *Minutes of meetings*, 28 Sept. 1967.
102 *Malay Mail*, 7 Nov. 1967.
103 SCCC, *Minutes of meetings*, 30 Nov. 1967 and *NYSP*, 30 Nov. 1967.
104 *NYSP*, 30 Dec. 1967.
105 *SCJP*, 22 Apr. 1968.
106 SCCC, *Minutes of meetings*, 30 Oct. 1968 and *Malay Mail*, 31 Oct. 1968 and interview with Tan Keong Choon, *Pioneers of Singapore*, p. 160.
107 *Sunday Times*, 16 Mar. 1969, *NYSP*, 31 Oct. 1970 and *ST*, 31 Oct. 1970.
108 *ST*, 1 Sept. 1971 and see Tregonning.
109 Interview with Tan Eng Joo, *Pioneers of Singapore*, p. 24.
110 *New Nation*, 12 Oct. 1971, *ST*, 13 Oct., 21 Oct., 1 Nov., 6 Nov. 1971 and *New Nation*, 22 Nov. 1971.
111 *ST*, 1 Dec. 1971, *New Nation*, 9 Dec. 1971 and *ST*, 11 Jan. 1972.
112 *ST*, 12 Jan. 1972.
113 *ST*, 1 Feb. 1972.
114 *ST*, 22 Sept. and 29 Oct. 1973.
115 Huff, p. 291 and p. 352, Krause, Koh and Lee, p. 6 and p. 9.
116 *NYSP*, 22 Nov. 1967.
117 *ST*, 5 Dec. 1967.
118 *ST*, 15 Dec. 1967, *NYSP*, 28 Dec. 1967 and *ST*, 2 Feb. 1968.
119 *NYSP*, 31 July 1968.
120 Huff, pp. 342–3.
121 Mirza, p. 125.
122 Cheng Lim Keak 1985, p. 88.
123 *ST*, 1 May 1974 and *NYSP*, 29 June 1974.
124 *BT*, 28 July 1978.
125 *ST*, 30 Nov. 1978.
126 *NYSP*, 1 May 1970, *ST*, 29 June 1974, *ST*, 3 July 1974 and *New Nation*, 3 July 1974.
127 *ST*, 30 May and 13 June 1970.
128 *ST*, 13 June 1970.
129 Rodan 1989, pp. 70–1.

130 See Turnbull, p. 312. Mirza observed that by the late 1980s state entrepreneurship generated half of the indigenous GDP. For a list of state-owned enterprises, see pp. 114–9 of his book.

131 Mirza, pp. 256–62.

132 *ST*, 17 Mar. 1977.

133 Goh Keng Swee in *The Mirror*, 1977, Vol. 13, No. 27, pp. 1–2.

134 *ST*, 1 Apr. and 11 Apr. 1977, *Sunday Times*, 29 May 1977 and *BT*, 23 Aug. 1977.

135 *BT*, 1 June 1978.

136 *ST*, 5 Feb. 1979.

137 Interview with Lim Kee Ming, 20 March 1997.

138 SCCCI, *80th anniversary publication*, p. 473.

139 *ST*, 26 June and 10 July 1979 and *BT*, 24 July 1979.

140 *ST*, 7 July 1980 and 23 Jan. 1981.

141 *Sunday Mail*, 27 June 1971.

142 SCCCI, *80th anniversary publication*, p. 489.

143 *ST*, 21 Feb. 1981.

144 *SCJP*, 11 Mar. 1966, *Malay Mail*, 31 Mar. 1966, *ST*, 24 Apr. 1970 and *ST*, 10 Sept. 1971.

145 *Eastern Sun*, 1 Apr. 1969 and *ST*, 11 Apr. 1969.

146 *ST*, 12 Apr. 1969, *ST*, 3 Nov. 1969, both *ST* and *NYSP*, 1 Aug. 1972 and 1 Dec. 1972.

147 *ST*, 28 Jan. and 13 Mar. 1970.

148 *NYSP*, 14 Sept. 1967.

149 *NYSP*, 29 Sept. 1967.

150 *NYSP*, 8 Nov. 1968 and 14 Oct. 1969, *SCJP*, 1 Apr. 1971, *NYSP*, 23 Oct. 1972 and *NYSP*, 23 Apr. 1978.

151 *New Nation*, 23 Sept. 1979, *NYSP*, 31 Mar. and 3 Sept. 1982 and *ST*, 12 and 18 Oct. 1982.

152 *ST*, 3 Nov. 1982.

153 *Singapore Monitor*, 15 Sept. 1983, *ST*, 3 Oct. 1983 and *ST*, 26 Mar. 1984.

154 Regnier, p. 241.

155 Interview with Tan Keong Choon, 29 July 1996.

156 Ibid.

157 *New Nation*, 31 May 1979.

158 *ST*, 13 May and 29 May 1981.

159 *BT*, 18 June 1981.

160 Lee Kuan Yew quoted in Josey, p. 448.

161 Ibid., p. 554.

162 *ST*, 16 Mar. 1971.

163 *Sunday Mail*, 16 Mar. 1969.

164 Lee Kuan Yew in *The Mirror*, Vol. 8, No. 47, pp. 1–4.

165 See Cheng Lim Keak, p. 128.

166 *ST*, 3 May 1966.

167 *NYSP*, 7 Mar. 1971.

168 Chiew 1987, p. 58.
169 Huff, p. 354.
170 *NYSP*, 1 June 1974.
171 *ST*, 7 Apr. 1978.
172 *ST*, 8 Apr. 1978.
173 *ST*, 1 June 1977.
174 *ST* and *NYSP*, 29 Apr. 1978.
175 *ST*, 17 Feb. 1979.
176 *ST*, 14 Aug. 1979.
177 Interview with Pang Say Sock, SCCCI secretariat, 1977–1985, 18 Jan. 1997.
178 *SCJP*, 17 August 1979 and Turnbull, pp. 301–2.
179 *ST*, 7 Sept. 1979.
180 Interview with contemporary Chamber leader, 14 Nov. 1996.
181 *Sunday Times*, 23 Sept. 1979.
182 SCCCI, *Annual Report 1980*, pp. 61–2.
183 Interview with Pang Say Sock, SCCCI secretariat, 1977–1985, 18 Jan. 1997.
184 Minchin, pp. 225–6.
185 Kwok, pp. 18–22.
186 *ST*, 2 Oct. 1981.
187 *SCJP*, 11 Oct. 1982.
188 *ST*, 15 Sept. 1983, *ST*, 2 Feb. 1984 and *Singapore Monitor*, 6 June 1984.
189 *New Nation*, 26 Oct. 1982.
190 *ST*, 27 Oct. 1982.
191 Ong Teng Cheong quoted in *ST*, 25 Aug. 1984.
192 Krause, Koh and Lee, pp. 6–9.
193 Mirza, p. 59 and Krause, Koh and Lee, p. 16.
194 The Generalized System of Preferences was a system in which exports from countries classified and recognized as developing economies to developed countries were taxed at lower than standard rates.
195 Rodan 1989, pp. 124–39 and p. 198.
196 Mirza, pp. 104–9.
197 Minchin, p. 244.
198 Rodan 1989, pp. 140–55.
199 Rodan 1989, pp. 189–92.
200 Ibid., pp. 140–55.
201 Minchin, pp. 203–5.
202 Tremewan, pp. 56–7.
203 The *NYSP* and the *SCJP* were forced to cooperate in 1982 in the Singapore News and Publications Limited (SNPL). In 1984, the SNPL and the Times Group were forced to merge into the Singapore Press Holding (SPH), thereby uniting all newspapers in one organization. SPH was controlled and managed by the PAP government who put some of its trusted people, such as former minister Lim Kim San, in charge of it (Seow 1998, pp. 119–25, and Turnbull, p. 320).
204 Turnbull, p. 319.
205 See Lydgate.

206   *ST,* 30 Sept. 1981 quoted in Chua, p. 61.
207   Chua, pp. 75–7.
208   *BT* and *ST,* 19 Mar. 1979.
209   *ST,* 20 Mar. 1979.
210   *BT,* 6 Sept. 1979.
211   *ST,* 6 Sept. 1979.
212   *BT,* 6 Sept. 1979.
213   *BT,* 8 May 1980.
214   The six were: the Singapore Rope, Hardware and Paint Merchants Association, the Singapore Hardware Association, the Singapore Metal and Machinery Association, the Singapore Sanitary Ware Importers and Exporters Association, the Building Materials and Suppliers Association and the Singapore Ship-Chandlers Association.
215   *NYSP,* 10 Mar. 1981 and *ST,* 13 Mar. 1981.
216   *ST,* 28 Dec. 1981.
217   SCCCI, *Annual Report 1981,* p. 104.
218   *ST,* 29 Jan. 1982.
219   SCCCI, *Annual Report 1983,* p. 4.
220   *BT,* 30 June and 11 July 1984.
221   *BT,* 11 July 1984.
222   *ST,* 12 July 1984.
223   *New Nation,* 7 Feb. 1975.
224   *ST,* 11 Jan. 1977.
225   *BT,* 20 Jan. 1978.
226   *BT,* 16 Feb. 1979.
227   *FEER,* 30 Mar. 1979, pp. 24–5.
228   Ibid.
229   Interview with Pang Say Sock, SCCCI secretariat, 1977–1985, 18 Jan. 1997.
230   *NYSP,* 3 Oct. 1981.
231   *Sunday Nation,* 4 Oct. 1981.
232   *Sunday Times,* 4 Oct. 1981.
233   *SCJP,* 4 Oct. 1981.

Chapter 6

1   Newly elected SCCCI president Kwek Leng Joo, *BT,* 12 Feb. 1993.
2   Interview with Tan Eng Joo, 5 Aug. 1996.
3   Interview with Kwek Leng Joo, 20 Mar. 1997.
4   *ST,* 12 Feb. 1993.
5   *BT,* 12 Feb. 1993.
6   This biographical sketch was also based on an interview with Kwek Leng Joo, 20 Mar. 1997, *ST,* 11 and 12 Feb., 2 May 1993 and 11 Apr. 1994, http://www.cdl.com.sg/cdl2.nsf/corporate-management.shtm, and *Who is Who in Singapore,* p. 197.
7   *BT,* 16 Mar. 1993.

8   *ST*, 16 Mar. 1993.
9   This biographical sketch was based on: *Who is Who in Singapore*, p. 402, and an interview with Tay Beng Chuan, 3 Feb. 1998.
10   Interview with Kwek Leng Joo, 20 Mar. 1997.
11   *ST*, 2 Apr. 1993.
12   *ST*, 16 Apr. 1993.
13   Interview with Tay Beng Chuan, 3 Feb. 1998.
14   Interview with Kua Soon Khe, former Executive Secretary of the SCCCI, 6 June 1996.
15   *BT*, 30 June 1993.
16   *Sunday Times*, 22 Aug. 1993.
17   Interview with Lee Peng Shu, July 1996.
18   *Sunday Times*, 22 Aug. 1993.
19   Interview with Tan Eng Joo, 5 Aug. 1996.
20   Lee Hsien Loong, or BG Lee as he was habitually referred to in conversation and in newspaper reports, is the eldest son of Lee Kuan Yew. Born in 1952, he received a Chinese-language education while being tutored in English and Malay. For his tertiary education he attended Trinity College at Cambridge University where he read mathematics. He also studied computer systems, nuclear physics and business administration, amongst others at Harvard University. After a spectacular rise through the ranks, he first achieved public prominence when he was appointed to head the emergency rescue operation handling the Sentosa cable car disaster of January 1983. The year after he entered politics, he was elected PAP MP and later became Minister of State as an understudy to Goh Chok Tong and Tony Tan at their respective ministries of defence and trade and industry (Minchin, pp. 204–5 and Lee Kuan Yew, pp. 118, 221–2).
21   *ST*, 16 Mar. 1991.
22   *Xin Min*, 21 Feb. 1985.
23   *ST*, 22 and 23 Feb. 1985.
24   Krause, Koh and Lee, pp. 6–10.
25   Rodan 1989, p. 189.
26   *BT* and *ST*, 1 Mar. 1985.
27   *BT*, 9 Mar. 1985.
28   *BT*, 16 Mar. 1985.
29   *Singapore Monitor*, 15 Mar. 1985.
30   *ST*, 16 Mar. 1985.
31   *ST*, 20 and 28 Aug. 1985.
32   *ST*, 2 Oct. 1985.
33   Rodan 1993, pp. 89–90.
34   For Lee Hsien Loong, the chairmanship of the Economic Committee was his first test as a political leader and policy maker.
35   Singapore Economic Committee various sections, and *Sunday Times*, 26 Jan. 1986.
36   *ST*, 10 Feb. 1986.
37   *BT*, 14 Mar. 1986.

38 The government set up the Feedback Unit in 1985 as an extra-parliamentary body, which is however headed by a PAP MP. It has four stated objectives: to receive suggestions from the public on national problems, to gather information on existing policies, to facilitate prompt response by government departments to public complaints, and to instigate public information programmes.

39 *ST*, 2 Mar. 1987.

40 *ST*, 17 Mar. 1987.

41 *ST*, 25 Jan. 1983.

42 *Singapore Monitor*, 27 June 1983.

43 Ibid.

44 *ST*, 28 Feb. 1985.

45 *Singapore Monitor*, 4 June 1985.

46 Two hundred guests represented the Associated Chinese Chambers of Commerce and Industry of Malaysia (ACCCIM), which held its annual dialogue with the SCCCI as part of the programme. Others represented Chinese business organizations from Thailand, the Philippines, Hong Kong, Macau and Brunei. The People's Republic of China honoured the Chamber by sending a delegation headed by the Chairman of the Council for the Promotion of International Trade (*ST*, 17 Sept. 1986).

47 *Xin Min*, 20 Sept. 1986.

48 *ST*, 18 Sept. 1986.

49 *ST*, 22 Sept. 1986.

50 *Lianhe Zaobao*, 22 Sept. 1986.

51 *Sunday Times*, 21 Sept. 1986.

52 Interview with Linn In Hua, 25 Mar. 1997. This biographical sketch was also based on *ST*, 20 Mar. 1987 and *BT*, 24 June 1987.

53 *BT*, 13 Jan. 1987 and *ST*, 14 Jan. 1987.

54 The same principle held true for council member Chew Keng Juea who represented the See Hoy Chan Company of the well-known Teochew Teo family in the SCCCI (*ST*, 9 Feb. 1987).

55 *BT*, 6 Mar. 1987 and *ST*, 19 Mar. 1987.

56 Interview with Kwek Leng Joo, 20 Mar. 1997.

57 *BT*, 17 Mar. 1987, *Xin Min*, 23 May 1987 and *ST*, 3 Mar. 1987.

58 *Lianhe Wanbao*, 16 Mar. 1987 and *Xin Min*, 15 Mar. 1987.

59 *ST*, 17 Mar. 1987.

60 *Singapore Business*, June 1987, reprinted in *BT*, 24 June 1987.

61 Ibid.

62 Interview with Linn In Hua, 25 Mar. 1997.

63 Interview with former SCCCI Executive Secretary Kua Soon Khe, 26 Oct. 1996.

64 *New Paper*, 12 Jan. 1989.

65 *New Paper*, 31 Oct. 1989 and *BT*, 1 Nov. 1989.

66 *New Paper*, 10 and 14 May 1990.

67 *ST*, 17 Mar. 1981.

68 *ST*, 6 Oct. 1981.

69   *ST*, 15, 27, 28 Jan. and 1 Mar. 1980 and *Singapore Monitor*, 8 Dec. 1983, *ST*, 18 Oct. 1984 and 14 June 1985.

70   *ST*, 1 Mar. 1980, 8 Mar. 1982 and 29 Apr. 1983, *NYSP*, 5 Apr. 1980, *BT*, 31 July 1982, *ST*, 27 Apr. and 1 June 1983.

71   *BT*, 15 and 19 Aug. 1983 and *Singapore Monitor*, 22 Aug. and 3 Nov. 1983.

72   The TWI scheme was an American training program developed during World War II. First introduced in Singapore in 1954, it was actively promoted by the government between 1968 and 1978 (*BT*, 14 Dec. 1983). *NYSP*, 6, 9 and 30 Apr. 1982, *ST*, 14 Dec. 1983, *BT*, 24 Sept. and 16 Oct. 1984, *Lianhe Wanbao*, 9 Feb. 1984.

73   Interview with Linn In Hua, 25 Mar. 1997.

74   *BT* and ST 29 Jan. 1985.

75   *ST*, 27 Sept. 1985.

76   *BT* and *ST*, 8 July 1986, *ST*, 4 Feb. 1987 and *Sunday Times*, 22 Feb. 1987.

77   *BT*, 13 May 1987

78   *ST*, 1 June 1988.

79   *ST*, 30 June 1988.

80   *ST* and *BT*, 16 Sept. 1988 and *ST*, 1 Oct. 1988.

81   *BT*, 11 Mar. 1989.

82   *ST*, 10 Jan. 1990.

83   Interview with MC member Lee Peng Shu, early July 1996.

84   *Sunday Times*, 18 Mar. 1979.

85   *FEER*, 20 Aug. 1982, pp. 46–7.

86   *ST*, 5 Sept. 1983 and 12 Oct. 1984.

87   Regnier, pp. 28–9.

88   *BT*, 14 July 1984, *Singapore Monitor*, 25 July 1984 and 31 May 1985 and *BT*, 23 July 1985.

89   *ST*, 30 Aug. 1986.

90   *BT*, 8 Apr. 1988.

91   *ST*, 3 Feb. 1986, BT, 13 Aug. 1986, *Lianhe Zaobao*, 1 Apr. 1987, and *ST*, 1 Oct. 1988.

92   *ST*, 8 Nov. 1986 and *ST*, 1 June 1988.

93   *BT,* 21 Feb. 1991.

94   *ST*, 4 Mar. and *BT*, 8 Apr. 1988.

95   *ST*, 1 Aug. 1988.

96   *ST*, 2 Mar. and 13 June 1989.

97   See *ST*, 10 Mar. 1990. Leading by example was Linn In Hua's own company and others included Tay Beng Chuan, Ng Kok Lip, John Lu and Tan Eng Joo. See also *BT*, 21 Feb. 1991.

98   *BT*, 27 Sept. 1988.

99   *ST*, 15 Aug. and 23 Aug. 1989.

100   *ST*, 26 June 1986.

101   *Xin Min*, 15 Mar. 1987, *BT* and *ST*, 24 Mar. 1987.

102   *BT*, 25 Mar. 1987 and *Lianhe Zaobao*, 1 Apr. 1987.

103   *ST*, 2 Apr. 1987.

104 Ibid.
105 *Sunday Times*, 5 Apr. 1987.
106 *ST*, 16 Feb. 1987.
107 *ST*, 23 Feb. 1987, *BT*, 6 Nov. and 16 Dec. 1987.
108 *BT*, 23 Dec. 1987 and *ST*, 24 Dec. 1987.
109 *BT* and *ST*, 17 Aug. 1988.
110 *BT* and *ST*, 7 Sept. 1988.
111 *BT*, 28 Dec. 1988.
112 *BT* and *ST*, 15 Nov. 1991.
113 *ST*, 20 Aug. 1985.
114 *BT*, 13 Oct. 1988.
115 *ST*, 14 Oct. 1988.
116 *BT*, 14 Oct. 1988.
117 *BT*, 19 Oct. 1988.
118 *ST*, 11 Mar. 1989.
119 *BT*, 2 Apr. 1991.
120 *BG Lee*, quoted in *ST*, 16 Mar. 1991.
121 *ST*, 16 Apr. 1991.
122 *BT*, 16 Apr. 1991.
123 See *BT*, 16 Apr. 1991. A number of years later Tan clashed with the International Chamber over this issue when it was the turn of the latter to put up the president. He objected to the local Chinese candidate forwarded because he worked for a Hong Kong based colonial company. Tan tried to force the issue but failed and stepped down from the Federation six months later (interview with Mr. Hayward, Executive Director of the SICC, 10 Feb. 1998).
124 Interview with Mr. Hayward, Executive Director of the SICC, 10 Feb. 1998.
125 *ST*, 8 Nov. 1985.
126 *ST*, 8 July 1985 and *Asiaweek*, 4 Oct. 1985.
127 *ST*, 19 Sept. 1985.
128 *Asiaweek*, 4 Oct. 1985.
129 *ST*, 18 Dec. 1985.
130 *ST*, 3 Jan., 5 May, 26 June and 26 July 1986.
131 *Asian Wall Street Journal*, 8 Sept. 1986.
132 *Lianhe Zaobao*, 1 Apr. 1987.
133 *ST*, 2 Apr., 16 Apr. and 19 June 1987.
134 *ST*, 31 May 1988.
135 *BT* and *ST*, 17 Aug. 1988 and *BT*, 7 Sept. 1988.
136 *ST*, 10 Apr. 1989.
137 *ST*, 9 June 1989 and 10 June 1989.
138 *ST*, 15 Aug. 1989 and 23 Aug. 1989.
139 *ST* and *BT*, 24 Aug. 1989.
140 *ST*, 30 Apr. 1988.
141 *BT*, 16 Feb. and 14 Aug. 1989 and *ST*, 9 Feb. 1991.
142 Interview with Tan Eng Joo, 5 Aug. 1996.

143 Lee Kuan Yew had stepped down from the position of Prime Minister in 1990 and had taken on the job of Senior Minister.

144 SCCCI 1992, pp. 23–9.

145 Ibid., p. 35.

146 *Lianhe Zaobao* editorial of 14 Aug., in *ST,* 16 Aug. 1991.

147 *ST,* 13 Aug. 1991.

148 Ibid.

149 SCCCI 1992, p. 49.

150 *ST,* 13 Aug. 1991.

151 The Second WCEC was indeed held in 1993 in Hong Kong (*ST,* 23 Nov. 1993), and the conventions have been held regularly every alternate year since then.

152 *ST,* 24 Dec. 1992 and 30 Jan. 1993.

153 *BT,* 12 Feb. and 16 Mar. 1993 and *ST,* 16 Apr. 1993.

154 *ST,* 15 Mar. 1993.

155 See Tong and Chan.

156 *ST,* 24 Apr. 1993.

157 *ST,* 12 and 14 May 1993.

158 *Asiaweek,* 9 June 1993.

159 *ST,* 28 May 1993.

160 *ST,* 10 July 1993.

161 *ST,* 23 May 1993.

162 *Asiaweek,* 21 June 1996.

163 *Pereira,* pp. 67–73.

164 *ST,* 26 May 1993.

165 *ST,* 29 Jan. 1986.

166 *ST,* 2 Feb. 1986.

167 *ST,* 30 Aug. 1986.

168 *ST,* 30 May 1987.

169 SFCCA, *Members' Directory,* 1997, p. 5.

170 *ST,* 30 Dec. 1987.

171 *ST,* 20 Dec. 1990.

172 *ST,* 18 Feb. 1991.

173 Chua, pp. 34–5.

174 *ST,* 15 Nov. 1991.

175 *ST,* 28 Apr. 1992.

176 *ST,* 28 May and 14 Aug. 1992.

177 *ST,* 29 Oct. 1992.

178 *ST,* 24 May 1993.

179 *ST,* 29 Mar. and 25 Nov. 1996.

180 *Lianhe Zaobao,* 21 Sept. 1986.

181 *Xin Min,* 15 Mar. 1987.

182 *ST,* 2 Apr. 1987.

183 *ST,* 20 Mar. 1987.

184 *ST,* 9 Apr. 1987.

185 *Xin Min,* 15 Mar. 1987 and *Lianhe Zaobao,* 1 Apr. 1987.

186 *ST*, 31 Oct. 1987 and 4 May 1989.
187 *ST*, 18 Oct. 1989.
188 *ST*, 28 Nov. 1989.
189 *ST*, 20 Dec. 1990.
190 See *Government White Paper*, quoted in Chua, p. 32. For a critical evaluation of these values, see Chua 1995, Chapters 1 and 5. David Brown 1993 and 1994 analyzes this development in the wider perspective of the "corporatist management of ethnicity in Singapore".
191 *Lianhe Zaobao*, 18 Feb. 1991.
192 Interview with SCCCI Council Member Lee Peng Shu, early July 1996, and *BT*, 20 July 1993 and *Sunday Times*, 22 Aug. 1993.
193 Interview with contemporary SCCCI member, 18 Jan. 1997.
194 *ST*, 21 July 1993.
195 SCCCI, *Directory of members of the 48th and 49th council*.
196 *ST*, 2 Dec. 1994.
197 SCCCI, *Directory of members of the 48th council*.
198 *ST*, 26 Feb. 1997.
199 *ST*, 24 July 1991.
200 *ST*, 29 May and 23 June 1996.
201 *ST*, 23 Nov. 1993.
202 *ST*, 25 Nov. 1993
203 *Asia Wall Street Journal*, 25 Jan. 1996.
204 *The Economist*, 16 Mar. 1996.
205 *ST*, 8 Nov. 1996.
206 Ibid.
207 A group constituency is formed by the electoral committee by combining a number of constituencies and having their combined electorates vote for a team of candidates.
208 Interviews with Gwee Yee Hean, 23 Jan. 1997, Kua Soon Khe, 20 Jan. 1998.
209 In the immediate aftermath, Tang Liang Hong was prosecuted on libel charges. Having fled Singapore, he was convicted *in absentia* and remains in exile.
210 *ST*, 4 Jan. 1997.
211 Interview with Tay Beng Chuan, 3 Feb. 1998.

Epilogue

1 Speech by President S.R. Nathan at the SCCCI 2001 Chinese New Year Celebration. From http://www.istana.gov.sg/sp-010124.html.
2 Speech by BG (NS) George Yeo at the SCCCI 95th Anniversary Celebrations and Sun Yat Sen Nanyang Memorial Hall Fund-Raising Dinner. From http://www.mti.gov.sg/public viewed on 4 Feb. 2005.
3 *ST*, 14 Mar. and 19 June 2005.
4 *ST*, 14 Mar. 2005.

Bibliography

SCCCI sources

Singapore Chinese Chamber of Commerce: *Singapore Chinese Chamber of Commerce minutes of the monthly meetings, 1906 to 1971*, National Archives of Singapore.

_____ (1964): *Fifty-eight years of Enterprise: Souvenir Volume of the New Building of the Singapore Chinese Chamber of Commerce – 1964*. L.M. Creative Publicity, Singapore.

_____ (1966): *List of Association & Firm Members.*

_____ (1973): *Members & Trade Directory.*

Singapore Chinese Chamber of Commerce and Singapore, Department of Information (1959): *Singapore constitution exposition, Jan.–Feb., 1959; souvenir number, Singapore.*

Singapore Chinese Chamber of Commerce and Industry (1981): *75th Anniversary Souvenir Publication*. Singapore Chinese Chamber of Commerce and Industry, Singapore.

_____ (1985): *Trade & Industry Fair, '85, Singapore World Trade Centre, 27th July–4th August '85.*

_____ (1986): *80th Anniversary Souvenir publication*. Singapore Chinese Chamber of Commerce and Industry, Singapore.

_____ (1992): *First World Chinese Entrepreneurs Convention: A Global Network.* Singapore Chinese Chamber of Commerce and Industry, Singapore.

_____ (1993): *SCCCI delegation to the 2nd World Chinese Entrepreneurs Convention, Nov. 22–24, 1993.*

_____ (1995): *The Price of Peace: True Accounts of the Japanese Occupation.* Foong Choon Hon (ed.). Asiapac Books, Singapore.

_____ (1996): *90th Anniversary Souvenir Publication*. Singapore Chinese Chamber of Commerce and Industry, Singapore.

_____ (1997): *Roadmap for SMEs.*

_____ *Annual report*, 1979 through 2005.

_____ *Chinese Enterprise*, Newsletter of the SCCCI, various years.

_____ *Directory of the Singapore Chinese Chamber of Commerce and Industry*, various years.

_____ *Directory of Council Members*, various years.

Archival sources

Colonial Office file

CO 273: Original correspondence between the Colonial Office and the Foreign Office relating to the Straits Settlements and the Federated Malay States, 1838–1939.

CO 275: Proceedings of the Legislative Council of the Straits Settlements.

CO 537: Colonies general supplementary original correspondence, 1759–1955.

CO 717: Federated Malay States original correspondence, 1920–1951.

CO 940: Sessional papers of the Colonial Government of Singapore, 1946–1960.

CO 953: Original correspondence of the Colonial Office relating to Singapore, 1946–1951.

CO 991: Malayan Union and Singapore: registers of correspondence, 1946–1951.

CO 1022: Original correspondence of the Southeast Asia Department, 1950–1956.

CO 1030: Original correspondence of the Far Eastern Department relating to the Federation of Malaya and Singapore, 1954–1960.

Commonwealth Relations Office file

DO 169: Singapore and Malaysia political affairs.

Foreign Office files

FO 371: General correspondence political, 1914–1960.

FO 1091: File of the Office of the Commissioner General for the United Kingdom of Southeast Asia, 1955–1962.

Personal papers

Bloodworth collection, National Archives of Singapore.

Lee Kong Chian papers, National Archives of Singapore.

William Goode personal papers, Rhodes Library, Oxford.

Government and miscellaneous documents

All-Party Committee of the Singapore Legislative Assembly (1956): *Report on Chinese Education*. Government Printing Office, Singapore.

Commission of Inquiry into the Chinese Middle School Students' Secondary Four Examination Boycott (1962). National Library of Singapore, Southeast Asia Reading Room.

Department of Education, Colony of Singapore (1953?): *Supplement to the Ten-Year Programme, Data and Interim Proposals*. Department of Education, Singapore.

Government of Singapore (1964): *Communism in the Nanyang University*.

History of negotiations with the SCCC of the Ministry of Education, National Archives of Singapore.

Letter of SCCC to Select Committee dated 11 July 1966. In: *Report of the Select Committee on the Land Acquisition Bill*, pp. B12–B14.

Memorandum setting out heads of agreement for a merger between the Federation of

Malaya and Singapore, Cmd. (Singapore, Legislative Assembly) 33 of 1961, Government Printer, 1961.

Minutes of the Public Sessions of the Singapore Advisory Council, various dates.

Report of the Constitutional Commission, 1954. Government Printer, Singapore.

Secretariat of Chinese Affairs, National Archives of Singapore.

Singapore Economic Committee (1986): *The Singapore Economy: New directions: Report of the Economic Committee.* Ministry of Trade and Industry, Singapore.

Singapore Government Press statement, BYC/Infs OC. 91/59, p. 3.

Singapore Government Press statement, JK/MC.MA 93/60, p. 4.

Singapore Government Press statement MC.AP.8/66(FOR.) 6 Apr. 1966.

Tan Ee-Leong (1967): *Obituary of Lee Kong Chian for the Singapore China Society.*

United Nations Industrial Survey Mission (1963): *A Proposed Industrialization Programme for the State of Singapore.* United Nations, Commissioner for Technical Assistance, Department of Economic and Social Affairs.

Interviews

Over the course of three years, I conducted interviews with senior Chamber members, either in function or retired. Among them were seven presidents, a number of vice presidents and committee chairmen, dialect group leaders and management council members, as well as members and former members of the Secretariat. In addition, interviews were conducted with relatives or close associates of Chamber leaders, with long-time professional observers of the Chinese business community, and with two former government ministers.

The 1984 *"Pioneers of Singapore"* collection of the Oral History Department of the National Archives of Singapore is a collection of 73 life history interviews with Singaporean businessmen, politicians and artists.

Leaders of Singapore (Melanie Chew, 1996) and numerous interviews in newspapers and magazines provided more information.

Newspapers

English language newspaper research was conducted in the clippings collection of *The Straits Times*. The pre-1958 collection is held at the *New Straits Times* in Kuala Lumpur and dates back to 1938. The post-1958 collection held in Singapore contains a category on the Chamber. While most of the articles are from the *Straits Times*, there are also clippings from other newspapers. A thematic clipping collection at the library of the Institute of Southeast Asian Studies (ISEAS) was used to scan the English language press for information on the political, economic, social and cultural development of Singapore. For Chinese newspaper material I used the clippings library at Singapore Press Holdings. The collection comprises mostly *Nanyang Siang Pau* and *Sin Chew Jit Pao* articles, dating back to 1947. At the National Library of Singapore, I used the collection of the "Digest of the Vernacular Press" from the 1950s, which was prepared for the use of British colonial officials. In total, over 1,500 articles reporting on the Chamber were read, annotated and indexed in a timeline file system, which provided the backbone for the chapters.

Unpublished theses

Andersen, Robert Allan (1973): "The Separation of Singapore from Malaysia: A Study in Political Involution". Ph.D. dissertation, The American University, Washington, D.C.

Bellows, Thomas J. (1968): "The Singapore Party System: The First Two Decades". Ph.D. dissertation, Yale University.

Brøgger, Benedicte (2000): "Occasions and Connections: The Chinese Clan Associations as Part of Civil Society in Singapore". Ph.D. dissertation, Department of Social Anthropology, University of Oslo, Oslo.

Hsieh, Jiann (1977): "Internal Structure and Socio-Cultural Change: A Chinese Case in the Multi-Ethnic Society of Singapore". Ph.D. dissertation, University of Pittsburgh.

Lee, Su Yin (1995): "British Chinese Policy in Singapore, 1930s to Mid-1950s: With Particular Focus on the Public Service Career of Tan Chin Tuan". MA thesis, Department of History, National University of Singapore.

Leong, Stephen Mun Yoon (1976): "Sources, Agencies and Manifestations of Overseas Chinese Nationalism in Malaya, 1937–1941". Ph.D. dissertation, University of California Los Angeles.

Peritz, Rene (1964): "The Evolving Politics of Singapore: A Study of Trends and Issues". Ph.D. dissertation, University of Pennsylvania.

Sweeney, George (1973): "Political Parties in Singapore, 1945–1955". MA thesis, University of Hull.

Tan, Thomas Tsu-wee (1983): "Singapore Modernization: A Study of Traditional Chinese Voluntary Associations in Social Change". Ph.D. dissertation, University of Virginia.

Visscher, Sikko (2002): "Business, Ethnicity and State: The Representational Relationship of the Singapore Chinese Chamber of Commerce and the State, 1945–1997". Ph.D. dsissertation, *Vrije Universiteit*, Amsterdam.

Yen, Chen-Shen (1990): "Consequences of Socioeconomic Development in Taiwan, Singapore, and South Korea: Democracy or a Continuation of Authoritarianism?" Ph.D. dissertation, Purdue University.

Academic books and articles

Akashi, Yoji (1968): "The Nanyang Chinese Anti-Japanese and Boycott Movement, 1908–1928 — A Study of Nanyang Chinese Nationalism". In: *Journal of the South Seas Society*, Vol. XXIII, pp. 69–96.

Andaya, Leonard and Andaya Watson, Barbara (1982): *A History of Malaysia*. Macmillan Press, Basingstoke, London.

Arumugam, Raja Segaran (1975): "Education and Integration in Singapore". In: *Political and Social Change in Singapore*. (Ed.: Wu,Teh-yao) Institute of Southeast Asian Studies, Singapore, pp. 55–69.

Bailey, F. G. (1970): *Strategems and Spoils: A Social Anthropology of Politics*. Basil Blackwell, Oxford.

Ban, Kah Choon and Yap, Hong Kuan (2002): *Rehearsal for War: Resistance and the Underground War against the Japanese and the Kempeitai 1942–1945*. Horizon Books, Singapore.

Barr, Michael D. (2000): *Lee Kuan Yew: The Beliefs behind the Man*. Nordic Institute of Asian Studies Monograph Series, No. 85. Curzon Press, Richmond, Surrey.

Barth, F. (Ed.) (1969): *Ethnic Groups and Boundaries: The Social Organization of Culture Difference*. Little, Brown, Boston.

Bellows, Thomas J. (1970): *The People's Action Party of Singapore: Emergence of a Dominant Party System*. Yale University Southeast Asian Studies Monograph Series No. 14. Yale University Southeast Asian Studies, New Haven.

_____ (1993): "The Singapore Polity: Community, Leadership, and Institutions". In: *Asian Journal of Political Science*, Vol. 1, No. 1, June 1993, pp. 113–32.

Bloodworth, Dennis (1986): *The Tiger and the Trojan Horse*. Times Books International, Singapore.

_____ (199?): Transcript of an interview held with Sir William Goode. Rhodes Library, Oxford.

Blythe, W. (1969): *The Impact of Chinese Secret Societies in Malaya: A Historical Study*. Oxford University Press, London.

Brown, David (1993): "The Corporatist Management of Ethnicity in Contemporary Singapore". In: *Singapore Changes Guard*. (Ed.: Rodan, Garry) Longman Cheshire, Melbourne, pp. 16–33.

_____ (1994): *The State and Ethnic Politics in Southeast Asia*. Routledge, London, New York.

Brown, Rajeswary A. (1994): *Capital and Entrepreneurship in South-East Asia*. Macmillan, London.

Butcher, John and Dick, Howard (Eds.) (1993): *The Rise and Fall of Revenue Farming: Business Elites and the Emergence of the Modern State in Southeast Asia*. Macmillan, Sydney.

Campo, J. N. F. M. a (1992): *Koninklijke Paketvaart Maatschappij: Stoomvaart en Staatsvorming in de Indonesische archipel 1888–1914*. Verloren, Hilversum.

_____ (1993): "Perahu Shipping in Indonesia 1870–1914". In: *Review of Indonesian and Malaysian Affairs*. Vol. 27, Nos. 1 and 2, pp. 33–60.

Careem, Nicky (1979): "OCBC: Tan Chin Tuan's financial fortress". In: *Insight*, January 1979, pp. 8–18.

Chan, Heng Chee (1978): *The Dynamics of One-Party Dominance: The PAP at the Grass-Roots*. Singapore University Press, Singapore.

_____ (1996): "Political Developments, 1965–1979". In: *A History of Singapore*. (Eds.: Chew, Ernest C. T. and Lee, Edwin) Oxford University Press, Singapore, pp. 157–81.

Chan, Kwok Bun (Ed.) (2000): *Chinese Business Networks: State, Economy and Culture*. Prentice Hall, Singapore.

Cheah, Boon Kheng (2003): *Red Star over Malaya: Resistance and Social Conflict during and after the Japanese Occupation of Malaya, 1941–1946*. Singapore University Press, Singapore.

Cheng, Lim-Keak (1985): *Social Change and the Chinese in Singapore*. Singapore University Press, Singapore.

Chew, Ernest C. T. and Lee, Edwin (Eds.) (1996): *A History of Singapore*. Oxford University Press, Singapore.

Chew, Melanie (1996): *Leaders of Singapore*. Resource Press, Singapore.

Chia, Felix (1994): *The Babas Revisited*. 3rd revised ed. Heinemann Asia, Singapore.

Chiew, Seen-kong (1987): "The Socio-Cultural Framework of Politics". In: *Government and Politics of Singapore*. (Eds.: Quah, Jon S., Chan, Heng Chee and Seah, Chee Meow) Oxford University Press, Singapore, pp. 45–67.

_____ (1995): "The Chinese in Singapore: From Colonial Times to the Present". In: *Southeast Asian Chinese: The Socio-Cultural Dimension*. (Ed.: Suryadinata, Leo) Times Academic Press, Singapore, pp. 42–66.

Chong Carino, Theresa (1998): *Chinese Big Business in the Philippines: Political Leadership and Change*. Times Academic Press, Singapore.

Chua, Beng Huat (1995): *Communitarian Ideology and Democracy in Singapore*. Routledge, London, New York.

Chui, Kwei-chiang (1977): *The Response of the Malayan Chinese to Political and Military Developments in China, 1945–1949*. Institute of Humanities and Social Sciences, College of Graduate Studies, Nanyang University. Research Projects Series, No. 4, October 1977.

_____ (1985): "The China Democratic League in Singapore and Malaya". In: *Review of Southeast Asian Studies*, Vol. 15, pp. 1–28.

_____ (1996): "Political Attitudes and Organizations, c.1900–1941". In: *A History of Singapore*. (Eds.: Chew, Ernest C. T. and Lee, Edwin) Oxford University Press, Singapore, pp. 66–92.

Chui, Kwei-chiang and Hara, Fujio (1991): *Emergence, Development and Dissolution of the Pro-China Organizations in Singapore*. Institute of Developing Economies, Tokyo.

Clammer, John R. (1980): *Straits Chinese Society: Studies in the Sociology of the Baba Communities in Malaysia and Singapore*. Singapore University Press, Singapore.

Clutterbuck, Richard (1984): *Conflict and Violence in Singapore and Malaysia 1945–1983*. Revised edition, Graham Brash Ltd, Singapore.

Comber, L. (1959): *Chinese Secret Societies in Malaya: A Survey of the Triad Society from 1800 to 1900*. Locust Valley, New York.

Cushman, Jennifer (1991): *Family and State: The Formation of a Sino-Thai Tin-Mining Dynasty 1797–1932*. Oxford University Press, Oxford.

Cushman, Jennifer and Wang, Gungwu (Eds.) (1988): *Changing Identities of the*

Southeast Asian Ethnic Chinese since World War II. Hong Kong University Press, Hong Kong.

Dick, Howard (1993): "Indonesian Economic History Inside Out". In: *Review of Indonesian and Malaysian Affairs*, Vol. 27 (1 and 2), pp. 1–13.

Donnison, F. S. V. (1956): *British Military Administration in the Far East 1943–46.* Her Majesty's Stationary Office, London.

Doraisamy, T. R. (1969): *150 Years of Education in Singapore.* Teachers' Training College, Singapore.

Douw, Leo, Huang, C. and Godley, Michael R. (Eds.) (1999): *Qiaoxiang Ties: Interdisciplinary Approaches to 'Cultural Capitalism' in South China.* Kegan Paul International in association with the International Institute for Asian Studies, Leiden and Amsterdam, London, New York.

Douw, Leo and Post, Peter (Eds.) (1996): *South China: State, Culture and Social Change during the 20th Century.* Royal Dutch Academy of Arts and Sciences, Amsterdam.

Drabble, John (1973): *Rubber in Malaya 1876–1922: The Genesis of the Industry.* Oxford University Press, Kuala Lumpur.

Drysdale, John (1984): *Singapore: Struggle for Success.* Times Books International, Singapore.

East Asia Analytical Unit (Ed.) (1995): *Overseas Business Networks in Asia.* Department of Foreign Affairs and Trade, East Asia Analytical Unit, Parkes, Australia.

Fong, Sip Chee (1979): *The PAP Story: The Pioneering Days.* Times Periodicals Ltd, Singapore.

Freedman, Maurice (1979): *The Study of Chinese Society: Essays by Maurice Freedman.* Stanford University Press, Stanford.

Gamer, Robert E. (1969): "Parties and Pressure Groups". In: *Modern Singapore.* (Eds.: Ooi, Jin-Bee and Chiang, Hai Ding) University of Singapore Press, Singapore, pp. 197–215.

_____ (1972): *The Politics of Urban Development in Singapore.* Cornell University Press, London.

George, Thayil Jacob Sony (1984): *Lee Kuan Yew's Singapore.* Eastern Universities Press, Singapore.

Giddens, Anthony (1971): *Capitalism and Modern Social Theory: An Analysis of the Writings of Marx, Durkheim and Max Weber.* Cambridge University Press, Cambridge.

Gillis, Elizabeth Kay (2005): *Singapore Civil Society and British Power.* Talisman, Singapore.

Godley, Michael R. (1975): "The Late Ch'ing Courtship of the Chinese in Southeast Asia". In: *Journal of Asian Studies*, Vol. 34, No. 2, pp. 361–85.

_____ (1981): *Overseas Chinese Enterprise in the Modernization of China, 1893–1911.* Cambridge University Press, Cambridge.

_____ (1999): "The Moral Economy of Profit: Diaspora Capitalism and the Future of China". In: *Qiaoxiang Ties: Interdisciplinary Approaches to 'Cultural*

Capitalism' in South China. Kegan Paul International in association with the International Institute for Asian Studies, Leiden and Amsterdam, London, New York, pp. 267–305.

Gopinathan, S. (1976): "Towards a National Education System". In: *Singapore: Society in Transition*. (Ed.: Hassan, Riaz) Oxford University Press, Kuala Lumpur, pp. 67–83.

Gough, Richard (2003): *The Jungle was Red: SOE's Force 136, Sumatra and Malaya*. SNP Panpac, Singapore.

Gwee, Yee Hean (1970): "Chinese Education in Singapore". In: *Journal of the South Seas Society*, Vol. 25, No. 2, pp. 100–27.

Hamilton, Gary G. (1985): "Why No Capitalism in China? Negative Questions in Historical, Comparative Research". In: *Max Weber in Asian Studies*. (Ed.: Buss, Andreas) E.J. Brill, Leiden, The Netherlands, pp. 65–89.

Harper, T. N. (1999): *The End of Empire and the Making of Malaya*. Cambridge University Press, Cambridge.

_____ (2001): "Lim Chin Siong and the 'Singapore Story' ". In: *Comet in our Sky: Lim Chin Siong in History*. (Eds.: Tan, Jing Quee and Jomo, K. S.) INSAN, Kuala Lumpur.

Heng, Pek Koon and Sieh Lee, Mei Ling (2000): "The Chinese Business Community in Peninsular Malaysia, 1957–1999". In: *The Chinese in Malaysia*. (Eds.: Lee, Kam Hing and Tan, Chee Beng) Oxford University Press, Shah Alam, pp. 123–68.

Hicks, George (1995): *The Comfort Women*. Heinemann Asia, Singapore.

Hicks, George and Redding, S. G. (1983): "The Story of the East Asian Economic Miracle". In: *Euro-Asia Business Review*, Vol. 2, Nos. 3–4, pp. 3–4.

Hill, Michael and Lian, Kwen Fee (1995): *The Politics of Nation Building and Citizenship in Singapore*. Routledge, London, New York.

Huang, Jianli (1995): "The Founding of the PRC and the Economic Concerns of Singapore Chinese Entrepreneurs". In: *Southeast Asian Chinese and China: The Politico-Economic Dimension*. (Ed.: Suryadinata, Leo) Times Academic Press, Singapore, pp. 161–92.

Huff, W. Gerald (1994): *The Economic Growth of Singapore: Trade and Development in the Twentieth Century*. Cambridge University Press, Cambridge.

Hyde, Francis E. (1973): *Far Eastern Trade, 1860–1914. A. &C. Black*, London.

Jackson, R. N. (1965): *Pickering, Protector of Chinese*. Oxford University Press, Kuala Lumpur.

Josey, Alex (1968): *Lee Kuan Yew: The Crucial Years*. 1980 edition, reprinted 1995 ed. Times Books International, Singapore.

Krause, Lawrence B., Koh, Ai Tee and Lee, Tsao Yuan (1987): *The Singapore Economy Reconsidered*. Institute of Southeast Asian Studies, Singapore.

Kua, Bak Lim (Ed.) (1995): *Who is Who in the Chinese Community of Singapore*. EPB Publishers, Singapore.

Kwok, Kian Woon (1994): "Social Transformation and the Problem of Social Coherence: Chinese Singaporeans at Century's End". (Working Papers, 124) Department of Sociology, National University of Singapore, Singapore.

Lau, Albert (1991): *The Malayan Union Controversy 1942–1948*. Oxford University Press, Singapore.

_____ (1998): *A Moment of Anguish: Singapore in Malaysia and the Politics of Disengagement*. Times Academic Press, Singapore.

Lee, Edwin (1991): *The British as Rulers: Governing Multi-racial Singapore 1867– 1914*. Singapore University Press, Singapore.

Lee, Kam Hing (1995): *The Sultanate of Aceh: Relations with Britain 1760–1824*. Oxford University Press, Kuala Lumpur.

Lee, Kuan Yew (1998): *The Singapore Story: Memoirs of Lee Kuan Yew*. Times Editions, Singapore.

Lee, Poh Ping (1978): *Chinese Society in Nineteenth Century Singapore*. Oxford University Press, Kuala Lumpur.

Lien, Ying Chow and Kraar, Louis (1994): *From Chinese Villager to Singapore Tycoon: My Life Story*. Times Books International, Singapore.

Lim, Choo Hoon (1979): "The Transformation of the Political Orientation of the Singapore Chinese Chamber of Commerce, 1945–1955". In: *Review of Southeast Asian Studies*, Vol. 9, pp. 3–63.

Lim, How Seng (1995): *Singapore Chinese Community and Entrepreneurs*. Singapore Society of Asian Studies, Singapore.

Lim, Pui Huen (1992): *Singapore, Malaysian and Brunei Newspapers: An International Union List*. (Institute of Southeast Asian Studies, Singapore, Library Series, 19) Institute of Southeast Asian Studies, Singapore.

Lind, Andrew W. (1974): *Nanyang Perspective: Chinese Students in Multiracial Singapore*. University Press of Hawaii, Honolulu.

Liu, Hong (1998): "Old Linkages, New Networks: The Globalization of Overseas Chinese Voluntary Associations and its Implications". In: *China Quarterly* Vol. 155 (1998), pp. 582–609.

Liu, Hong and Wong, Sin-kiong (2004): *Singapore Chinese Society in Transition: Business, Politics, & Socio-economic Change, 1945–1965*. Peter Lang, New York.

Low, James (1972): *The British Settlement of Penang*. Oxford University Press, Singapore.

Lydgate, Chris (2003): *Lee's Law: How Singapore Crushes Dissent*. Scribe Publications, Carlton North, Victoria.

Mackie, Jamie (1992): "Overseas Chinese Entrepreneurship". In: *Asian-Pacific Economic Literature*, Vol. 6, No. 1, pp. 41–64.

Mak, Lau Fong (1995): *The Dynamics of Chinese Dialect Groups in Early Malaya*. Asian Studies Monograph Series, 1. Singapore Society of Asian Studies, Singapore.

McVey, Ruth (Ed.) (1992): *Southeast Asian Capitalist*. Cornell University Press, Ithaca, New York.

_____ (1995): "Change and Continuity in Southeast Asian Studies". In: *Journal of Southeast Asian Studies*, Vol. 26, No. 1, pp. 1–9.

Menkhoff, Thomas (1993): *Trade Routes, Trust and Trading Networks: Chinese Small Enterprises in Singapore*. Breitenbach Verlag, Saarbrücken.

Minchin, James (1986): *No Man is an Island: A Study of Singapore's Lee Kuan Yew.* Allen & Unwin, Sydney & Boston.

Mirza, Hafiz (1986): *Multinationals and the Growth of the Singapore Economy.* St. Martin's Press, New York.

Nanda Graduates Friendly Association (1997): *Chen Liushi bai niandan jinian wenji* (Collected Works Commemorating the hundredth birthday anniversary of Tan Lark Sye). Global Publishing, Singapore.

Ng, Wing Chung (1992): "Urban Chinese Social Organization: Some Unexplored Aspects in Huiguan Development in Singapore, 1900–1941". In: *Modern Asian Studies*, Vol. 26, No. 3, July 1992, pp. 469–94.

Ownby, David and Somers Heidhues, Mary (Eds.) (1993): *"Secret Societies" Reconsidered: Perspectives on the Social History of Modern South China and Southeast Asia.* M. E. Sharpe, Armonk, New York.

Pan, Lynn (Ed.) (1998): *The Encyclopedia of the Chinese Overseas.* Archipelago Press and Landmark Books, Singapore.

Pang, Wing Seng (1973): The 'Double-Seventh Incident', 1937: Singapore Chinese Response to the Outbreak of the Sino-Japanese War. In: *Journal of Southeast Asian Studies*, September 1973, pp. 269–99.

Paul, Erik C. (1992): *Obstacles to Democratization in Singapore.* (Monash University, Centre of Southeast Asian Studies Working Papers, 78.) Centre of Southeast Asian Studies, Monash University, Clayton, Victoria.

Pereira, Alexius A. (2003): *State Collaboration and Development Strategies in China: The Case of the China-Singapore Suzhou Industrial Park (1992–2002).* RoutledgeCurzon, London and New York.

Plato (1987): *The Republic.* Second revised edition, translated and with an introduction by Desmond Lee. Penguin Books, London.

Pugalenthi, S. R. (1996): *Elections in Singapore.* VJ Times International, Singapore.

Purcell, Victor (1965): *The Chinese in Southeast Asia.* 2nd ed. Royal Institute of International Affairs, London.

Quah, Jon S., Chan, Heng Chee and Seah, Chee Meow (Eds.) (1987): *Government and Politics of Singapore.* Revised Edition. Oxford University Press, Singapore.

Regnier, Phillipe (1987): *Singapore: City-State in South-East Asia.* Translated English Edition ed. C. Hurst & Co., London.

Reid, Anthony (1988): *Southeast Asia in the Age of Commerce, 1450–1680.* Yale University Press, New Haven.

_____ (1993): "The Unthreatening Alternative: Chinese Shipping in Southeast Asia, 1567–1842". In: *Review of Indonesian and Malaysian Affairs*, Vol. 27, Nos. 1 and 2, pp. 13–32.

_____ (Ed.) (1996): *Sojourners and Settlers: Histories of Southeast Asia and the Chinese.* Allen & Unwin, St. Leonards.

Rodan, Garry (1989): *The Political Economy of Singapore's Industrialization: National State and International Capital.* Macmillan Press, Basingstoke, London.

_____ (1993): "Preserving the One-Party State in Contemporary Singapore". In: *Southeast Asia in the 1990s: Authoritarianism, Democracy and Capitalism.*

(Eds.: Hewison, Kevin, Robison, Richard and Rodan, Garry) Allen & Unwin, St. Leonards.

Rudolph, Jürgen (1998): *Reconstructing Identities: A Social History of the Babas in Singapore*. Ashgate, Aldershot.

Rutten, Mario (1994): *Asian Capitalists in the European Mirror*. (Comparative Asian Studies Series, 14.) Free University Press, Amsterdam.

Sam, King (1992): *Tiger Balm King: The Life and Times of Aw Boon Haw*. Times Books International, Singapore.

Sandhu, Kernial Singh and Wheatley, Paul (Eds.) (1983): *Melaka: The Transformation of a Malay Capital c. 1400–1980*. Oxford University Press, Kuala Lumpur.

Salaff, Janet W. (1988): *State and Family in Singapore: Restructuring a Developing Society*. Cornell University Press, Ithaca NY.

Seagrave, Sterling (1995): *Lords of the Rim: The Invisible Empire of the Overseas Chinese*. Bantam Press, London.

Seow, Francis T. (1994): *To Catch a Tartar: A Dissident in Lee Kuan Yew's Prison*. (Yale Southeast Asia Studies Monograph, 42.) Yale University Southeast Asia Studies, New Haven, Conneticut.

_____ (1998): *The Media Enthralled: Singapore Revisited*. Lynne Rienner, Boulder.

Shimizu, Hiroshi and Hirakawa, Hitoshi (1999): *Japan and Singapore in the World Economy: Japan's Economic Advance into Singapore, 1870–1965*. Routledge, London and New York.

Sim, Victor (1950): *Biographies of Prominent Chinese in Singapore*. Nan Kok Publication Company, Singapore.

Singapore Federation of Chinese Clan Associations (1997): *Members' Directory*, 1997.

Singapore International Chamber of Commerce (1997): *Annual Report 1996–1997*. Singapore International Chamber of Commerce, Singapore.

Skinner, G. William (1957): *Chinese Society in Thailand: An Analytical History*. Cornell University Press, Ithaca, New York.

Somers Heidhues, Mary (1992): *Bangka Tin and Mentok Pepper: Chinese Settlement on an Indonesian Island*. Institute of Southeast Asian Studies, Singapore.

Song, Ong Siang (1967): *One Hundred Years' History of the Chinese in Singapore*. Reprinted edition (Original Edition 1923, London). Oxford University Press, Singapore.

Sopiee, Mohamed Noordin (1976): *From Malayan Union to Singapore Separation: Political Unification in the Malaysia Region 1945–1965*. Second edition 1976 ed. Penerbit Universiti Malaya, Kuala Lumpur.

Spence, Jonathan D. (1990): *The Search for Modern China*. W.W. Norton & Company, New York, London.

Suryadinata, Leo (Ed.) (1995a): *Southeast Asian Chinese and China: The Politico-Economic Dimension*. Times Academic Press, Singapore.

_____ (1995b): "China's Economic Modernization and the Ethnic Chinese in ASEAN: A Preliminary Study". In: *Southeast Asian Chinese and China: The Politico-Economic Dimension*. (Ed.: Suryadinata, Leo) Times Academic Press, Singapore, pp. 193–215.

Sutherland, Heather A. (1989): "Eastern Emporium and Company Town: Trade and Society in Eighteenth Century Makassar". In: *Brides of the Sea: Port Cities of Asia from the 16th–20th Centuries*. (Ed.: Broeze, F.) New South Wales University Press, Kensington, pp. 97–128.

Suyama, Taku (1977): "Pang Societies and the Economy of Chinese Immigrants – A Study on the Communalism in Southeast Asia". In: *Review of Southeast Asian Studies*, Vol. 7, pp. 7–27.

Tan Chong Tee (1995): *Force 136: Story of a WWII Resistance Fighter*. Translated by Lee Watt Sim & Clara Show. Asiapac Books, Singapore.

Tan, Jing Quee and Jomo, K. S. (2001): *Comet in our Sky: Lim Chin Siong in History*. INSAN, Kuala Lumpur.

Tan, Thomas Tsu-wee (1985): "Political Modernization and Traditional Chinese Voluntary Associations: A Singapore Case Study". In: *Southeast Asian Studies*, Vol. 13, No. 2, pp. 67–79.

Tee, Ming San (1995): *The Singapore Successful Business Elite*. Cross Century Creative City, Singapore.

Tong, Chee Kiong and Chan, Kuok Bun (1994): *One Face, Many Masks: The Singularity and Plurality of Chinese Identity*. Paper prepared for the conference "The Last Half Century of the Chinese Oversea, 1945–1995" held at the University of Hong Kong, 19–21 December 1994.

Touwen, Jeroen (2001): *Extremes in the Archipelago: Trade and Economic Development in the Outer Islands of Indonesia, 1900–1942*. KITLV Press, Leiden.

Tregonning, K. G. (1967): *Home Port Singapore: A History of Straits Steamship Company Limited, 1890–1965*. Oxford University Press for Straits Steamship Co. Ltd., Singapore.

Tremewan, Christopher (1994): *The Political Economy of Social Control in Singapore*. The Macmillan Press Ltd., Basingstoke.

Trocki, Carl A. (1979): *Prince of Pirates: The Temenggongs and the Development of Johor and Singapore 1784–1885*. Institute of Southeast Asian Studies, Singapore.

_____ (1990): *Opium and Empire: Chinese Society in Colonial Singapore*. Cornell University Press, Ithaca, New York.

Turnbull, Mary (1977): *A History of Singapore*. Oxford University Press, Oxford.

Twang, Peck Yang (1998): *The Chinese Business Elite in Indonesia and the Transition to Independence 1940–1950*. Oxford University Press, Kuala Lumpur.

Vaughan, J. D. (1879): *The Manners and Customs of the Chinese of the Straits Settlements*. Reprinted in Oxford in Asia Paperbacks in 1974 ed. Oxford University Press, London.

Vennewald, Werner (1994): *Technocrats in the State Enterprise System of Singapore*. (Working Paper, 32) Asia Research Centre, Murdoch University, Perth.

Visscher, Sikko (2002a): "Actors and Arenas, Elections and Competition: The 1958 Election of the Singapore Chinese Chamber of Commerce". In: *Journal of Southeast Asian Studies*, Vol. 33, No. 2 (June 2002), pp. 315–32.

_____ (2002b): "Merchants, Empires and Emperors: Global and Local Factors in Elite Composition and Elite Representation of Chinese Businessmen in

Colonial Singapore; 1819–1945". In: *Entrepreneurship and Institutions in Europe and Asia, 1500–2000*. (Eds.: de Goey, F. and Veluwenkamp, J. W.) Aksant Publishers, Amsterdam, pp. 167–92.

_____ (2003): "Brokering Change, Changing Brokers: The Chinese Business Elite and Decolonization Politics in Singapore, 1945–1965". In: *Capital and Knowledge in Asia: Changing Power Relations*. (Eds.: Dahles, H. and van den Muijzenberg, O.) RoutledgeCurzon, London, New York, pp. 111–30.

Vogel, Ezra F. (1989): "A Little Dragon Tamed". In: *Management of Success: The Moulding of Modern Singapore*. (Eds.: Sandhu, Kernial Singh and Wheatley, Paul) Institute of Southeast Asian Studies, Singapore, pp. 1049–66.

Wang, Gungwu (1981): "Chinese Politics in Malaya". In: *Community and Nation; Essays on Southeast Asia and the Chinese*. Heinemann Educational Books, Selangor. Previously published in China Quarterly, Vol. 43.

_____ (1990): "Merchants without Empire: The Hokkien Sojourning Communities". In: *The Rise of Merchant Empires: Long-distance Trade in the Early Modern World, 1350–1750*. (Ed.: Tracy, James D.) Cambridge University Press, Cambridge, pp. 400–21.

_____ (1998): *The Nanhai Trade: The Early History of Chinese Trade in the South China Sea*. First published in 1958 by the *Journal of the Malayan Branch of the Royal Asiatic Society*. Times Academic Press, Singapore.

Ward, A. H. C., Chu, Raymond W. and Salaff, Janet (Eds.) (1994): *The Memoirs of Tan Kah Kee*. Singapore University Press, Singapore.

Wee, Mon Cheng (1972): *The Future of the Chinese in Southeast Asia*. Second Edition, 1972. University Education Press, Singapore.

Who is Who in Singapore. Second edition, 2003, WhosWho Publishing, Singapore.

Wickberg, Edgar (1994): "The Chinese as Overseas Migrants". In: *Migration: The Asian Experience*. (Eds.: Brown, Judith and Foot, Rosemary) Macmillan Press, London, pp. 12–37.

Williams, Lea (1952): "Chinese Entrepreneurs in Indonesia". In: *Explorations in Economic History*, Vol. 5, No. 1.

Willmott, D. (1960): *The Chinese of Semarang*. Cornell University Press, Ithaca, New York.

Wilson, Dick (1972): *Solid as a Rock: The First Forty Years of the Oversea-Chinese Banking Corporation*. Oversea-Chinese Banking Corporation, Singapore.

Wolters, O. W. (1967): *Early Indonesian Commerce: A Study of the Origin of Srivijaya*. Cornell University Press, Ithaca, New York.

_____ (1970): The Fall of Srivijaya in Malay History. Lund Humphries, London.

Wong, Lin Ken (1960): "The Trade of Singapore 1819–1869". In: *Journal of the Malayan Branch of the Royal Asiatic Society*, Vol. XXXIII, No. 4, December 1960, pp. 5–315.

Wong, Ting-hong (2003): "Education and State Formation Reconsidered: Chinese School Identity in Postwar Singapore". In: *Journal of Historical Sociology*, Vol. 16, No. 2, pp. 237–65.

Wong, Siu-lun (1985): "The Chinese Family Firm: a Model". In: *Britsh Journal of Sociology*, Vol. XXXVI, No. 2, pp. 58–72.

_____ (1995): "Business Networks, Cultural Values and the State in Hong Kong and Singapore". In: *Chinese Business Enterprise in Asia*. (Ed.: Brown, Rajeswary A.) Routledge, London, pp. 136–53.

Wu, Xiao An (2003): *Chinese Business in the Making of a Malay State, 1882–1941: Kedah and Penang*. RoutledgeCurzon, London and New York.

Xinjiapo Zhonghua Zongshanghui bangpai lunzheng lai long qu mai. (The Singapore Chinese Chamber of Commerce, the origin and development of the dialect group controversy) (1969). International Times Publishing, Singapore.

Yap, Pheng Geck (1982): *Scholar, Banker, Gentleman Soldier: The Reminiscences of Dr. Yap Pheng Geck*. Times Books International, Singapore.

Yen, Ch'ing-hwang (1985): "Ch'ing Protection of the Returned Overseas Chinese after 1893, with special reference to the Chinese in Southeast Asia". In: *Review of Southeast Asian Studies*, Vol. 15, pp. 29–42.

_____ (1986): *A Social History of the Chinese of Singapore and Malaysia, 1800–1911*. Oxford University Press, Singapore.

_____ (1995a): Ch'ing China and the Singapore Chinese Chamber of Commerce, 1906–1911. In: *Southeast Asian Chinese and China: The Politico-Economic Dimension*. (Ed.: Suryadinata, Leo) Times Academic Press, Singapore, pp. 133–60.

_____ (1995b): *Community and Politics: The Chinese in Colonial Singapore and Malaysia*. Times Academic Press, Singapore.

Yeo, Kim Wah (1973a): "The Anti-Federation Movement in Malaya, 1946–48". In: *Journal of Southeast Asian Studies*, Vol. 4, No. 1, pp. 31–51.

_____ (1973b): *Political Development in Singapore 1945–1955*. Singapore University Press, Singapore.

Yeo, Kim Wah and Lau, Albert (1996): "From Colonialism to Independence, 1945–1965". In: *A History of Singapore*. (Eds.: Chew, Ernest C. T. and Lee, Edwin) Oxford University Press, Singapore.

Yong, Ching-fatt (1985): "Some Thoughts on the Creation of a Singaporean Identity among the Chinese: The Pre-PAP Phase, 1945–59". In: *Review of Southeast Asian Studies*, Vol. 15, pp. 52–60.

_____ (1987): Tan Kah Kee: *The Making of an Overseas Chinese Legend*. Oxford University Press, Singapore.

_____ (1994): *Chinese Leadership and Power in Colonial Singapore*. Times Academic Press, Singapore.

Index